# THE HANDBOOK OF
# CACTI
## AND
# SUCCULENTS

# THE HANDBOOK OF
# CACTI
## AND
# SUCCULENTS

## CLIVE INNES

**WARD LOCK LIMITED · LONDON**

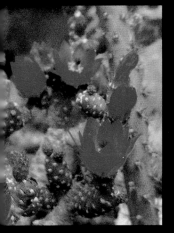

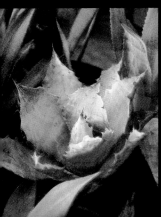

A QUINTET BOOK

First published in Great Britain in 1988 by
WARD LOCK LIMITED
8 Clifford Street, London W1X 1RB
an Egmont Company

Innes, Clive
    The handbook of cacti and succulents
    1. Cacti. Cultivation
    I. Title
    635.9'3347


ISBN 0-7063-6703-0

This book was designed and produced by
QUINTET PUBLISHING LIMITED
6 Blundell Street
London N7 9BH

ART DIRECTOR: Peter Bridgewater
DESIGNER: Alan Marshall
EDITORS: Louise Bostock, Patricia Bayer
PHOTOGRAPHS: Clive  Innes/Holly Gate
International

Typeset in Great Britain by
Central Southern Typesetters, Eastbourne
Manufactured in Hong Kong by
Regent Publishing Services Limited
Printed in Hong Kong by
Leefung-Asco Printers Limited

# Contents

# Foreword

Clive Innes is so well known in the world of cacti and succulents that no introduction is really necessary. This is so for many good reasons: his long and tireless work for various societies over so many years, the remarkable exhibitions of cacti and succulents — enjoyed by so many people — for which he has been responsible and the enormous scope of his knowledge. Not everyone is aware of how widely Clive has travelled in search of the plants he loves, or his generosity in distributing rare species to eager and grateful enthusiasts.

It has been my great privilege to have known Clive for many years, to have visited him at his nursery, to have heard him lecture and to sit on the Governing Council of the Royal Horticultural Society with him. The longer I have known him, the more I have come to appreciate his knowledge of and affection for cacti and succulents. It was therefore a very great pleasure to learn that *The Handbook of Cacti and Succulents*, beautifully illustrated throughout, is to be published. There is an ever-growing number of lovers of these plants who, I know, will be fascinated by this publication, and will undoubtedly wish to acquire it.

It would not be an idle compliment to say that, in my opinion, there is no-one today with a broader knowledge of these plants, or a greater ability to translate his practical experience into such highly accessible prose.

L. MAURICE MASON V.M.H.

RIGHT: *Cephalophyllum regale*

# Preface

VERY FEW PEOPLE go through life without a hobby. Many have an instinctive desire to collect – stamps, coins, antiques and so on – and those with a particular feeling for gardening, in its broadest sense, find the collecting together of plants for the sheer pleasure of growing them something which inspires and stimulates the imagination for years on end. Very few groups of plants hold a greater fascination than succulents, and once caught up by the lure of these exotics, seldom is its attraction displaced.

My own interest in succulents began many years ago, and the enthusiasm and allurement have never worn off, or even worn thin. Contrariwise, succulents have provided endless pleasure and enjoyment, together with a constant absorbing challenge to learn more and more about them and to understand them better. Recalling those earlier days, I remember how great a problem it was to obtain plants in any great variety, and perhaps even more difficult to acquire the right type of book to tell me what I wanted to know, and in a language which I, as a layman, could understand. They were certainly few and far between. In this age we are extremely fortunate in being able to procure many authoritative works relating to cacti and the other succulents generally. Sometimes the botanic terms used can be confusing to the beginner; botanical descriptions are essential but the vocabulary of the botanic world is not exactly that used in everyday language and therefore sometimes difficult to follow. The recognition of a plant – its genus, and specific status – is what most collectors aspire to determine, but would not with to dissect the plant, the flower, its fruits, its seeds to ascertain the correct nomenclature.

Through these pages I shall endeavour to simplify the process, making reference primarily to those aspects most readily appreciated and discernible to the layman, and the beginner.

I would be the last person to question the deliberations and research activities of botanists as I have too many close and respected friends within their ranks. The fact remains, however, that the botanic world is seemingly one of change, even turmoil, especially in the realm of nomenclature – the thinking of botanists and horticulturalists does not always run on parallel planes, differing opinions can exist, and undoubtedly one can be complementary to the other. While we have devoted botanists engaging continually in research, and horticulturalists using their skill and imagination to better explain to the world of 'collectors' those things which contribute to their hobby, the fascination of succulents will never fade.

Clive Innes

Conditions – geographical and environmental – have been taken seriously into consideration with the division of the chapters. Perhaps it will be found that certain species mentioned are not usually referred to as succulents and this might cause controversy – perhaps this is all to the good. I am nevertheless convinced there is sufficient factual information available which confirms their inclusion, that they should be accepted as succulents, sometimes terrestrial, sometimes epiphytic. Succulent plants have more far-reaching associations than we may generally acknowledge.

What the plant is, to which genus or family it belongs, where it comes from, what it looks like, what peculiarities are of primary importance, the flower colour – these and other obvious aspects are my main consideration, and I hope that I have been successful in meeting this challenge.

I hope this book will stimulate even more interest in this vast group of wonderful plants – succulent species of the Cactaceae and many other obvious and sometimes obscure plant families.

C.F.I.
*Holly Gate, Ashington, Sussex.*

RIGHT: *Puya alpestris*

# General Distribution

THE WORLD OF SUCCULENT PLANTS is one of sheer fascination, unaccountable beauty, extraordinary allurement and distinctive charm. Yet these features, which make succulents not only among the most diverse of all groups of plants but also among the most popular, have come into being mainly through the slow evolutionary processes by which they have adapted to harsh conditions – conditions under which most other plants would perish. It is this that has forced them to take on the curious shapes and modes of growth that give them their great appeal.

In spite of their diversity, all succulents (including cacti) have one thing in common: the ability to store water. All the evolutionary changes they have undergone have been in order to modify themselves to achieve this one end. Yet in fact there are only three parts of plants which can be adapted to storing water – the leaves, the stems and the roots. Succulents are, therefore, loosely grouped together according to whether they are stem succulents, leaf succulents or root succulents. The majority of cacti are typical stem succulents, as are many species of the Asclepiadaceae and Euphorbiaceae. The majority of species of Crassulaceae and Mesembryanthemaceae are typical leaf succulents. Examples of typical root succulents – in which the root system is tuberous and is generally referred to as a 'caudex' – come from a wider range of families including some, perhaps, unexpected ones: the Convolvulaceae, Cucurbitaceae, Euphorbiaceae and others.

This essential peculiarity – the ability to store water in leaves, stems or roots – brings together a host of plants from all over the world that are generally accepted as succulents. Some are cacti; others look like cacti and are easily mistaken for them because of their similarity of form, yet have no direct relationship with cacti, having merely evolved a similarity of appearance in order to adapt to a similar mode of existence. All, however, have in common the ability to resist climatic and environmental conditions and changes so extreme that they would destroy any plants that had not made these adaptations. Changes, for example, from midday temperatures well over 100°F/37°C, to night temperatures below freezing – changes which regularly occur within successive 24-hour periods.

Most people think of succulents, particularly cacti, as plants of the dry, arid, even desert, regions of the world. Though many do indeed come from these regions, the statement is not true of succulents in general. Succulents can be found in almost every part of the world, literally from the Arctic through the northern hemisphere to the Equator, and southward to the Antarctic; they are found equally in the eastern and western hemispheres. In fact, they are found anywhere where the conditions might be described as those of privation.

To delve in detail into the worldwide distribution of succulent plants would require many volumes – large volumes at that – but a brief yet reasonably precise survey is useful since, by showing how and where plants grow in the wild, one can gain a pretty fair idea of how to treat them in cultivation.

It is generally accepted that cacti are indigenous to the New World – as for that matter are many species of other succulent plants. Most of the non-cacti succulents occur in Africa, Asia and Australia; a few are endemic to many European countries. Thus the succulents are an extensively distributed group. They range through the temperate zones where periods of warmth and cold alternate by the seasons, to areas where temperature variations occur between day and night. By contrast, there are the torrid regions of many tropical and sub-tropical countries with their parched landscapes and relatively high temperatures which persist continuously throughout the year, knowing no seasons as such – a perpetual summer with its awful implications of drought and famine.

Europe, including Britain where native sedums are to be found, is the natural home of several species of the Crassulaceae. Throughout southern France, Spain and Portugal are others of the same family – *Sempervivum, Crassula, Aeonium* and *Greenovia*, as well as Asclepiads, represented by *Caralluma* and *Ceropegia*, to mention but a few. The Iberian Peninsula, together with the Canary Islands and Madeira, still offer splendid scope for the adventurous plantsman! It is quite usual to find cacti, agaves, aloes and other exotics established and thriving on rock faces in southern Europe and also cultivated in gardens. None of these is native to those regions; they have become naturalized over the years, and thrive in their adopted environment.

To travel through the Americas would provide a continuous presentation of succulents varying from country to country. The USA is rich in species. California, on its borders with Nevada in the region of the Clark Mountains, provides *Yucca* and *Agave* together with *Coryphantha, Mammillaria* and many members of the great Opuntia family. Arizona is the home of the giant saguaro *Carnegia gigantea* and species of *Ferocactus* and *Mammillaria*. In the south of Texas are *Echeveria, Dudleya* and *Bursera* species. Utah has its own particular cactus, originally called a *Utahia* (now *Pediocactus*), a rarity of the Cactaceae.

Moving into the exotic Baja California, still mainly a wild peninsula, even with modern development gradually encroaching, with well-provided highways pushing down from the north and up from the south, the desert regions still hold the major attraction. Temperatures vary considerably on the Baja, with warm, comfortable conditions along the Pacific Coast, while bordering the Gulf of California on the east, oppressive heat is characteristic. Exciting plant life abounds from end to end. *Fouquieria columnaris* (the boogum tree sometimes wrongly referred to as the elephant tree) can be found in forests in Baja California, also *Pachycormus* (the true elephant tree), rare species of *Echinocereus, Mammillaria, Dudleya, Agave,* endemic species from the many off-shore islands, *Ferocactus* and *Opuntia,* including the very rare *O. invicta* and *Stenocereus eruca,* the creeping devil, with its long spiny branches trailing many feet in length.

On the other side of the Gulf of California, in Sonora – on the dry plateau or mountain slopes – cacti and succulents dominate the landscape. *Opuntia,* the prickly pear – the cholla – in all its many forms abound, vying with the *Agave* for prominence, both a menace to any unwary traveller. Mexico is the so-called home of cacti – by far the greatest number of species is congregated there, and this becomes increasingly apparent as one travels through the country. *Echinocereus, Mammillaria, Coryphantha, Neobesseya, Ferocactus, Pachycereus* and many other genera are encountered journeying southward, and several *Cereus* species, usually referred to as the organ-pipe cactus, adorn the roadside.

Alongside the Gulf of California plants usually attributed to Baja California are to be seen: *Lophocereus, Echinocereus* and *Mammillaria.* Below Guaymas the coastal strip becomes arid, often devoid of rainfall for months or years on end with only the moisture from the fogs, which descend on the area almost daily, bringing some relief from the continual drought. Here are what are really only survivors of persistent hardship – *Wilcoxia, Rathbunia, Peniocereus, Opuntia* and *Ferocactus,* together with *Pedilanthus* and a few epiphytic bromeliads. Through Sinaloa to Durango, *Mammillaria senilis* is found on high rock faces, content to accept near-freezing conditions at times, as well as many differing forms of *Agave, Yucca* and *Dasylirion.* Heading inland toward Coahuila are *Ariocarpus,* that look so very rock-like as to be well nigh indistinguishable from the real rocks, *Echinocereus, Turbinocarpus, Thelocactus, Lophophora, Astrophytum* – and near to Monterrey the beautiful *Agave victoriae-reginae,* found on the precipitous mountain slopes of the Huasteca Canyon close to Santa Catarina. Around Saltillo, mountains rising to over 6000 ft/1828 m offer foothold to *Echeveria* species, together with cacti such as the beautiful white *Mammillaria plumosa,* clinging to minute cracks in the rock faces. Many of the most ornamental and distinctive cacti are found in Mexico. Hidalgo is the home of *Cephalocereus senilis,* where it is found on steep limestone hillsides. Beyond Mexico City species of *Heliocereus* abound. To the extreme south are new vistas of interest. The moist tropical zones of Chiapas and Tabasco are the beginning of the chain of rain forests which extend southward into Central America. Here are some of the truly epiphytic cacti – *Epiphyllum, Hylocereus* and *Selenicereus* climbing and clambering through the forest trees, *Disocactus, Cryptocereus* and other lesser-known but indisputedly exotic species.

And on to Central America – to Guatemala with its lush jungle coastlines and high rugged mountains, and while epiphytes are usually associated with this still unspoiled countryside, species of *Myrtillocactus, Stenocereus, Heliocereus, Rhodocactus, Acanthocereus* and *Nyctocereus* also abound. From the forest areas of Guatemala and Honduras comes *Wilmattea minutiflora,* a monotypic genus of epiphytic cactus. Farther south the land narrows toward Costa Rica and Panama. The climate of Costa Rica is most variable – humid and hot in the lowlands, while the highlands provide a reasonably temperate climate. Rain forests cover much of the country and here again the emphasis is on epiphytic genera – the monotypic *Eccremocactus bradei, Cryptocereus, Epiphyllum, Rhipsalis, Selenicereus* and *Weberocereus. Acanthocereus, Pedilanthus, Yucca* and *Agave* grow on the drier mountain slopes.

The tropical zones of South America gradually reveal new and different succulents. In the endless rain forests of Amazonia, very much of which is still unexplored, are numerous bromeliads and other epiphytes in endless assortment and variety – *Strophocactus wittii,* the strap cactus, very rare indeed and almost unknown in cultivation, while in more northerly coastal regions of South America is *Melocactus* – the Turk's cap cactus. Further epiphytic species occur in Ecuador and Colombia, as do the more columnar varieties of *Borzicactus, Armatocereus* and *Acanthocereus.*

Peru is something different again, with its extremes of humid rain forests and barren Andean mountain slopes – of sullen heat and bitter cold. There are enormous contrasts in this remarkable country. It has been more thoroughly explored in recent years than other parts of South America, leading to the discovery of many new species of cacti – *Matucana, Neoporteria, Oroya, Mila, Borzicactus, Espostoa, Brownineia* and *Melocactus* – and *Opuntia* now providing a contrasting group *Tephrocactus,* a miniature section of the Opuntieae.

Chile, though so close to Peru, is different yet again, a long narrow strip of coastal plain and numerous off-shore islands bounded from north to south by the Andes rising to snow-covered heights. Here many genera of cacti flourish: *Copiapoa, Eriosyce, Browningia, Eulychnia, Neoporteria, Austrocactus, Corryocactus, Neowerdermannia* and *Oreocereus.* Of the other succulents only a few are indigenous and these include *Portulaca, Calandrinia, Ullucus* and *Kalanchoë.* The inland state of Bolivia is the home of *Lobivia* (an anagram of Bolivia), *Weingartia, Gymnocalycium, Quiabentia* (another unusual member of the Opuntieae), *Rebutia, Sulcorebutia* and others. Paraguay has many species similar to surrounding countries – *Parodia, Notocactus, Monvillea, Echinopsis* and the non-cactaceous *Chorisia*.

The south and east of Brazil provide some of the most popular of all cacti – *Schlumbergera, Hatiora, Rhipsalis, Lepismium* and *Buiningia* – to mention just a few of the choicest and, in some instances, the rarest. Further inland many important discoveries have been made, during the last two decades, of species which have caused excitement and interest to botanists and amateurs alike – *Uebelmannia, Discocactus, Melocactus, Gymnocalycium, Notocactus*; these, and others, are still a talking point with many enthusiasts and open up a continual and extensive sphere for further research.

On the higher mountain slopes of southern Argentina, almost at snow-line level, is the elusive opuntia-like *Maihuenia*, while Patagonia as a whole provides many important members of the Cactaceae. In northern Argentina, where it joins borders with Paraguay, and in Uruguay, are species of *Trichocereus, Gymnocalycium, Pfeiffera, Parodia, Echinopsis* and *Oreocereus*, with some of the more xerophytic genera of Bromeliaceae – *Puya, Bromelia* and *Abromeitiella*.

The West Indian islands – from Curaçao and Trinidad in the south to the northerly islands of the Bahamas – provide an ever-fascinating profusion of exotic succulents. The drier mountain slopes of many of these islands abound with agaves – and it is worth noting that a great number of the islands have agave species differing from the neighbouring islands, almost a matter of one island, one species. Other succulents of consequence include *Jatropha, Pedilanthus, Portulaca, Kalanchoë, Furcraea, Sansevieria, Plumiera* (the 'franzipani'), *Chorisia, Peperomia* and *Talinum*. In many, if not all, of these islands, the contrasting temperatures between coastal areas and mountain heights, between the leeward and windward coasts, produce varying plant characteristics – *Melocactus* and *Pilosocereus* appear on the coastal fringe – usually not penetrating further than 50 to 100 yd/45 to 90 m from the shores of the Atlantic Ocean and the Caribbean Sea. Cuba is the home of *Dendrocereus* and *Leptocereus*. *Harrisia, Hylocereus* and *Selenicereus* are found in many of the islands, as are *Rhipsalis* species and *Rhodocactus*, one of the few cacti with true leaves.

The Galapagos Islands, a sanctuary of protected flora, have as endemics many attractive and sought-after plants – *Brachycereus, Jasminocereus* and some 'deluxe' species of *Opuntia* – all exclusive to these remarkable islands.

The continent of Africa offers the greatest diversity of the 'other' succulents. The Old World still holds a glory all its own when it comes to plant life, and succulents in paricular have a high place of honour. The countries bordering the Mediterranean and the Red Sea from Morocco to Somalia, much of which is arid and semi-desert – produce species of *Caralluma, Euphorbia, Kalanchoë* and *Jatropha*, while Somalia is the home of the rare *Pseudolithos*, the

*Trematosperma* and *Pterodiscus*. The off-shore and almost inaccessible island of Socotra is another 'Galapagos' – even more so. Only one botanic expedition has been possible for many years and that was almost an accident. Rarities exist in wild array – *Adenium, Caralluma, Echidnopsis, Edithcolea, Dendrosicyos, Dorstenia* and *Pedalium*, to mention but a few.

Many of the desert regions of Arabia have their endemic species of *Caralluma* and other members of the Asclepiadaceae, especially *Euphorbias*, shrunken and leafless so as to provide the smallest possible area through which moisture can evaporate. Further south, in East Africa, are countries of extremes – areas of savannah, of humid mountain slopes and valleys where hosts of succulents of many genera capture the eye: *Pelargonium, Stapelia, Huernia, Caralluma, Lithocaulon, Merremia, Turbina, Gerardanthus, Kedostris, Corallocarpus, Momordica*. Kenya in particular is the home of many remarkable succulents; *Pyrenacantha* with its huge swollen trunk, species of Euphorbiaceae (*Synadenium* and *Dorstenia* are but two), while many species of the Asclepiadaceae, *Gynura, Stenadenium, Adenium* and *Adenia*, together with *Aloe* and *Sansevieria*, are native to Tanzania.

On the west coast a totally different character of succulent is dominant. The West African countries of Nigeria and Ghana have peculiar forms of Euphorbia indigenous to their respective countries, together with *Kalanchoë, Aloe, Jatropha, Stephania* and *Cissus*.

It is best to consider Namibia apart from South Africa – because it covers so vast an area. Much of this terrain remains comparatively unknown botanically – though what is known is enthralling. An endless array of Aloes and Mesembryanthemums colours the landscape, backed up by Euphorbias together with *Ammocharis* and *Haemanthus* of the Amaryllidaceae; *Pachpodium* species, Asclepiadaceae represented by *Decabelone, Duvalia, Hoodia, Hoodiopsis, Huerniopsis, Piaranthus, Stapelia, Tavaresia* and *Trichocaulon*. Here too is the baobab tree *Adansonia digitata, Commiphora, Othonna, Ipomoea, Adromischus, Cotyledon, Kalanchoë, Acanthosicyos* – a rare cucurbit – together with unusual succulent forms of *Pelargonium* and *Sarcocaulon*. One of the world's wonders comes from Namibia – *Welwitschia* – a huge desert plant giving the effect of a gigantic bulbous species, believed by some botanists to be the 'original' flowering plant. The various succulents from this vast countryside include many rarities such as *Dolichos, Moringa, Ceraria, Cissus* and *Chamaegigas*.

In South Africa each province seems to provide different dominant succulents. Because the seasons are in complete contrast from east to west, there is a never-ending opportunity to enjoy flowering succulents at almost any time. Mesembryanthemaceae or Ficoidaceae or Aizoaceae – whichever naming is most acceptable (they are all the same) – abound throughout most provinces from Cape Province in the south to Natal and Transvaal in the east. Aloes also are an eye-catching feature. In addition, many other succulents endemic to the south – *Stapelia, Kinepetalum, Luckhoffia, Orbea, Pectinaria, Stultitia* and the tuberous-rooted *Brachystelma* – are representative of the Asclepiadaceae, as well as species of the *Senecio, Othonna, Kalanchoë, Kedostris* and *Melothria*. The elephant's foot *Testudinaria elephantipes* and other Dioscoreaceae are also from South Africa, and Liliaceae and its associated families, Hyacinthaceae and Asphodelaceae in their many varied forms – *Bowiea, Bulbine, Chamaealoe, Drimia, Gasteria, Haworthia* – in addition to *Aloe* already mentioned, help to garnish the picture.

Madagascar, 250 miles/400 km off the east coast of Africa, is the homeland of some of the most beautiful and awe-inspiring of all plant species – and many are succulents. This is a large island, nearly 1,000 miles/1,600 km in length, mountainous in the north, with rain forests toward the east and vast plateaux in the centre. In recent years extensive exploration by diligent botanists has resulted in many new succulents being recorded. Some expeditions were made only just in time, before the area was deliberately cleared for agricultural purposes. *Aloe, Kalanchoë* and *Euphorbia* species – many having the distinctive quality of being of miniature growth – and *Rhipsalis* were found, the last being one of the few true cacti found outside the Americas. To elaborate on the flora of Madagascar would be an encyclopaedic task, but a few plants must be mentioned. *Pachypodium, Cynanchum, Stapelianthus, Trichocaulon, Adansonia, Senecio, Corallocarpus, Seyrigia, Xerosicyos, Alluaudia, Decarvia, Didierea, Jatropha, Lomatophyllum, Adenia, Peperomia, Uncarina, Cyphostemma* – these and many others constitute what is undoubtedly one of the grandest conglomerations of plant life to be found anywhere in the world.

Australia has a number of succulent plants, most of which are rare in cultivation and yet not difficult to rear successfully once obtained. *Dischidia, Hoya, Sarcostemma, Adansonia, Bulbine, Xanthorrhoea, Kingia, Anacampseros, Calandrinia, Portulaca, Myrmecodia* and *Hymenanthera* are representative of the many species within these and other genera, and it is likely that future exploration could provide an ever-increasing list of such exotic succulents.

Many parts of Asia have relatively few succulents. The sub-continent of India has *Sansevieria, Ceropegia, Caralluma, Dischidia, Hoya, Arthrocnemum, Kalanchoë* and *Coleus*, while far away to the east the Philippines also provide *Dischidia* and *Hoya*. Japan has a few indigenous species related to the Crassulaceae – *Meterostachys* and *Orostachys* – and from the regions of the Himalayas and China are still further members of the Crassulaceae – *Sempervivella* and *Sinocrassula*.

Finally, Malaysia and the Indonesian archipelago all have romantic vegetation, the monsoons providing tropical forests containing a profusion of exotics. This is one of the principal homes of the orchid, but nevertheless succulents do feature prominently. All are epiphytic or semi-epiphytic, or at least have an association with the forest regions. A number of *Hoya* species, succulent *Impatiens, Senecio, Kalanchoë, Coleus, Hydnophytum* and *Myrmecodia* – the ant tuber – all grow here. If for no other reason, this region deserves mention on account of the last two genera.

More clarification will be given when individual species and genera, so briefly surveyed here, are described more fully in the chapters that follow.

*Cacti and Succulents in a Spanish Garden*

# A~Z
## OF
## CACTI

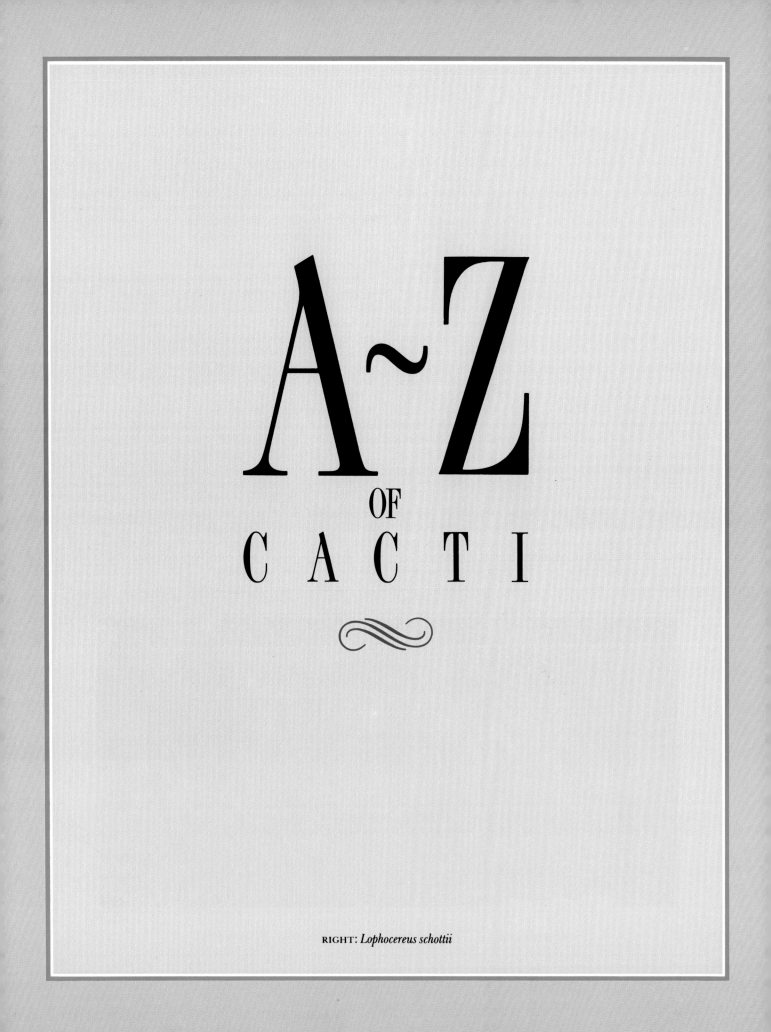

RIGHT: *Lophocereus schottii*

**Acanthocalycium** Backeb. are globular plants usually with very many acute ribs, long spines and colourful flowers.
*Acanthocalycium spiniflora* (Sch.) Backeb. (syn. *Echinocactus spiniflorus* Sch.) Type species from Argentina. Globular to cylindric with about 20 ribs, large white areoles with up to 20 spreading spines, reddish-yellow. Flowers about 1½ in/ 4 cm long and broad, rose red. *A. violaceum* (Werd.) Backeb., also from Argentina with dark green body and about 20 ribs, areoles with up to 15 yellowish-brown spines and lilac-purple flowers.

*Acanthocalycium auranticum*

*Acanthocalycium auranticum* Rausch. Native of Catamarca, Argentina, at 9,900 ft/3,000 m altitude, has 10-16 ribs, pronounced areoles with only few spreading spines and yellowish-orange flowers.

**Acanthocereus** (Bgr.) Br. & R. includes species with varying habits, some erect, others clambering.
*Acanthocereus columbianus* Br. & R. A semi-erect plant, later clambering, native of Colombia. Branches consist of three-angled joints about 3 in/8 cm wide with large areoles having about 8 short radial spines and 2 thick central spines. Very large flower about 10 in/25 cm long, white.
*Acanthocereus pentagonus* (L.) Br. & R. (syn. *Cactus pentagonus* L.) Type species. A long clambering plant, rooting at tips and forming further growths and colonizing. Stems three to five angled with regular areoles along the margins and many short acicular spines. Large flower up to 8 in/20 cm long, white with spreading petals. Tube covered with brownish felt. Very widely distributed throughout some of the southerly states of USA, the eastern coast of Mexico as far as Guatemala, and parts of the West Indies. Also known in parts of northerly South America. Other species are recorded from Mexico, *A. subinermis* Br. & R., and *A. occidentalis* Br. & R., having much the same characteristics as the type species.

**Acantholobivia** Backeb. consists of globular or oval-shaped plants. Now considered synonymous with *Lobivia*, only the flower tends not to open widely, and is borne on the sides of the plant. Very colourful.
*Acantholobivia incuiensis* Rauh & Backeb. A globular or caespitose plant with 16-20 ribs somewhat undulated with very pronounced areoles having many spines, the centrals being much longer than the radials. Flowers carmine-red. Native of southern Peru between Chala and Coracora at 11,815 ft/ 3,600 m altitude. The type species is *A. tegeleriana* Backeb. from central Peru.

**Acanthorhipsalis** (Sch.) Br. & R. are mostly epiphytic on forest trees, stems flattened and sometimes to four-angled, mostly short, occasionally elongated. Crenate margins with spiny areoles. Flowers mostly orange or reddish-orange. Indigenous to Bolivia, Argentina and Peru.
*Acanthorhipsalis crenata* (Br.) Br. & R. Very flat branches and narrow stems, much crenated. Largish areoles with wool and spines. Flower reddish, small. From high altitudes near Yungus, Bolivia.
*Ancanthorhipsalis incahuasina* Card. Another Bolivian species, little known in cultivation. Long flattened or three-winged branches, less spiny than others of the genus. Flower purported to be reddish-orange.

*Acanthorhipsalis monocantha*

*Acanthorhipsalis monocantha* (Gris.) Br. & R. Similar to the preceding but with more robust habit, sometimes semi-erect, then pendent stems, often to four-winged with spiny areoles. Flower rich orange (records of Br. & R. and Borg are incorrect in stating this has a white flower). A decorative species of easy culture. Northern Argentina.

**Anisocereus** (Br. & R.) Backeb. is now divided and included within **Pterocereus** and **Escontria**.
*Anisocereus gaumeri* (Br. & R.) Backeb. *(Escontria)* An erect slender plant with usually three, sometimes four angles, very winged. Areoles small and far apart with many slender

brownish spines. Flower greenish-yellow to 2 in/5 cm long, tube with leafy scales. Fruit very large, deep red with small bristles. From southern Mexico.

*Anisocereus lepidanthus* (Eichl.) Backeb. *(Pterocereus)* (syn. *Cereus lepidanthus* Eichl.) A little-known species from Guatemala. An erect plant, rarely branched, having seven to nine low ribs. Areoles very small with many central and radial spines. Flowers up to 3 in/8 cm long, whitish. Flower tube and ovary with thin scales.

*Ancistrocactus* Br. & R. are comparatively small globular plants with deep-set, notched ribs arising from a very fleshy frequently quite long taproot. All are natives of the USA and Mexico. Current thinking tends to refer the four species to *Ferocactus*, but for this record they are listed separately.

*Ancistrocactus crassihamatus* (Web.) L. Benson (syn. *Glandulicatus crassihamatus* Backeb.) An attractive compact plant about 6 in/15 cm across with fairly deeply notched ribs with areoles bearing several long spines of reddish-brown. Flowers are a rich purple, slightly paler on the edges of the petals. From Mexico.

*Ancistrocactus scheerii* (Salm-Dyck) Br. & R. A rather squat, columnar plant to about 4 in/12 cm high. It has yellowish spines and greenish-yellow flowers about 1¼ in/ 3 cm long. Found in both Mexico and the USA (Texas). It is inclined to be variable – one such recognized form being *Ancistrocactus scheerii* f. *megarhiza* (Rose) Krainz (syn. *Ancistrocactus megarhizus* [Rose] Br. & R.) Plant with long fleshy tap roots. Stems usually solitary, sometimes in clusters, globular to 3 in/8 cm high ribs in spirals, divided into dark green tubercles to 2 in/5 cm high. About 20 pectinate, pale, radial spines, spreading, and four central spines, the lower ones being stouter and longer and strongly hooked. Flower funnel-shaped, small with short tube from the base of the long tubercles. A rare species from near Victoria, Mexico.

*Ancistrocactus uncinatus* Gal. (Beus.) (syn. *Glandulicactus uncinata* [Gal.] Backeb.) Type species. Short cylindrical plant to about 8 in/20 cm high with 13 ribs having strong tubercles undulate. Areoles with many hairs and spines, the central spine and three lower radial spines are prominently hooked. Flowers brownish. From western Texas to central Mexico. This was included with the genus *Ferocactus*, then transferred by Backeberg to a new genus created for this and one other species because they had glands in the areole which secreted a honey-like substance. These glands were often elongated and gave the effect of stunted spines. The actual status of this plant is still in doubt.

*Aporocactus* Lem. is the popular 'rat's tail cactus' consisting of slender-stemmed creeping plants, sometimes vine-like and invariably pendent, regardless of the fact that aerial roots develop on some stems. All known species are reputedly of Mexican origin, but escapes have become established in parts of Central and South America. Some species have been cross-pollinated with species of other genera, *Epiphyllum* in particular, thereby providing most interesting, useful and floriferous cultivars with *Aporocactus*-like stems, and flowers resembling *Epiphyllum*. Referred to as × *Aporophyllum*.

*Aporocactus flagelliformis* (L.) Lem. The best-known of this genus. It would appear certain that the original home of the species was Mexico, although suggestions have been made that it might be native of South America. This seems unlikely as it is very well known in southern Mexico, but escapes may have become established in parts of South America. The soft, spiny and pendent branches have 10 to 12 ribs, very inconspicuous being closely covered by many soft spines from areoles set about ¼ in/6 mm apart. The flowers are diurnal, crimson and zygomorphic, lasting for up to four days.

*Aporocactus flagriformis* (Zucc.) Lem. From Oaxaca in southern Mexico. A creeping species, branching freely with occasional aerial roots from slender stems. Ribs 10 or 11 with smaller areoles and fewer spines than *A. flagelliformis*. This gives the effect of a more open and less densely covered stem – one of the main obvious differences between the two species when not in flower. Flower is dark crimson, up to 4 in/10 cm long and broader than the former.

*Aporocactus leptophis* (De Cand.) Br. & R. An epiphytic species from Oaxaca, southern Mexico, and having more slender stems than others of the genus with seven or eight ribs. Areoles not so closely set, but with many stiff spines. Has reddish flower with suggestion of lilac shading. A rare plant in cultivation.

*Aporocactus martianus*

Other species recorded include *Aporocactus conzatti* and *Aporocactus martianus*. *Aporocactus mallisonii* is a cultivar derived from *Aporocactus flagelliformis* × *Heliocereus* (possibly *H. speciosus*), and sometimes known as × *Heliaporus smithii* Rowley. The *Aporocactus-Heliocereus* complex has still to be better appreciated. There is possibly a greater kinship between the two genera than has, as yet, been determined.

*Arequipa* Br. & R. concerns principally plants rather globular in shape, from a somewhat confined area around Arequipa, Peru, which gave the genus its name, and to part of northern Chile. Certain characteristics link this genus with *Matucana*.

*Arequipa leucotricha* (Phil.) Br. & R. (syn. *Echinocactus leucotrichus* Phil.) The type species. A globose sometimes semi-elongated plant having from 10 to 20 ribs, close-set areoles with many spines, up to 20, the centrals being about 1¼ in/3 cm long. Flowers on long slender tube, red. Other species are described which appear almost identical, if not synonymous to the species and include *A. rettigii* (Quehl) Br. & R., *A. erectocylindrica* Rauh & Backeb.

*Ariocarpus* Scheidw. are curious, somewhat gnarled plants with prominent rock-like tubercles. Extremely slow-growing.

*Ariocarpus agavoides*

*Ariocarpus agavoides* (Cast.) Anderson (syn. *Neogomesia agavoides* Cast. A monotypic genus now absorbed into *Ariocarpus*.) Thick fleshy root. Tubercles only few, spreading, semi-erect, horny, giving the effect of a miniature *Agave*. Areoles roundish on upper surface of tubercle just below the tip, woolly. Flower deep purplish-pink, funnel-shaped. A unique species from Tamaulipas, Mexico.

*Ariocarpus fissuratus* (Engelm.) Sch. (syn. *Roseocactus fissuratus* Sch. A. Bgr.) There is no justification for separating this from other species of *Ariocarpus*. The genus *Roseocactus* has never been totally accepted by some. It has a thick turnip-like root. Tubercles triangular and thick, scarcely showing above the ground in its habitat. Plant about 6 in/15 cm or more diameter, the whole surface fissured and warty and generally almost flat. Areoles contain many hairs. Flowers from the centre areoles, purplish-pink. From western Texas and northern parts of Coahuila and Zacatecas, Mexico. *A. lloydii* Rose is closely related to this species, has somewhat rounded surface with generally larger tubercles and is possibly only a variant. Referred to as 'Living Rock'.

*Ariocarpus retusus* Scheidw. Type species. Widely distributed in Coahuila, Zacatecas and San Luis Potosi in Mexico.

Globular plants with somewhat flattened or depressed surface, about 5 in/12 cm or more diameter, greyish, with wool at the centre. Tubercles very horny up to 2 in/5 cm long, generally three-angled and tending to overlap one another. Flowers from the axils of the young tubercles at the centre, white. Associated with rocky, stony places and often almost covered by sand leaving only the tips of tubercles visible.

*Armatocereus* Backeb. includes a number of tree-like cerei, closely linked to *Lemaireocereus*. The flower tube, ovary and fruit are spiny.

*Armatocereus humilis* (Br. & R.) Backeb. A low-growing trailing plant from Dagua Valley, Colombia, having elongated stems, four to five ribs, spreading with rooting branches. Areoles bear white felt, spines about 15. Nocturnal white flowers.

*Armatocereus laetus* (H. B. & K.) Br. & R. (syn. *Cactus laetus H. B. & K.*) Type species. At one time included within the genus *Lemaireocereus*. An erect plant to 20 ft/6 m high, tree-like with many branches, bluish-green. Ribs about eight somewhat prominent, areoles with brownish-grey spines about 1¼ in/3 cm long. Flowers nocturnal, white to 3 in/8 cm long. Indigenous to southern Ecuador and Peru.

*Arrojadoa* Br. & R. non Mattf. Cylindrical stems, generally slender with low ribs and many small spines. An apical pseudocephalium develops from which the flowers arise. An interesting genus consisting of only a few known species, all from Brazil.

*Arrojadoa canudosensis* Buin. & Bred. A tall erect species from Canudos, Bahia, Brazil, to over 3¼ ft/1 m high, branching from the base with cephalium of brown bristles and white hairs in which the flowers are produced. Stems continue to grow through the cephalium with the existing cephalium persisting, thus forming bristly rings around the stem. About 14 ribs, areoles close-set with white felt and to 15 brown radial spines and eight usually upward-pointing central spines. Flowers tubular, pinkish-green.

*Arrojadoa penicillata* (Gurke) Br. & R. A slender erect plant from Bahia, Brazil, about 6½ ft/2 m high with many branches often becoming bushy. About 10 low ribs with closely set areoles bearing short spreading spines. Brownish bristles develop at terminal ends of joints forming a thick ring around the stem. Flowers rose-pink.

*Arrojadoa rhodantha* (Gurke) Br. & R. (syn. *Cereus rhodanthus* Gurke) Type species from Piauhy, Brazil, where it is found in very arid areas. Semi-erect, then clambering, cylindrical stems in joints with about 12 ribs, dark green; small areoles having brown slender spines. Flowers from terminal ends, pink about 1¼ in/3 cm long surrounded by brownish bristles which persist and form a ring around each joint.

*Arthrocereus* Bgr. are generally small-growing species with very spiny stems. Flowers develop from near the top of the stems, nocturnal. This is possibly very closely related to *Setiechinopsis*.

*Arthrocereus microsphaericus* (Sch). Bgr. A small species from near Rio de Janeiro, Brazil, with slender somewhat prostrate stems jointed with many low ribs and spiny. Small whitish nocturnal flowers usually at terminals of joints.

*Arthrocereus rondonianus* Backeb. & Voll. A rare species from Diamantian, Brazil, small creeping plant with cylindrical stems to 28 in/70 cm long, areoles with numerous bright yellowish spines. Flowers purplish-pink.

**Astrophytum** Lem. includes only a few much sought-after plants. Mostly with a greyish, somewhat globular body with only 5-10 ribs. Flowers are large and yellow.

*Astrophytum myriostigma* Lem. (syn. *Echinocactus myriostigma* S-D) Type species. A well-loved species, commonly known as the 'bishop's cap'. A globular plant usually solitary with few ribs, four sometimes up to eight, very broad and covered with woolly scales. Areoles along the ridges, sometimes woolly and pronounced. Flower yellow. Native to northern central Mexico. There are a number of varietal forms. *A. myriostigma* var. *strongylogonum* is a fat form of the species with more rounded ribs. *A. myriostigma* var. *columnare*, a white columnar plant with somewhat paler flowers. *A. myriostigma* var. *quadricostata* which is typical of the species but with only four ribs, and this has been known to revert to the normal five. *A. myriostigma* var. *nuda* is similar in every respect only having no whitish scales and presenting a greenish appearance.

*Astrophytum asterias*

Other species include *A. asterias* (Zucc.) Lem., a very distinctive plant, commonly known as the 'bishop's mitre', a very sought-after species. *A. ornatum* (De Cand.) Web. has a number of forms; along with *A. capricorne* (Dietr.) Br. & R. and its varieties, theese are the only members of this genus which are heavily spined.

**Austrocactus** Br. & R. includes only a few species which are sometimes likened to the North American Echinocerei. Low-growing plants, somewhat cylindrical with hooked central spines and colourful flowers. Patagonia, south Argentina.

*Austrocactus bertinii* (Cels.) Br. & R. (syn. *Cereus bertinii* Cels.) Type species of this interesting and rare genus, body olive-green to about 12 in/30 cm or more high, 10-12 prominent ribs, felted areoles bearing up to 15 slender spreading radial spines and four-five slender, very hooked blackish central spines up to 1¼ in/3 cm long. Large flower to 4 in/10 cm diameter, pinkish-yellow with red stigma lobes. *A. dusenii* (Web.) Br. & R. is very similar, branching from near the base, rose-pink flowers.

*Austrocactus patagonicus* (Web.) Backeb. A taller plant, often reaching 20 in/50 cm high. It has up to 16 radial spines and four centrals. Flowers of pinkish-white about 1½ in/4 cm across with rich violet stigmas.

**Austrocephalocereus** (Backeb.) Backeb. Tall-growing cerei with superficial pseudocephalium, which develops on one side of the stem.

*Austrocephalocereus dybowskii*

*Austrocephalocereus dybowskii* (Goss.) Backeb. An attractive much-branched plant from Bahia, Brazil. Tall cylindrical stems nearly 13 ft/4 m high, branching freely from the base, forming clusters. Branches with over 20 ribs with closely set areoles bearing long white hairs and few yellowish radial and central spines, the centrals protruding horizontally, about 1¼ in/3 cm long. Nocturnal white flowers 1½ in/4 cm long, rising from the white pseudo-cephalium.

*Austrocephalocereus purpureus* (Gurke) Backeb. (syn. *Cereus purpureus* Gurke) Type species. An erect columnar plant, unbranched, to over 10 ft/3 m high with broad low ribs 12-16, depressions above each areole, elongated areoles with white wool and many spines, radials about 18, acicular, short; centrals about 10, 2 in/5 cm long, brown. Pseudo-cephalium on one side of the stem, nocturnal white flowers.

**Aztekium** Böd. is so-named because of its resemblance to Aztec sculpture. An unusual and quite rare species.

*Aztekium ritteri*

*Aztekium ritteri* (Boed.) Boed. (syn. *Echinocactus ritteri* Boed.) A monotypic genus for this one species from Nuevo Leon, Mexico. A small globular plant, sometimes grouping. Having 9–11 rather spiral ribs with small glandless areoles having short hairs. The surface has many furrows, and notches at each areole. Spines insignificant. The whole plant gives the effect of being hard and similar to species of Ariocarpus, dark dull green with small white flowers. A rare species in cultivation.

**Backebergia** Bravo is a monotypic genus. Often tree-like, it bears a very bristly cephalium with nocturnal flowers.

*Backebergia militaris*

*Backebergia chrysomallus* (Lem.) Backeb. (syn. *Pilocereus chrysomallus* Lem.) Sometimes called *B. militaris*. A very large columnar species with many branches up to 18 ft/ 5½ m high. Branches with many ribs, up to 14, dull greyish-green. Mature growths develop a brown cephalium eventually covering the whole apex which becomes larger as

the plant grows taller. Flowers from the cephalium, about 1¼ in/3 cm long, creamy-white. A plant of exceptional attraction – cuttings of flowering stems will root easily and the cephalium will continue to grow. Endemic to more southerly parts of Mexico around Oaxaca and Puebla.

**Bergerocactus** Br. & R. is a monotypic genus with slender, heavily spined stems. The flowers are borne laterally and are diurnal.

*Bergerocactus emoryi*

*Bergerocactus emoryi* (Engelm.) Br. & R. (syn. *Cereus emoryi* Engelm.) A sprawling species with bright green cylindrical stems and branches having many ribs and completely covered with long golden-yellow spines, often with over 30 to an areole. Flowers creamy-white with very spiny fruits. Distributed in more southerly areas of California and into northwesterly parts of Baja California, Mexico, in coastal regions.

**Blossfeldia** Werd. include some of the more miniature species of the Cactaceae, mostly multi-headed with whitish scattered areoles and no perceptible spines.
*Blossfeldia liliputana* Werd. The type species from north Argentina. Small flattish-circular plants, greyish-green with minute greyish woolly areoles and totally unarmed. Flower whitish-pink produced near to the crown, diurnal. *B. minima* Ritt. is similar and likely to prove synonymous.

**Borzicactus** Ricco. This genus along with many others (*Matucana, Submatucana, Oroya, Arequipa, Denmoza*, etc.) has been the subject of much research by botanists on both sides of the Atlantic and to date no all-embracing formula has yet been produced which is generally acceptable to all. Many of the original generic names will die hard, and while there is no intention to ignore the work of very eminent scientists, for the purpose of this record the better-known generic title is being used. *Borzicactus* has now absorbed many other genera, including *Akersia, Bolivicereus, Borzicactella, Clistanthocereus, Loxanthocereus, Hildewintera* and *Seticereus*.

*Borzicactus acanthurus* (Vaup.) Br. & R. Low-spreading procumbent plant from Matucana, Peru, with long branches up to 12 in/30 cm long and about 1½ in/4 cm diameter. Stems with about 18 low rounded ribs, small woolly areoles and numerous yellow short bristly spines, with a few somewhat longer centrals. Flowers red. At one time included within the genus *Loxanthocereus*. Also seemingly legitimately placed is *B. roezlii* (Haage Jr.) Backeb. with pronounced rounded ribs, up to 20 radial spines and one central protruding horizontally. Flowers reddish, from toward end of stem.

*Borzicactus auriespina*

*Borzicactus auriespina* (Ritt.) Kimn. (syn. *Hildewintera auriespina* [Ritt.] Ritt.) A beautiful plant of easy culture. The generic names of *Winteria* Ritt. and *Winterocereus* Backeb. have also been used in connection with this species. A cylindrical stem, of pendent habit, branching freely from the base, slender with many ribs and a profusion of golden-yellow spines completely covering the body of the plant. Flowers orange-reddish, with protruding yellow stigma, diurnal. Native of Bolivia.

*Borzicactus fieldianus* (Br. & R.) Kimn. (syn. *Clistanthocereus fieldianus* [Br. & R.] Backeb.) A tall-growing plant, forming thickets to 16-20 ft/5-6 m in height, many elongated branches which often tend to become pendent and almost prostrate. Ribs six-seven, broad and stout, pronounced, large circular areoles with about eight whitish spines of unequal length, some to over 2 in/5 cm long. Flowers from terminal ends of branches, reddish.

*Borzicactus gracilis* (Akers & Buin.) Kimn. (syn. *Loxanthocereus gracilis* [Akers & Buin.] Backeb.) Originating from Peru at over 9,800 ft/3,000 m altitude in the Andes. When first introduced was included in the genus *Maritimocereus* which was erected for this particular plant. A low decumbent species, branching quite freely with about 10 or 11 low ribs, tubercled. Areoles bearing 10 small protruding spines, greyish. Flowers zygomorphic, diurnal, orange-red.

*Borzicactus icosagonus* (H. B. & K.) Kimn. (syn. *Seticereus icosagonus* H. B. & K.) A species which originates from northern Peru and Ecuador. A grouping plant with somewhat erect stems and about 20 ribs, transversely furrowed. Close-set areoles with numerous needle-like spines and long red-orange flowers.

*Borzicactus roseiflora* (Buin.) Kimn. (syn. *Akersia roseiflora* Buin.) An interesting columnar species from Peru. Erect with many ribs and yellowish-brown spines. Flowers somewhat tubular-campanulate, bright rose-pink.

*Borzicactus samaipatanus* Card. (syn. *Bolivicereus samaipatanus* Card.) A most imposing plant from Bolivia, branching freely from the base, very erect. Branches with up to 16 low, transverse ribs with prominent brown woolly areoles and numerous golden-yellow radial acicular spines. Flowers are deep red, diurnal.

*Borzicactus sextonianus* (Backeb.) Kimn. has been transferred from *Loxanthocereus*. It grows to well over 3¼ ft/1 m long with about 13 deeply notched ribs. 1-2 central and up to 30 radial spines. Flowers are deep red 2-2½ in/5-6 cm long.

**Brachycereus** Br. & R. Short-stemmed plants from the Galapagos Islands, with close-set areoles and many acicular spines.

*Brachycereus thouarsii* (Web.) Br. & R. (syn. *Cereus thouarsii* Web.) Type species. One of the few endemic species of the Galapagos Islands where it is fairly widely distributed. A rare plant in cultivation. Stems to about 3¼ ft/1 m high and branching from base. Ribs about 20, with closely set areoles bearing numerous bristly spines about 1¼ in/3 cm long which completely cover the branches, so dense is the formation. Flower nocturnal, whitish.

**Brasilicereus** Backeb. is allied to *Cephalocereus*. Tree-like plants, all from Brazil.

*Brasilicereus phaeacanthus* (Gurke) Backeb. (syn. *Cereus phaeacanthus* Gurke) An erect slender plant, branching freely from the base, endemic to Bahia, Brazil. Branches have about 12 ribs, low and narrow, closely set white woolly areoles with numerous brownish spines to ½ in/1.5 cm long. The flowers are white, funnel-shaped and nocturnal.

**Browningia** Br. & R. are attractive erect plants, sometimes branching at the top. Stems with numerous ribs and very spiny.

*Browningia candelaris* (Meyen) Br. & R. (syn. *Cereus candelaris* Meyen.) Type species. Erect tall tree-like, from high altitudes in northern Chile and southern Peru. Stems to over 13 ft/4 m high forming a stout trunk and branching at the top. Many rounded ribs with pronounced areoles bearing numerous brownish-black spines. Flowers pinkish-white, nocturnal. Other species include *B. altissima* (Ritt.) Buxb. with erect, almost spineless, prominently ribbed stems and nocturnal whitish flowers, earlier known as *Gymnanthocereus altissimus* Ritt. and originates from Cajamarca, Peru. *B. pil-*

*leifera* (Ritt.) Hutch. and hitherto known as *Gymnanthocereus pilleifera* Ritt. from Balsas, Peru, with small greenish-white flowers at terminals of branches.

*Browningia nobilis* Buxb. (syn. *Azureocereus nobilis* Akers & Johns.) A very imposing species from Peru, erect, columnar with few branches, bluish-green, many low but prominent ribs having woolly areoles and long deflexed spines. Flowers nocturnal from upper areoles, white. Another species, perhaps synonymous, is *B. hertlingianus* (Backeb.) Buxb. Has bright bluish stems and long yellow spines.

**Buiningia** Buxb. is a species of particular interest and attraction, segregated from *Coleocephalocereus* as its flowers and seeds are more similar to *Melocactus*. Plants with pseudocephalium.

*Buiningia brevicylindrica* (Buin.) Buxb. (syn. *Coleocephalocereus brevicylindrica* Buin.) A fascinating plant, short cylindrical stem with about 17 broad acute ribs, having pronounced areoles bearing approximately 10 spreading radial spines and three or four centrals, yellowish but becoming greyish.

Cephalium develops firstly across three or four ribs eventually spreading and covering half the stem with yellowish bristles set in thickish yellowish-white wool which becomes blackish with age. Flowers small, yellowish-green.

*Buiningia aurea*

*Buiningia aurea* (Ritt.) Buxb. is very similar in many respects to *Buiningia brevicylindrica*, offsets freely from the base with heavily spined plantlets. Both species are from southern Brazil and are closely allied to *Coleocephalocereus*.

*C*

**Calymmanthium** Ritt. includes only two species from Peru. Tall erect plant, their unique characteristic among cacti is undoubtedly the flowers with a double perianth – one within the other.

*Calymmanthium substerile*

*Calymmanthium substerile* Ritt. Type species. A rare plant from Peru and Bolivia, erect, branching from the base four to five-angled, fresh green with large areoles and spines of unequal length. Also recognized is *C. fertile* Ritt. with three to four-angled branches.

**Carnegia** Br. & R. is a monotypic genus which develops tree-like proportions. Of extremely slow growth.

*Carnegia gigantea*

*Carnegia gigantea* (Engelm.) Br. & R. (syn. *Cereus giganteus* Engelm.) One of the most spectacular plants of the cactaceae – the giant saguaro of Arizona. This species also occurs near Kino Bay, Sonora. A huge columnar cactus, stout, with many ribs and areoles felted and spiny. For many years the plant remains simple, then branches with thick ascending growths – can become up to 50 ft/15 m tall. Flowers up to 5 in/12 cm long, white, short tube with small but broad scales. Fruits red. Woodpeckers make their nests within the body of the plant; when deserted they are occupied by other forms of bird life.

***Castellanosia*** Card. was erected for one species with upper areoles having brownish-grey bristles and the lower areoles with awl-shaped spines.
*Castellanosia caineana* Card. Type species. A tall-growing species to about 16 ft/5 m or more. Stems cylindrical with nine rounded ribs. Pseudocephalium develops toward top of branches. Flowers deep red, diurnal, somewhat funnel-shaped. A species from Bolivia which has close association with *Browningia*.

***Cephalocereus*** Pfeiff. at one time included many species. Through recent reclassifications now reduced to monotypic status.
*Cephalocereus senilis* (Haw.) Pfeiff. (syn. *Cactus senilis* Haw.) Type species. A well-known and attractive plant from the limestone hills of eastern Hidalgo, Mexico. A tall-growing cactus up to 45 ft/14 m high, columnar, with numerous ribs and densely covered with white bristles and thick long whitish wool. Has become known as the 'old man cactus'. Pseudocephalium develops when the stems are about 20 ft/6 m tall. Flower rose-pink about 2 in/5 cm long, tube with few scales. Nocturnal flowering. This species has the distinctive quality of having a similar attractive appearance from seedling stage through to maturity.

***Cereus*** Mill. are tall, stately plants, generally much-branched. All with nocturnal flowers and generally red fruits.

*Cereus chalybaeus*

*Cereus chalybaeus* Otto. From northern Argentina and Uruguay. Attains 10 ft/3 m tall, stems bluish-green with 5–6 ribs, areoles with black radial and central spines. Flowers white.
*Cereus jamacaru* De Cand. One of several of this large genus which are very well known in cultivation. Tall-growing to 32 ft/10 m high, branching freely, bluish-green erect

branches with up to six ribs having large areoles and many spines – on mature plants these become very long. Flowers on long tube, white, nocturnal to about 10 in/25 cm long. Widely distributed in Bahia, Brazil. This is often confused with *C. peruvianus* (L.) Mill., a plant to be seen in many parts of southeastern South America, and not necessarily native to Peru, which its name would suggest. Stems are dark green, usually four to nine ribs, dark brownish-black spines. Flowers also white, large, nocturnal. The type species of the genus is *C. hexagonus* (L.) Mill. from more northerly regions of South America, which has generally six-angled stems, thin ribs, small felted areoles and short spines. Flowers are very large, nocturnal, white.

***Cleistocactus*** Lem. are slender plants of erect or clambering habit. The flower is the main characteristic, the perianth tube being almost closed and only the stamens and style protrude.
*Cleistocactus baumannii* (Lem.) Br. & R. (syn. *Cereus baumannii* Lem.) Type species. Plants having erect stems with many ribs and closely set areoles bearing numerous very short brownish spines, from yellowish areoles with orange-red diurnal flowers, endemic to Argentina. *C. Strausii* (Heese) Backeb. is possibly the best known of the genus, having greyish areoles and white spines. Flowers reddish, diurnal. Mountainous areas of Bolivia.
*Cleistocactus brookei* Card., better known as *C. wendlandiorum* Backeb. from western Argentina. One of the finest of the genus, with very short golden-yellow spines and deep orange flowers, the bright green stigma just protruding. A very rewarding group which are easy in cultivation and begin to produce flowers when about 30 in/75 cm tall.
*Cleistocactus chrysocephalus* Ritt. A tall-growing plant with many cylindrical branches, characterized by 11-14 low ribs and areoles bearing about 15 radial spines and six centrals. Branches develop very long cephaliums, consisting of yellowish-brown bristly spines. Flowers reddish about 2 in/5 cm long. Endemic to Bolivia.

***Coleocephalocereus*** Beckeb. were separated from *Cephalocereus* on account of the naked funnel-shaped flowers emanating from the bristly woolly pseudocephalium borne in a groove.
*Coleocephalocereus fluminensis* (Miqu.) Backeb. (syn. *Cereus fluminensis* Miqu.) Type species. Found on rocky cliff faces near the coastline of Rio de Janeiro, Brazil, tall, erect or clambering, densely branched. Stems have about 12-17 ribs, acute, with closely set areoles and short acicular yellow spines. Pseudocephalium on only one side of the terminal ends consisting of dense white wool and yellowish bristles. Flowers nocturnal, pinkish-white. *C. goebelianus* (Vaup.) Backeb., endemic to the states of Bahia and Minas Gerais, Brazil, is possibly the largest of this genus, often to 20 ft/6 m high. Stems with up to 25 ribs, closely set areoles with about 16 radial spines and about six to eight stiff straight centrals. Cephalium covers half the stem consisting of whitish wool and dark brown sometimes black bristles. Flowers pinkish-

white. Other more recent introductions include *C. decumbens* Ritt. from Minas Gerais, Brazil, a smaller-growing species somewhat decumbent in habit. *C. paulensis* Ritt. is another densely branching and clambering plant from the island of Ilhabela near São Paulo, Brazil.

***Copiapoa*** Br. & R. contains many of the most spectacular globular cacti, all originating from Chile. The title is derived from the provincial name, Copiapo. It includes many species, some of which might possibly be considered synonymous with others, or alternatively be reduced to varietal status.
*Copiapoa marginata* (S-D) Br. & R. (syn. *Echinocactus marginatus* S-D) The type species from the coastal hills of Antofagasta, Chile, is a clustering plant, sub-cylindrical, about 12 low ribs and very closely set areoles from which emanate up to 10 spines of unequal length, one usually much longer than the others. Flowers yellow, from the crown of the plant which becomes closely set with many brownish hairs. *C. cinerea* (Phil.) Br. & R. from near Taltal, western Chile, is one of the most distinctive species, somewhat cylindrical whitish-grey stem, dense white wool in the apex, about 18 broad ribs with closely set areoles and black spines. Flowers yellow. Two distinct varieties of *C. cinerea* are recognized, *C. cinerea* var. *dealbata*, usually with long spines, singly from the areoles; *C. cinerea* var. *columna-alba* has generally shorter spines than the species, taller and white.
*C. longistaminea* Ritt. is yet another outstanding plant, with greyish-green body, somewhat flattened with white wool at the apex, round areoles with brownish felt and three to six brownish spines, generally spreading. *C. krainziana* Ritt. is exceptional on account of its covering of fine, white, hair-like bristles and golden spines.

***Corryocactus*** Br. & R. are short erect plants with prominent ribs and large diurnal flowers, very symmetrical, borne from the upper areoles.
*Corryocactus brevistylus* (Sch.) Br. & R. (syn. *Cereus brevistylus* Sch.) Type species. A tall-growing plant to about 10 ft/3 m high and branching freely from the base forming thickets. Slender branches with about 6 pronounced ribs, large, roundish, areoles about 1¼ in/3 cm apart with dense wool and about 15 brownish spines of unequal length. Flowers large, about 4 in/10 cm diameter, yellowish. Indigenous to the mountainous areas of southern Peru at altitude of nearly 9,900 ft/3,000 m. A Bolivian species, *C. melanotrichus* (Sch.) Br. & R. is a smaller growing plant from barren hills around La Paz at over 9,900 ft/3,000 m, with yellow spines and a large yellow flower.
*Corryocactus squarrosa*, previously known as *Erdisia squarrosa* (Vaup.) Br. & R. From the highlands of Peru at an altitude of over 6,250 ft/2,000 m. Long slender stems to 6½ ft/2 m having about eight ribs with fairly closely set areoles from which emanate about 15 yellowish spines of unequal length, longest to about 1½ in/4 cm. Flowers at terminal ends of stems, yellowish-red. Other species include *Corryocactus*

*tenuiculus* Hutchinson with orange-red flowers.
***Coryphantha*** (Engelm.) Lem. is a large genus of more or less globular plants. Require a good sunny position. Their prominent tubercles are a main feature.

*Coryphantha calochlora*

*Coryphantha calochlora* Böd. A rare species from Mexico. It has a globular body, more or less covered with many turbercles – 12–15 spines to each areole and deep reddish flowers.
*Coryphantha organensis* D. Zimm. With cylindrical stems, clustering freely, yellowish-green with pronounced tubercles. Areoles with numerous spines, radials about 35, stiff, straight, whitish; centrals about 12, straight, stout, yellowish. Flowers pale pink. Endemic to the area of the Organ Mountains, New Mexico, USA. ·
*Coryphantha pulleineana* (Backeb.) Glass (syn. *Neolloydia pulleineanus* Backeb.) With elongated growth and very long fleshy tuberous roots. Pronounced tubercles with many radial and central spines, centrals being much longer, straight, brownish-black. Flower yellow or golden-yellow from near the apex. From San Luis Potosi, Mexico.
*Coryphantha pusilliflora* Bremer. A newly introduced species from Coahuila, Mexico. A plant about 5 in/12 cm high, 2-2½ in/5-6 cm wide with tubercles arranged in spirals. 18-20 radial spines and one central. The magenta and whitish flowers are funnel-shaped.
*Coryphantha scheeri* (Kuntze) L. Benson. A rather elongated plant to 6 in/15 cm long and 3½ in/9 cm diameter at base, solitary, sometimes clustering, pronounced tubercles and densely spined. Radial spines one to five, slightly hooked or curved, spreading irregularly 1 in/2½ cm long, centrals thickish, about 1 in/2½ cm long, light brown with red tips, spreading. Flower to 2¾ in/7 cm diameter, yellowish with reddish markings. Two varietal forms are recorded, *C. scheeri* var. *valida* (Engelm) L. Benson and *C. scheeri* var. *robustispina* (Schott) L. Benson. The latter now has specific status as *Coryphantha robustispina* (Schott) Br. & R. All from high elevations in Chihuahuan Desert, southeast Arizona, Texas, and in parts of Chihuahua in Mexico.
*Coryphantha sneedii* (Br. & R.) Berg. var. *leei* (Rose) L. Benson. This variety is synonymous with *Escobaria leei* Rose

ex. Boed. A choice miniature-growing species from lime-stone rock ledges in Rattlesnake Canyon, New Mexico. Rarely solitary, generally clusters freely, densely covered with small whitish spines. Flowers pinkish-white.

*Coryphantha sulcolanata* Lem. (syn. *Mammillaria sulcolanata* Lem.) Type species, a somewhat sub-globose plant, usually clustering about 2 in/5 cm high and 2½ in/6 cm diameter. Tubercles five-angled at base, conical above with wool in axils of young plants. About 10 radial spines of unequal length up to ⅝ in/16 mm long, brownish with black tips. Flower about 1½ in/4 cm long, pinkish. Hidalgo, Mexico.

*Coryphantha strobiliformis* var. *strobiliformis* (Poselger.) L. Benson, the other variety being *C. strobiliformis* var. *orcuttii* (Rose) L. Benson. Plants usually clustering, cylindrical to about 7 in/18 cm high, tubercles regularly arranged in spirals, with numerous radial spines, up to 30, acicular, several centrals, usually tipped brown or blackish and one protruding horizontally. Flowers pale pink, about 1 in/ 2.5 cm diameter lasting several days. This plant is found at fairly high altitudes in limestone soil, and is native to Arizona, New Mexico and Chihuahua, Mexico.

**Cryptocereus** Alex. is a genus created for what is undoubt-edly one of the most fascinating discoveries of recent years, and to which, since, has been transferred another species. At first considered to be one of the Epiphyllanae on account of the stem being similar to certain *Epiphyllum* species. Develops long branches and has many aerial roots. The rick-rack stem forms a unique characteristic of the genus which includes three species.

*Cryptocereus imitans*

One other species is recorded, *Cryptocereus imitans* (Kimn. and Hutch.) Backeb. Said to be endemic to Costa Rica. Has the same rick-rack stem growth, but bears white flowers and now reclassified as *Weberocereus imitans* Buxb.

**Dendrocereus** Br. & R. is a monotypic genus – columnar plants with few ribs. Flowers nocturnal, often to 8 in/20 cm long.

*Cryptocereus anthonyanus*

*Cryptocereus anthonyanus* Alex. A true epiphyte from south-ern Mexico – in the regions of Chiapas and reputedly also in Costa Rica. Originally discovered growing on the roof of a native's hut, and some time elapsed before the actual habitat was determined. An outstanding exotic flower of brick-red sepals and yellow throat. Nocturnal flowering and only slightly scented. The elongated stems develop many aerial roots which enable it to trail or hang pendent from trees. A desirable species of easy culture.

*Dendrocereus nudiflorus*

*Dendrocereus nudiflorus* (Engelm.) Br. & R. (syn. *Cereus nudi-florus* Englem.) Type species. A very rare species from Cuba, scarcely known in cultivation. A tree-like plant up to 33 ft/10 m high with woody trunk and many terminal branches. Branches dull green with three to five ribs, very pronounced and areoles with many spines. Mature growth is stout and sturdy, while young immature branches tend to be weak and small jointed. Flowers whitish.

***Denmoza*** Br. & R. is an anagram of Mendoza, Argentina, signifying its place of origin. Somewhat cylindrical plants with very straight parallel ribs and clusters of uneven reddish-brown curved spines.
*Denmoza rhodacantha* (S-D) Br. & R. (syn. *Echinocactus rhoda-canthus* S-D) Globular-cylindric, becoming more elongated with age. With straight ribs somewhat undulated, grey-felted areoles about ¾ in/2 cm apart each bearing about 10-11 curving red spines. Flowers red with style protruding beyond the petals and stamens. Endemic to the western mountainous areas of Argentina. *D. erythrocephala* (K Sch.) Berg. is very similar but with more slender spines and bristly hairs at areoles, also from Argentina.

***Discocactus*** Pfeiff. is a genus of consequence due in no small degree to the many expeditions which have resulted in the discovery of a number of new species during the last two decades. The names of Buining and Horst are particularly associated with such expeditions and they, probably more than any others, have been instrumental in introducing new species of *Discocactus*, *Melocactus*, and other of the more rare, little-understood Brazilian plants. The genus is characterized by the body of the plant, being globose and somewhat flattened; the cephalium which is more apparent with some species than with others; the large nocturnal white fragrant flowers, and the naked fruits.

*Discocactus horstii*

*Discocactus placentiformis* (Lehm.) Sch. (syn. *Cactus placenti-formis* Lehm.) The type species. Low, globular, bluish-green plant, with woolly cephalium. Has about 10-14 broad, low ribs, and six to eight areoles on each rib bearing usually six, sometimes seven stout recurved dark brownish spines and rarely one solitary central spine. Large white flower, fragrant. Endemic to Brazil. *D. heptacanthus* (Rodr.) Br. & R. from Mato Grosso, Brazil, is about 5 in/12 cm diameter with

up to 12 rather tuberculate ribs and areoles bearing usually seven stout recurved radial spines. Cephalium bristly, and flower white, large, scented. *D. alteolens* Lem. from Brazil, a very flattish plant with few ribs and few spines. A very rare species with the typical large white scented flower.

One of the most fascinating plants to be discovered in recent years is *D. horstii* Buin. & Bred., a small Brazilian species with up to 20 acute ribs having closely set areoles and minute 'comb-like' spines. The plant body measures about ¾-1¼ in/2-3 cm diameter, reddish-greyish-green with pronounced woolly cephalium from which large white nocturnal flowers emerge.
Several more species of *Discocactus* have been discovered in more recent years. *D. magnimammus* Buin. & Bred. is a heavily spined plant from Mato Grosso, Brazil, about 6 in/15 cm broad, 2½ in/6-7 cm high with a white-tufted crown and terminal flowers of pale pinkish-white. *D. bolivi-ensis* Backeb. from La Cruz, Bolivia, is much the same size, a cephalium to 1½ in/4 cm high without bristles or spines and with white flowers. *Discocactus lindaianus* Diers & Esteves from Goias, Brazil has a flattish, globular stem about 3 in/8 cm high and to 7 in/17 cm across, greyish-green, a few radial spines and one central. The cephalium is 1 in/2-3 cm high, 2 in/5 cm wide. The flowers are greenish-white.

***Disocactus*** Lindl. is a much-branching epiphytic group, having flattened stems and branches, sometimes terete. Flowers diurnal. Indigenous to Central America. Of easy culture, and providing a most desirable flowering plant.
*Disocactus alatus* (Swartz) Kimn. A true epiphytic species with lanceolate stems having crenate margins. Small yellowish-cream flowers with slender style and five stigma lobes. From mountainous regions of Jamaica. Long known as *Pseudorhipsalis alata* (Swartz) Br. & R.

*Disocactus biformis*

*Disocactus biformis* Lindl. Long-branched species with fleshy, flattened stems with slightly serrate margins. Long slender flower, magenta with purple style and four white stigma lobes. From Guatemala and Honduras.

*Disocactus eichlamii*

*Disocactus eichlamii* (Weing.) Br. & R. Tends to branch from the base with wider and more serrated stems than *D. biformis*. Flowers bright red, about 1½ in/4 cm long. Style protrudes with five stigma lobes. From Guatemala.

*Disocactus himantocladus* (Roll.-Goss.) Kimn. Stems flat and elongated, branching freely with small creamy-pink flower with white style and four stigma lobes. Endemic to Costa Rica. Known as *Pseudorhipsalis himantoclada* (Roll.-Goss.) Br. & R. until transferred to *Disocactus*.

*Disocactus macranthus*

*Disocactus macranthus* (Alex.) Kimn. & Hutchinson. An attractive, easy-flowered epiphytic species. Long strap-like stems with slightly crenate margins. The flower is sweetly scented, yellowish-cream and floriferous, usually in winter months. Widely known as *Pseudorhipsalis macrantha* Alex. until transferred to the genus *Disocactus*. From high altitudes in Chiapas, Mexico, and possibly also in Guatemala.

*Disocactus nelsonii* (Br. & R.) Lindinger. From high altitudes in south Chiapas and Guatemala. Many-branched elong-

ated species with flattened stems, margins obtusely crenate. Flower purplish-pink on tube up to 1 in/3 cm long, and short-lived. Rare in cultivation. This once constituted a monotypic genus, *Chiapasia*, now merged with *Disocactus*. Stigma yellow.

*Disocactus nelsonii*

*Disocactus nelsonii* var. *hondurensis* Kimn. A distinctive variety of the species, branching from the base and with larger flowers. Stigma purple. From Honduras.

*Disocactus quezaltecus*

*Disocactus quezaltecus* (Standl. & Steyerm.) Kimn. From Guatemala. Originally *Bonifazia quezalteca*. *Disocactus acuminatus* (Cuf.) Kimn., from Costa Rica and Guatemala. Earlier known as *Pseudorhipsalis acuminata*. Both are recognized species and are possibly distinctive – but bear certain pronounced similarities to others.

*Disocactus ramulosus* (Salm-Dyck) Kimn. A much-branching species with thin, flattened stems, terete at base. New growth commences reddish and gradually changes to green. Stems crenate with small lobes. Has small open flower, pinkish-cream. Widely distributed species. Guatemala, Costa Rica and other parts of the West Indies. Originally *Rhipsalis ramulosa* until incorporated within the genus *Disocactus*.

Among the most recent transfers to *Disocactus* are the genera *Wittia* and *Wittiocactus*. A transfer which carries a degree of uncertainty!

*Disocactus amazonicus* (Schum.) Hunt (syn. *Wittia amazonica* Schum.) Flattened branches, coarsely crenated. Flower small ¾-1¼ in/2-3 cm long, magenta, almost cylindrical on very short tube. From northeastern Peru near to the Brazil frontier.

*Disocactus panamensis* (Br. & R.) Hunt. Very flattened branches, elongated, dark green with low crenations. Flower purple or magenta with protruding style and stamens. From near Chepo in Panama, and distributed in northerly South American countries.

**Eccremocactus** Br. & R. is a monotypic genus of considerable interest and having unique characteristics. Epiphytic with pendent habit. The low branches are flat and thick. From the dense forest regions of Costa Rica, usually at low altitudes.

*Eccremocactus bradei*

*Eccremocactus bradei* Br. & R. Light dull green branches with regular slightly crenate margins. Flower pinkish-white or creamy-white, nocturnal. Short tube only about ⅜ in/1 cm long. A rare species in cultivation, most easily recognized by the very broad, thick, strap-like stems, often to 12 in/30 cm long and pendent habit.

**Echinocactus** Link & Otto. was once a large genus, now reduced to only a very few species. Globular plants, barrel-shaped, with many ribs and comparatively small flowers.

*Echinocactus grusonii*

*Echinocactus grusonii* Hildm. One of the best-known species in cultivation, referred to as Golden Barrel. Very large globular plant, light green body with many ribs up to nearly 40. Areoles with golden-yellow spines up to 2 in/5 cm long. Flowers are embedded in deep felt, yellowish, opening in full sunlight. From central Mexico in the region of San Luis Potosi through to Hidalgo.

*Echinocactus ingens*

*Echinocactus ingens* Zucc. A tall species found in Hidalgo, Mexico, reaching over 3¼ ft/1 m high and wide. It has about 50 ribs, closely set areoles bearing brownish spines. Flowers at crown of plant, yellow, about 1 in/2.5 cm long.

*Echinocactus platyacanthus* Link & Otto. Type species. A nearly globular species, large and bright green with woolly apex. Ribs very acute, about 30 and having brownish, later becoming greyish, spines, the radials four, short and spreading and three or four central spreading spines about 1¼ in/3 cm long. Flowers about 1¼ in/3 cm long. Known only from eastern Mexico.

*Echinocactus texensis* Hopff. (syn. *Homalocephala texensis* (Hopff.) Br. & R. Usually globose, but often very much depressed, almost flattened, to about 12 in/30 cm diameter with 13 to 27 ribs, acute but with only few white-felted areoles having about 6 radial spines to 1½ in/4 cm long, spreading and recurved with long solitary central about 2½ in/6 cm long. Flowers to 2½ in/6 cm long, reddish in the lower part, pinkish above. Native of southeast New Mexico, Texas, and parts of northern Mexico. A species which is now becoming exceedingly rare, even in habitat.

**Echinocereus** Engelm. includes species all endemic to North America. The stems vary considerably from one species to another, some cylindrical, others oval or roundish. Many are free-branching from the base, others tend to remain solitary. Usually with many ribs and very spiny, rarely spineless or nearly so. All have exceptionally colourful flowers, generally large.

*Echinocereus brandegeei* (Coult.) Sch. An uncommon plant from the low hills bordering the coastline of south Baja California. A clumping species sometimes with very elongated stems. Ribs with many tubercles, and areoles bearing very stout longish spines. Radial spines about 12, acicular and spreading with long rigid centrals usually four. Flowers purple with whitish wool and spiny areoles on the ovary.

*Echinocereus delaetii* Gurke. A remarkable species very much resembling a small *Cephalocereus senilis*. Native to a restricted area north of Parras de la Fuente in Coahuila, Mexico. Densely clustering plant almost completely covered with long whitish hairs from the areoles which also have a few reddish stiff spines. Flowers pink, the ovary also being hidden by clusters of long white bristles.

*Echinocereus engelmannii*

*Echinocereus engelmannii* (Parry) Rümpl. One of the more variable species as far as the spines are concerned – these can be yellow, brown, even black, and either straight or slightly curled. Clustering plants, to 4 in/10 cm tall and about 2½ in/6 cm wide with up to 14 ribs. Radial spines about 12, and 2–6 centrals. Flowers are a rich purplish-red to almost 3 in/8 cm across. Found in areas of California bordering Nevada and further south into northern districts of Mexico. *E. blanckii* Palmer is another variable species. It comes from Tamaulipas, Mexico, has slender, often elongating stems, few ribs and areoles bearing 8–9 radial spines and usually a single central. Flowers are violet-red, to about 2¾ in/7 cm across.

*Echinocereus fendleri* (Engelm.) Rümpl. A well-known species from southern states of the USA and northern Sonora and Chihuahua, Mexico. Can be extremely variable. Clustering with erect stems from the base of prominent ribs, somewhat undulate. Areoles with up to 10 spreading radial spines and one central. Flowers from the upper part of the stems, large, deep purple.

*Echinocereus knippelianus*

*Echinocereus knippelianus* Liebn. A more or less globular plant with a blackish-green body about 2 in/5 cm wide. Only a few ribs and spines, producing pinkish flowers about 1½ in/4 cm long. From Coahuila, Mexico.

*Echinocereus pectinatus* Engelm. One of the best-known species. It is found in more southern states of USA and parts of Mexico. It only rarely offsets, the stems about 6 in/15 cm tall, to 2¾ in/7 cm wide, areoles elongated with spines arranged comb-like, differing in colour from white to yellow and brownish. Flowers purplish-red. There is also a very choice form – *E. pectinatus* var. *neomexicanus* L. Bens. which is a wider plant, many pinkish-grey spines and bright yellow flowers to about 4 in/10 cm long and opening wide to 4½ in/12 cm across or more.

*Echinocereus pulchellus* (Mart.) Sch. A comparatively small-growing species from western Puebla and Hidalgo, Mexico, where they are found growing flat to the ground. Stems are simple, somewhat cylindrical, greyish-green with about 12 ribs divided into tubercles. Areoles with only two or three short spines, yellowish and deciduous. Flowers pinky-white about 1½ in/4 cm diameter. An unpublished *E. aguirrei* is synonymous. This species is very similar to *E. amoenus*

(Dict.) Sch. and the two are frequently confused.

*Echinocereus russanthus* Weniger. A species long confused with *E. chloranthus*. Found in a restricted area of Brewster County, Texas, USA. Stems cylindrical to over 8 in/20 cm long, branching profusely from the base. Ribs about 11 to 18, low, narrow with very indistinct tubercles. Areoles with white wool when young with up to 45 slender bristle-like spines completely covering the body of the plant. Flowers brownish-red, funnel-shaped with long yellowish style.

*Echinocereus sciurus* (K. Brand.) Br. & R. A dense-clumping species from south of Baja California, Mexico. Stems slender 8 in/20 cm long, ribs about 12 to 15, low and divided into tubercles. Areoles closely set with up to 18 radial spines which are longer than the centrals. Flower bright cerise with greenish filaments and dark green pistil.

*Echinocereus stoloniferus* Marsh. An almost unique species on account of its habit of producing stolons from which develop the offsets. Somewhat cylindrical plant with many ribs and areoles with dense whitish spines, closely set together. Flowers yellow. Rather rare in cultivation. Sonora, Mexico.

*Echinocereus viridiflorus*

*Echinocereus viridiflorus* Engelm. The type species of the genus. Small almost globular plants, either simple or clustering with 14 low ribs and elongated areoles. Radial spines about 16 with centrals usually two or three in a row. Flowers greenish. Native of New Mexico and parts of Texas and the Dakotas, USA.

**Echinofossulocactus** Lawr. is perhaps better known as *Stenocactus*. Mostly heavily spined plants, all globular in shape and generally considered difficult to identify. Easy culture, requiring really good light for successful flowering.

*Echinofossulocactus coptonogonus* (Lem.) Lawr. (syn. *Echino-cactus coptonogonus* Lem.) Type species. A globular plant, somewhat depressed, to 4 in/10 cm high and 3 in/8 cm broad having 10 to 14 stout acute ribs. Areoles well apart and three to five rigid, incurved flattened spines. Flowers white and purplish. Native to the region of San Luis Potosi, in Mexico.

*Echinofossulocactus multicostatus* (Hild.) Br. & R. A most attractive species, globose with over 100 narrow wavy ribs. Areoles few with six to nine spines, the three upper ones being somewhat flexible, elongated and erect, the lower spines being short and spreading. Flowers pinkish-white about 1 in/2½ cm long. From near Rio Nazas in Durango and also Saltillo, Coahuila, Mexico.

*Echinofossulocactus pentacanthus* (Lem.) Br. & R. A handsome species, somewhat globose, dark green. Has up to 45 sinuous ribs with only few areoles to each rib. Spine cluster consists of three upper, elongated flat spines and two lower, more slender and shorter with occasionally a single central. Flowers large, deep purple with white margins. Endemic to the region of San Luis Potosi and Hidalgo, Mexico.

This genus consists of a great number of 'names'. Species are inclined to be so variable so as to cause confusion and duplication. Certainly an attractive and unusual group with the unique characteristic of wavy ribs.

*Echinopsis/Lobivia hybrids*

**Echinopsis** Zucc. has been the subject of considerable taxonomic interest in recent years. Certain genera have been merged, including *Trichocereus*, but this with many is still not readily acceptable. *Pseudolobivia* is now united with *Echinopsis*. Many of the species are very well known in cultivation, and have proved popular houseplants. Some species have been used for cross-pollination with plants of other genera, notably *Lobivia*, resulting in some remarkably attractive cultivars with a great many different coloured flowers.

*Echinopsis ancistrophora* Speg. (syn. *P. ancistrophora* [Speg.] Backeb.) From Salta and Tucuman, Argentina, have rather flattened plant body, about 18 ribs with somewhat sunken areoles bearing seven radial spines and one hooked central. Flowers white.

*Echinopsis aurea* Br. & R. (syn. *P. aurea* [Br. & R.] Backeb.) A compact species from Cordoba, Argentina, having about 14 ribs, areoles with short brownish wool and 10 radial spines to ⅜ in/1 cm long, centrals about four and longer than radials. Flowers lemon-yellow.

*Echinopsis eyriesii* (Turp.) Zucc. (syn. *Echinocactus eyriesii*

Turp.) The type species. A popular species originating from southern Brazil, Uruguay and Argentina. Generally of clustering habit, short globular plants with many pronounced acute ribs, areoles bearing whitish wool and to 18 very short spines. Flowers from side of plant to 10 in/25 cm long, pure white, scented, lasting only one day. *E. multiplex* (Pfeiff.) Zucc. with which *E. eyriesii* is often confused, is endemic to southern Brazil. It differs in respect to the spine formation, viz. up to 15 ascending radial spines about ⅜-¾ in/1-2 cm long and four or five even longer central spines. Flower lilac-pink. *E. leucantha* (Gill.) Walp. is an oblong plant to 12 in/30 cm high, having about 12-15 ribs, close-set areoles with eight somewhat curved brown radial spines and one elongated curved central to 4 in/10 cm long. Large flower about 6½ in/16 cm long, white.

*Echinopsis kermesina*

*Echinopsis mammillosa* var. *kermesina* (Krainz.) Friedr. (syn. *Pseudolobivia kermesina* Krainz.) Very similar in appearance to *Echinopsis* as far as the body is concerned. Plant about 4½ in/12 cm diameter, glossy green having about 20 ribs, areoles furnished with yellowish wool, about 15 radial spines with brownish tips and four to six reflexed centrals to ¾ in/2 cm long. Flowers from crown of plant, deep carmine-red. Native of Argentina.

**Encephalocarpus** Berg. is monotypic. The body of the plant is covered with leaf-like thick tubercles. The spines that develop are insignificant and soon fall.
*Encephalocarpus strobiliformis* (Werd.) Berg. (syn. *Ariocarpus strobiliformis* Werd.) A small globular plant, sometimes simple, often clustering and forming groups. Tubercles numerous and densely imbricate and with a keel at the back surface, terminating in a point with a small areole on the inner side, with wool and insignificant spines, scale-like, which makes it distinctly different to species of *Ariocarpus*. Flowers purple with fringed edges and yellow stigma.

Endemic to Tamaulipas, Mexico. A rare and desirable species resembling a pine cone, its closest relation would appear to be *Pelecyphora aselliformis* – and these might deservedly be united in one genus.

**Epiphyllum** (Herm.) Haw. non Pfeiff. are mostly epiphytic with thin flattened stems, occasionally three-winged. The areoles are very small, and while soft spines are seen at seedling stage, they rapidly disappear as mature growth develops, and to all intents and purposes the stems are spineless. All have large or very large flowers, usually white or cream, perfumed and mainly nocturnal-flowering. Indigenous to many parts of Central and South America, Mexico and the West Indies. Some species have been used for hybridizing, resulting in an extraordinary array of numerous beautiful cultivars.
*Epiphyllum anguliger* (Lem.) Don. Another rick-rack species. Much-branched with bright green stems and marginal lobes which are generally more pointed than *E. darrahii*. Scented white flower on stout tube, style and stigma lobes white. A popular species endemic to Mexico. Another species, *E. gertrudianus*, seems to be very similar to *E. anguliger* and *E. darrahii* and might be an intermediate form.
*Epiphyllum cartagense* (Web.) Br. & R. A very distinct species from Costa Rica. A true epiphyte with short, sometimes elongated stems, bright green in colour and slightly toothed or crenate margins. Flower white with reddish tube. Style pale pink or whitish and bright yellow stigma lobes. Still uncommon in cultivation.
*Epiphyllum caudatum* Br. & R. Has elongated lanceolate stems, tapering toward the tip and the stalk. Develops into a many-branched plant, the older stems becoming terete. Leaf margins undulating without spines. Has white flowers about 2¾ in/ 7 cm long. Little is known of this species from authoritative sources, and many pertinent characteristics of this species have not been recorded. Endemic of Mexico from the region surrounding Oaxaca.

*Epiphyllum chrysocardium*

*Epiphyllum chrysocardium* Alex. One of the most outstanding discoveries of recent years from the northern region of

Chiapas, Mexico, in tropical rain forests. So wide is the stem and so deeply crenated, it was at first thought to be a 'tree fern'. Stem to 12 in/30 cm wide and deep-set lobes about 6 in/15 cm long which gradually taper toward the tip. Very large flower, pure white with rich golden filaments; this feature provides the name, which translated means 'heart of gold'. A unique and very desirable species requiring more care than most of this genus. At one time included temporarily in the genus *Marniera* (Backeb.) created for this and *E. macropterum*.

*Epiphyllum crenatum* (Lindl.) G. Don. A very popular and well-known species from Honduras and Guatemala. Has been used extensively in cross-pollinating with species of other genera to develop many beautiful *Epiphyllum* cultivars. Has thick glaucous branches, stiff, strong and erect, with fairly deep crenations along the margins. Flowers are diurnal, creamy-white and about 6 in/15 cm wide. Sweetly scented, lasting many days.

*Epiphyllum darrahii* (Schum.) Br. & R. One of 4 rick-rack stemmed species. The marginal lobes are generally rounded, usually obtuse. Flower creamy-white on long tube, very fragrant. Very long style, pure white and eight stigma lobes. Endemic to Mexico.

*Epiphyllum grandilobum* (Web.) Br. & R. Many-branched plant with broad stems and deeply lobed margins. This large-growing species is still rare in cultivation and has not proved of easy flowering. Flower is large, white and nocturnal. These develop on a curved tube, are about 10 in/26 cm wide, funnel-shaped. Style protruding beyond stamens, with many yellowish stigma lobes. Indigenous to Costa Rica.

*Epiphylllum guatemalense* Br. & R. Strong-growing species with flat, bright green, fairly wide and soft stems with rounded crenations. Very large flower, white, up to 9½ in/24 cm diameter. The yellow style has 12-13 deep yellow stigma lobes. Indigenous to Guatemala. This might also be a variety of *E. phyllanthus*; Kimnach proposes *Epiphyllum phyllanthus* var. *guatemalense* (Br. & R.) Kimn. In cultivation a most floriferous species.

*Epiphyllum hookeri* Haw. Long thin light green stems with pronounced crenations on the margins. Flower white up to 6 in/15 cm wide, nocturnal. Long style about 16 cm long, magenta or purplish, perhaps shaded orange at base and apex. About 14 yellow stigma lobes. Doubt exists as to whether this species, together with *E. stenopetalum* and *E. strictum*, are synonymous. However, Kimnach does not recognize these other two species, and gives varietal status to *Epiphyllum hookeri*, viz.: *Epiphyllum phyllanthus* var. *hookeri* (Haw.) Kimn. Indigenous to Trinidad and Tobago, Guyana, Venezuela.

*Epiphyllum lepidocarpum* (Web.) Br. & R. One of the rarest species of this genus with thickish and rather narrow stems having slight crenations along the margins. Medium-sized white flower with white style and yellow stigma lobes. Nocturnal. From isolated area near Cartago, Costa Rica.

*Epiphyllum macropterum* (Lem.) Br. & R. A species of doubtful authenticity – possibly synonymous with *E. thomasianum* and with *E. thomasianum* var. *costaricense* (which would not appear to justify varietal status). In keeping with the synonyms, it is widely distributed throughout Costa Rica, Guatemala and southern Mexico.

*Epiphyllum oxypetalum* (De Cand.) Haw. Possibly synonymous with *E. latrifons*. Recorded from Mexico and Guatemala where it is indigenous, and also escapes in Brazil and Venezuela. A much-branched plant with flattened thin stems, tapering toward the apex, and wavy margins. Nocturnal-flowering with long curved tube (hence this species sometimes called the Dutchman's pipe). Flower white and cream. Style thick and long, about 8 in/20 cm and stigma lobes cream. A very popular plant of easy culture.

*Epiphyllum phyllanthus* (L.) Haw. Widely distributed in many parts of Central and South America – Brazil, Peru, Bolivia, Panama, Guyana, Trinidad and Tobago. Has elongated stems, usually flattened, light green with a very definite purplish margin. Flower up to 12 in/30 cm long, slender and scented, white in colour. Slender tube and long slender rose-pink style and about 10 white lobes. Nocturnal-flowering.

*Epiphyllum phyllanthus*

*Epiphyllum phyllanthus* var. *boliviense* (Web.) Backeb. Differs from the species in the wider stronger stem, and flowers much larger and inclined to be luminous. Beautiful scent. Endemic to Bolivia.

*Epiphyllum phyllanthus* var. *colombiense* (Web.) Backeb. Smaller flower than the species – to about 4 in/10 cm long – short tube with pinkish style having five to seven white lobes. From Colombia, Ecuador, Costa Rica and Panama.

*Epiphyllum phyllanthus* var. *rubrocoronatum* Kimn. Long slender branches, flower similar to species but with larger style which is pinkish-orange below and deep red or purplish above and has 10-13 orange lobes. Endemic to Panama, Colombia and Ecuador.

*Epiphyllum pittieri* (Web.) Br. & R. Stems are flattened and thin, the margins coarsely toothed. Flower white and small, up to 6 in/15 cm long and only 5 in/9 cm wide. Shortish style about 5 in/12 cm with 13 cream-coloured lobes. Beautifully scented, with perfume resembling that of hyacinths. Considered by Kimnach to be a variety of *Epiphyllum phyllanthus* and recorded by him as *Epiphyllum phyllanthus* var. *pittieri* (Web.) Kimn.

*Epiphyllum pumilum* (Vpl.) Br. & R. A branched species, very long stems becoming terete with elongated flattened branches, some tapering toward the apex, others rounded. Has only small flowers about 2 in/5 cm, white and fragrant. Style slender to 2¾ in/7 cm long, white.

*Epiphyllum stenopetalum* (Forst.) Br. & R. Many characteristics similar to the foregoing – flower, style and stigma lobes apparently identical. Distribution given as Oaxaca, Mexico. This species is still of doubtful status.

*Epiphyllum strictum* (Lem.) Br. & R. Seemingly distinctive on account of its very stiff upright green stems, elongated and having slightly serrated margins. White flower on long slender tube, with rose or red style, and yellow stigma lobes. Very easy in cultivation, grows rapidly and is most floriferous. Distribution: Guatemala, Panama and southern Mexico.

*Epiphyllum thomasianum* (K. Schum.) Br. & R. Having stem characteristics similar to those of *E. oxypetalum*. Flower from curved tube, large whitish-cream, up to 10 in/25 cm wide. Fragrant and nocturnal. Style up to 12 in/30 cm long and 17 stigma lobes, cream or yellow. From Mexico, Guatemala and Nicaragua where it is widely distributed.

This genus has been considered fairly extensively on account of the problems which still exist in nomenclature. Other species recorded, *Epiphyllum ruestii*, *E. gigas*, and *E. costaricense*, are of obscure origin and are also doubtful, and therefore not mentioned further.

**Epithelantha** Br. & R. have a particular interest for collectors. Plants which are uncommon and much sought-after. Plants are densely spined, the flowers mostly from the crown of the plant.

*Epithelantha micromeris*

*Epithelantha bokei* L. Benson. Stems similar to those of *E. micromeris*. Spines from areoles in four or five series, generally longer forming a dense covering over the body of the plant. Flowers pale pink. At altitudes of up to 3,950ft/ 1,200 m on limestone hillsides in Texas.

*Epithelantha micromeris* (Engelm.) Web. (syn. *Mammillaria micromeris* Engelm.) Type species. A very small species, usually clustering, sometimes simple. Almost globular up to about 2 in/5 cm in diameter, having small, low-set tubercles arranged in spirals. Spines numerous in two or three series. Flower from near the apex of the plant, small, pinkish-white to light pink. The 'button cactus' from western Texas and parts of northern Mexico.

**Eriocereus** (Bgr.) Ricco. have their counterpart in the genus *Harrisia* which includes a number of West Indian species, all with yellowish fruits. *Eriocereus* have red fruits, and originate generally from South America. Now includes *Roseocereus*.

*Eriocereus bonplandii*

*Eriocereus jusbertii* (Rebut) Ricco. From Argentina, has more or less an erect stem, about 2 in/5 cm thick and 5–6 ribs with deep furrows between. Greyish areoles are set well apart bearing about 7 radial spines and 1 or more centrals of brownish-black. Flowers appear in late evening, white with greenish-brown outer petals, about 7 in/18 cm long.

*Eriocereus martinii* (Lab.) Ricco. A well-known species from Argentina, much-branched, clambering to 6½ ft/2 m or more. Branches with about 4–5 angles, areoles with a row of short radial spines and 1 long stout central. Flower very large to 8 in/20 cm, nocturnal, white. *E. tortuosa* (Forb.) Ricco., also from Argentina around Buenos Aires, has about 7 low rounded ribs, areoles with up to 10 awl-shaped spines spread radially and 1 much longer central. Flowers whitish-pink. *E. bonplandii* (Parm.) Ricco., with 4-angled stems, areoles about ¾ in/2 cm apart with 6–8 acicular spines to 1½ in/4 cm long, reddish-grey. Flowers nocturnal, white.

*Eriocereus tephracanthus* (Lab.) Backeb. [syn. *Cereus tetracanthus* (Lab.)] The type species endemic to Bolivia. An erect plant with many low ribs having somewhat sunken woolly areoles and several brownish-tipped spines. Flowers funnel-shaped, white, on long tube with swollen reddish scales and white hairs in the axils. The flowers are very beautiful and large, sometimes to over 6 in/15 cm long.

***Eriosyce*** Phil. is a small genus of large globular to semi-columnar plants with many ribs and spines, and very woolly at the apex.
*Eriosyce ceratites* (Otto) Br. & R. A large-growing plant to 3¼ ft/1 m high, native of Chile with 25 or more ribs and up to 20 long, thick, blackish spines, mostly straight but some curved. The apex of the plant becomes very woolly with age. Flowers from the top of the plant, about 1½ in/3-4 cm long, yellowish-red.

***Erythrorhipsalis*** Berg. are epiphytic with slender and rounded stems and branches, firstly erect, then becoming pendent. Well-distributed areoles bearing many bristles. Terminal, regular flowers. Monotypic genus, very closely allied to *Rhipsalis*.

*Erythrorhipsalis pilocarpa*

*Erythrorhipsalis pilocarpa* (Löfgr.) Berg. Stems dark greyish-green to purplish. Mostly elongated branches with terminal branches in whorls. Becomes pendent with maturity. Flowers pinkish-cream, scented. Of easy culture. Brazil.

***Escobaria*** Br. & R. are closely allied to *Coryphantha*. Generally small-growing, cylindrical, quite heavily spined, scaly flowers. Full sun essential for successful flowering.
*Escobaria chaffeyi* Br. & R. An interesting species, cylindrical to 4½ in/12 cm long and 2½ in/6 cm diameter with many short light green tubercles having a narrow groove above. Radial spines numerous, stiff and bristly, together with several shorter centrals, pure white but tipped brown, which almost envelop the body of the plant. Flowers about ⅝ in/15 mm long, cream or pale pink. Native of Zacatecas, Mexico.

***Escontria*** Rose is a genus of two species. Tall, columnar branched plants bearing day-flowering blooms. Both native of Central America.
*Escontria chiotilla* (Web.) Rose (syn. *Cereus chiotilla* Web.) Type species. A tall-growing plant up to 23 ft/7 m high. The main stem is usually short with numerous weak branches, having seven or eight acute ribs. Areoles very close together with many short, somewhat flattened spines and one that is very much longer. Flower creamy-yellow, the tube and ovary with many overlapping scales. Endemic to southern Mexico.

***Espostoa*** Br. & R. includes many columnar species with pseudocephalium. Areoles with longish spines and white hairs and usually small nocturnal flowers, with short style and stamens.
*Espostoa lanata* (H. B. & K.) Br. & R. (syn. *Cactus lanatus* H. B. & K.) The type species from hills of Ecuador and Peru at an altitude of over 6,250 ft/2,000 m. A white-haired columnar plant to over 13 ft/4 m high, often branching freely in habitat. Over 20 ribs, rounded with large areoles bearing numerous brownish needle-like spines inter-mingled with long white hairs. Pseudocephalium develops at tops of branches through which the reddish flowers emerge. *E. melanostele* (Vaup.) Berg. from Peru is a more robust plant producing a brownish cephalium through which the pinkish-white flowers appear.

***Eulychnia*** Phil. includes a few interesting and attractive species, erect, branching, sometimes procumbent with many ribs, spines and very small flowers.
*Eulychnia acida* Phil. A tall-growing, tree-like plant, to over 10 ft/3 m high, sometimes with different habit, with shorter branches, becoming procumbent. Stems have about 12-13 low but broad ribs, areoles with many spines of unequal length protruding almost horizontally, some very long to almost 6 in/16 cm. Flowers rather top-shaped, about 2 in/5 cm long, pinkish-white.
*Eulychnia castanea* (Sch.) Backeb. (syn. *Cereus castaneus* Sch.) Type species for this species from Aconcagua, Chile. Shrubby plant, spreading from the base with long cereoid stems having low rounded ribs, yellow-greyish spines, flower pinkish-white on very hairy tube.

***Facheiroa*** Br. & R. is a somewhat obscure genus originally created for one species. It has been proposed that the genus should be merged with *Thrixanthocereus*, but the title still persists and newer discoveries may support its retention.
*Facheiroa publiflora* Br. & R. The type species which has its origin on the Serra de Cannabrava, Bahia, Brazil. An erect, tall, much-branched plant, lightish to greyish-green. Ribs about 15, the brown-felted areoles bearing up to 12 brown radial acicular spines and usually four centrals somewhat longer than the radials. Branches with long brownish-red pseudocephalium consisting of masses of brownish-red

hairy bristles extending from the top downward, flowers small, whitish, nocturnal. *F. ulei* (Gurke) Werd. is another rare member of this genus from Serra do Ignacio, Brazil, its pseudocephalium reputedly brown and very soft.

***Ferocactus*** Br. & R. is a popular group of plants of easy culture. It now embraces the genus *Hamatocactus.* Globular plants with fierce spination bearing flowers with a very short tube, borne around the crown of the plant.

*Ferocactus acanthodes* (Lem.) Br. & R. One of the most attractive of all this genus. Globular becoming cylindrical with age up to 10 ft/3 m high. With numerous ribs, 27 or more, very acute and large areoles densely brown-felted and numerous spines. The radials somewhat weak and usually spreading, the centrals rather flattened, slender, spreading and tortuously curved, white, pink, yellowish or red. It is these which make the species so beautiful. Flowers yellow or pale orange about 2½ in/6 cm long from near the crown of the plant. Endemic to the arid areas of southeastern California, southern Nevada, Arizona, and parts of northern Baja, California.

*Ferocactus emoryi*

*Ferocactus emoryi* Backeb. From Arizona and northern areas of Mexico in Sonora. A large plant to 5 ft/1.5 m high, greyish-green in colour, about 32 ribs with large oval areoles bearing 5–8 radial spines and 1 central, all reddish or white and 2½ in/6 cm long, the central one hooked. Flowers are reddish-tipped with yellow, about 2½ in/6 cm long.

*Ferocactus latispinus* (Haw.) Br. & R. Plant globular, somewhat depressed to 1½ in/4 cm high and about 1½ in/4 cm in diameter. Usually with 21 ribs, but up to 23, sometimes much less. Large areoles with 6–10 pinkish-white radial spines, rather slender and four or more stout centrals, brownish or reddish, all straight except one which is very flattened and decidedly hooked. Flowers purplish. Widely distributed in Mexico and possibly Guatemala.

*Ferocactus mesae-verdae* (Boissev. & C. Davidson) N.P. Taylor (syn. *Coloradoa mesae-verdae* Boissev. & C. Davidson). Something of a controversial transfer to *Ferocactus.* A small globular species about 2½ in/6 cm high and 3 in/8 cm broad, ribs 13 to 17 set with areoles having brown or greyish wool. Radial spines 8–10 and only rarely a single central. Flowers creamy-yellow with brownish midrib. A rare species from southerly slopes of dry hills, Mesa Verde cliffs in Colorado, and possibly in New Mexico, Utah and Arizona.

*Ferocactus setispinus* (Engelm.) L. Benson (syn. *Hamatocactus setispinus* [Engelm.] Br. & R.) A fibrous rooted plant up to 6 in/15 cm high, darkish-green. Ribs usually 13, thin, high and undulate on the margins. 12–16 slender spines, central spines one to three longer than radials and hooked. Large flower to 2¾ in/7 cm long, yellow with red throat. Distributed in southern Texas and throughout northern Mexico. A very popular and easily cultivated plant. *Ferocactus hamatacanthus* (Mühlpf.) Br. & R. is also a recent transfer from *Hamatocactus.*

*Ferocactus viridescens*

*Ferocactus viridescens* Br. & R. Found in southern California and Baja. A more or less globular species to about 18 in/45 cm tall and 12 in/30 cm thick with many ribs, and mostly heavily spined. Flowers yellowish-green, 1¼–1½ in/3–4 cm long from around the crown of the plant.

*Ferocactus wizlizeni* (Engelm.) Br. & R. (syn. *Echinocactus wislizenii* Engelm.) Type species. Globular at first becoming cylindrical with age and reaching a height of 6½ ft/2 m or more. Ribs 25 or more with large elliptical areoles with brownish felt with many thread-like radial spines and several reddish or white central spines, one of them being slightly hooked and much stouter than the others, strongly flattened. Flowers yellow about 2½ in/6 cm long. A widely distributed species from Texas to Arizona and in parts of Sonora and Sinaloa, Mexico.

A number of other Mexican species of *Ferocactus* are of particular note: *F. fordii* (Orcutt) Br. & R., one of the smaller-growing plants from Baja California, which has rose-pinkish flowers. *F. schwarzii*, a very rare species from

Ranche del Padre, Sinaloa. *F. gatesii* Lindsay, which is native of the islands in Los Angeles Bay on the west coast of Baja California, beautifully spined with red flowers. These and many more make this one of the most popular genera of large-growing plants.

**Frailea** Br. & R. consists of a great number of relatively small-growing species, globular, sometimes becoming elongated and branching. Many tuberculate ribs and small spines. Flowers small from apex of plant. Flowers can be pollinated without opening.

*Frailea cataphracta* (Dams.) Br. & R. (syn. *Echinocactus cataphractus* Dams.) The type species which is native of Paraguay. Small globose to about ¾ in/2 cm diameter, dull velvety purplish-green with about 10-15 low ribs with flattened tubercles and under each a crescent-shaped band, maroon-coloured. Spines very small and adpressed. Flowers pale yellow, open in full midday sunshine. *F. asterioides* Werd. is synonymous with *F. castanea* Backeb. – very similar to *F. cataphracta* but with even smaller spines on a reddish-brown body. *F. pumila* (Lem.) Br. & R. is caespitose, deep green, with up to 15 ribs and areoles with yellowish-brown spines, radials about 14, centrals only one or two, flowers yellow. *F. gracillima* (Lem.) Br. & R. has greyish-green stems covered with minute bristly spines, flower yellow – a species from Paraguay. *F. matoana* Buin. & Bred. from the southern part of Mato Grosso in Brazil is one of the more recent discoveries, being globose with depressed crown to only 1 in/25 mm diameter, reddish to dark brown with 15 ribs divided by transverse minute furrows into small globular tubercles. Areoles with small spines to ⅛ in/4 mm long, brown and flower yellow.

*Frailea phaeodisca*

*Frailea phaeodisca* Speg. A dwarf species from Uruguay with a dark greyish-green body only about 1¼–1½ in/3–4 cm across. 30 ribs, few minute spines which are all appressed arising from small brownish areoles. Flowers yellow from near the crown of the plant. This has also been considered a variety of *F. pygmaea* Br. & R.

**Gymnocalycium** Pfeiff. is a popular genus of mainly globular plants, often solitary but sometimes caespitose, ribs either rounded or acute which are divided into tubercles. Flowers usually bell-shaped, sometimes more funnel-shaped, flower tube with broad scales having naked axils. Includes many species.

*Gymnocalycium bruchii*

*Gymnocalycium bruchii* (Speg.) Hoss. A clustering species, each body only about 1½ in/4 cm wide, dark-green, spines about 12 and pale pink flowers about 1¼ in/3 cm across. A plant of easy and rewarding growth!

*Gymnocalycium denudatum* (Link & Otto) Pfeiff. The type species of this important genus. Native of southern Brazil. Plant body is glossy dark green, somewhat depressed, about 6 in/15 cm diameter with five to eight broad, low ribs, tubercles hardly discernible, and to about eight slender, rather curved adpressed radial spines. Flowers from apex of plant, white. *G. westii* Hutchis. from Bolivia, has about 14 somewhat spiralled ribs, areoles yellowish felted having about 11 radial spines, white, erect or slightly curved and four centrals, all tipped brown. Flowers bright golden-yellow. *G. horstii* Buin., a Brazilian species, has many similar characteristics to *G. denudatum*. Plant dark glossy green with about six broad well-defined ribs, felted areoles having spreading radials and often one long central. Flowers peach-pink, lasting for several days. A varietal form, *G. horstii* var. *buenekeri* Buin. found about 125 miles/200 km north of the species has much darker rose flowers. *G. chuquisacanum* Card. from Chuquisaca, Bolivia, is greyish-green with 13 ribs consisting of very pronounced tubercles, grey-felted areoles with about seven spreading curved radial spines and one central to nearly 1¼ in/3 cm long curved upward, all greyish with brown tips. Flowers pinkish. *G. platense* (Speg.) Br. & R. from near Cordoba, Buenos Aires, Argentina, about 4 in/10 cm diameter, bluish-green, with about 10-14 ribs divided by transverse furrows forming tubercles, the areoles with usually seven radial adpressed spines. Flower whitish.

*Gymnocalycium kieslingii* Ferrari. From Argentina, has a greyish-green globose body scarcely 1 in/2.5 cm tall, 2-4 in/5-10 cm across. It has whitish spines and white flowers tinged with green. There are also f. *alboareolatum* and f. *castaneaum* described by Ferrari.

*Gymnocalycium mihanovitchii* (Fric & Gurke) Br. & R. Native of Paraguay. Body reddish-greyish-green with eight sharp ribs divided by transverse furrows above and below the areoles which have small radial spines. Flowers yellowish-green. The variety *G. mihanovitchii* var. *friedrichiae* has rose-pink flowers. Interest has also centred around the freak forms of the species where the plant body is either red, orange, yellow or white, generally referred to as *G. mihanovitchii* 'Hibotan'. These colorations are due to chlorophyll deficiency and the plant can only exist when grafted. Many other species would deserve mention if space permitted. *G. saglione* (Cels.) Br. & R. from Catamarca, northern Argentina, is important. Globular often to 12 in/30 cm in diameter, up to 32 ribs, low and broad, divided into large round tubercles, large areoles with about 10 outward-curved spines and usually 1 central. Flowers pinkish-white. *G. saglione* var. *tilcarense* Backeb. was segregated and placed in a new genus *Brachycalycium;* it has now been re-united with *Gymnocalycium.*

## Haageocereus

**Haageocereus** Backeb. includes a large number of species varying considerably in many respects one from the other. Generally they are associated with yellowish-golden spines and undoubtedly many attractive plants are involved, but it would nevertheless seem to be of doubtful origin.

*Haageocereus decumbens* (Vaup.) Backeb. A clambering sprawling plant from southwest Peru and northwest Chile where it is found on rocky hillsides. Slender branches with about 20 low ribs almost hidden by numerous golden-yellow spines, about 30 radials and five centrals. Flowers whitish. *H. setosus* (Akers) Backeb. is a beautiful species with yellow spines. The stem has many white hairs and reddish flowers. *H. acranthus* (Vaup.) Backeb. represents a number of species with coarser spines, stems densely covered with yellowish woolly areoles and numerous yellowish radial spines. Flowers whitish. Endemic to Peru.

**Harrisia** Britt. is allied to *Eriocereus,* and the species are frequently confused. More or less columnar plants, sometimes inclined to trail. Flowers are nocturnal.

*Harrisia gracilis* (Mill.) Britton (syn. *Cereus gracilis* Mill.) Type species. A tall-growing and much-branched species from Jamaica, dark green with up to 11 ribs, somewhat rounded with shallow depressions between. Areoles far apart with many white spines tipped black. Flowers large, white with brownish-green scaly tube. Better known as *H.*

*Harrisia guelichii*

*repandus.* Somewhat rare in cultivation.

*Harrisia guelichii* (Speg.) Br. & R. From Argentina. A slender, rather sprawling plant with several branches and 3–4 pronounced ribs, shallowly grooved between. The greyish-white areoles develop short radial spines and one longer central – all greyish, tipped black. Flowers are about 10 in/ 25 cm long, white with greenish outer petals, nocturnal.

**Haseltonia** Backeb. is a monotypic genus closely linked to *Pilosocereus.* Flowering is nocturnal. A much sought-after species.

*Haseltonia hoppenstedtii* (Web.) Backeb. (syn. *Pilocereus hoppenstedtii* Web.) A doubtful genus, probably better called *P. hoppenstedtii.* A very attractive rare plant, tall, slender and erect to 32 ft/10 m high. Has many ribs, often up to 20, with areoles close together and the whole body covered with whitish spines. In maturity the terminals develop a pseudocephalium. Flower whitish, bell-shaped. From southern Mexico.

**Hatiora** Br. & R. A much-branched slender bushy plant. Spineless with numerous small joints. Closely related to *Rhipsalis,* indigenous to Brazil.

*Hatiora bambusoides* (Web.) Br. & R. With clavate joints, somewhat elongated to 1½ in/4 cm long. Flower similar to the preceding, orange and flowering from the terminals. Sometimes confused with *Hatiora salicornioides,* but the shape of joints is a very ready method of identification.

*Hatiora cylindrica* Br. & R. A more robust species with cylindrical joints up to 1¼ in/3 cm long. Light green with reddish markings. Flower light orange, or yellowish-orange, larger than that of the two other species. Rare in cultivation.

*Hatiora epiphylloides* (Campos-Porto & Werd.) Heath (syn. *Pseudozygocactus epiphylloides* Backeb.) A many-segmented plant, the little joints being generally club-shaped but flat, about 1 in/2½ cm long, ½ in/1 cm wide. Flowers from tips of branches, small, yellow. From São Paulo, Brazil. *Hatiora epiphylloides* f. *bradei* Heath is very similar, but the individual joints are smaller, only to about ½ in/1 cm long. These are among the choicest of epiphytic cacti.

*Hatiora herminiae* (Campos-Porto & Castell) Backeb. From Campos do Jordao, Brazil. One of the most sought-after of this genus. The areoles have one to two bristles and lovely deep pink flowers, ¾ in/2 cm long.

*Hatiora salicornioides*

*Hatiora salicornioides* (Haw.) Br. & R. With club-shaped small branches, dark green. An epiphyte on forest trees. Flowers yellowish-orange, small to about ¼ in/10 mm long.

**Heliabravoa** Backeb. is a monotypic genus from Mexico. The one species, *H. chende* (Goss.) Backeb. was originally included under *Lemaireocereus*. It has a stem to 23 ft/7 m tall and to 4 in/10 cm thick, seven to nine ribs, a few radial and one central spine. Flowers are white, pinkish externally, 1½-2 in/4-5 cm long.

**Heliocereus** Br. & R. includes six beautiful flowering species – diurnal. Some have been used to cross-pollinate with species of *Epiphyllum* to produce the many exotic orchid cacti.

*Heliocereus elegantissimus* Br. & R. An interesting clambering plant with decumbent habit. Branches light green, usually three- or four-angled, the ribs being strongly undulate. Areoles are well apart, large, brownish-yellow felted. Spines very short in two series, the radials acicular, white and bristly, the inner ones very stiff. Flowers deep scarlet to about 6 in/15 cm diameter. A distinctive variety is recorded, *H. elegantissimus* var. *stenopetalum* Bravo, which has many similarities to the species, but with a greater number of ribs, up to seven, and flowers somewhat zygomorphic, smaller than the species and with very narrow petals. It would seem also that the colour is different, this being given as purplish-red. Both are from the same area of Mexico, on the highway between Durango and Mazatlan, at an altitude of between 6,500 ft/2,000 m and 8,200 ft/2,500 m.

*Heliocereus heterodoxus* Standl. & Steyerm. Discovered in Guatemala, but possibly indigenous to Mexico in Chiapas. Clambering species with three-angled stems, slender with slight prominences. Large flower with reddish colourings, 1½-2 in/4-5 cm wide. Rare and almost unknown in cultivation.

*Heliocereus luzmariae* L. Scheinvar. A new epiphytic species discovered in southern Mexico. Usually with three to four winged stems or seven-ribbed to about 2 ft/60 cm long and 1½ in/4 cm wide. Stems are pale green – flowers a rich metallic purplish-red, 5 in/12 cm long and across.

*Heliocereus speciosus* (Cav.) Br. & R. (syn. *Cactus speciosus* Cav.) Type species. A deservedly popular species from central to southern Mexico. A semi-erect plant with up to 5 ribs, somewhat undulating and large felted areoles with numerous yellowish spines. Flowers rich scarlet to 6½ in/16 cm long.

**Hylocereus** (Berg.) Br. & R. is of wide distribution from western Mexico to Panama, parts of the West Indies and northerly countries of South America. All are climbing plants, usually with three-angled stems, the areoles bearing varying numbers of shortish spines, some species totally spineless. Flowers large, mostly scented, usually white, rarely red. Night-flowering. Some species have striking similarities and would cause bewilderment to the amateur, hence those detailed have obvious and very apparent differences.

*Hylocereus calcaratus*

*Hylocereus calcaratus* (Web.) Br. & R. From the forest regions around Port Limon in Costa Rica. A unique species with fresh green and near-spineless three-angled stems and exceptionally prominent marginal lobes. A climbing plant of considerable attraction. Large creamy-white, perfumed flowers on matured specimens. Has long stout scaly tube. It is worthy of note that the flower was not described until very recent years.

*Hylocereus escuintlensis* Kimn. A long trailing epiphyte from Guatemala. Stems are three-angled, dark green bearing large creamy-white flowers, the tepals greenish-yellow, about 12 in/30 cm long and 14 in/35 cm across.

*Hylocereus ocamponis*

*Hylocereus ocamponis* (Salm-Dyck) Br. & R. A Mexican species, but escapes do occur in central and northerly South American countries. While new growth commences green, the stems very quickly change to greyish-blue, and it is this peculiarity which makes it distinctive. Invariably three-angled with hard horny margins. A fast-growing climber with very elongated stems and having short pines. Aerial roots develop at the joints and along the stems. Very large cream flowers up to 12 in/30 cm wide, scented. Night-flowering. Must not be confused with *H. broxensis* which it resembles in stem colour and growth, but the flowers are very different.

*Hylocereus stenopterus* (Web.) Br. & R. From the Vallee de Tuis in Costa Rica. A much less robust species with dull greenish stems, three-angled with small but pronounced areoles. Apparently of much slower growth than most of the other species. Has the distinction of having reddish flowers, only shared by one other of this genus, *H. extensus* – a small flower only to 4½ in/12 cm long. Nocturnal. Reported to be rare in habitat and most certainly rare in cultivation.

*Hylocereus undatus*

*Hylocereus undatus* (Haworth) Br. & R. Very similar to *H.*

*triangularis* and *H. tricostatus* and might well be synonymous. One of the best-known and most easily cultivated species indigenous to many tropical and sub-tropical areas. Possibly originated from the West Indies, but now widely cultivated even in southern France and Spain. Stems usually three-angled, green with hard horny margins on mature growth and very small spines. A clambering, almost untidy plant with its long stems and branches forming masses like a hedge, for which purpose it is used in some places. Flowers very large and scented, cream in colour and nocturnal. Grown extensively in China and other Far Eastern countries where it is known as the 'moon flower'.

*J*

**Jasminocereus** Br. & R. includes only species from the Galapagos Islands. So-named because of its perfumed jasmine-like flowers.

*Jasminocereus galapagensis* (Web.) Br. & R. (syn. *Cereus galapagensis* Web.) The type species is a tree-like plant with many branches composed of short joints. Ribs about 15 with closely set brown-felted areoles bearing many slender, sometimes bristle-like brown spines varying in length. Flowers on slender tube, funnel-shaped, brown with yellowish stripes. Other species have been recorded. *J. sclerocarpus* Sch. is undoubtedly synonymous with the type. *J. howellii* and its variety *delicatus*, which may be distinctive, is also mentioned but little is known of it.

*L*

**Lasiocereus** Ritter includes only two species – columnar plants, often tree-like.

*Lasiocereus rupicola* Ritter. The type species from Peru – 10-13 ft/3-4 m high, about 2 in/5 cm or more thick and many very bumpy ribs and about 20 yellow spines to an areole, these being radial, plus about 12 centrals. Flowers are pure white and about 2 in/5 cm long – the outer petals with long black tips.

**Leocereus** Br. & R. contains a few species of slender growth, clambering, almost vine-like, cylindrical stems with very indistinct ribs, small flowers on scaly tube, the scales having hair-like bristles in the axils.

*Leocereus bahiensis* Br. & R. The type species is native of Joazeiro, Brazil. Long, slender and trailing with about 12 low ribs, closely set areoles and numerous radial, few central yellowish spines, all spreading. Flowers about 1½ in/ 4 cm long, white. *L. glaziovii* (Sch.) Br. & R. from Minas Gerais, Brazil, with about 12 ribs, small elongated white-felted areoles and numerous brownish spines; flower about 2½ in/6 cm long, white. *L. melanurus* (Sch.) Br. & R. is also endemic to the same region; there seems little to distinguish this from *L. glaziovii*, and it is possibly synonymous.

**Lepismium** Pfeiff. is closely related to *Rhipsalis*, differing only because the ovary is sunken in the stem margin or they are considered transitional species. There is doubt that this feature justifies segregation, all the more so on account of the several *Rhipsalis* species which have been transferred by Backeberg to *Lepismium* for only meagre reasons. All species and varieties are endemic to Brazil, and possibly also Peru.

*Lepismium cruciforme* (Vel.) Miqu. Usually saxicolous, rooting freely along the branches. Generally three- or four-angled, sometimes flattened branches, purplish-green or reddish, elongated with margins slightly undulate. Areoles sunken in margins. Flower white and fruit purple or red.

Varieties of the species are on record, but in most instances the similarities are so apparent that even varietal status is not justified.

*Lepismium cruciforme* var. *anceps* (Web.) Backeb. Would appear to be distinct as branches are invariably flattened. Flower pink with purple fruits.

*Lepismium cruciforme* var. *cavernosum* (Lindb.) Backeb. Has stouter branches and more green. Flower white with purple fruits.

*Lepismium cruciforme* var. *myosurus* (S-D) Backeb. Has shorter and narrower stems than the species. Flower generally pink.

*Lepismium myosurus*

*Lepismium cruciforme* var. *vollii* (Backeb.) Backeb. Appears to have no differences at all to the species.

*Lepismium dissimile* Lindb. An unusual species of distinction. Free branching with hairy stems and close-set areoles. At first erect, then pendent with many aerial roots. Branches can become four- or five-angled with areoles alternating. Pinkish flowers and reddish fruits. This species is possibly synonymous with *L. pacheo-leonii* (Löfgr.) Backeb. While there is recorded a varietal form, *L. dissimile* var. *setulosa*, it would appear to have precisely the same characteristics as the species. Endemic to Brazil.

*Lepismium epiphyllanthoides* (Backeb.) Backeb. Having stems terete at base, but branches in whorls, stout, but short with indentations similar to certain growth on some *Epiphyllanthus* species. Very rare in cultivation; has yellowish-creamy flowers.

*Lepismium floccosum* (S-D) Backeb. Long slender stems, with many branches, of pendent growth. Areoles with white tufts of wool and largish flowers, white or creamy-yellow. Fruit pinkish-white. Brazil.

*Lepismium gibberulum* (Web.) Backeb. Has thickish stems and branches, pale green or yellowish-green developing in whorls. Areoles almost indiscernible. Flowers pale pink and white fruits. Endemic to Organ Mountains, Brazil.

*Lepismium grandiflorum*

*Lepismium grandiflorum* (Haw.) Backeb. Stems usually erect, smooth and terete. Young branches commence with deep green hairy growth, but gradually become smooth and reddish about the areoles. Very free-flowering with largish creamy-pinkish blooms and pinkish-purple fruits. Brazil. An outstanding species.

*Lepismium megalanthum* (Löfgr.) Backeb. Similar to *L. grandiflorum*, dark green stems and branches and with large flowers up to 1½ in/4 cm diameter. Fruit pinkish-white.

*Lepismium neves-armondii* (K. Sch.) Backeb. Elongated stems with branches in whorls. Flowers in profusion, whitish with slight orange coloration in the throat. Fruits whitish-yellow. Brazil, in state of Rio de Janeiro.

*Lepismium paradoxum* S-D. Large-growing species with link-like stems and branches developing in whorls. With many aerial roots from the glossy-green joints. Flower is white and fruit white. From the state of São Paulo, Brazil.

*Lepismium pittieri* (Br. & R.) Backeb. A distinctive and rare species from Venezuela, usually with cylindrical branches, but sometimes flattened. Develops bushy habit. Flower greenish-yellow and white fruits.

*Lepismium pulvinigerum* (Lindb.) Backeb. A robust-growing species, at first erect but becoming pendent with very long branches. Branches olive-green with purple markings around the areoles. Flowers creamy-white, fruits red. Central Brazil. There is no great difference between this and *L. grandiflorum*, which may be synonymous or a variety.

*Lepismium puniceo-discus*

*Lepismium puniceo-discus* (Lindb.) Backeb. Very slender pendent branches, pale green. Large flowers, creamy-white with pronounced orange-coloured stamens. Fruit deep yellow at maturity. Brazil.

*Lepismium trigonum* (Pfeiff.) Backeb. Three-angled joints make this species distinctive. Stems broad and very branched with prominent areoles, sometimes woolly. Stems are olive or dull green, except on young growth which commences bright green. Large pinkish-white flowers and red fruits. From the state of São Paulo, Brazil.

*Lepismium tucumanensis* (Web.) Backeb. Much-branched species of pendent habit, often in whorls. Young growth generally terete with reddish areoles, but older growth becomes angular and turns from bright green to dull or yellowish-green. Flowers pinkish-white, fruits deep pink or red. From Tucuman, Argentina, also Bolivia and Paraguay.

The *Rhipsalis-Lepismium* complex presents a fascinating study. Many differing opinions will always be expressed as many misnamed species have been distributed throughout the world. One fact emerges, that there are too many similarities to keep the two genera apart; while the 'sunken ovary' of the *Lepismium* presents a distinguishing feature, this should not serve as reason for division.

**Leptocereus** Br. & R. includes a number of slender-branched, rather tree-like species, all of which are uncommon. Day-flowering, the flowers somewhat scaly and bristly.

*Leptocereus assurgens* (C. Wright) Br. & R. (syn. *Cereus assurgens* C. Wright) Type species. A clambering, untidy plant up to 10 ft/3 m high with many branches. Usually four-angled having areoles with brown acicular spines up to 3 in/8 cm long. Flowers white and fruits with clusters of short spines. A rare plant in cultivation from northwestern coast of Cuba on limestone rock.

*Leptocereus leonii* Br. & R. A tree-like species with decidedly rounded trunk up to 16 ft/5 m high. Branches freely, slender, elongated and having six to eight ribs, bright green. Ribs are crenate with the areoles at the depressions having up to 12 yellowish spines. Flower pinkish-white. From Sierra de Anafe, Cuba. Extremely rare in cultivation.

**Leuchtenbergia** Hook. is a monotypic genus of a solitary, very unusual plant with elongated tubercles carrying papery, terminal spines. Can be propagated from seeds, but rather slow-growing.

*Leuchtenbergia principis*

*Leuchtenbergia principis* Hook. Type species. An unusual, fascinating plant with invariably long taproots. Plants to 6 in/15 cm high usually solitary but sometimes clustering. The elongated tubercles are the feature of the species, these are erect and up to 4½ in/12 cm or more long, three-angled. Spines from the almost truncate tip of the tubercle, thin and papery with several radials and one or two longer centrals to almost 4 in/10 cm length. Flowers golden-yellow, lasting several days, scented. From northern Mexico and certain more central areas. Sometimes called the 'agave cactus'.

**Leucostele** Backeb. includes only the species for which this genus was erected.

*Leucostele rivierei* Backeb. A tall columnar plant, rarely branching, up to 6½ ft/ 2 m high. Branches with many distinct ribs, areoles woolly with long white spines densely arranged. Flowers from near terminal ends, diurnal, said to be reddish. South America.

**Lobivia** Br. & R. is composed of many species, globular or somewhat cylindric, usually clustering freely. It is sometimes difficult to associate one species with another, the more so as some would seem on the one hand more similar to *Echinopsis*, and on the other hand to *Rebutia*. It would certainly appear a difficult genus and further research might well produce a new classification. All species have colourful flowers. The generic title is an anagram of Bolivia, the country where many of the species originate, but more recent exploration has located closely allied plants in Peru. It is similar to *Echinopsis*, *Trichocereus* and other South American genera. It has more recently absorbed the well-known *Chamaecereus*.

*Lobivia aureiflorus* Backeb. (syn. *Mediolobivia aureiflora* [Backeb.] Backeb.) From Salta, Argentina, at over 6,500 ft/ 2,000 m altitude. Stems dark greenish-red usually clustering freely. Ribs not too distinct, tubercles irregularly disposed. Areoles have about 20 whitish-brown bristly spines. Large flowers bright orange with whitish throat. *L. aureiflorus* var. *rubriflora* (Backeb.) Backeb. differs in respect of the flower colour which is rosy-red.

*L. aureolilacina* Card. From Chuquisaca, Bolivia. Very spiny, the radials somewhat pectinate, the centrals subulate, strong, whitish-grey and slightly hooked at tip. Flowers very beautiful, lilac and yellow.

*Lobivia backebergii*

*Lobivia backebergii* (Werderm.) Backeb. Only very rarely clusters – the body is more or less globular with about 15 spirally arranged ribs which are notched. It has 5–7 yellowish-brown spines – all radials. Flowers appear from the side of the plant, pale carmine–red about 2 in/5 cm long. Native of Bolivia.

*Lobivia cariquinensis* Card. From Cariquina, Bolivia, at about 12,800 ft/3,900 m altitude. A clustering plant with golden-yellow spines and orange-yellow flowers, and which might well be a variety of *L. pentlandii*.

*Lobivia cinnabarina* (Hook.) Br. & R. From the Bolivian Andes, has about 20 irregular ribs with 8–10 backward-curved radial spines and two or three centrals, grey, slender. Flowers to 1½ in/4 cm diameter, bright scarlet.

*L. ferox* Br. & R. From Oruro, Bolivia. A large species, solitary to about 12 in/30 cm diameter or more with many very long upcurved spines, the centrals being to 6 in/15 cm long. Flowers reddish.

*Lobivia intermedia* Rausch. From Challuanca, Peru, with dark green stem, armed with many slender radial and central spines, centrals being much longer and somewhat curved. Flowers bright scarlet.

*Lobivia jajoiana* Backeb. Has a long taproot, a somewhat cylindrical body with up to 18 spirally notched ribs. Spines are many, both radial and centrals – one of the centrals pointing upward and hooked. Flowers vary in colour – reddish shades, yellow, orange, about 2½ in/6 cm long and beautifully scented. From Jujuy, Argentina.

*Lobivia larae* Card. From Cochabamba, Bolivia. About 5 in/ 12 cm diameter with spreading incurved spines, flower

funnel-shaped, lilac and magenta. A rare species.

*Lobivia leptacantha* Rausch. Also from Peru at Paucartambo at 9,900 ft/3,000 m altitude. Bright green stems with long brownish-yellow spines and large flowers, somewhat variable colourwise, either reddish-orange or yellowish-orange. A group of very easily cultivated plants, decorative, with pleasing appearance of stem and flower alike.

*Lobivia pentlandii* (Hook.) Br. & R. (syn. *Echinocactus pentlandii* Hook.) The type species which is of Bolivian origin. Stems simple or caespitose, greyish-green with about 12 ribs deeply crenate, forming tubercles. Areoles with about five to eight radial spines, brownish and curving backward. Funnel-shaped flowers about 1½ in/4 cm long, reddish-orange.

*Lobivia silvestrii*

*Lobivia silvestrii* (Speg.) Rowl. (syn. *Chamaecereus silvestrii* [Speg.] Br. & R.) One of the most popular and well-known cacti from mountainous regions of Tucuman, Argentina. Plant consists of small joints forming prostrate clusters. Joints with six to nine ribs and soft white spines. Flowers, large for the plant, to about 2¾ in/7 cm long, orange-red. Easy in cultivation and readily propagated by rooting the small joints.

*Lobivia zudanensis* Card. Greyish-green stem to about 6 in/ 15 cm diameter, heavily spined from grey-felted areoles with centrals being up to 3 in/8 cm long. Flowers deep blood-red. Native of Zudanez-Tarabuco, Bolivia.

**Lophocereus** Br. & R. includes just four species from Mexico and the USA. Somewhat columnar plants and developing a pseudocephalium with maturity. All species are night-flowering. Of easy culture.

*Lophocereus schottii*

*Lophocereus schottii* (Engelm.) Br. & R. (syn. *Cereus schotti* [Engelm.]) Type species. A columnar spreading plant forming clusters usually branching from the base. Stems dull to fresh green with five to seven ribs. Non-flowering areoles with greyish-brown felt and few short spines. Flowering areoles with numerous bristles at terminal areas of stems, these thickening and almost forming a cephalium. Flowers white to 1½ in/4 cm long. Large fruits about 1¼ in/3 cm diameter. There are varieties with only trifling differences to the species.

**Lophophora** – there are 3 specific titles recorded, all of similar habit. Plants are bluntly ribbed with low tubercles.

*Lophophora williamsii*

*Lophophora williamsii* (Lem.) Coult. (syn. *Echinocactus williamsii* Lem.) Type species. Spineless globular plants of dull bluish-green colour, having thickened taproot. Ribs varying from about 7 to 13, not very prominent and few areoles with tufts of thick hairs. Flowers pink. Endemic to parts of central Mexico to southern Texas. Called the 'Mescal button' or 'Peyote'. The narcotic extracted is said to cause hallucinations.

Other species of this genus include *L. ziegleri* and *L. lewinii* but these are possibly only variants. All are rare species.

**Lymanbensonia** Kimn. is a monotypic genus erected for an unusual shrubby species with two to three angled stems. Best grown in full sun.
*Lymanbensonia micrantha* (Vaup.) Kimn. (syn. *Acanthorhipsalis micrantha* Br. & R.) A relatively rare species from high altitudes in Peru. Stems flat or three-winged, branching freely. Flowers small, tubular-campanulate, purplish-red.

**Maihuenia** Phil. includes five species rarely encountered in cultivation. Similar to many dwarf *Opuntia* species, but with no glochids. Flowers more or less terminal on the short stems, these have no perianth tube. All are winter-hardy in Europe.
*Maihuenia poeppigii* (Otto) Web. One of the outstanding miniature species of the Opuntieae indigenous to the high mountains of Chile. A shrubby prostrate plant forming masses with cylindrical joints to about 2½ in/6 cm long, slender with small cylindrical leaves and three spines to each areole. Flowers yellow at terminal ends. Other species include *M. valentinii* Speg. from Chubut, southern Argentina, with whitish or creamy-yellow flowers, and *M. patagonica* (Phil.) Br. & R. with white flowers. All are of similar appearance and habit and exceedingly rare in cultivation.

*Mammillaria varieties*

**Mammillaria** Haw. This genus constitutes one of the largest of the Cactaceae. Considerable interest is centred around these species, and while existing grouping appears to be poorly founded, constant investigation and study are undertaken to ensure the best system of classification. In recent years several new discoveries have been made which have increased its already popular appeal.

*Mammillaria anniana* Glass & Foster. A more recently discovered species from Tamaulipas in Mexico. Plants are mostly solitary to about 2 in/5 cm high and across. They have 14 radial, ½ in/1 cm long, stiff yellowish spines and five to nine centrals. The flowers are ½ in/1 cm long and they are a pale yellow.

*Mammillaria boolii*

*Mammillaria boolii* Lindsay. From near San Carlos Bay in Sonora, Mexico. A small species scarcely more than 1¼ in/3.5 cm high and the same across – the white spination almost obliterates the green of the body. Flowers are pinkish. There is a theory that this might well be an annual in habitat – germinating, growing to maturity, flowering and fruiting all in one year.

*Mammillaria candida* Scheidw. A most attractive and popular species from San Luis Potosi, Mexico. Usually considered a solitary plant, but occasionally caespitose. Plant body, to 3 in/8 cm diameter or more, covered completely by white spines, globose. Areoles with scant white wool and numerous radial spines, 50 or more, slender, spreading, white; centrals to 12, stiff, whitish with one protruding. Flower funnel-shaped, pinkish with brownish markings. There are supposedly varietal forms: *M. candida rosea* which tends to have pinkish tips to the spines particularly toward the crown of the plant, and *M. candida* var. *caespitosa*, so-named due to its consistently caespitose habit and other minor differences. Whether or not these varieties are valid is much in doubt as it would seem the species itself has similar variations.

*Mammillaria fittkaui* Glass & Foster. Species from rocks near north shore of Lake Chapala, Jalisco, Mexico. Stem cylindric 1½-2 in/4-5 cm diameter, clustering. Tubercles in spirals, terete with rounded apex. Areoles with little wool having seven to nine radial spines, acicular, white about ⅛ in/5 mm long; centrals four, yellowish brown, three hardly distinguishable from the radials, protruding horizontally, slightly longer and hooked. Flower about ⅜ in/1 cm diameter, whitish-pink and slightly darker midrib.

*Mammillaria garessii* Cowper. From southwest of Matachic, Chihuahua, Mexico, in rock crevices. A solitary or clustering species to 3 in/8 cm long and to 2 in/5 cm diameter, having dullish grey-green tubercles up to ⅓ in/8 mm long. Areoles with wool and up to 22 radial spines, whitish, spreading, somewhat adpressed, acicular and interlacing; usually only one central, stiff, reddish-brown, acicular, hooked and protruding at sharp angle. Flowers whitish-pink.

*Mammillaria glassii* Foster. Discovered in Nuevo Leon near the village of Dieciocho de Marzo, Mexico. A clustering species, globose to 1¼ in/3 cm diameter, tubercles in 8–13 spirals, pale green, ⅓ in/8 mm long, axils with thin whitish bristles. Radial spines 50-60 about ⅜-½ in/1-1½ cm long, fine, white ascending and interlaced; six to eight sub-central spines spreading and mingling with radials; one central, brownish, hooked about ⅛ in/5 mm long, protruding horizontally. Flowers forming ring around crown, somewhat funnel-shaped, pale pink.

*Mammillaria goldii*

*Mammillaria goldii* Glass & Foster. A miniature species from north of Nacozari, Sonora, Mexico, at over 3,300 ft/1,000 m elevation. Small stem, simple, rarely caespitose to 1 in/2½ cm diameter, sub-globose. Tubercles in spirals, ⅛–⅓ in/5-7 mm long, dark green sometimes pinkish at base. Areoles with up to 45 radial spines, pectinate, thin, white and interlacing. Flower funnel-shaped to 1-1½ in/3-4 cm diameter, lilac-pink.

*Mammillaria halei* Brandeg. (syn. *Cochemiea halei* [Brandeg.] Walton) Current opinion has veered toward the uniting of this species and other of the *Cochemiea* with *Mammillaria*. Usually clustering stems, very erect to 12 in/30 cm long and to 2¾ in/7 cm diameter. Tubercles very short, axils woolly. Radial spines to 20, about ¼ in/10 mm long, three or four centrals about ⅝ in/25 mm long – all straight. Flowers toward the centre, 2 in/5 cm long, yellowish with scarlet lobes. An attractive plant from the offshore islands of Baja California, Mexico, particularly Magdalena Island. Other species within this complex include *M. setispina* (Coult.) Walton, *M. pondii* (Greene) Walton and *M. poselgeri* (Hild.)

Br. & R., all having many similar characteristics and all originating from Baja California.

*Mammillaria longiflora*

*Mammillaria longiflora* Br. & R. (syn. *Krainzia longiflora* [Br. & R.] Backeb.) A choice species from Puerto Coneto, Durango, Mexico. Usually solitary, sometimes clustering, stems about ¼ in/3 cm in diameter, smallish tubercles, closely set and almost hidden by spines, radials about 30, acicular to ½ in/12 mm long, yellowish, spreading; centrals four, reddish-brown, one much longer and hooked at the tip. Flowers borne freely at the crown, about ¾ in/2 cm long, pink with slightly purplish throat. This species, together with *Mammillaria guelzowiana* Werd. also from Durango and having large rich reddish- purple flowers, has recently been transferred to the genus *Mammillaria*.

*Mammillaria longimamma* De Cand. (syn. *Dolichothele longimamma* [De Cand.] Br. & R.) A clustering species, pale fresh green with prominent elongated tubercles. Spines from areoles at tip of tubercles, radials up to 12 acicular, spreading, central spines one to three protruding horizontally, all yellowish, centrals with blackish tips. Flowers to 2½ in/6 cm long, bright yellow. Native of parts of central Mexico.

*Mammillaria mainae* K. Brandeg. An uncommon plant found between Nogales and Hermosillo, Sonora, Mexico, usually in the shade of shrub. Stem globose, somewhat flattened to 3 in/8 cm diameter, frequently clustering. Tubercles pale green to dark green having about 10 radial spines, yellowish with brown tips, widely spreading; central spines few, stout, hooked at tip. Flowers from upper part of plant, about ¾ in/2 cm long, with open throat, pinkish-white.

*Mammillaria microcarpa* Engelm. A well-known species of wide distribution from Texas to Arizona and to Sonora, Mexico. Stem globose, often forming clusters to 3 in/8 cm high, tubercles smallish greyish-green with up to 30 radial spines, white with blackish tips, rigid and spreading to ½ in/12 mm long; centrals one to three, brownish to ¾ in/

2 cm long, hooked. Flowers from near the crown about 1 in/2½ cm long, somewhat funnel-shaped, purplish with sometimes whitish edges.

*Mammillaria nelsonii* Br. & R. (syn. *Oehmea nelsonii* [Br. & R.] Buxb.) A globose plant to 2 in/5 cm diameter with about 15 white acicular radial spines ¼ in/8 mm long and spreading, several centrals similar to radials but one longer and strongly hooked. Flowers yellowish.

*Mammillaria nivosa* Link. An interesting and unusual West Indian species distributed in the Virgin Islands. A clustering species to 5 in/12 cm or more diameter with long tubercles about ⅜ in/10 mm long with white wool in axils. Spines about 14, acicular up to ½ in/15 mm long, golden-yellow. Flowers creamy-white. An uncommon and rare species, its spines give the effect of an almost golden-yellow plant.

*Mammillaria oliviae*

*Mammillaria oliviae* Orc. From Arizona. More or less globular in shape and fairly densely covered with spines which are white or brownish. Flowers are purplish-red and edged in white.

*Mammillaria pectinifera* Web. (syn. *Solisia pectinata* [B. Stein.] Br. & R.) A rare but well-known plant, native of Tehuacan, Puebla, Mexico. Plants solitary to 1¼ in/ 3 cm diameter covered entirely by overlapping white spine clusters. Tubercles hatchet-shaped, low and small with narrow elongated areoles and numerous slender spines, all radials, white and arranged comb-like, pectinate. Flowers yellowish.

*Mammillaria plumosa* Web. A densely clustering species from Coahuila, Mexico, from quite high altitudes. It becomes a mass of whitish feathery-spined individual heads, globular in shape, no central spines, flowers of greenish-white or yellowish, about ½ in/1½ cm long and wide. *M. schiedeana* Ehrenb. is of similar habit, although occasionally the odd solitary plant is seen. The small bodies are densely covered with fine hair-like golden-yellow or whitish spines, up to 75 radials to an areole and no centrals. Flowers about ¾ in/2 cm long, yellowish-white. Hidalgo, Mexico.

*Mammillaria pottsii* Scheer. An elongated species of wide distribution from Texas, Chihuahua, Coahuila, etc. Stems cylindrical to 6 in/15 cm long, usually forming clusters from base and stem. Tubercles almost hidden by spines, radials about 30 white, short spreading; centrals six to twelve, stout and longer than radials, greyish with brown tips; axils with wool. Flowers from below the crown, small, about ⅜ in/ 1 cm long, magenta or purplish.

*Mammillaria pringlei* K. Brandeg. Native of San Luis Potosi, Mexico. A rather large species, generally solitary, globose to 6½ in/16 cm high and 3 in/8 cm diameter with dull greenish tubercles, conic, the axils woolly. Radial spines to 20 spreading; central spines about seven, much stouter and longer than radials and very much recurved, all deep yellow. Flowers about ⅜ in/10 mm long, red.

*Mammillaria santaclarensis* Cowper. Native of Santa Clara Canyon in Mexico, west of Cuidad Juarez to Chihuahua Highway. Somewhat cylindrical stem up to 6½ in/16 cm long with soft green tubular tubercles becoming conical at the base. Radial spines about 30 on mature plants, acicular, stiff and straight to ½ in/12 mm long, yellowish-white, about 10 spreading and adpressed toward the base of the plant; centrals one to four strongly hooked, acicular, stout, reddish-brown and protruding horizontally. Flower ½ in/ 1½ cm long, pale pink with darker midrib.

*Mammillaria schumannii* Hild. (syn. *Bartschella schumannii* [Hild.] Br. & R). An uncommon plant, usually clustering to about 2½ in/6 cm high, somewhat globular to short-oblong with ungrooved large rounded tubercles, axils slightly woolly and no bristles. Radial spines to about 15, spreading, stout, central spines slightly hooked. Flower about 1½ in/ 4 cm diameter, short and hidden among the tubercles, dark pink to violet-rose. Distributed in more or less coastal areas from La Paz to Todos Santos, Baja California, Mexico.

*Mammillaria senilis*

*Mammillaria senilis* Lodd. (syn. *Mamillopsis senilis* [Lodd.] Weber) A most attractive plant, even without flower, but more so when in full bloom. Native of mountainous regions of Chihuahua and Durango Mexico, at altitudes of 6,500 ft/2,000 m or more, often in almost bare rock crevices and enduring very low temperatures. Stems to about 3-3½ in/8-9 cm high, sometimes longer and to 2½ in/6 cm diameter, rarely simple, more generally clustering freely.

Tubercles about ⅛ in/4 mm long with numerous pure white spines to ¾ in/2 cm long. Flowers about 2½ in/6 cm long and almost the same diameter, red or orange-red.

*Mammillaria tetrancistra* Engelm. (syn. *Phellosperma tetrancistra* [Engelm.] Br. & R.) A globular plant, somewhat cylindrical, solitary or caespitose and very spiny. Has large fleshy taproot which branches. Tubercles rounded and elongated with numerous radial spines, acicular, whitish and tipped brown; centrals one to four, brown or blackish and longer than radials, usually hooked. Flower to 1½ in/4 cm, purplish.

*Mammillaria hahniana*

There are many more deserving mention, made very popular by their pleasing appearance and flowers. *M. zeilmanniana* Boed. is grown mainly as a pot plant in certain parts of Europe and is most attractive with its masses of purplish flowers. *M. spinosissima* Lem. has a variety of spine colours, densely covering the plant body and with rings of flowers, pink to reddish, around the crown. *M. hahniana* Werd. is another deservedly popular plant, densely covered with white spines and long flexible bristles and producing a ring of carmine flowers near to the apex. This is a specialist genus which has inspired enthusiasm and research by laymen as well as botanists.

**Matucana** Br. & R. includes several species or varieties originating from Peru. Current opinion suggests that these should be merged into the genus *Borzicactus* due basically to flower characteristics. The plants here are generally globular, but some becoming short-cylindrical with age. Numerous broad and low tuberculate ribs, usually with many spines and slender tubular flowers.

*Matucana aurantiaca* (Vaup.) Buxb. (syn. *Submatucana aurantiaca* (Vaup.) Backeb.) A beautiful species from Catamarca, Peru, having about 16 ribs, areoles somewhat elliptical and 15 or more reddish-brown spreading spines, some to ⅜ in/ 1 cm long and one even longer. Flowers from the crown of the plant, tubular, scarlet.

*Matucana haynei* (Otto) Br. & R. (syn. *Echinocactus haynei* Otto) The type species which is native of Matucana in central Peru. Mostly globular plants to about 4 in/10 cm diameter with dense spine formation, white with brownish tips, to over 1¼ in/3 cm long. Flowers orange-red or even deeper red on a long slender tube.

Many new discoveries have been made during the last few years due to the extensive efforts of Rauh, Ritter, Lau and others. Varying characteristics have been noted with many of the newer plants, but it may well be determined that some are varietal forms of *M. haynei*. However, newer species include *M. blancii* Backeb. from Rio Parron, Cordillera Blanca, Peru, a very densely spined stem covered with numerous whitish spines, flowers reddish. *M. herzogiana* Backeb. from Cordillera Negra, Peru, with yellowish-white somewhat curved and spreading bristle-like spines and scarlet flowers. *M. variabilis* Rauh & Backeb. from Churin, Oyan, Peru. *M. crinifera* Ritt. from Machua Huari, Peru. *M. yanganucensis* Rauh & Backeb. from Casma Pass, Peru. All have very similar characteristics as far as spination is concerned. *M. winterae* Ritt. from Santiago de Chuco, Peru, while similar in spination generally, has a distinctly different-coloured flower, lilac-red. *M. madisoniorum* (Hutch.) Rowl. very much resembles a *Lophophora*, greyish-green body with a few areoles, sometimes with very long spines. Flowers reddish. *M. madisoniorum* var. *pujupattii* Lau & Don. from Puente de 24 Julio, on the River Maranon, Peru, is similar in many respects, but the stem has a beautiful bluish-white bloom, flowers red. This species and variety were previously included in *Submatucana*.

*Matucana myriacantha*

*Matucana myriacantha* (Vaup.) Buxb. A somewhat flattened species, but generally globular in shape with about 26 ribs. Spines yellowish becoming greyish – about 25 radials and 10 centrals, these being longer than the radials at about 1 in/2.5 cm long. Flowers are a bright golden-yellow or orange-red, to 3 in/8 cm long. Native of Peru.

**Mediocactus** Br. & R. are clambering plants having much the same character as *Hylocereus*. Long slender branches usually three-angled, with short spines and many aerial roots. Considered to be a genus midway between *Hylocereus* and *Selenicereus* and having a resemblance to both genera.

Fairly widely distributed in South America – Peru, Colombia, Bolivia, Brazil and Argentina. All species are rare in cultivation.

*Mediocactus coccineus* (Salm-Dyck) Br. & R. The type species of this genus. Originates from Brazil, but also found in northern Argentina. A climber, sometimes clambering, having dark green stems, usually three-angled, with knobby projections below the areoles and very small spines. Large flowers, white and funnel-shaped. Night-flowering. The specific name would suggest red flowers, but this is possibly more appropriate to the fruits.

*Mediocactus megalanthus* (Schum.) Br. & R. A rare epiphyte from Peru, originally discovered in Loreto, but now reported elsewhere in Peru and Bolivia. Forms masses of stems which tend to hang pendent rather than climb. Stems are 3-angled with undulating margins and brownish spines. Flowers are considered to be among the largest of the Cactaceae – up to 15 in/38 cm long – white, scented and night-flowering.

Other species are recorded, but their identity is much in doubt. *Mediocactus hassleri* is of interest, having the appearance of *Selenicereus* with rounded stems, but there is doubt about its authenticity.

**Melocactus** Link & Otto is a distinctive genus, the species of which are often referred to as the 'Turk's cap' cactus. Several are indigenous to North America and the West Indies, and there are many which are native of South America. Some of the more recent discoveries have been in Brazil. All species with cephalium.

This is one of the earliest groups of cacti introduced into cultivation; for many years they had the generic title of *Cacti* (e.g., *Cactus broadwayii* etc.) until the existing title of *Melocactus* was established finally in 1827.

*Melocactus bahiensis*

*Melocactus bahiensis* (Br. & R.) Werderm. From Bahia, Brazil, has a body about 6 in/15 cm diameter, 10–12 ribs and a few central spines. The cephalium consists of densely set brownish bristles. Flowers are pink, and measure to about 1 in/2.5 cm long.

*Melocactus broadwayii*

*Melocactus broadwayii* Br. & R. A West Indian species from the Windward Islands and Tobago. Very shallow rooted with somewhat flattened base, pale green up to 6 in/15 cm long, 6 in/15 cm broad at the base and narrowing toward the cephalium. Ribs 14 to 18 with areoles regularly set about ⅜ in/1 cm apart, 8–10 radial spines and usually one central, all yellowish-brown. Cephalium about 2½ in/6 cm diameter and eventually to 1-2 in/3-5 cm high consisting of densely set soft brown bristles and whitish wool. Flowers small, purplish. This is one of the many recorded species from these parts of the West Indies. *M. intortus* (Mill.) Br. & R. is very similar in most respects, but invariably with a longer cephalium more rounded at the top having lilac-pink flowers.

*Melocactus matanzanus* Leon. One of the choicest species, always small and producing its cephalium after about six years. Stem fresh green, 4 in/10 cm high and 3 in/8 cm broad with wide shallow ribs. Areoles with short reddish spines. Cephalium bright orange composed of dense bristles and white wool. Flowers deep pink. This is one of the several species endemic to Cuba; most are rare in cultivation and would appear, in most cases, to be somewhat smaller in growth than those from other parts. *M. acunai* Leon, with wide somewhat acute ribs, armed with long spreading rigid spines. *M. harlowii* Br. & R. with light green body with narrow low ribs, closely set areoles with up to 16 spines, spreading and some curved. *M. guitartii* is the rarest of these Cuban species, about 4 in/10 cm broad and 4½ in/12 cm high, densely armed with long spreading and protruding spines.

*Melocactus melocactoides* De Cand. A charming, medium-sized species from coastal areas of Brazil, particularly around the regions of Rio de Janeiro, Bahia and Pernambuco. Sometimes called *M. violaceus* Pfeiff. (the two are synonymous). Fresh green stem with about 10 broad obtuse ribs, areoles about six to each rib, bearing about five to eight

radial spines, brownish-grey to about ⅜ in/1 cm long, sometimes a little curved. Cephalium compact with white wool and brownish bristles and deep pink flower. *M. neryi* Sch. from the state of Amazonas, Brazil, is very similar, but with pronounced terete spines all curved and spreading outward; rose-pink flowers. *M. erythracanthus* Buin. & Bred. from western slopes of Serra do Espinhaco, Bahia, Brazil, a recent discovery with globose body, about 12 sharp pronounced ribs, rounded areoles and seven yellowish-brown spines, one of which is bent downward about 5 in/13 cm long. Small tubular flower, lilac-red. *M. giganteus* Buin. & Bred. from Serra Santo Inacio, Bahia, Brazil, is another discovery which has about 15 ribs, greyish areoles with greyish-brown spines – eight radials about 7 in/18 cm long and one central about 7½ in/17 cm long slanting upward. Flower deep lilac.

One of the most outstanding discoveries has been *M. glaucescens* Buin. & Bred. with greyish-blue body. Native of the western slopes of Serro do Espinhaco, Bahia, Brazil, with about 11 ribs, areoles have eight greyish spines, radials spreading and one curved downward, one central protruding, somewhat ascending, with slightly hooked tip. Flower red.

*M. cremnophilus* Buin. & Bred. from Serro do Espinhaco, Bahia, Brazil, a dark green plant about 5½ in/14 cm diameter with up to 13 somewhat obtuse ribs, slightly sunken areoles with eight to nine radial spines of varying lengths, one lower one directed downward to 2½ in/7 cm long. Central spines four, the lower one directed downward to 1½ in/4 cm long, the other three about 1¼ in/3 cm long. Flower carmine-red.

**Micranthocereus** Backeb. includes a few fascinating plants, mainly rare in cultivation with distinctive pseudocephaliums from which many small flowers emerge.

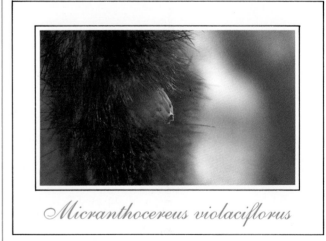

*Micranthocereus violaciflorus*

*Micranthocereus polyanthus* (Werderm.) Backeb. (syn. *Cephalocereus polyanthus* Werderm.) The type species from near Caetete, Bahia, Brazil. A low slender plant branching from the base, the stems being almost completely covered with whitish-yellowish spines, and even more so toward the apex where the pseudocephalium develops and many rose-red flowers are borne. *M. violaciflorus* Buin. from Minas Gerais, Brazil, is a recent introduction of considerable merit, slender stems with many ribs and short rather interlaced spines. The pseudocephalium extends well down one side of the stem consisting of brownish-red-purplish bristles and white wool with reddish-purplish flowers. *M. auriazureus* Buin. & Bred. native of Grao Mogol, Minas Gerais, Brazil, at an altitude of about 3,250 ft/1,000 m. A tall slender plant to just over 3¼ ft/1 m, bluish-grey body with 18 rounded ribs and areoles with yellow wool and many yellowish-brown spines of unequal length. Pseudocephalium develops with thickening whitish wool from which the lilac-pinkish flowers emerge.

**Mila** Br. & R. are Peruvian plants, caespitose with small yellowish flowers. The generic name is an anagram of Lima, the capital of Peru.
*Mila caespitosa* Br. & R. The type species from near Santa Clara on the low hills bordering Remac Valley. Small plant to about 6 in/15 cm high and clumping freely. About 10 ribs with straight margins, areoles densely brown-felted with 20 radial spines and several longer centrals, all yellowish-brown. Flowers about ⅝ in/1½ cm long, at apex of stems. *M. densiseta* Rauh. & Backeb. also from central Peru is rather longer, up to 10 in/25 cm, heavily spined with typical yellow flowers. Other species include *M. kubeana* with whitish spines and *M. nealeana*, a smaller species with soft whitish spines.

**Monvillea** Br. & R. are night-flowering plants with slender, semi-erect stems and flowers on long slender tube. The peculiarity of the flower is centred in the stamens which instead of being in definite rows are scattered over the throat.
*Monvillea campinensis* Backeb. A species to 16½ ft/5 m tall, but somewhat straggling in habit – the stems being quite slender. It has 7–9 ribs and is quite spiny. Flowers are about 4 in/10 cm long, whitish. It is found in the district of São Paulo, Brazil.
*Monvillea cavendishii* (Monv.) Br. & R. (syn. *Cereus cavendishii* Monv.) The type species from Brazil, Paraguay and northern Argentina. A tall-growing plant, generally branching from the base with about nine low rounded ribs bearing small areoles and to 12 brownish spines. Flower whitish, about 4½ in/12 cm long, nocturnal. *M. spegazzini* (Web.) Br. & R. from the Chaco Territory, Argentina, is a distinctive species, bluish-green stems, marbled white and grey, three-angled with pronounced tubercles, areoles with black spines, flower whitish-pink. *M. diffusa* Br. & R., native of the hillsides of Catamayo Valley, Ecuador, is a tall species having eight ribs bearing areoles with about 10 radial and one to three central black-tipped greyish spines.

**Morangaya** Rowl. is a genus erected for a single species with distinctive characteristics.

*Morangaya pensilis* (K. Brandeg.) Rowl. (syn. *Cereus pensilis* K. Brand.) By some considered 'half-way' between *Echinocereus* and *Aporocactus*, seemingly having characteristics of both. Native of Baja California in the high mountains of Sierra de la Laguna. Stems erect or semi-erect, sometimes pendent to nearly 10 ft/3 m long. Ribs 8–10 with fairly close-set areoles having about eight radial spines and one central. Flowers orange-red about 2½ in/6 cm long, rather narrow. Tube and ovary with bristly spines and whitish or brownish wool. Fruit globular about ¾ in/2 cm diameter.

**Myrtillocactus** Cons. includes just four species from Central America. Several flowers develop from a single areole.

*Myrtillocactus cochal*

*Myrtillocactus cochal* (Orc.) Br. & R. A branching species with bluish-green stems and branches. Ribs 6–8, deeply furrowed inbetween. Spines to 2 in/5 cm long. Flowers appear by day, often several together, pure white. This is very close to *M. geometrizens*. Native of Baja California, Mexico.
*Myrtillocactus geometrizens* (Mart.) Cons. (syn. *Cereus geometrizens* Mart.) Type species. A well-known Mexican species from the regions of San Luis Potosi to Oaxaca, having edible fruits which when dried resemble raisins. Young seedlings are frequently used for grafting stock. Popular in collections. A tree-like plant with short blue-green trunk and many branches above. Ribs five or six, very pronounced, areoles well apart with strong blackish spines, the central spine usually being more elongated. Flowers small from the upper part of the areole, creamy-yellow. Fruits bluish.

**Neoabottia** Br. & R. is a somewhat obscure genus of two species, only one of which is occasionally encountered in cultivation.
*Neoabottia paniculata* (Lam.) Br. & R. (syn. *Cactus paniculata* Lam.) Type species. The only representative of this obscure

genus. Rarely met with in cultivation. Apparently quite widely distributed in Haiti and Cuba and has a striking resemblance to certain species of *Leptocereus* and *Dendrocereus,* all from the same areas. A tree-like plant often to 33 ft/10 m high. Branches from the top, the branches being four ribbed and strongly winged with somewhat crenate margins. Many brownish-grey spines at well-spaced areoles. Cephaliums develop on terminal ends. Flowers nocturnal, white, short and tubular.

***Neobesseya*** Br. & R. is a genus belonging somewhere between *Neolloydia* and *Coryphantha. N. arizonica* Hester has now been transferred to *Coryphantha.* A Cuban species, originally described by Britton and Rose as *Coryphantha cubensis,* and transferred by Backeberg to *Neolloydia,* and now known as *Escobaria cubensis.* It seems likely that all other species will likewise be included under *Escobaria.*

*Neobesseya asperispina*

*Neobesseya asperispina* (Boed.) Boed. From Mexico, from valleys in the mountains south of Saltillo, also in the state of Nuevo Leon. A rather small plant, darkish green with pronounced tubercles with few spines about 12, somewhat spreading and greenish-yellow flowers with deeper midrib and ciliate margins.

*Neobesseya macdougallii* (Alex.) Kladiwa (syn. *Ortegocactus macdougallii* Alex.) One of the most outstanding discoveries of recent years and only now becoming generally known in cultivation. Native of Oaxaca near the village of San Jose Lachiguiri, Mexico, where is was discovered by T. Mac-Dougall growing on limestone rocks. Stem short-cylindric to globose, frequently solitary, often clustering with distinctive bluish-grey-green body. Tubercles rhomboidal ⅝ in/ 12 mm in diameter, spirally arranged. Areoles bearing wool in their upper part, radials about seven mostly black or black-tipped to ⅜ in/10 mm long and one central to ⅛ in/ 5 mm long. Flower about 1¼ in/30 mm long and 1 in/

25 mm diameter, bright clear yellow on short pale green tube. Just where this species should be placed is still in doubt. It has the peculiarity of a woolly ovary and this would seem to provide a reason for complete separation.

*Neobesseya missouriensis* (Sweet) Br. & R. (syn. *Mammillaria missouriensis* Sweet.) From mountains in Missouri, North Dakota, Colorado, Oklahoma and possibly elsewhere in the more southerly states of the USA. Plants are usually solitary, and frequently clustering. Stem globose about 2 in/ 5 cm diameter with tubercles somewhat spiralled, ¼-⅝ in/ 10-15 mm long. Invariably all spines are radial, occasionally one central, up to 20 in all, grey, acicular, pubescent. Flowers are yellow, somewhat insignificant but quite fragrant.

***Neobuxbaumia*** Backeb. is a Mexican genus of six species. Tree-like columnar plants. Flowers are either diurnal or nocturnal.

*Neobuxbaumia tetetzo* (Web.) Backeb. (syn. *Pilocereus tetetzo* Web.) Type species. Originally included with *Pilocereus,* with which it could well be reunited, or with *Pachycereus.* An erect columnar species with greyish-green stems and many rounded ribs, areoles well-armed with many spines. Flowers somewhat small, rather cylindrical and not widely opening. From the limestone slopes of Cerro Guiengola, near Oaxaca, Mexico.

*Neobuxbaumia euphorbioides* (Haw.) Buxb. (syn. *Rooksbya euphorbioides* [Haw.] Backeb.) An obscure species rarely encountered in cultivation. A tall columnar plant to about 16½ ft/5 m high. Stems with eight acute ribs, somewhat crenate and very closely set areoles, white-felted and with few small spines. Flower diurnal, reddish. Native of Mexico around Tamaulipas.

***Neodawsonia*** Backeb. is a tree-like species, bearing rather small flowers and subsequently rather hairy fruits. There are three species, all from Mexico.

*Neodawsonia apicicephalium* (Dawson) Backeb. (syn. *Cephalocereus apicicephalium* Dawson) Type species. An erect columnar plant, rounded stems with numerous ribs having closely set areoles and many short spines. Mature growth develops pronounced woolly rings around the stems due to the annual displacement of the terminal cephalium from which the nocturnal pink flowers emerge. A rare and desirable species from Cerro Guiengola, near Tehuantepec, Oaxaca, Mexico.

***Neolloydia*** Br. & R. are plants with attractive spination and large colourful flowers. Closely allied to *Coryphantha* and *Escobaria.*

*Neolloydia ceratites* (Quehl.) Br. & R. A Mexican species usually solitary but also forming clusters. Stem to 4 in/10 cm long with somewhat four-angled tubercles spirally arranged. Radial spines about 20, white and more or less spreading about ½ in/15 mm long; centrals five or six and slightly longer with blackish tips. The flower is large and purple.

*Neolloydia conoidea*

*Neolloydia viereckii*

*Neolloydia conoidea* (De Cand.) Br. & R. (syn. *Mammillaria conoidea* De Cand.) Type species. A clustering species, sometimes solitary with tubercles in spiral rows, somewhat obtuse with woolly axils. Spines numerous almost completely obscuring the plant. Radial spines whitish, 25 or more, spreading ⅜ in/10 mm long; central spines longer to 1¼ in/3 cm long, blackish. Large flowers, purple. Native of northern Mexico.

*Neolloydia erectrocentra* (Coult.) L. Benson (syn. *Echinocactus erectrocentrus* Coult.) An attractive plant about 4½ in/10 cm diameter and to 3½ in/14 cm tall, somewhat ovoid, greyish-green. Many low ribs made up of closely set tubercles bearing about 14 radial spines and one or two elongated erect centrals, these often being somewhat swollen toward the base. Pinkish flowers to about 2 in/5 cm long with green style. From southwest Arizona, USA.

*Neolloydia grandiflora* (Otto) Berg. One of the most outstanding of this genus from Tamaulipas, Mexico. Usually solitary, cylindrical to 4½ in/12 cm or more high, brownish-green, small tubercles with whitish wool in the axils; radial spines about 25, yellowish-brown, spreading horizontally and few centrals, sometimes absent, blackish. Large beautiful reddish-purple flowers from crown of plant.

*Neolloydia matehualensis* Backeb. A rare plant from south of Matehuala in San Luis Potosi, Mexico. Stems bluish-grey and somewhat elongated with soft tubercles and many radial but few central spines. It bears large pinkish-purple flowers.

*Neolloydia unguispina* (Engelm.) L. Benson. A unique species completely covered by elongated, somewhat twisted spines almost hiding the entire body of the plant. Globular, sometimes short-cylindrical, to about 4½ in/12 cm high and 2½ in/7 cm diameter, pale green with rather obscure low ribs.

Spines whitish, the radials about 25 widely spreading and the four to eight central spines being much stouter and longer, some turning upward, others downward and all somewhat curved. Flowers red. A desirable and rare species from states of Chihuahua and Zacatecas, Mexico. These last two species are recent transfers from *Echinomastus*.

*Neolloydia viereckii* (Werderm.) F.M. Knuth. A transfer from *Gymnocactus*. A Mexican species, somewhat globular in shape with many tubercles set in 15 or more rows. Spines white below, brownish above and black-tipped – the radials are more or less white and about 20 in number from each areole. Flowers pale purplish-pink.

*Neolloydia warnockii* L. Benson. A little-known species from the Chihuahuan Desert in Mexico and parts of Texas, where it grows on limestone hills at 3,000-4,000 ft/900-1,200 m altitudes. Stems solitary to 4 in/10 cm long and 2½ in/7 cm diameter with long tubercles and elliptic areoles. Radial spines about 14, brownish, spreading irregularly at low angles; centrals about four, some straight and one protruding horizontally. Flowers about 1 in/25 mm diameter, pinkish.

Other species of this genus include *N. mariposensis* (Hester) L. Benson, from near the town of Mariposa, Texas; *N. intertexta* (Engelm.) L. Benson, from widely distributed regions of Arizona, Texas and northern Mexico.

This genus illustrates some of the difficulties of nomenclature. The non-botanist could easily accumulate plants under various names only to find that they were all the same!

**Neoporteria** Br. & R. is a large genus which has absorbed several other genera such as *Pyrrhocactus*, *Horridocactus*, *Neochilenia* and others from South America. Mostly globular or slightly elongated plants.

*Neoporteria jussieui* (Monv.) Br. & R. (syn. *Neochilenia jussieui* [Monv.] Backeb.) A native of Chile, globular plant, blackish-greenish-red, slightly woolly at top with no spines, about 14 acute ribs divided into pronounced tubercles, yellowish-felted areoles armed with seven or more dark brown spreading radial spines and one central to 1 in/2½ cm long. Flowers from near the apex, pale pink with darker midrib. *N. fusca* (Mühlpf.) Backeb. from the Chilean Andes, dark green with 12 ribs, somewhat tubercled, areoles with brownish spines, about seven radials and four centrals, flowers yellow. *N. esmeraldana* (Ritt.) Backeb. from Esmeraldas, northern Chile, purplish-reddish stem and numerous tubercles; areoles woolly with up to 12 brownish radial spines, with or without centrals. Flower yellowish. *N. residua* (Ritt.) Backeb. from near Antofagasta, northern Chile, about 3 in/8 cm diameter with about 12 ribs, blunted tubercles, areoles having many brownish spines, about 12 radials and five or more centrals, flower yellowish.

*Neoporteria paucispinosa* Donald & Rowl. (syn. *Islaya paucispinosa* Rauh. & Backeb.) Globular plants from Chala, Arequipa, Chile. Stem reddish-grey about 3 in/8 cm diameter with about 12-16 ribs, pronounced areoles with stiff spreading greyish-brown spines. Flowers from apex of plant, golden-yellow. Other species include *N. Islayensis* Donald & Rowl., *N. bicolor* Donald & Rowl. and others which have many characteristics in common, and the more they are grown together in cultivation the more similar they appear to be.

*Neoporteria subgibbosa* (Haw.) Br. & R. (syn. *Echinocactus subgibbosus* Haw.) The type species for which this genus was created. A somewhat cylindrical-shaped plant to 12 in/30 cm high with about 20 ribs, close-set areoles and numerous brown acicular spines, mostly straight. Flowers at apex, pinkish-red. Native of Valparaiso, Chile.

**Neoraimondia** Br. & R. constitutes a monotypic genus. The distinctive characteristic is the areoles. These are considerably enlarged, being brown-felted, thick and often becoming elongated and branching, producing a bristly cephalium effect.

*Neoraimondia macrostibas* (Sch.) Br. & R. A tall species branching from the base, very spiny, 12 or more to each areole, some elongated to 9½ in/24 cm long. Flowering areoles become very enlarged. Flowers about 1½ in/4 cm long, white. Endemic to desert area of western Peru. This is a very rare species, of which little is known in cultivation.

**Neowerdermannia** Fric includes a few species, from widely varying localities, which are specifically recognized, but in fact appear very similar.

*Neowerdermannia vorwerkii* (Fric) Backeb. The type species originating from around Lake Titicaca in Bolivia and Jujuy in Argentina. A globular plant with about 16 ribs divided into low tubercles; the areoles centred in the depressions between the tubercles bear about 10 spreading somewhat curved spines, one upper spine being much longer and hooked. Flowers pinkish-white. *N. chilensis* Backeb. from Chile is very similar, and reputedly has flowers of varying colours.

**Nopalxochia** Br. & R. is very closely related to *Epiphyllum*, with which it is often confused. The genus was originally erected for *Nopalxochia phyllanthoides* (DC.) Br. & R. and subsequently other species have been included. All epiphytic with reddish or pink flowers. All species from Central America, although escapes have naturalized in northern parts of South America.

*Nopalxochia ackermannii* Haw. For a long period considered a hybrid, but in recent years, collections have been formed in southern Mexico as wild plants, and therefore the species now appears to be recognized. This certainly differs considerably from the hybrid varieties named *Epiphyllum ackermannii*, in particular as far as stem growth is concerned. Stems, usually flattened and thin with slightly-crenate margins, sometimes three or four angled; branches freely, mostly from the base. Flowers crimson, diurnal. Style rosepink, short, and white stigma lobes.

*Nopalxochia conzattianum* MacDoug. With firm strong branches, thick with pronounced crenations along the margins and areoles. Flower is bright red with short tube. Style red with purplish stigma lobes about five to six. From about 6,000 ft/2,000 m in rain forest in the Mixe district, Mexico. Still a great rarity for which *Pseudonopalxochia* Backeb. was created, but is now considered invalid.

*Nopalxochia horichii* Kimn. A native of Costa Rica – a pendulous plant growing to 2 ft/60 cm long, three-angled at the base of the stems, then becoming flattened to 1½ in/4 cm across, the margins serrated. Flowers funnel-shaped, rosepink, 5 in/13 cm across at the tips. A true epiphyte.

*Nopalxochia macdougallii* (Alex.) Marsh. Elongated flattened stems, thickish with pronounced crenations and areoles. Generally of pendent habit, branching from the base. Flower lilac-rose, medium-sized with stoutish style and up to six to nine short stigmas about ¼ in/5 mm long. From near Cerro Hueitepec, Chiapas, southern Mexico. A dayflowering species, still rare in cultivation. When discovered it was considered to have differing characteristics to *Nopalxochia*. *Lobiera* Alex. was created, and it was known as *Lobiera macdougallii* Alex.

*Nopalxochia phyllanthoides*

*Nopalxochia phyllanthoides* (DC.) Br. & R. Branches freely, terete at base, but generally flattened and thin above. Stems bright green with crenate margins. Flowers are shades of pink about ¾-1¼ in/2-3 cm wide on short tube ¾ in/2 cm long. Long slender style with five to seven stigma lobes. A very decorative houseplant of easy culture.

A hybrid of this species, *Nopalxochia* (sometimes *Epiphyllum*) × *'Deutsche Kaiserin'*, has proved one of the most exceptional examples of remarkable hybridizing, resulting in an outstanding plant which has been popular for many generations.

***Notocactus*** (K. Sch.) Bgr. constitutes one of the most popular genera of the Cactaceae. It has been subject to careful study and research, and has been subdivided into other genera, viz., *Brasilicactus* and *Eriocactus*, but now the trend is to reunite these, together with *Malacocarpus Wigginsia*, into a single genus, *Notocactus*. Generally globular plants, sometimes semi-cylindrical or short-columnar, all free-flowering; some bloom as very young plants. Mentioned here are only those which have been included in *Brasilicactus, Eriocactus, Notocactus* or *Malacocarpus*.

*Notocactus brevihamatus* (W. Haage) Buxb. A small species, the body to about 2 in/5 cm wide and with over 20 ribs. Radial spines about 16 and 1 or more centrals of pale yellow tipped with brown. Flowers bright yellow, about 1½ in/4 cm long with yellow stigmas. From Rio Grande do Sul, Brazil.

*Notocactus claviceps*

*Notocactus claviceps* (Ritt.) Krainz. From Paraguay and Brazil. The body almost club-shaped – more or less cylindrical to about 20 in/50 cm tall, 4½ in/12 cm or so wide, often narrowing toward the base. Areoles with many slender short yellowish spines and flowers of sulphur-yellow, 1½–2 in/4–5 cm across.

*Notocactus ottonis* (Lehm.) Bgr. (syn. *Cactus ottonis* Lehm.) The type species from Brazil. Usually clustering, with bright green bodies having about 10-15 ribs; areoles with yellowish radials and brownish centrals about ¼ in/1 cm long. Flowers golden-yellow with reddish stigma and lobes, the tube covered with brown hairs. Widely distributed throughout Brazil, Uruguay, Paraguay and Argentina. There are a number of varieties of the type. *N. rutilans* Dan.

& Krainz from Uruguay, has elongated bluish-green body, tubercled, areoles with brownish-red-tipped spines; flowers pale purplish with yellowish throat. *N. scopa* (Spreng.) Bgr., endemic to Brazil and Uruguay, is one of the most attractive of the genus, whitish slender spines from white woolly areoles. Flower from the centre, bright yellow with red stigma. *N. mammulosus* (Lem.) Bgr. from Brazil, Uruguay and Argentina. A globular species with up to 25 ribs, strongly tuberculate and covered by numerous almost interlocking spines. Flowers golden-yellow with reddish-brown stigma. *N. leninghausii* (Haage. Jr.) Bgr. with pale green body and up to 40 low ribs, closely set areoles and numerous golden spines, large golden-yellow flowers. A

*Notocactus uebelmannianus*

south Brazilian plant included in *Eriocactus*. *N. uebelmannianus* Buin. from the Rio Grande do Sul, Brazil. Body globose, somewhat depressed, dark green, with about 16 ribs having chin-like tubercles; areoles bear about six adpressed whitish spines, the lowest being the longest. Flower reddish-purple about 2 in/5 cm diameter. *N. uebelmannianus* var. *flaviflorus* Buin. is similar in all respects except the flower is golden-yellow. *N. magnificus* (Ritt.) Krainz is another outstanding species from Serra Geral, Rio Grande do Sul, Brazil, with greyish-green body, pronounced ribs with closely set areoles and hairy spines, flowers clustering at the apex, yellow. *N. herteri* Werderm., another distinctive plant, native of Uruguay, having many ribs, tubercled, slender spines and reddish-purple flowers. *N. buiningii* Buxb. has peculiar differences with bluish-green body, wavy undulating ribs, stiffish radiating spines and yellow flowers. Native of Uruguay on the borders with Brazil, southwest of Livramento-Riviera. *N. graessneri* (K. Sch.) Bgr., also from Rio Grande do Sul, at one time included in the genus *Brasilicactus*, densely spined, with masses of long yellowish hairy spines adpressed against the body of the plant and with almost greenish flowers. *N. minimus* Fric. & Krzgr. is one of the more recent discoveries with smallish semi-cylindrical body, grouping freely with large yellow flowers.

*Notocactus sellowii* Theun. (syn. *Malacocarpus sellowii* Sch.) A globular species from Brazil, Uruguay and Argentina, about 6 in/15 cm diameter with woolly apex. Ribs about 20, acute and slightly undulate on margins, pale green. Areoles well apart bearing about six straight spines to ¾ in/2 cm long. Flowers from the top, yellow. *N. erinaceus* (Haw.) Schaefer, with strongly undulate ribs, areoles with about eight yellowish radial spines to ¾ in/2 cm long and one central. Flowers large to about 2½ in/6 cm diameter. This is possibly synonymous with *N. corynodes* S-D, which it certainly resembles in many characteristics, both being from Brazil, Uruguay and Argentina. *N. langsdorfii* (Lehm.) Br. & R. from central and southern Brazil is more oblong in shape, developing a very woolly crown, ribs about 17 with slender spreading spines, the central over ¾ in/2 cm long. Flowers yellow.

**Nyctocereus** (Berger) Br. & R. is either erect or trailing with slender, elongated stems and mainly terminal nocturnal flowers. There are six species recorded. All of easy culture. *Nyctocereus serpentinus* (Lag. & Rodr.) Br. & R. (syn. *Cereus serpentinus* DC.) An erect then spreading plant, forming clumps, creeping and hanging to sometimes 10 ft/3 m long. Stems slender, pale green. Ribs 10 or 12, low and rounded with closely set areoles, somewhat felted with about 12 white bristle-like spines. Flowers usually from the upper areoles, whitish, about 6½ in/16 cm long, tube with bristles and areoles on ovary. Has very large seeds. Possibly from eastern Mexico, but it has been so much cultivated througout Mexico that its natural habitat is in doubt. Sometimes called the 'snake cactus'.

**Obregonia** Fric is closely allied to *Strombocactus* and by some considered synonymous. Spines only occur on young plants, then disperse.
*Obregonia denegrii* Fric. A unique plant, looking somewhat like an artichoke. Discovered in the valley of Jaumave, Tamaulipas, Mexico, having characteristics peculiar to itself and for which a monotypic genus was created. Stem usually simple, sometimes clustering, about 4½ in/12 cm diameter, greyish-green, tubercles rather leaf-like, thick and flat above, strongly keeled below, spines and wool almost obsolete. Areoles at tips of tubercles, with few bristles. Flower funnel-shaped, white.

**Opuntia** (Tournf.) Mill. includes many sub-genera, sections or series. Most species become tree-like, others remain dwarf or prostrate. Roots are invariably fibrous, but there are a few with tuberous roots frequently resembling a caudex. All North American species are of easy culture, in fact there are those which have proved almost totally hardy in protected areas of northern Europe. Others from South America and the West Indies frequently prove more of a challenge! In recent years a number of well-known genera have been absorbed by *Opuntia*, including *Nopalea, Tephrocactus, Corynopuntia, Micropuntia, Maihueniopsis*. In the following list, the original generic title (sub-genus or section) is shown in brackets.

*Opuntia aciculata*

*Opuntia aciculata* Griff. From Texas, grows to about 3¼ ft/ 1 m in height and widely spreading. It has obovate joints of dark green about 8 in/20 cm long and these are closely set with large brown areoles. Flowers are golden-yellow. There is also its var. *orbiculata* Backeb., which has more rounded joints, but still densely set with brown areoles, the flowers are a deep red.
*Opuntia arbuscula* Engelm. (*Cylindropuntia*) A bush-forming species with numerous slender cylindrical branches becoming woody. Terminal joints have low indistinct tubercles, sometimes with very small leaf-like growths and long yellowish-brown spines with sheath to 1½ in/4 cm long. Flower greenish-yellow, somewhat tinged rose. Distributed originally throughout much of Arizona and Sonora, Mexico, but now becoming more localized.
*Opuntia articulatus* (Pfeiff.) var. *syringacanthus* Backeb. One of several botanical varieties of the species – all are from Argentina. Stems are almost globular, quite small and forming open clusters. It has a few rather flexible spines from each areole, often to ¾ in/2 cm long. Flowers are white. One of the many species originally included under *Tephrocactus*.
*Opuntia basilaris* Engelm. & Bigelow (*Platyopuntia*) A popular and still rather rare species, referred to as the 'beaver tail cactus', forms compact clumps to about 10 in/25 cm high and spreading. Joints very attractive, obovate, blue-green to purplish with numerous areoles. Flower purplish. There are varietal forms. *O. basilaris* var. *cordata* would appear to be only an even more attractive form than the type material, having a heart-shaped pad. *O. basilaris* var. *treleasii* (Coult.) Toumey is similar to the species but with generally more narrow elongated pads. *O. basilaris* var. *brachyclada* (Griff.) Munz from high elevations is a low-growing rather dwarf plant having miniature pads com-

pared with the species and pinkish-rose flowers. All are from California/Nevada/Arizona border areas.

*Opuntia bigelovii*

*Opuntia bigelovii* Engelm. (*Cylindropuntia*) A rare species, referred to as the 'teddy bear cactus'. Intensely spined on cylindrical joints having many tubercles and armed with golden-yellow spines, many from an areole. Flowers yellowish-green. Usually growing in rocky mountainous areas up to nearly 3,300 ft/1,000 m in southwestern states of the USA, Sonora, Mexico, particularly on the coastal regions of the Gulf of California, and Baja California. One of the most beautiful of the genus.

*Opuntia bradtiana* K. Brandeg. (*Grusonia*) A cylindrical-stemmed plant forming thick clusters, to 6½ ft/2 m high. Stems pale green with tuberculate ribs and heavily spined, particularly at the apex. The spines often to 20 or more are pale yellow on young growth but becoming white, not sheathed. Flower yellow and fringed. A difficult species to establish in cultivation, especially from cuttings, so while it is common in Coahuila, Mexico, its habitat, it is rarely seen in collections.

*Opuntia brasiliensis* (Willd.) Haw. (*Brasilopuntia*) A well-known species widely distributed in Brazil, Argentina, Peru and other South American countries. Tall erect plant to 13 ft/4 m high with cylindrical main stem, flattened branches and many bright green flat, thin, terminal joints with few spines. Flowers yellow from terminal joints, fruit yellow. This species is very similar to *O. argentina* Gris. which has greenish-yellow flowers and red fruits.

*Opuntia cochenillifera* (L.) Mill. (*Nopalea*) Tall plants with smooth rounded stems and branches and scarcely any spines. Joints very brittle and break away easily, dark glossy green with shaded diamond-shaped tubercles. Flower orange-red with pinkish stamens and greenish stigma lobes which, with the style, protrude beyond the petals. A well-known species, originally cultivated for the production of cochineal, the insect being reared on these plants. Its origin is possibly in southern Mexico or Central America.

*Opuntia erinacea* var. *ursina* (Weber) Parish (*Platyopuntia*) A low-growing plant forming clumps. Plants semi-erect

bearing flattened oblong joints with large, somewhat tuberculate areoles and numerous spines, almost pure white and giving the effect of very long hairs up to 5½ in/14 cm long. These hairs are in fact elongated spines, very flexible and usually from the bases of the lower joints. Flowers generally pink, but sometimes yellow. From northern Arizona areas of the Mojave Desert and the Clark Mountains in California. This is a species of distinctive qualities; the long hairy form is known by horticulturalists as *O. erinacea* var. *ursina* f. *senilis.*

*Opuntia floccosa* S-D (*Tephrocactus*) One of the very attractive species from Peru. Plant consists of oblong joints with long white hairs from the areoles hiding the joints almost entirely. Flower yellow. *O. lagopus* (K. Sch.) and other similar species are possibly synonymous, the main difference seeming to be in the colour of the hairs.

*Opuntia galapageia* Hens. (*Platyopuntia*) A very rare and beautiful species from the Galapagos Islands which in habitat grows into a large compact bush-like plant. Joints oblong-elongated, dark green with pronounced felted areoles and numerous long golden-yellow-brownish spines. Flowers yellow. This is a spectacular cactus.

*Opuntia humifusa*

*Opuntia humifusa* Rag. From the USA, is an almost hardy species – the segments are oval in shape, spineless or with 1–3 whitish spines from the areoles, glochids brownish. Flowers bright yellow, slightly suffused reddish in the throat. *O. microdasys* (Lehm.) Pfeiff. is possibly the best known of all the genus. The oval segments vary from 3–6 in/8–15 cm long. Spines only very rarely produced, the glochid differing in colour according to the variety: var. *albispina* (white), var. *pallida* (yellow), var. *rufida* (reddish-brown). Flowers are very pale yellow to 2 in/5 cm across. All are native of northern Mexico.

*Opuntia ignescens* Vaup. (*Tephrocactus*) An interesting species from Peru with bluish-green erect or spreading joints, forming clusters. Joints somewhat pointed, few areoles covered with felt and numerous glochids with up to 15 erect, acicular yellow spines. Flowers scarlet from near the top of the joints.

*Opuntia invicta*

*Opuntia invicta* K. Brandeg. (*Corynopuntia*) A rare species from Baja California, Mexico, uncommon in cultivation. In habitat it masses into large clusters with club-shaped joints, dark green, strongly tubercled and armed with vicious red spines which become greyish with age. Flowers yellow. In many ways this resembles some species of *Echinocereus* for which it was mistaken when originally discovered.

From Baja California, |in |central regions around San Juanico.

*Opuntia leptocaulis* De Cand. (*Cylindropuntia*) A well-known species with very slender erect stems forming thickets. The bright green stems branch freely, often at right angles and the new joints tend to be very brittle. Areoles often almost spineless but bearing a few minute leaves which quickly fall. Where spines are apparent they are small, yellowish-white and very short, usually in small clusters. Flowers greenish-

*Opuntia kleiniae*

yellow. There are certain species very close, particularly *O. kleiniae* De Cand. with which it i sometimes confused. Varietal forms of *O. leptocaulis* are recorded, and *O. leptocaulis* var. *longispina* Engel. deserves mention on account of the very long spines, yellowish-brown. All are endemic to Mexico and certain of the southern states of the USA.

*Opuntia miquelii* Monv. (*Austrocylindropuntia*) An uncommon species from Chile with cylindrical bluish-green stems to about 3¼ ft/1 m high with many branches. New growth is bright green, turning bluish with age, having flattened tubercles, areoles rounded and pronounced with many glochids and up to 12 spines in clusters. Flower pale or rose-pink about 2½ in/5 cm diameter.

*Opuntia molfinoi* Speg. (*Maihueniopsis*) An uncommon species endemic to Argentina from high altitudes of over 9,900 ft/3,000 m. Prostrate, densely branched with many small oval joints, small areoles bearing glochids and few minute spines, often absent. Flowers at terminal ends, pinkish.

*Opuntia pachypus* Schumm. (*Austrocylindropuntia*) A rare species from Peru and possibly Ecuador, in habitat a tall much-branching plant over 10 ft/3 m high, cylindrical, dark green, tubercles slightly elevated with numerous short yellowish-white spines from depressed woolly areoles. Flowers rather small, red, to about ¾ in/2 cm diameter developing near the tips of the plant. Not often seen in cultivation.

*Opuntia camanchica*

*Opuntia phaeacantha* Engel. Has rounded flat segments to 6 in/15 cm or more round. Its variety *camanchica* is probably the better-known, and this has areoles of almost white bristles and yellow glochids. Flowers can be variable, but usually in yellowish shades, to 3½ in/9 cm long. This is from Colorado and Arizona, and can be considered hardy subject to protection from excess rain in winter.

*Opuntia pulchella* Engelm. (*Micropuntia*) An interesting and desirable miniature species with large 'bulbous' caudex-like tuber much of which is usually below ground. Stems develop from the caudex with small joints somewhat elliptical with tubercles and many spines, mostly whitish or greyish-white; such growths come from an areole with glochids and which are ultimately deciduous. Flowers in varying shades of pink to purple. Associated with sandy plains and deserts in Nevada, Arizona and California at about 3,280-4,250 ft/1,000-1,300 m elevation. The type locality is given as Walker River, Nevada.

Opuntia pycnantha

Opuntia pycnantha Engelm. (*Platyopuntia*) A low-growing species forming clumps with oblong joints having numerous areoles and spines. The yellowish-brown glochids are a feature, being heavily massed in the upper part of the areole, the spines developing from the lower part. The flower is reputed to be yellow, but this cannot be confirmed. An uncommon species rarely seen in cultivation, from the region around Magdalena Bay in the south of Baja California, Mexico.

Opuntia quimilo Sch. (*Platyopuntia*) A large branching species from northern Argentina with obovate joints, large and thick, dark greyish-green, only few areoles and usually a solitary spine from each areole about 5½ in/14 cm long. Large flowers, to about 2½ in/7 cm diameter, bright red. This can grow to large dimensions in cultivation and it is reputed that in habitat it can reach to 13 ft/4 m high and cover many square feet/metres.

Opuntia ramosissima Engelm. (*Cylindropuntia*) A distinctive species with greyish stems and branches forming either large or frequently miniature bushes. Stems slender and angled giving the effect of being covered with rough diamond-shaped sections. Often spineless, but sometimes with long yellowish-golden sheathed spines. Flower pink, with a suggestion of purplish. A rare species from Nevada, Arizona and California borders on low mountain slopes. This is almost a non-succulent, the stems being very woody and becoming more so with age, quickly dehydrating and therefore difficult to cultivate from cuttings.

Opuntia rubescens S-D (*Consolea*) Representative of a group of *Opuntias* endemic to the West Indies. Backeberg recognizes the genus *Consolea* Lem., erected for those species with erect continuous stems, unjointed and branching from opposite or alternate sides of the main stems, giving the effect of a cross (cruciform). Flowers variable, usually yellow, but sometimes reddish. Two distinctive forms are found, one with quite long spines, the other totally spine-

less, but this is not considered sufficient reason for giving even varietal status. Endemic from Antigua to Dominica.

Opuntia spegazzinii

Opuntia salmiana Parm. (*Austrocylindropuntia*) A very slender erect bushy plant from Brazil, Argentina and Paraguay. Elongated cylindrical terete stems, greenish-purple having small woolly areoles, yellowish glochids and few spines. Flowers yellowish-white with red fruits. *O. spegazzinii* Web. is possibly only a variety, having pure white flowers, as also

Opuntia ipatiana

is *O. ipatiana* with lilac-pink flowers. *O. colubrina* is very similar, but inclined to be far more bush-like in habit and with larger bright yellow flowers.

Opuntia subterranea R.E. Fries (*Tephrocactus*) A very rare and unusual species from northern Argentina and Bolivia. Very thick tuberous root, stem usually solitary, occasionally branching, cylindrical to only 1½-2 in/4-5 cm long with many low dark green tubercles, very small areoles with few short whitish spines, adpressed. Flowers whitish-brown.

Opuntia subulata (Muehl.) Engelm. (*Austrocylindropuntia*) A popular well-known species originating from Chile and Argentina, it has been widely naturalized in parts of southern Europe. Large plant to 13 ft/4 m high, bright

*Opuntia exaltata*

green, cylindrical, developing many long pointed cylindrical leaves near the apex of branches. Has yellow flowers near terminal ends. *O. exaltata* Berg., which is distributed widely in Peru, Chile, Bolivia and Ecuador, is also very similar, but with very tuberculate dark green stems and reddish flowers.

*Opuntia versicolor*

*Opuntia versicolor* Engelm. (*Cylindropuntia*) An erect bush-like species to 10-13 ft/3-4 m high. Main stems quickly become woody and branching freely with terminal joints in whorls about 8 in/20 cm long. Joints cylindrical, somewhat tuberculate, with few areoles having many spines with sheaths. Flowers in many colours, yellow, pink, purplish, reddish or sometimes brown, hence its name. Widely distributed throughout parts of Arizona and northern Mexico. This is another instance where variations within the species do not justify varietal status.

*Opuntia vestita* S-D (*Austrocylindropuntia*) A very popular plant which originates from Bolivia. Somewhat erect stems

with many branches forming clusters. Joints are cylindrical, rather slender, with rounded areoles having short wool, few spines and long white hairs, also quickly deciduous minute leaves. Flowers red from near the terminal ends of the joints.

**Oreocereus** (Bgr.) Riccob. includes several cereoid plants with large areoles usually developing long hair. This genus has a close relationship with *Borzicactus* and a new classification might well bring about a merger of the two genera.

*Oreocereus celsianus*

*Oreocereus celsianus* (Lem.) Riccob. (syn. *Pilocereus celsianus* Lem.) The type species from the Andes, Bolivia, Peru and Chile. Sturdy stems, branching freely from the base, sometimes semi-prostrate. Branches with 10 obtuse ribs, divided into tubercles, areoles with long hairs and several straight rigid yellow spines protruding horizontally. Flowers from the top of the branches, red, diurnal. Other species include *O. hendriksenianus* Backeb. from Peru and Chile with much wool and golden spines, orange-red flowers. *O. trollii* (Kupp.) Backeb. is another beautiful plant almost entirely covered with whitish hair and wool and yellow spines, having carmine-red flowers.

*Oreocereus doelzianus* (Backeb.) Borg (syn. *Morawetzia doelziana* Backeb.) Native of southern and central Peru. An erect slender plant, branching freely from the base, and forming groups. Ribs about 10, low, bearing prominent woolly areoles having about 20 yellowish-brown erect spines. Flowers from the cephalium at apex, zygomorphic, carmine-red.

**Oroya** Br. & R. are all Peruvian species, named after the type locality – Oroya – and include a number of semi-globose plants with elongated areoles and widely spreading spines. Flowers from the crown, short, funnel-shaped. This is another genus with a close affinity to *Borzicactus*.

*Oroya peruviana*

*Pachycereus pringlei*

*Oroya peruviana* (Sch.) Br. & R. (syn. *Echinocactus peruvianus* Sch.) The type species for which the genus was erected. A globose depressed plant, deep green with broad ribs having humped tubercles and long narroow areoles, small somewhat pectinate radial spines, few centrals stronger than the radials. Flowers from near top, yellowish, with very short tube. From south of La Oroya, Peru. *O. neopuervianus* Backeb. from northeast of La Oroya, a larger plant with more ribs and less pronounced tubercles, flowers yellowish. *O. borchersii* (Boed.) Backeb. from Cordillera Negra at 13,000 ft/4,000 m altitude. Stem short-cylindrical or somewhat globular and depressed, light green, with rather broader areoles having deep yellow to brownish-red spines evenly distributed. Flowers greenish-yellow. Other recognized species include *O. laxiareolata* Rauh & Backeb. from Mantero Valley, south of La Oroya and *O. subocculta* Rauh & Backeb., also from Mantero Valley. There is a great similarity of characteristics and it is feasible that some will be reduced to synonymity or varietal status.

**Pachycereus** (Bgr.) Br. & R. is now confined to just a few species of tall columnar, tree-like plants. Cultivation is not difficult, but any suggestion of cold can prove injurious to the plants.

*Pachycereus pringlei* (S. Watson) Br. & R. (syn. *Cereus pringlei* S. Watson) One of the largest species of columnar cacti, frequently to 40 ft/12 m tall. Usually with short trunk, then branching freely with ascending stems. Ribs up to 15 somewhat obtuse, very large areoles, brown-felted with many spines. Young branches are almost bluish-grey with only few spines, but become more green and more heavily spined with growth. Flowering areoles very large. Flower tube and ovary covered with small scales and brownish hairs, flower whitish about 3 in/8cm long. Widely distributed throughout Mexico in western Sonora, parts of Baja California and offshore islands in the Gulf of California.

**Parodia** Speg. comprises many species of globular plants with distinct ribs, woolly areoles and highly coloured spines. Most species of easy culture, producing flowers as quite young plants.
*Parodia chrysacanthion* (Sch.) Backeb. Has numerous golden-yellow spines, glistening and shining, densely set. Flowers golden-yellow.
*Parodia microsperma* (Web.) Speg. (syn. *Echinocactus microspermus* Web.) The type species, the specific name suggests small seeds, and this feature is general of all *Parodia* species. It was earlier known as *Hickenia microsperma* Web. Stem globose or short-cylindrical to about 4 in/10 cm diameter. Ribs are divided into low tubercles, spirally arranged, areoles with about 10-25 white acicular spreading radial spines and three or four reddish-brown centrals, the lower one being hooked at tip. Flowers from crown, golden-yellow. A most attractive species from Tucuman, Argentina.
*Parodia microthele* Backeb. Has light green stem, pronounced areoles, whitish spines and orange-red|flowers.

*Parodia sanguiniflora* Fric ex Backeb. Endemic to Cochabamba, Bolivia, at an altitude of over 6,500 ft/2,000 m. Has thick white radial spines and brown centrals which are hooked at the tip. Flowers large, blood-red.

*Parodia nivosa* Fric ex Backeb. A very beautiful 'white' species, densely covered with whitish spines and having deep reddish flowers at the crown.

*Parodia setosa*

*Parodia setosa* Backeb. From northern Argentina. Grows to about 10 in/25 cm high and 4½ in/12 cm across. Ribs number about 35 and very spiny. Flowers arise from the crown of the plant, deep red in colour.

There are over 40 recognized species, native of Bolivia, Argentina, Brazil and Paraguay. They are, without exception, rewarding plants for the layman.

**Pediocactus** Br. & R. is an interesting genus which has become increasingly enlarged due to extensive research, and in consequence has absorbed certain monotypic genera for long associated with rare and desirable species. The genus also includes *P. bradyi* L. Benson from Coconino County in Arizona and elsewhere at high elevations with yellowish flowers, *P. knowltonii* L. Benson from near La Boca, Colorado.

*Pediocactus papyracantha* (Engelm.) L. Benson (syn. *Toumeya papyracantha* [Engelm.] Br. & R.) Somewhat elongated stem, ovoid or short-cylindrical with low spiral tubercles. Areoles with thin papery, flexible white spines, centrals longer than the radials. Flower from the terminal about 1 in/2.5 cm long, white with brownish midribs. A rare species from grasslands at elevations of over 6,500 ft/2,000 m in Arizona and northern New Mexico.

*Pediocactus paradinei* (B.W. Benson) B.W. Benson (syn. *Pilocanthus paradinei* B.W. Benson & Backeb.) From high elevations up to nearly 6,500 ft/2,000 m in Navajoan Desert and parts of northern Arizona. An unusual and rare plant, usually solitary, sometimes in pairs or even 3 together, some-

what globular about 1½ in/4 cm diameter. Circular areoles with straw-coloured centrals, about six hairlike, and up to 20 flexible radial spines, straight or curving. Flower about ¾ in/2 cm diameter, white with pinkish midrib.

*Pediocactus peeblesianus* (Croizat) L. Benson (syn. *Navajoa peeblesiana* Croizat) From desert hillsides at high altitudes up to 17,500 ft/1,600 m or more in Navajoan Desert, northern Mexico. A very rare species, stem globose, greyish-green, and in habitat often only the crown of the plant is visible, up to 1½ in/4 cm diameter and 2½ in/6-7 cm high. Areoles circular with three to seven radial spines and usually one central pale grey, flexible and curving slightly upward. Flower about ¾ in/2 cm in diameter, yellowish.

*Pediocactus polyancistrus*

*Pediocactus polyancistrus* (Engelm. & Big.) G.K. Arp (syn. *Sclerocactus polyancistrus* [Engelm. & Big.] Br. & R.) An oblong stem up to 12 in/30 cm long with up to 17 ribs, undulate, areoles with up to 20 spreading acicular white radial spines and several long centrals, some erect and flattened, others rounded and hooked. Flowers magenta, nearly 3 in/8 cm diameter. Distributed in some desert areas of California and Nevada, possibly western Arizona.

Other species of *Sclerocactus* have been transferred to *Pediocactus*, *S. whipplei* (Engelm.) Br. & R., *S. glaucus* (Schum.) L. Benson, *S. pubispinus* (Engelm.) Br. & R. and *S. wrightiae* L. Benson.

*Pediocactus sileri* (Engelm.) L. Benson (syn. *Utahia sileri* [Engelm.] Br. & R.) An exceptionally rare plant long cherished as a *Utahia* – and found to be rather difficult in cultivation, but nevertheless much sought after. Ovoid plant, to about 4½ in/12 cm long and 4 in/10 cm diameter with pronounced tubercles having circular areoles and densely spined, three to seven centrals, brownish-black and 10 to 12 radials, greyish, spreading. Flower yellowish with reddish markings about ¾-1¼ in/2-3 cm diameter. This unique plant is found in Utah and northern Arizona.

*Pediocactus simpsonii*

*Pediocactus simpsonii* (Engelm.) Br. & R. (syn. *Echinocactus simpsonii* Engelm.) Type species. Plant globular somewhat depressed to about 6 in/15 cm diameter and to 4½ in/12 cm high, with many tubercles, radial spines up to 30 each areole, spreading, creamy-white; centrals reddish-brown about eight, spreading. Flowers massed in crown of plant and surrounded by brown or whitish wool, pinkish-white to pinkish-magenta. A rare species from Arizona and other more southerly states.

**Pelecyphora** Ehrenb. is a monotypic genus embracing one of the most attractive of Cactaceae. The comb-like spine formation is the outstanding feature.
*Pelecyphora aselliformis* Ehrenb. Interesting species from San Luis Potosi, Mexico, with cylindric stem, clustering, covered with strongly flattened tubercles providing a 'hard' surface to the plant. Areoles at the top of tubercles, long and narrow; radials thick, arranged comb-like, pectinate. Flower from apex at axil of tubercle, purple.

**Peniocereus** (Berger) Br. & R. includes a few very slender stemmed semi-erect species with few or several ribs.
*Peniocereus greggii* (Engelm.) Br. & R. (syn. *Cereus greggii* Engelm.) Type species. A plant of considerable interest. When not in flower it is totally unimpressive, but in full bloom creates a wonderful effect. Root system very fleshy, frequently having enormous tubers. Stems slender, four to six angles, somewhat crenulate ribs and areoles with very small black acicular spines. Stems are greyish, looking almost like twigs. Flowers toward the terminal ends on slender tube, set with small scales, petals pure white about 4½ in/12 cm diameter, opening at night but remaining in flower for much of the following day. Native to parts of Arizona, Texas and New Mexico and also northern Sonora.
   Other species of this genus are recorded in Mexico, *P. marianus* from Topolobampo, Sinaloa, *P. johnstonii*, native to Baja California, and also *P. diguetti* (*Neoevansia diguetii*) from south of Guaymas and also reported from Topolobampo in Sinaloa, seemingly always in close proximity to coastal areas. All have the same characteristics of large

tuberous roots and slender straggling twiggy stems with beautiful flowers.

**Peireskiopsis** Br. & R. are shrubby tree-like plants with flat, lanceolate leaves. Similar to *Pereskia* except that they have glochids.
*Peireskiopsis spathulata* (Otto) Br. & R. An erect-growing shrubby plant with few branches. Glaucous stems with thick dark green spatulate leaves to about 2 in/5 cm long. Few areoles, woolly and having only occasional spines. The brownish glochids appear on the upper portion of the areole. Flower bright red. From southwestern Mexico. This species is used extensively for grafting. Other *Peireskiopsis* species are recorded, some very similar to the above. *P. velutina* Rose is outstanding on account of the velvet-like soft stems and leaves and yellow flowers.

**Pereskia** (Plum.) Mill. are characterized by the leaf-covered branches.

*Pereskia aculeata*

*Pereskia aculeata* (Plum.) Mill. A very much-branched vine-like shrub with long elliptical dark green leaves. Very spiny, usually two or three together. Flowers creamy-yellow produced in clusters. A widely distributed species, particularly in southern Mexico and the West Indies.
*Pereskia humboldtii* Br. & R. A slender erect species from southern Peru, with rounded stem and thin branches with generally few spines. Leaves oblong, rather elongated about 1½ in/4 cm long, solitary and arranged alternate. Flowers in clusters at terminal end of branches, reddish.
*Pereskia sacharosa* Gris. A tree-like plant to over 20 ft/6 m high with succulent stems and branches, heavily spined. Leaves about 4 in/10 cm long and very pointed. Flowers in clusters, usually pink with hard large fruit about 1½ in/ 4 cm diameter. A native of Argentina and Paraguay, and while similar to *P. aculeata* (Plum.) Mill. in many respects, has different flower colour.

**Pfeiffera** S-D have long-angled branches, with many spines, usually with pendent habit. Epiphytic. Whether this genus is rightfully placed is still uncertain, but seems to be allied to Rhipsalidinae. Northern Argentina.

*Pfeiffera ianthothele* (Mon.) Web. Elongated stems, bright green, usually three to five ribs with many spines. Of pendent habit. Flowers yellowish-cream from small ovary. Has distinctive fruits, similar to a miniature gooseberry, purplish-pink, and many black seeds.

Other species of this genus are now recorded including *P. stricta*, *P. gracilis* and *P. taragensis*. It would appear that the first two named are synonymous with each other and probably also with *P. taragensis*.

**Pilosocereus** Byl. & Rowl. includes species recorded previously under *Pilocereus*, *Cipocereus* and *Cephalocereus*. Includes many columnar plants, some from North America and the West Indies, others from South America. Mostly erect, tall, developing pseudocephaliums.

*Pilosocereus glaucescens* Lab. An erect, branching plant with dark-bluish rounded ribs, somewhat inflated, close-set areoles with numerous whitish bristles and hairs. Spines of varying length, 12 or more radials and about six more centrally disposed, yellowish-brown. Whitish woolly pseudocephalium develops on one side of the branches from which the flowers emanate. This species is of Brazilian origin and has also been referred to as *Pseudopilocereus glaucescens* (Lab.) Buxb.

*Pilosocereus nobilis*

*Pilosocereus nobilis* (Haw.) Byl. & Rowl. Sometimes referred to as a *Pseudopilosocereus*. It comes from the West Indies frequenting areas near to the sea and invariably among low bushes. A tall species with 5–7 ribs, brownish-yellow spines and pinkish-purple flowers 1½–2½ in/4–6 cm long, followed by reddish fruits.

*Pilosocereus leucocephalus* (Roul.) K. Schum. An erect plant to 16½ ft/5 m high, many branches from the base and ascending. Branches dull green with 12 low ribs, areoles with about 10 acicular spines. Flowering areoles develop on one side of the branch terminals and form a pseudocephalium of long white hairs often to 4 in/10 cm long from which the flowers protrude. From eastern parts of Sonora and Chi-

huahua, Mexico.

Many other species of this genus are available; *P. palmeri* Rose from Victoria, eastern Mexico, is a well-known species which develops an extraordinarily beautiful cephalium of thick white wool. Other species are natives of South America.

**Polaskia** Backeb. is a monotypic genus, the flowers of which have small perianth tubes covered with leaf-like scales.

*Polaskia chichipe* (Goss.) Backeb. (syn. *Cereus chichipe* Goss.) Type species. A tree-like plant growing up to 16½ ft/5 m high. Usually with short trunk and branching freely at the top. Branches greenish-grey with undulate, acute ribs, 9–12, areoles with six to seven greyish spines and one longer central. Flowers small, greenish-yellow, and diurnal. Spiny reddish fruit, globose, about ¾ in/2 cm diameter. Native to Mexico.

**Pterocactus** MacDoug. & Mir. is closely allied to *Opuntia*.

*Pterocactus kuntzei*

*Pterocactus kuntzei* Sch. An unusual species on account of its very large tuberous root, forming almost a caudex. Has erect slender stems, sometimes quite elongated, soft, greyish-purple and only about ⅜ in/1 cm in diameter. Areoles with numerous minute white adpressed spines. Flowers yellow. *P. tuberosus* (Pfeiff.) Br. & R. is very similar in most respects and is possibly synonymous.

*Pterocactus marenae* (Pars.) Rowl. An interesting species with thick tuberous roots and short, elongated, slender-cylindrical stems about 5½ in/14 cm long and branching freely. Stems dark grey-green with many areoles and downward-pointing spines. Flower pure white at the terminal ends of the pencil-like branches. This has a similar appearance to that of the *Wilcoxia*, and is from Sonora near to Kino Bay on the Gulf of California.

**Quiabentia** Br. & R. is closely related to both *Opuntia* and *Pereskia*. Stems have a number of branches in whorls. Leaves are persistent.

*Quiabentia zehntneri* Br. & R. A species of Brazilian origin. A very shrubby plant, cylindrical stem and horizontal branches usually in whorls. Leaves fleshy. Large felted areoles with numerous acicular whitish spines, glochids on upper part of areole. Flowers large, red, at terminal ends of branches. Rare in cultivation, closely resembling *Peireskiopsis* but with even more succulent stems and branches. Other species are recognized including *Q. chacoensis*, also a native of Brazil, and *Q. pereziensis* Backeb., a tree-like species from Perez, Bolivia, at 5,250 ft/1,600 m.

**Rathbunia** Br. & R. includes a few Mexican species of columnar growth, usually found in fairly dense scrub country. Flowers are diurnal.

*Rathbunia alamosensis*

*Rathbunia alamosensis* (Coult.) Br. & R. (syn. *Rathbunia sonorensis* or *Cereus sonorensis*) The type species. A large sprawling plant forming clusters with stems to 10 ft/3 m in length. Occasionally somewhat erect in growth, columnar with five to eight ribs, obtuse. Areoles with many straight and spreading spines, greyish. Flowers scarlet to 4 in/10 cm long, tube and ovary with few spines and tufts of felt. Globular red fruits about 1½ in/4 cm diameter. Distributed in many parts of Sinaloa and southern Sonora, especially in the area around Alamos.

**Rebutia** Sch. comprises a great number of small, globular plants, mostly caespitose with flowers of varying colours. All are very easy in cultivation, rewarding inasmuch as they produce flowers within a year or two of germination. Some species have been included in the genus *Aylostera* which is currently united with *Rebutia*. The genus is currently undergoing intense research, and it is expected that a complete reclassification will be forthcoming in the near future.

*Rebutia aureiflora*

*Rebutia aureiflora* Backeb. This was originally included in the now obsolete genus of *Mediolobivia*. A clustering species with dark-green body – up to 16 radial spines and to 4 centrals. Flowers can vary in colour, but generally yellowish, occasionally in shades of red or purplish, about 1½ in/4 cm across. Found in Argentina (Jujuy, Salta).

*Rebutia heliosa*

*Rebutia heliosa* Rausch. from Tarija, Bolivia. One of the more unusual species in particular because of its spination which is in a comb-like formation. The individual body of the plant is small and it is set around with 38 rows of tubercles. Flowers are orange with a whitish throat, about 1½ in/4 cm across. A very porous soil is essential to grow this species to perfection as it possesses a taproot – hence very careful watering is necessary.

*Rebutia minuscula* Sch. The type species from Tucuman,

northern Argentina. A very popular and well-known plant, clustering, bright green bodies about 2-2½ in/5-6 cm diameter, low ribs consisting of rounded tubercles, areoles with numerous very small whitish spines. Flowers red. *R. krainziana* Kesselr., which is native of Bolivia, has distinctive white woolly areoles with minute white spines and large red flowers. *R. senilis* Backeb. from Salta, Argentina, is typified by the dense covering of whitish bristle-like spines, flowers carmine-red. A variety, *R. senilis* var. *kesselringiana*, is similar but with yellow flowers.

*Rebutia marsoneri*

Another yellow-flowering species is *R. marsoneri* Werd. from the Jujuy province of northern Argentina, the body being dark green with brownish-yellow spines. *R. fiebrigii* (Gurke) Br. & R. (syn. *Aylostera fiebrigii*), a Bolivian species to about 2½ in/7 cm tall, dark glossy green, 15-18 spirally arranged ribs divided into tubercles with numerous bristly white spines from the areoles, flowers orange-red. *R. calliantha* Bew., a globular species with whitish areoles and whitish spines, has lilac-pink flowers and comes from Argentina.

In recent years a number of new species have been discovered, considerably extending the scope for research and study and in this respect the names of Donald and Buining are most prominent. Newer species include *R. kariusiana* Wess.; *R. calliantha* var. *kariusiana* Buin. & Don. with deep pink flowers, and *R. albiflora* Ritt. & Buin. having white flowers.

**Rhipsalidopsis** Br. & R. is a shrubby species, usually erect, but becoming somewhat pendent with maturity. Has joints or segments, somewhat flattish but with three, sometimes to five, angles. Considerable doubt exists as to whether this should be retained within the Rhipsalidinae as it would appear closer to Epiphyllanae. *Schlumbergera* species have been transferred to *Rhipsalidopsis*.

*Rhipsalidopsis rosea*

*Rhipsalidopsis rosea* (Lag.) Br. & R. A popular species from the state of Parana in southern Brazil. Flowers rose-pink, flowering in late spring. One of the parents of a number of popular hybrids with *Schlumbergera* species. Produces lilac, orange and magenta flowers.

*Rhipsalidopsis gaertneri* (Regel) Moran (syn. *Schlumbergera gaertneri* [Regel] Br. & R.) The well-recognized Easter cactus. Flattened and rather fleshy joints, with slightly crenated margins. Stem is bright green, and the margins often have a purplish effect. Flower develops at the apex of the segments, brick red to scarlet. Almost regular flowers. A varietal form is recorded, *Rhipsalidopsis gaertneri* var. *makoyana*, the difference being that longish bristles develop on the joints. The species also have this habit, so there seems little reason to recognize the variety.

Hybrids of *Rhipsalidopsis* have been produced, mostly due to the skill of Graeser, the best-known being *Rhipsalidopsis Graeseri* and *R. × Elektra*.

**Rhipsalis** Gaertn. are a most varied group with many diverse forms, some thread-like, others with flattened branches – angled, twisted, indented ribs – and while these give some indication, it is still most difficult to determine some species from others. Flowers are small, usually white, cream or pinkish, and produced freely along the length of the stems.

Many different *Rhipsalis* names appear in various authoritative works, and it is apparent that a great number must be synonyms. The majority of species are epiphytic.

*Rhipsalis aculeata* Web. Fresh green slender stems with closely set areoles, having much wool and many white bristles. Flower creamy-white or pinkish and purplish-black fruit. A rare species from northern Argentina.

*Rhipsalis angustissima* Web. A rare species from Costa Rica with narrow elongated flattened branches, tapering at the apex. Widely serrate margins, dark green becoming reddish-green. Main stems terete. A unique species, often wrongly considered synonymous with *R. coriacea* Polak. and *R. leiophloea* Vpl. Flowers whitish-pink and fruits white.

*Rhipsalis boliviana* (Britt.) Lauterb. Stems somewhat angled at the base with yellowish bristles at the areoles. Branches elongated and flattened, narrow with broad crenations – reddish-green having similar appearance as *Lepismium cruciforme* var. *anceps*. Flowers whitish-yellow and fruit white. From the rain forests of Bolivia.

*Rhipsalis burchelli* Br. & R. Much-branched, slender, pencil-shaped and becoming dichotomous. Flower white. Brazil near São Paulo.

*Rhipsalis campos-portoana* Löfgr. Long pendent cylindrical stems with small clusters of short branches at the terminal ends. Flower white. Serra de Itatiaya, Brazil. A rare species.

*Rhipsalis capilliformis* Web. Thread-like branches hang pendent. A graceful species. Flower creamy-white and numerous. Near São Paulo, Brazil.

*Rhipsalis cassutha* Gaert. Very variable species – generally long, slender, cylindrical stems and pendent. Young growth has white bristles at areoles. Flower creamy-white. Widely distributed in Mexico, South and Central America, the West Indies, Madagascar, Sri Lanka and Africa.

*Rhipsalis cassuthopsis* Backeb. Also known as *R. cassythoides*. Closely akin to *R. cassutha* but generally with more slender stems and branching freely. Flowers white and rather small even for *Rhipsalis*. Brazil.

*Rhipsalis cereoides* Backeb. & Voll. Stems invariably three-angled, joints short, occasionally elongated. Margins firm and precise. A species of considerable interest with whitish flowers. Brazil.

*Rhipsalis cereuscula*

*Rhipsalis cereuscula* Haw. Elongated cylindrical stems with clusters of small branches. Flower white to creamy-pink. Brazil, also in Uruguay.

*Rhipsalis clavata* Web. Pendent elongated branches, narrowly clavate. Very distinctive. Flower white. Brazil.

*Rhipsalis coralloides* Rauh. An interesting species from Madagascar with rounded stems, fairly robust and branching freely. Pinkish-cream flowers toward the apex of the stems. *R. saxicola* Graf is similar and might by synonymous.

*Rhipsalis cribrata* (Lem.) Rümpl. Slender stems, much-branched, elongated with short terminal branches in whorls. Flower creamy-white. Brazil, near São Paulo, Rio de Janeiro and Minas Gerais.

*Rhipsalis crispata* (Haw.) Pfeiff. Stems terete below. Branches freely with shortish pale fresh green joints, flattened and crenate. Flower creamy-white, rather small and white fruits. *R. goebeliana* (Hort.) Backeb. would appear to be a synonym for *R. crispata*.

*Rhipsalis crispimarginata*

*Rhipsalis crispimarginata* Löfgr. Pendent species with terete stems below and many-branched with oblong or roundish joints, bright green with undulating and crenate margins. Flowers creamy-white and white fruits. The obvious twisted, undulated margins make identification possible. Endemic to Rio de Janeiro, Brazil.

*Rhipsalis cuneata* Br. & R. Elongated stems and branches, thin and flattened, joints cuneate at base. Leaf-like margins are deeply crenate. Has white flowers. Little known in cultivation. Bolivia.

*Rhipsalis elliptica* Lindb. Quite large joints, elliptic in shape and only slightly crenate margins. Joints usually reddish. Of pendent habit, and free-flowering. Yellow flowers and reddish fruits. *R. chloroptera* Web. and *R. elliptica* var. *helicoidea* are so similar in every respect they should be considered synonymous. Endemic to state of São Paulo, Brazil, and possibly widely distributed in neighbouring states.

*Rhipsalis fasciculata* (Willd.) Haw. One of the most floriferous *Rhipsalis* species with many interesting characteristics. Widely distributed, being found in Brazil, also Madagascar – and it is likely that *R. pilosa* and *R. madagascarensis* are synonyms. Another Madagascan species has been recorded, *R. horrida*, and while this has certain peculiarities, it would appear nevertheless to be synonymous. Stems somewhat cylindrical and branching freely, many areoles with numerous hairs or bristles. Flower quite large, white with pinkish stamens. An outstanding but rare species.

*Rhipsalis gonacarpa* Web. A rare species having much the same appearance as *R. rhombea*, but with more lanceolate joints, dark green becoming purplish. Usually flattened, but sometimes three-angled and crenate, undulating margins. Flower white and narrow blackish fruits. From the region of São Paulo, Brazil.

*Rhipsalis handrosoma* Lindbg. For many years a species diffi-cult to locate – often confused with *Lepismium grandiflorum* but stems are less robust and brighter green in colour. Free-flowering with creamy-pinkish flowers. From the Organ Mountains, Brazil. A rarity in cultivation.

*Rhipsalis heteroclada* Br. & R. Much-branched, stiff rounded stems with purple shading on tips and areoles. Flower white. Brazil.

*Rhipsalis heptagona* Rauh & Backeb. A fascinating species still rare in cultivation. Stems very distinctly ribbed with five to seven somewhat irregular ribs. Flowers whitish. Peru.

*Rhipsalis houlletiana*

*Rhipsalis houlletiana* Lem. A very popular free-flowering species, generally with terete stems below and thin, flat and leaf-like above, about ½-1½ in/2-4 cm broad, pale fresh green, pronounced crenations with largish creamy flowers, bell-shaped. Fruits dark red. Widely distributed in southern Brazil.

*Rhipsalis jamaicensis* Britt. & Harr. Of pendent habit with thin angular stems and elongated dull green joints about ½-1¼ in/2-3 cm broad. Margins slightly crenate. Flowers yellowish-cream, sometimes greenish, fruits white. Rare in cultivation and liable to be confused with certain *Rhipsalis* species transferred to *Disocactus*. *R. coriacea* Polak. and *R. purpusii* Weing. are too similar to justify distinct status and should be considered synonymous.

Doubt also exists in respect to *R. leiophloea* Gris. and while this has certain similarities to *R. jamaicensis*, it is closer to *R. ramulosa* (now *Disocactus ramulosa*) and is possibly synonymous.

*Rhipsalis leucorhaphis* K. Sch. A much-branched species with many aerial roots. Stems usually terete, but ribs are only apparent when plant is not in growth. Areoles subtended by small bract – bristles occur on young growth. Flowers white with red fruits. Paraguay and northern Argentina.

*Rhipsalis lindbergiana* K. Sch. Elongated pencil-shaped stems, pendent, prolific growth. Areoles with hairs. Flower pinkish-white. Rio de Janeiro, Brazil. *R. densiareolata* and *R. erythrocarpa* are possibly synonymous.

*Rhipsalis linearis* K. Sch. Stems pale green, flattened, rarely three-angled. Has bushy, prostrate habit and branches free-ly. The leaf-like joints are slightly serrated. Flowers white and white fruits. Southern Brazil, Paraguay, northern Argentina and Uruguay.

*Rhipsalis loefgrenii* Br. & R. Has long slender dull green or purplish-green stems with many aerial roots, small areoles and large bract. White flowers with purple fruits. A rare but interesting species, little known in cultivation. Brazil.

*Rhipsalis lorentziana* Gris. A species known by name only in cultivation, very rare and interesting. A forest plant from northwest Argentina and parts of southern Bolivia. Base of stems terete, branches flattened and thin about ½ in/2 cm wide, serrated margins. Flower large and white with purple fruits.

*Rhipsalis lumbricoides* (Lem.) Lem. Slender angled stems, terete when growing, elongated and rooting freely. A much-branched species with white bristles at areoles. Flower white and fruit white. Found in Uruguay, Argentina and Paraguay. An unusual species not often met with in cultivation.

*Rhipsalis mesembryanthemoides* Haw. Stems cylindrical and usually densely shrubby. Flower white or pinkish. Brazil.

*Rhipsalis micrantha*

*Rhipsalis micrantha* (H. B. & K.) De Cand. A clambering bushy species with flattened or three to four-angled stems, light green with pronounced crenations along the margins. Small areoles. Tends to be a reluctant flowerer. Flowers white or cream and fruit usually pure white. Ecuador and northern Peru.

*Rhipsalis minutiflora* K. Sch. A very thin slender-stemmed species, similar to *R. cassutha* but with fewer areoles and no bristles. Flowers freely with relatively minute flowers, whitish-pink. Brazil.

*Rhipsalis oblonga* Löfgr. Main stems terete at base becoming flattened above. Branches freely with narrow oblong-shaped joints, deep green, sometimes purplish, margins crenate. Very free-flowering, pinkish-white with white fruits. Species of easy culture from Ilha Grande, Brazil.

*Rhipsalis pachyptera* Pfeiff. Robust stems, often terete below, with many large wide elongated or rounded joints, thick, deep green or purplish-green with margins crenate. A really spectacular species often developing many buds at one areole. Flower creamy-yellow and white fruits. Widely distributed in southern Brazil.

*Rhipsalis paranganiensis* (Card.) Kimn. A flattened or three-angled branched species, stems become elongated and only semi-pendent. Strongly crenate with small spines at areoles. Flower reddish, small. Discovered in Paragani, Ayopaya, Bolivia at 7,900 ft/2,400 m. Previously included under *Acanthorhipsalis*.

*Rhipsalis penduliflora* N. E. Br. Long slender stems, rarely branching, dull green with inconspicuous bristles especially on young growth. Free-flowering with pinkish-white flowers particularly from upper areoles of stems. Brazil.

*Rhipsalis pentaptera* Pfeiff. Stems and branches deep green, stiff with usually 6 distinct ribs, areoles with small white bristles and bracts. Very free-flowering on more pendent branches, flower creamy-pink with white fruit. From Uruguay and southern Brazil.

*Rhipsalis platycarpa* (Zucc.) Pfeiff. A much-branched species. Joints flattened and broad, somewhat elongated, with broad crenate margins – dark green, sometimes purplish. Flowers usually from the upper areoles, whitish-yellow or greenish and greenish fruits. From the Organ Mountains, Brazil.

*Rhipsalis prismatica* Rümpl. Elongated branches with upper branches much shorter and often angled. Flower white. Brazil.

*Rhipsalis pulchra* Löfgr. Long slender stems of bright green, much-branched, usually in whorls. Distinct minute red areoles. Has a reddish flower and ovary. An interesting species from the Organ Mountains, Brazil.

*Rhipsalis rhombea* (S-D) Pfeiff. A popular and well-known species almost resembling *Schlumbergera* in appearance. Stems terete or slightly angled with flattened branches and joints about ½ in/2 cm broad, dark green or purplish, pronounced crenate margins. Flowers freely at areoles, small, creamy-white with red fruits. Southern Brazil.

*Rhipsalis robusta*

*Rhipsalis robusta* Lem. non. Lindb. A much-branched species with large rounded flattened or 3-winged joints, hard,

slightly crenate, reddish-green with pronounced midnerve. A distinct species with some similarities in appearance to *R. pachyptera*. Flower whitish with white fruits. Brazil and possibly Peru.

*Rhipsalis roseana* Berg. Has fleshy flattened joints and stems with distinct crenations, whitish areoles along the crenate margins, giving the effect of notches. Flowers small, creamy-yellow. An attractive species, little known in cultivation. Colombia, parts of Ecuador and northern Peru.

*Rhipsalis russellii*

*Rhipsalis russellii* Br. & R. Erect-growing species with many branches. Joints flattened and rounded, crenate, dark green with purplish margins, sometimes the whole joint becomes reddish-green. Flowers very small, often with many at one areole. Fruit purple. Brazil.

*Rhipsalis shaferi* Br. & R. Stiff erect cylindrical stems, later pendent – with purplish tips and sometimes at areoles. Lower branches often with bristles, upper branches without. Flower white or greenish-white. Paraguay, Brazil and Argentina.

*Rhipsalis simmleri* Beauv. A species with cylindrical stems, pendent and much-branched. Lower branches smooth, upper angled, short and slightly hairy. Flower white and

*Rhipsalis sulcata* Web. Stems 5-angled, elongated and wide with few areoles. Branches freely with few flowers, pinkish-white, but large for *Rhipsalis* species. Origin uncertain, but possibly Peru or Ecuador.

*Rhipsalis teres* (Vell.) Steud. Stems elongated and strong, blotched red when mature. Much-branched and semi-erect, areoles pinkish, particularly when young. Flower creamy-yellow. Brazil, eastern states.

*Rhipsalis tonduzii* Web. A free-growing bushy species, usually elongated stems and branches with pronounced 3 to 5 angles, occasionally flattened on young growth. Stems grey-green with closely set areoles with small whitish flowers and white fruits. Costa Rica. *R. wercklei* Berg. is possibly a variety or synonymous.

*Rhipsalis triangularis* Werderm. A species very similar to *R. cereoides* with more elongated triangular stems, slightly cre-

nated. White flowers. Brazil.
*Rhipsalis virgata* Web. Elongated stems, first ascending, then pendent. Terminal and upper branches shorter. Areoles small and few hairs. Flowers from sides of stem, white. Near São Paulo, Brazil.

*Rhipsalis warmingiana*

*Rhipsalis warmingiana* K. Sch. Stems elongated and strap-like, often flattened, but usually 3-angled with crenate margins. Large flowers, bell-shaped, white; deep red or black fruits. Well-known species from Brazil, of easy culture.

There are many 'names' of *Rhipsalis* which may, or may not, justify recognition. A great deal of research has yet to be undertaken before definite conclusions can be reached. Another genus which is growing as new species and varieties are discovered in the rain forests of South America.

**Rhodocactus** (Bgr.) Knuth is a genus of about 15 species. Bushy and often clambering with colourful flowers. There is very close affinity between *Pereskia* and *Rhodocactus;* the division was probably made on the basis of flower colour. 'Rhodo' suggests pinkish-rose-coloured. Since some species within *Pereskia* also have flowers of this colour, the 'splitting' seems unjustified, at least on these grounds.
*Rhodocactus grandifolius* (Haw.) Knuth. An exceptionally free-growing species with erect thick stems developing tree-like proportions, fleshy, becoming woody with age. Leaves oblong narrowing at the base. Usually 2 or more spines at the areoles. Flowers particularly attractive, deep lilac-rose, usually in clusters at terminals of branches. Large pear-shaped fruit. This species is widely distributed, particularly in the West Indies.
*Rhodocactus moorei* (Br. & R.) Knuth. A stout-stemmed bushy plant indigenous to Brazil to about 3¼ ft/1 m high, freely branching with up to 4 long spines of unequal length to 2½ in/7 cm long, somewhat black or yellow-tipped black. Leaves almost round and tapering at tip. Flowers in clusters at apex, large to nearly 2 in/5 cm diameter, rich purple-red or magenta. Fruits green with 1 to 3 seeds. One of the most spectacular of this tribe; young, short cuttings root very quickly and flower easily and profusely.

**Samaipaticereus** Card. comprises two tall, tree-like species from Bolivia. Plants have only a few ribs and spines. Flowers nocturnal.
*Samaipaticereus corroanus* Card. An elegant columnar species which can attain 10 ft/3 m in height with a girth of about 6 in/15 cm. 4–6 spines and white flowers about 2 in/5 cm long developing from near the tops of the stems.
*Samaipaticereus inquisivensis* Card. Rather taller with fewer ribs, brownish areoles with up to 11 long spines. Flowers also white, and scented.

**Schlumbergera** Lem. is a popular group of plants which includes the Christmas cactus. This genus now includes species originally recorded within *Zygocactus* and *Epiphyllanthus*. Flowers zygomorphic or actinomorphic. Stem segments or joints flat, oval in shape, thin or thick and fleshy, with or without marginal teeth.
*Schlumbergera candida* (Löfgr.) Hövel (syn. *Epiphyllanthus candidus* (Löfgr.) Br. & R.) Not a great deal is known of this species, said to originate from Mt. Itatiaya at very high altitudes with spiny, terete joints and white flowers. Not known in cultivation and could be a variant.
*Schlumbergera orssichiana* Barthlott & McMillan. A more recent discovery with leaf-like flattened joints to 2 in/5 cm long, 1½ in/4 cm wide, strongly toothed on either side. Flowers zygomorphic, to 3½ in/9 cm long and broad, the petals not reflexed, magenta or carmine-red. Filaments white with yellow anthers. Brazil.

*Schlumbergera opuntioides*

*Schlumbergera obtusangula* (Schum.) Hunt (syn. *Epiphyllanthus microsphaericus* (Schum.) Br. & R. and *E. obtusangulus* (Lindb.) Bgr.) has slender *Opuntia*-like segments, slightly elongated and minutely spiny. Flowers zygomorphic, purple and lilac-rose. Mt. Itatiaya, Brazil, *Schlumbergera opuntioides* (Löfgr. & Dusen) Hunt (syn. *Epiphyllanthus obovatus* (Engelm.) Br. & R.) Sometimes better known as

*Epiphyllanthus opuntioides* (Löfgr. & Dusen) Moran. A much-branched miniature plant, with small *Opuntia*-like segments, dark green and fleshy. Flower purple and lilac. Zygomorphic. Found at high altitudes on Mt. Itatiaya, Brazil, where the distribution appears limited.

*Schlumbergera russelliana* (Gardner) Br. & R. The type species. An epiphyte growing on trees or sometimes on rocks in rich humus, having a semi-erect habit, but sometimes pendent. Joints are flat and thin, somewhat elongated and narrow. Flower reddish. Originating from the Organ Mountains, Brazil, but now almost extinct in habitat. Only a few plants are to be found in cultivation; it is a rather difficult plant to maintain. One of the parents of the well-known Christmas cactus which takes its stem characteristic from this parent.

*Schlumbergera truncata*

*Schlumbergera truncata* (Haw.) Moran (syn. *Zygocactus truncatus* (Haw.) Schum.) With sharply serrated dark green segments – the teeth are very apparent. Flower zygomorphic to about 2½ in/7 cm long, reddish-magenta with white filaments and purplish style. From the Organ Mountains in eastern Brazil. This is also one of the parents of the typical Christmas cactus. The species is rare in cultivation. *S. truncata* var. *delicatus* Backeb. & Borg is the white-flowered form with rich magenta style.

Of the great many hybrids, the Christmas cactus is the most popular – *Schlumbergera* × *buckleyi* (T. Moore) Tjaden, also known as *S.* × *bridgesii* Löfgr. A great many other lovely cultivars are now seen in a wide range of colours including yellow.

**Selenicereus** (A. Bgr.) Br. & R. is a genus of clambering epiphytic or saxicolous vines, usually developing roundish stems, if only with age. Has distinct rib and spine characteristics which give guidance in determining the species. Very widely distributed in parts of east, west and south Mexico and parts of the West Indies. In general they are very easy in cultivation. Stem cuttings of some species are used extensively for grafting purposes, especially to develop *Schlumbergera* 'standards'.

*Selenicereus grandiflorus*

*Selenicereus grandiflorus* (L.) Br. & R. From Jamaica, Cuba and possibly Haiti. Commonly referred to as the Queen of the Night, due to its outstandingly large white flower and nocturnal habit. One of the finest but not the largest flower of this genus, about 8–8½ in/20–22 cm wide. Stems which are dark green or bluish-green have five and eight ribs with small acicular brownish spines, occasionally up to ⅜ in/1 cm long. A prolific and rampant grower and the best known of this genus. Rooted cuttings of about 8–9½ in/20–24 cm long make excellent grafting stock.

*Selenicereus hamatus* (Scheidw.) Br. & R. Sometimes referred to as *S. rostratus* with which it is synonymous. Indigenous to east Mexico, but also reported from south Mexico. The stems are bright fresh green in colour, three- or four-angled and having very prominent lobes or projections at intervals along the margins. Spines usually absent, especially on young growth, but they may develop on very matured growth which will, with age, gradually become rounded. Large white nocturnal flowers, but only on matured plants. In cultivation, flowers are rarely seen.

*Selenicereus innesii*

*Selenicereus innesii* Kimn. From St. Vincent in the West Indies. This has previously been referred to as *Pseudoseleni-*

*cereus*. A long trailing, semi-pendent plant with stems and branches 3 ft/90 cm or more long with several pronounced ribs. Flowers are either male or female, but can be 'normal'; white when fully open, when it more closely resembles flowers of *Aporocactus*.

*Selenicereus macdonaldiae*

*Selenicereus macdonaldiae* (Hook.) Br. & R. From Central America, has long stems of clambering habit, with 5 or 6 ribs bearing raised tubercles. Areoles are brownish with only very few short spines. A free-flowering plant with large white or creamy flowers 10 in/25 cm wide, and often 12 in/30 cm or more long – the outer segments are reddish-brown.

*Selenicereus pteranthus* (Link & Otto) Br. & R. Synonymous with *S. nycticalus*. Species of Mexican origin with large dark green or bluish-green stems with four to six ribs and a few short blackish spines. A fast and rampant grower, having the largest of all flowers of this genus, up to 12 in/30 cm long, white and beautifully scented.

*Selenicereus testudo*

*Selenicereus testudo* (Karw.) Buxb. (syn. *Deamia testudo* [Karw.] Br. & R.) Other names have been associated with this plant, more recently that of *Deamia diabolica*, but all are considered synonymous with the species. The stems can be most varied in length with three to four or even six ribs with narrow margins armed with many spines, mostly on areoles set close together. This is very apparent in young growth. In habitat it is most usual for it to clamber over rock faces or up trees where it proves to be very much an epiphyte, often losing its original root system completely. The large creamy-white flower is up to 8 in/20 cm or more long. An exotic diurnal species, which was previously a monotypic genus, sometimes called the 'tortoise cactus' on account of its sometimes curious method of growth. Found throughout south Mexico and Central America to Colombia. Only in recent years has it become generally known in cultivation. *Selenicereus wercklei* (Web.) Br. & R. Has a striking resemblance to certain *Rhipsalis* species. Large white flowers about 6 in/15 cm long, but this is rarely seen even in habitat. A true epiphyte, branching with long slender stems, scarcely discernible ribs and no spines. Aerial roots appear along the length of the stems. Endemic to Costa Rica, near Miravalles.

**Setiechinopsis** (Backeb.) de Haas includes a very popular and well-known species for long associated with the genus *Echinopsis* to which it certainly does not belong. Slender plants with very long flower tube having bristle-like elongated scales.

*Setiechinopsis mirabilis* (Speg.) de Haas (syn. *Echinopsis mirabilis* Speg.) The type species from the Province of Santiago del Estero, Argentina. An erect cylindrical plant to about 6 in/15 cm tall, dull greyish-yellowish-green with 11 ribs, slightly undulated having up to 14 slender radial spines and 1 erect central. Flowers from near the apex, white.

**Stenocereus** (A. Bgr.) Riccob. has in recent years absorbed several other genera including *Hertrichocereus, Isolatocereus, Machaerocereus, Marginatocereus, Marshallocereus* and others beside. In general, they are columnar plants or species with sometimes prostrate, elongated stems.

*Stenocereus aragonii* (Web.) Buxb. (syn. *Marshallocereus aragonii* [Web.] Backeb.) Originates from westerly regions of Costa Rica and represents one of the few columnar types of cacti in that country. A tall-growing plant having many terminal branches with six to eight large rounded ribs. Brown-felted areoles with about 10 greyish spines, the centrals to 1¼ in/3 cm long. Flowers yellowish-white to 3 in/8 cm long.

*Stenocereus beneckei* (Ehrenb.) Backeb. (syn. *Hertrichocereus beneckei* [Ehrenb.] Backeb.) A shrubby species, erect and much-branched up to 16½ ft/5 m high. Branches greyish-green with eight ribs strongly tuberculate. Small black-felted areoles with up to 5 brown acicular spines. Flowers small, brownish-white, diurnal. From the area around Guerrero, central Mexico. This is a monotypic species which perhaps is warranted on account of its peculiar tuberculate ribs and small flower.

*Stenocereus dumortieri* (Scheidw.) Buxb. (syn. *Isolatocereus dumortieri* [Scheidw.] Backeb.) A tall erect plant up to

50 ft/15 m, branching freely. Main stems usually woody with age, branches dark bluish-green with six ribs or even more, many areoles, grey-felted with numerous spines, yellowish. Flower small about 2 in/5 cm long, diurnal, whitish. Fruits small, oblong and spineless. From central Mexico.

*Stenocereus eruca* (Brand.) Gibson & Horak (syn. *Cereus eruca* Brand.) Commonly called the 'creeping devil' on account of its lengthy crawling branches reaching to sometimes 50 ft/15 m in length. From Baja California, Mexico, including Magdalena Island. Of prostrate growth with large thick very spiny branches. Ribs about 12, large areoles having about 20 spines of unequal length to 1¼ in/3 cm long. Flowers yellowish-cream, 4½ in/12 cm long on long tube which has scales on the lower part. Large spiny berry-like fruits.

*Stenocereus gummosus*

One other species is recognized, *S. gummosus* (Engelm.) Gibson & Horak, which generally has more compact and erect growth with less vicious spines, also native to Baja California, Mexico, and off-shore islands.

*Stenocereus marginatus* (De Cand.) Buxb. (syn. *Marginatocereus marginatus* [De Cand.] Backeb.) Tall erect stems, rarely branching, to 23 ft/7 m high. Stems dark dull green with five or six acute ribs and white-cushioned areoles which form an almost continuous line on the ridges. Spines small. Flower funnel-shaped, very compact about 1½ in/4 cm long from ovary to tip and globular fruits about 1½ in/4 cm diameter covered with wool and spines. Fairly widely distributed in central Mexico.

*Stenocereus stellatus* (Pfeiff.) Riccob. (syn. *Cereus stellatus* Pfeiff.) Columnar plant branching freely from the base, pale bluish-green with up to 12 low obtuse ribs. Areoles

with many radial and central spines, centrals often 2½ in/6 cm long. Flowers toward the apex, diurnal, small, bell-shaped, reddish about 1½ in/4 cm long. Ovary with small scales and bristly spines, rather woolly. Red spiny globular fruits about 1¼ in/3 cm diameter. From more southerly regions of Mexico.

*Stenocereus thurberi*

*Stenocereus thurberi* Buxb. A widely distributed species from south Arizona to Sonora and Baja California. A stout much branched plant forming huge clusters to 23 ft/7 m high. Branches dark brownish-green with many low ribs, often 15 or more. Large circular brown-felted areoles with numerous spines up to 2 in/5 cm long. Flowers large, whitish, fruits spiny. A popular species in cultivation.

**Stephanocereus** Bgr. at one time included with *Cephalocereus*. Has the peculiarity of developing an apical cephalium consisting of masses of wool and bristles, forming a ring around the stem, through which the stem continues its growth after flowering.

*Stephanocereus leucostele* (Gurke) Bgr. (syn. *Cereus leucostele* Gurke) The type species originating from the deserts of southern Bahia, Brazil. An erect plant with 13–15 low ribs, numerous whitish spines, the radials spreading, centrals longer. Flowers at the top of the plant in the woolly bristly cephalium, nocturnal, white with yellow stamens and stigma lobes. A plant which closely resembles *Arrojadoa* species.

**Stetsonia** Br. & R. is a unique genus containing only one species. An erect plant with pronounced ribs and stiffish spines, endemic to northwest Argentina.

*Stetsonia coryne* (S–D) Br. & R. Stems columnar, tree-like, in habitat up to several yards/metres high. Stems pale green having seven to nine obtuse ribs, areoles with wool and up to 10 stout greyish-black spines of unequal length. Flowers white on longish tube, slightly scaly, nocturnal.

**Strombocactus** Br. & R. is closely allied to *Turbinocarpus*, and further research might well see a merger of the two genera.

*Strombocactus disciformis*

*Strombocactus disciformis* (De Cand.) Br. & R. (syn. *Mammillaria disciformis* De Cand.) A somewhat flattened semi-globose plant to 2–2½ in/5–7 cm diameter. Tubercles thick, imbricate and spineless in maturity. Flower whitish from centre or near-centre of plant. The peculiarities of this plant resulted in the erecting of a genus to include just the one species from Mineral del Monte in central Mexico.

**Strophocactus** Br. & R. is a monotypic genus of great interest – still considered one of the most novel of all cactus species. This unique plant comes from the area of Manaos, Brazil, and is said to be widely distributed in the swampy forests of the Amazon. Rarely encountered in collections. *Strophocactus wittii* (Schum.) Br. & R. This remarkable species with flattened climbing stems achieved by almost continual aerial roots on the midnerve of the branch, and having numerous closely arranged areoles with resultant numerous spines, is an important example of the 'unusual' in the realm of cacti. Sometimes called the strap cactus on account of its strap-like stems. This epiphyte has white flowers, with red sepals, about 10 in/25 cm long. Tube elongated. Night-flowering. Records suggest this could possibly be the link between *Epiphyllum* and *Selenicereus*. It is currently recorded as *Selenicereus wittii* (Schum.) Rowl.

**Sulcorebutia** Backeb. constitutes a genus of plants mainly from Bolivia. At first many of the species were considered *Rebutia*, and named such. It would now seem that the genus has a greater affinity to *Weingartia*. Plants are caespitose, small and somewhat tuberculate, usually with pronounced areoles and spines, flowers very colourful.
*Sulcorebutia steinbachii* (Werd.) Backeb. The type species

from Colomi, Bolivia. A small globular plant, usually caespitose with darkish green body, tuberculate ribs having groove on upper surface of tubercle, long narrow areoles with small spreading brownish spines. Flower deep red. *S. arenacea* (Card.) Ritt. has dark brownish-green body, areoles with whitish spines, tipped brownish and golden-yellow flowers. Native of Ayopana, Bolivia. *S. rauschii* Frank, one of the newest discoveries from near Zudanez, Chuquisaca, Bolivia, having a blackish-green-grey body, ribs divided into round flattened tubercles, small elongated areoles set with black adpressed spines. Flowers magenta-rose with white throat. *S. tiraquensis* (Card.) Ritt. from Tiraque to Monte Puncu at over 9,850 ft/3,000 m, densely covered with bristle-like spines to over ½ in/1 cm long, yellowish-red and flowers reddish.

This species can be variable particularly in respect to spine colours. *S. totorensis* (Card.) Ritt., native of the region around Totora, has long dark red spines and deep red flowers. *S. glomeriseta* (Card.) Ritt. is a yellow-flowering species from Rio Cotacajes, Ayopana, Bolivia, densely covered with numerous whitish bristle-like spines. *S. candiae* (Card.) Buin. & Don. has a dark green body with yellowish pectinate spines from pronounced areole and yellowish flowers. From Tiquirpaya, Ayopana, Bolivia. Another very similar plant, *S. menesesii* (Card.) Buin. & Don., found at 5,250 ft/1,600 m near Naranjito, Ayopana, Bolivia, with pinkish-white pectinate spines, somewhat bristle-like, flowers yellow. Other popular and well-known species include *S. kruegerii* (Card.) Ritt. with yellow flowers and likewise the same flower colour from *S. caineana* (Card.) Don.

**Tacinga** Br. & R. is closely linked with *Opuntia*. Tall-growing species with spines and glochids.

*Tacinga funalis*

*Tacinga funalis* Br. & R. An erect cylindrical branched species from Bahia, Brazil. Tall-growing plant with greyish-blue stems and branches and scarcely discernible ribs. Areoles have short glochids, deciduous and sometimes soft brownish spines. Flowers usually at terminal of branches, reputedly nocturnal, green or greenish-white. This is still a rare species, not too frequently seen in cultivation. The monotypic genus was erected for this one species.

**Thelocactus** (K. Schum.) Br. & R. is a popular genus of beautifully flowering plants. Globular and spiny, the spines developing from prominent tubercles.

*Thelocactus hexaedrophorus*

*Thelocactus bicolor*

*Thelocactus bicolor* (Gal.) Br. & R. One of the best-known of the genus, widely distributed from south Texas to central Mexico. This, and its varieties, are now referred to as *Ferocactus*. Plants solitary, globose to conical to 4½ in/12 cm or more high and 2½ in/7 cm diameter. Ribs about 8 or 10, broad and tubercled. Spines are colourful, reddish-brown or yellowish – radials up to 18 widely spreading 1¼ in/3 cm long, central spines about four ascending and protruding, straight to 2 in/5 cm long. Flowers about 2½ in/6 cm long and broad, purplish-pink. *T. bicolor* var. *flavidispinus* Backeb. from Texas, has shorter, fewer spines which are yellow.
*Thelocactus conothele* (Reg. & Klein) Knuth. From the region around Jaumave, Tamaulipas, Mexico. Plant solitary, about 5 in/13 cm or more diameter, light green and somewhat cylindrical in shape, tubercles with 14–16 whitish radial spines spreading; centrals usually 4, one of which extends horizontally. Flowers pinkish-white. Two outstanding varieties are recognized. *T. conothele* var. *argenteus* Glass & Foster has a greater number of spines, which are 'shredding' and of silvery appearance and flowers lilac-pink. *T. conothele* var. *aurantiacus* Glass & Foster also has a greater number of spines than the type plant and is somewhat brownish with rich orange-yellow flowers. *T. saussieri* (Weber) Berg. is very similar to the species and possibly synonymous.

*Thelocactus hexaedrophorus* (Lem.) Br. & R. (syn. *Echinocactus hexaedrophorus* Lem.) Type species. A globose somewhat flattened plant, dark greyish-green, strongly tubercled, overall to 5 in/14 cm diameter. Prominent tubercles, six-sided arranged in spirals with up to nine rigid spreading radial spines of unequal length to ⅝ in/18 mm long; and one central spine, erect to 1¼ in/3 cm long. Flower 2 in/5 cm or more diameter, pinkish-purple. A variety, *T. hexaedrophorus* var. *fossulatus* (Scheidw.) Backeb. with bluish ribs divided into thick large tubercles with four to five thick spines. Flowers white, flushed pink. Both the species and the variety are from the region around San Luis Potosi, Mexico.
*Thelocactus leucacanthus* (Zucc.) Br. & R. A clustering plant from near Ixmiquilpan, Hidalgo, Mexico. Also currently included in *Ferocactus*. Ribs to 13, often spiralled and obtusely tubercled with up to 20 yellowish-grey radial spines, spreading or recurved of unequal length, some to 1½ in/4 cm long; central spine blackish-grey to 2 in/5 cm long. Flowers bright yellow. A pleasing form, *T. leucacanthus* var. *schmollii* Werd. from north of Bernal, Queretaro, Mexico, has prominent tubercles on a smallish stem and almost pectinate spines with deep red flowers.
*Thelocactus nidulans* (Quehl.) Br. & R. Distributed in many parts of Coahuila, Mexico, particularly around Saltillo and Parras. Somewhat flattened body to 4 in/10 cm high and 8 in/20 cm or more diameter, silvery-grey or bluish-grey with about 20 wavy ribs, divided into tubercles with long, shredding silvery-white spines. Flowers to 1½ in/4 cm long, yellowish-white.
*Thelocactus rinconensis* (Poselg.) Br. & R. Native of Nuevo Leon near Rinconada, Mexico. A globose somewhat flattened plant about 3 in/8 cm high and to 5½ in/14 cm diameter. Ribs spiralled with strong tubercles. Tubercles angled and flattened with few spines, usually three. Flowers white.

*Thelocactus tulensis*

**Thelocactus tulensis** Br. & R. A Mexican species from Tamaulipas, reaches about 4½ in/12 cm high with ribs formed by conical warts closely set together. Radial spines 6–8, 1–2 centrals. Flowers pink with deeper central line on petals.

**Thrixanthocereus** Backeb. includes species of erect habit, often with long bristle-like hairs at the base of the plant, particularly when young. Forms pseudocephalium on one side at top of branches with nocturnal flowers from older part of pseudocephalium.
*Thrixanthocereus blossfeldiorum* (Werd.) Backeb. (syn. *Cephalocereus blossfeldiorum* [Werd.]) From Peru. A tall species, sometimes branching from the base, 20 straight ribs with woolly areoles set with whitish-brownish bristly spines. The pseudocephalium develops at the terminal ends of mature stems and extends downward with masses of brownish-whitish bristles and whitish wool. Flowers nocturnal, somewhat funnel-shaped. Other species include *Thrixanthocereus senilis* Ritt. from Ancash, Peru, a distinctive plant covered with white silvery bristly spines and hairs, older growth tends to develop long yellowish spines also, these often with reddish-brown tips. Flowers emanating from the pseudocephalium, purplish-red, nocturnal.

**Trichocereus** (Bgr.) Riccob. is one of the best-known genera which for long was recognized as including principally columnar plants. It is now, however, considered by some authorities to be synonymous with *Echinopsis*, and certain species have already been transferred to that genus. For this record certain species are being included, even if transferred to *Echinopsis*. The genera *Helianthocereus* and *Soehrensia* are now united with *Trichocereus*. Plants of easy culture. Young plants of some species are to be recommended for grafting purposes.
*Trichocereus bruchii* (Br. & R.) Ritter (syn. *Soehrensia bruchii* [Br. & R.] Backeb.) Originates from Tucuman, Argentina. Large greyish-green plant with about 50 ribs or more, tuberculate, areoles with whitish wool and spreading, sometimes protruding spines. Flowers deep red, from near the

crown of the plant.
*Trichocereus grandiflorus* (Br. & R.) Backeb. (syn. *Helianthocereus grandiflorus* [Br. & R.] Backeb.) Also from Argentina. Small clustering plant, stems with about 14 ribs and about 15 yellowish radial spines. Flowers pink. This has now been renamed *Trichocereus rowleyi* Kiesling.

*Trichocereus huasha*

*Trichocereus huasha* (Web.) Br. & R. (syn. *Helianthocereus huasha* [Web.] Backeb.) A clump-forming species with many semi-erect cylindrical stems, having about 12–18 low rounded ribs. Areoles closely set with numerous acicular yellowish-brown spines. Flowers variable in colour, yellow or red. Native of Catamarca, Argentina.
*Trichocereus macrogonus* (S–D) Riccob. (syn. *Cereus macrogonus* S–D) An erect plant, somewhat bluish-green having seven low rounded ribs with large areoles about ¾ in/2 cm apart, radial spines short, acicular, brown and one longer central about ¾ in/2 cm long. Flowers nocturnal, whitish. *T. pachanoi* Br. & R., native of Ecuador, has about six ribs, dark green; above each areole a deep horizontal depression, only very few spines, usually small, occasionally to ¾ in/2 cm long. Flowers near to terminal, white, nocturnal. *T. pasacana* (Web.) Br. & R., endemic to Argentina and Bolivia – a well-known species with about 25 or more pronounced ribs, areoles with long yellowish stiff spines. Flowers whitish.

**Turbinocarpus** (Backeb.) Buxb. & Backeb. are among the choicest of miniature cacti. Very variable in spination, attractive flowers. A sought-after group.
*Turbinocarpus pseudopectinatus* (Backeb.) Glass & Foster (syn. *Normanbokea pseudopectinata* [Backeb.] Klad. & Buxb.) Plant

body usually simple with closely set very small four-angled tubercles and minute pectinate slender whitish spines, arranged comb-like. Flowers from apex of plant, pinkish-white to yellowish-white. A northern Mexican species.

*Turbinocarpus schmiedickeanus* (Boed.) Buxb. & Backeb. (syn. *Echinocactus schmiedickeanus* Boed.) Type species. Diminutive species, globular, about 1–1½ in/3–4 cm broad, dark greyish-green having many tubercles. The feature of this plant is the small crown covered with rather long, thick, slightly curved spines. Flowers pale pink with deeper pinkish midrib. San Luis Potosi and Tamaulipas, Mexico.

*Turbinocarpus valdezianus* (Moëller) Glass & Foster (syn. *Normanbokea valdeziana* [Moëller] Klad & Buxb.) A very miniature plant, almost completely globular and covered entirely with minute plumose spines. Flowers borne from the apex and range in colour from white to purple. Grows on limestone rock faces around San Luis Potosi and Nuevo Leon, Mexico.

A number of other species of this genus are of considerable interest, all miniatures and uncommon in cultivation. *T. pseudomacrochele* (Backeb.) Buxb. & Backeb. has dark green body, hair-like spines and large pink flowers. *T. schwarzii* (Shurly) Backeb. with pointed tubercles and heavier spines. *T. polaskii* Backeb. from Matehuala, San Luis Potosi, Mexico, resembles a small *Lophophora* with few soft curved spines and large pink and white flowers. *T. lopho-*

*Turbinocarpus lophophoroides*

*phoroides* (Werd.) Buxb. & Backeb. from near Las Tablas, San Luis Potosi, Mexico, very similar in appearance to *Lophophora*, grey-green body somewhat larger than that of *T. polaskii*, flowers large and white-blushed pink.

## U

**Uebelmannia** Buin. includes some of the newest discoveries of recent years and its introduction caused great interest. Most species are still rare in cultivation. All known species are of Brazilian origin.

*Uebelmannia pectinifera*

*Uebelmannia pectinifera* Buin. An extraordinary plant with a globose or cylindrical body to about 6 in/15 cm diameter. Dark reddish-brown in actual colour, but with a white scaly covering giving the effect of a greyish-bluish-white body. Ribs 14–18, areoles very closely set with pectinate blackish perpendicularly arranged spines, almost comb-like. Areoles in crown of plant somewhat felted and with greyish-white wool from which the small yellow flowers are borne. From an altitude of 3,300 ft/1,000 m in Minas Gerais, Brazil. *U. pectinifera* var. *pseudopectinifera* Buin. is similar to the species but with non-pectinate greyish-black spines, untidily spreading, flowers yellow. From the vicinity of Diamantina, Minas Gerais, Brazil.

*U. gummifera* (Backeb. & Voll.) Buin. (syn. *Parodia gummifera* Backeb. & Voll.) is an interesting plant, thought to be identical to *Echinocactus centeterius* Pfeiff. and from the same habitat, Minas Gerais, Brazil. Dull greenish body with many ribs, tubercled, areoles with about seven spines, of the two centrals one points upward, the other down. Crown of plant woolly, flowers small, yellow. *U. buiningii* has a reddish body with ribs strongly tubercled, few whitish spines and yellowish flowers. *U. meninensis* Buin. is almost completely covered with pronounced tubercles and two stiff spines from each areole.

## V

**Vatricania** Backeb. includes only one species from Rio Grande Valley, Bolivia, at an altitude of 3,900 ft/1,000 m or more. Similar to *Cephalocereus* and *Espostoa*.

*Vatricania guentheri* (Kupp.) Backeb. (syn. *Cephalocereus guentheri* Kupp.) An erect columnar plant branching from the base. Branches with about 27 somewhat tubercled ribs; areoles have yellowish wool and about 15 bristly yellowish-brown spines and one central. Flowers nocturnal, about 2½ in/7 cm long, whitish-pink, arising from the pseudo-cephalium which develops on one side of the branch.

**Weberbaureocereus** Backeb. are distinctive plants, and were once originally included with *Trichocereus*. Their branches very spiny. Flowers somewhat curved at base and tube very scaly.

*Weberbaureocereus fascicularis* (Meyen) Backeb. (syn. *Cereus fascicularis* Meyen) From high altitudes in southern Peru and Chile. Erect slender plant with about 16 low ribs; areoles with brownish felt and numerous brownish-yellow spines, the centrals being stouter and longer than the radials. Flowers about 4 in/10 cm long, pinkish-white from near the ends of the branches. Other species are *W. rauhii* Bakeb., a very lovely plant with creamy-yellow flowers at the branch tips, and *W. seyboldianus* Rauh & Backeb., a Peruvian species with deep red flowers.

**Weberocereus** Br. & R., Slender-stemmed epiphytic cacti comprising only four species having many aerial roots to encourage both climbing and pendent habit. All species are from Costa Rica where they grow in dense rain forests, and in the Province of Colon in Panama frequenting tree thickets. Have certain resemblances to *Rhipsalis*, only the flower, while not as exotic as so many of the Hylocereaneae, is larger and generally more colourful than those of *Rhipsalis*.

*Weberocereus biolleyi*

*Weberocereus biolleyi* (Web.) Br. & R. Originally considered as a *Rhipsalis* due to the almost round or only slightly angled stems, spineless and with aerial roots. Found in the area of Port Limon in Costa Rica growing from the branches of forest trees. Nocturnal-flowering. Small flowers, pinkish, up to 2 in/5 cm long. This interesting plant remains one of the lesser-known species in cultivation.

*Weberocereus glaber*

*Weberocereus glaber* (Eichal.) Rowl. Slender, usually, three-angled stems, bright green and glaucous, the margins having pronounced projections from which the areole is born. Spines are few and small. The flower seems to appear at the apex of the stem or at the upper areoles. White in colour, about 4 in/10 cm long, tube having many brownish spines. Night-flowering. Fruit becomes brick-red. Widely distributed in Guatemala.

*Weberocereus tonduzii* (Web.) Rowl. From the area of El Copey in Costa Rica where its distribution is seemingly restricted. Has 3–4-angled stems, developing a bushy habit. Branches are deep green in colour and have straight margins with small areoles at regular intervals, and aerial roots. In habitat the stems have short spines which are about ⅛ in/3 mm long, but these are not usually observed with the cultivated plants. Flower white and generally free-flowering, with a short tube having dark spines and wool. A rare species.

*Weberocereus trichophorus* Johns. & Kimn. A forest species from Costa Rica, from the area of Peralta in the province of Limon. Rampant growth with six to seven-angled stems with spines and many blackish hairs at the areoles. Has many aerial roots and is nocturnal-flowering with smallish bloom to 2½ in/6 cm long and pink in colour. Very attractive species.

*Weberocereus tunilla* (Web.) Br. & R. Another Costa Rican species from southwest of Cartago. Has slender four-angled greyish-green stems, occasionally flattened – sometimes with three or five angles and up to 12 stiff spines at each areole. Of climbing habit with only few aerial roots. The funnel-form flower is up to 2½ in/7 cm long, rose-pink or purplish-pink with short tube. Night-flowering. Uncommon in cultivation. One other species is recorded, *Weberocereus panamensis*, usually with triangular stems and white flower.

*Weingartia* Werd. are globular plants with turnip-like roots, but having a small 'neck' between the body of the plant and the root. Very tubercled with numerous spines. Possibly related to *Sulcorebutia*.

*Weingartia fidaiana* (Backeb.) Backeb. (syn. *Echinocactus fidaiana* Backeb.) The type species from Bolivia. Globular or somewhat oval olive-green body with flattened tubercles and pronounced woolly areoles bearing about eight brownish-yellow spines. A dwarf-growing variety with orange-yellow flowers. *W. westii* (Hutch.) Don. from south of Potosi in Bolivia at 11,500 ft/3,500 m altitude. Somewhat elongated and offsetting freely from near the base; strongly tubercled with about 14 brownish spines of unequal length. Flowers golden-yellow.

*W. torotorensis* Card., a native of Mina Asientos, Bolivia, is heavily tubercled with numerous yellowish spines and rose-pink flowers. *W. neocummingii* Backeb., also known as *W. cummingii*, from Peru and Bolivia, has very pronounced tubercles and orange-yellow flowers.

*Weingartia multispina*

*Weingartia multispina* Ritt. From Bolivia. Semi-globular in shape, about 5½ in/14 cm in diameter with the ribs resolved into tubercles. Numerous spines of brownish-yellow ⅜–¾ in/1–2 cm long. Flowers are borne near the crown of the plant and last several days, opening by day and closing at night. The flowers are ¾in/2 cm or more long, and are golden-yellow.

   *Weingartia* is a genus undergoing considerable revision which might well result in its being merged with *Sulcorebutia*.

*Wilcoxia* Br. & R. is yet another genus in a state of turmoil. The proposal to include this within *Echinocereus* does not appear to be totally acceptable, and it is treated separately here. More or less slender columnar plants, erect or sprawling. Flowers are either diurnal or nocturnal.

*Wilcoxia albiflora*

*Wilcoxia albiflora* Backeb. From coastal regions bordering the Gulf of California in Sonora, Mexico. It has pale green stems with fine but small spines and bears terminal flowers of white or very pale pink.

*Wilcoxia poselgeri* (Lemaire) Br. & R. (syn. *Echinocereus poselgeri* Lemaire.) Type species. Root system extremely tuberous. Stems elongated and slender with about 10 insignificant ribs, greyish-green. Areoles small with minute slightly adpressed spines, one central spine rather longer. Flowers purplish-pink with brilliant green style, 2 in/5 cm long. Tube and ovary with small spines and whitish hairs. A popular species endemic to southern Texas and parts of Sonora and Coahuila, Mexico.

*Wilmattea* Br. & R. is a monotypic genus. At one time incorporated with *Hylocereus* but due to certain flower differences a distinct genus was created.

*Wilmattea minutiflora* Br. & R. Native of Guatemala and Honduras. A true epiphyte with long slender stems, bright green in colour with few very small insignificant spines from pronounced areoles. Branches freely. A very small flower, white with pinkish markings, fragrant. The tube is almost unnoticeable. Night-flowering. A desirable and easily grown species, but still quite rare in cultivation.

*Zehntnerella* Br. & R. is a genus of Brazilian plants, tall and erect with very spiny ribs with small nocturnal flowers scattered along the upper ends of the branches.

*Zehntnerella squamulosa* Br. & R. The type species from east of Joazeiro, Bahia, Brazil. Stems long and slender branching from the base. Branches have about 18–20 low ribs, set closely together with small areoles and 15 or more brownish acicular spines, some to ¾–1¼ in/2–3 cm long. Flowers nocturnal, small, white.

# A~Z
## OF
## SUCCULENTS

**Abromeitiella** (BROMELIACEAE) are all natives of Argentina. Dwarf, terrestrial plants which quickly form dense 'cushions'.

*Abromeitiella chlorantha*

*Abromeitiella brevifolia* (Griseb.) Castell. A well-known species endemic to many parts of Bolivia and Argentina. Small compact rosette of elongated triangular leaves about 1¼ in/3 cm long, thick and fleshy with spineless margins. Clusters freely forming mats. Flowers cannon-shaped and bright green. *A. chlorantha* (Haum.) Mez., from the region of Tucuman, Argentina, has very small rosettes of elongated triangular leaves about ¾ in/20 mm long and pale green. Clusters freely forming mounds. Leaves very stiff with a small terminal spine and minutely toothed margins. Flowers greenish.

**Acanthosicyos** (CUCURBITACEAE) have caudiciform rootstock bearing thorn-covered branches and large edible fruits. Native of Namibia and Angola.
*Acanthosicyos horrida* Welw. Has long fleshy taproot with a tall, erect, leafless stem. The name implies a thorny plant, and this species has long thorns in pairs along the stem. Flower yellowish green. Fruit spiny, edible. From coastal regions, Namibia.

**Adansonia** (BOMBACACEAE) are tree-like plants from tropical Africa, Madagascar and Australia. Only few species, mostly with the same habit. Plants for the connoisseur!
*Adansonia digitata* L. A huge tree with trunk up to 60 ft/18 m high and of considerable girth. The swollen trunk consists of pulpous wood and with no growth rings. Leaves large digitate with leaflets, deciduous. Pendulous flowers, about 4 in/10 cm, white with purple stamens and long woody fruits, somewhat hairy about 9 in/25 cm long. Leaves and fruit are edible. This features very much in savannah areas in tropical Africa. Commonly known as the 'baobab tree', 'dead-rat tree' and 'monkey bread tree'. Other species have mainly the same characteristics, but flower colour varies.

**Adenia** (PASSIFLORACEAE) includes a number of caudiciform plants from tropical Africa, Madagascar and Burma – all with thorny stems and inconspicuous flowers.
*Adenia digitata* (Harv.) Engl. Large rounded caudex, sometimes malformed, having greyish skin. Erect fleshy stem from the caudex, slightly branching with digitate leaves in groups towards the terminal ends. This species is considered poisonous. Transvaal, South Africa.
*Adenia fruticosa* Burtt-Davy. Has very large, somewhat elongated caudex, usually deformed, brownish-green. Branches freely, rambling and climbing, fleshy, greenish to greyish-brown. Leaves globose-ovate and deciduous. Flowers yellowish and insignificant. Native to Transvaal, South Africa.
*Adenis globosa* Engl. Possibly the best-known of this remarkable genus. Has massive swollen caudex to about 3¼ ft/1 m thick, with the appearance of a large grey-green stone. Short branches, twig-like, develop from the top of the caudex, but sometimes to about 6½ ft/2 m long or more, furnished with stout and long thorns, all greenish-grey. Rarely with leaf, but sometimes, immediately following the rains, small narrow lanceolate leaves appear but soon fall. Grouped inflorescence with bright red, star-like, scented flowers. Tanzania.
*Adenia pechuelii* (Engl.) Harms. Usually with large fleshy caudex, rounded and long tap roots. Sometimes the thick base is more elongated, almost bottle-shaped, greenish-grey. Many stems and branches, somewhat spiny. Leaves lanceolate, deciduous. Small inflorescence with three flowers. Fruit pale pink. From Namibia.
*Adenia spinosa* Burtt-Davy. Massive swollen succulent trunk, partly subterranean, dull greyish-green to about 6½ ft/2 m high. Branches freely, usually from the upper part of the stem, but occasionally also from the lower parts. Branches armed with sharp straight spines. Leaves rather small, deciduous. Flower creamy-yellow which appears before the leaves. Transvaal, South Africa.
*Adenia venenata* Forsk. Thick, somewhat elongated fleshy stem to about 6½ ft/2 m high, with smooth greenish bark. Branches freely, greenish, rope-like and many tendrils. Leaves small and deciduous. Flowers yellowish-green. Endemic to Nigeria.

**Adenium** (APOCYNACEAE) are attractive flowering succulents with thick, fleshy, almost caudiciform-like stems. Found in many areas of Namibia, East Africa and Arabia.
*Adenium multiflorum* Kl. An attractive succulent shrub with thick swollen trunk to 10 ft/3 m high. Many branches, leaves at terminal ends, spirally arranged, simple, ovate-lanceolate, smooth, dark green, deciduous. Flower funnel-shaped, white with crimson edges. The milky sap is poisonous. From Zimbabwe and Transvaal, South Africa. Known as the Impala lily.

*Adenium obesum*

*Adenium obesum* Balf. f. Has thick, succulent caudex with many short fleshy branches to 6½ ft/2 m high. The swollen roots often protrude above ground. Leaves spirally arranged at branch terminals, glossy dark green, fleshy, obovate with pinkish midrib. When young, leaves often have minute hairs. Flowers numerous, showy with spreading petals, carmine-red. Sometimes called 'desert rose'. Kenya, Tanzania, Mozambique and other areas of East Africa. Other varieties of the species are known including var.swazicum from parts of East Africa.

*Adenium oleifolium* Stapf. A rare species with elongated tuberous caudex, pale brown skin. Branches develop from the upper portion, erect, fleshy. Leaves at end of branches in clusters, linear and narrowing into the stalk, glossy grey-green. Flowers pinkish-red with deeper red markings. A poisonous plant from Namaqualand.

Other *Adenium* species are recorded, mostly having the same characteristics with slight differences in leaf shape or flower colour.

**Adromischus** (CRASSULACEAE) has over 50 known species, primarily miniatures with small stems and rather insignificant flowers of white or brownish-red. Propagation easy from leaves or seeds.

*Adromischus bolusii* (Schoenl.) Bgr. Has small green spatulate leaves with waxy covering, margins have hard reddish edge. Flower red on unbranched inflorescence. Mosselbay and Riversdale, Cape Province, South Africa.

*Adromischus festivus* C. A. Smith. Small branches with grey-green and silver mottled leaves, cylindrical and truncate towards the apex. Graaff Reinet, Cape Province, South Africa.

*Adromischus roaneanus* Uitew. Erect, zig-zag stems, branching freely and becoming procumbent. Leaves round or oblong narrowed into a stalk, apex with a small spine, margins rounded, grey-green, covered by waxy mottlings. Flower whitish or purplish. Namaqualand and Cape Province, South Africa.

*Adromischus tricolor* Sm. Short stem with few branches, spindle-shaped leaves with silver and maroon markings.

Flower purplish-red. Clanswilliam Div. Cape Province, South Africa.

*Adromischus trigynus* (Burch.) v. Poelln. Short stems, clustering with leaves compressed, elliptical, light green with silver-grey and brownish-red markings. Flower purplish. Transvaal to Orange Free State, South Africa.

**Aeolanthus** (LABIATAE) is a small genus of tropical plants of which only one has found its way into cultivation. The others are mainly annuals and to a degree are succulents.

*Aeolanthus repens* Oliv. A very uncommon species of creeping habit, sometimes becoming semi-erect, stems somewhat angled and hairy. Small elongated fleshy leaves and purple flowers. Fairly well distributed in tropical Africa.

**Aeonium** (CRASSULACEAE) are indigenous to the Canary Islands, Madeira, parts of North Africa and the Cape Verde Islands, and parts of the Mediterranean.

All species have an attractive leaf structure in the form of a rosette. The flowering stem often dies after the seeds are formed.

*Aeonium arboreum* (L.) Webb & Berth. A popular species up to 3¼ ft/1 m high, erect and topped with rostte of thin leaves, ciliate on margins. Flowers in long racemes, golden-yellow. There are varieties of this species, *A. arboreum* var. *atropurpureum* with dark purple leaves, and variegated forms, var. *albovariegatum* and var. *luteo-variegatum* with white and yellow mottlings respectively.

*Aeonium nobile* Praeg. Very large rosette on short stem. Leaves darkish green and sticky. Flowers reddish or coppery colour – a most attractive species.

*Aeonium smithii* (Sims) Webb & Berth. A rarity with distinctive characteristics. Usually short stems which become covered with brownish hair when mature. Leaves undulated with many soft hairs, deep green with red stripes on both sides. Flower yellow.

*Aeonium simsii* (Sweet) Stearn. Short stemmed plant, grouping freely. Broad leafy rosette, grass-green with reddish lines and margins ciliate. Flowers golden-yellow.

*Aeonium tabulaeforme* (Haw.) Webb & Berth. Low, almost stemless species with almost flat rosette, growing on rock faces. Leaves narrow and spatulate, margins ciliate, fresh-green. Flower yellow.

**Afrovivella** (CRASSULACEAE) consists of a few species from high altitudes, similar in some respects to *Echeveria*.

*Afrovivella simensis* (Hochst.) Bgr. Small species with fleshy stem and many branches forming mats. Leaves in rosettes, oval and pointed with white spiny tip, and margins ciliate. Flower on long scape, in clusters, pink. Ethiopia and Somalia.

**Agave** (AGAVACEAE) is a large genus of rosette-forming plants. Some are comparative dwarfs, others develop giant proportions. Mostly of easy growth, but flowering often means the 'death' of the particular rosette.

*Agave americana*

*Agave americana* L. A well-known species having become naturalized in many parts of Europe, even in more protected areas of Britain. Seemingly of Mexican origin. Stemless rosettes producing offsets, greyish-green leaves, sometimes to 10 ft/3 m high. Inflorescence to 26 ft/8 m high with many branches and flowers to 3½ in/9 cm long. There are also most attractive varieties: *A. americana* var. *mediopicta* Trel. variegated form with yellow stripe down centre of leaves; *A. americana* var. *mediopicta* forma *alba* Hort. which has white centre stripe; *A. americana* var. *striata* Trel. with many cream or yellowish stripes in leaf centres; *A. americana* var. *marginata* Trel. yellow margins to greenish leaves.

*Agave attenuata* Salm-Dyck. Plants to 3¼ ft/1 m high, 'soft' leaves without spines or prickles, sometimes developing a trunk. Leaves up to 30 forming a rosette, smooth pale green. Inflorescence to 10 ft/3 m or more high with dense raceme of greenish-white flowers about 2½ in/6 cm long. From Hidalgo, Mexico.

*Agave bracteosa* S. Wats. A stemless species from near Monterrey, Nuevo Leon, Mexico, growing to about 16 in/40 cm high with peculiarity of the lower leaves recurving, upper leaves ascending abruptly with recurved tips. Leaves pale green, no spines but margins minutely denticulate. Inflorescence to 6½ ft/2 m high, flowers in dense spike about ⅛ in/3 mm long, creamy yellow.

*Agave couci* Trel. A large plant not unlike *A. americana*, having greyish-green leaves armed with reddish-brown marginal spines and terminal spine. Marginal spines rather triangular, those toward the top of the leaf are curved forward, the lower ones recurved. Long branched inflorescence with long yellow flowers. Endemic to Venezuela.

*Agave cundinamarcensis* Lem. From the area of Cundinamarca, Colombia. A stemless rosette plant with very thick leaves, first spreading horizontally, then curved toward the centre and finally recurving abruptly. Leaves greyish-yellow with blunted marginal spines and very short terminal spine.

Has a tall inflorescence, pyramid-like with creamy-yellow flowers.

*Agave filifera* Salm-Dyck. Stemless species from Hidalgo and San Luis Potosi, Mexico, with rosette to 20 in/50 cm high. Leaves to about 10 in/25 cm long, darkish green with white markings and numerous white threads along the margins and a long brown grooved spine ⅜ in/10 mm long at tip. Inflorescence to over 6½ ft/2 m high with yellowish-green flowers, two together. This is one of the most attractive of the genus with a number of varietal forms: *A. filifera* var. *compacta* J. Versch, a small rosette with short and broad leaves; *A. filifera* var. *filamentosa* (S-D) Baker, which is larger than the type and with much narrower leaves.

*Agave gracilipes* Trel. Stemless rosette of greyish-white smooth elongated leaves, stiff and tapering forming a hollow on the upper surface, terminal spine brownish, straight or flexuose. Margins with about 15 spines about ¾ in/20 mm apart, narrow-triangular, brownish. Inflorescence to 16½ ft/5 m high with ascending branches and yellow flowers about 1¼ in/30 mm long on stalks. Native to Sierra Blanca and Rock Creek, western Texas, USA.

*Agave karatto* Mill. One of the best representatives of the West Indian agaves. *A. dussiana* Trel. and *A. grenadina* Trel. are undoubtedly synonymous. The species is stemless with lanceolate leaves about 5 ft/150 cm long, hollowed on the upper surface. The wide green shining leaves have a black terminal spine somewhat recurved and margins with narrow triangular reddish spines. Inflorescence to 20 ft/6 m high with spreading branches and bright yellow flowers.

*Agave maculosa* (Rose) Hook. Species with rather tuberous root from southern Texas. Loose rosette of soft leaves up to 12 in/30 cm long, greyish-green with many brown markings, margins with small teeth. Inflorescence to 3¼ ft/1 m high or more with greenish-white sweet-scented flowers.

*Agave parrasana* Bgr. One of the most beautiful species with compact rosette. Leaves about 14 in/35 cm long, obovate, thick, fleshy and somewhat concave on upper surface, dull green with bluish-grey pruinose tapering to a brown terminal spine about ¾ in/2 cm long. Margins dentate, upper portion armed with stout curved reddish spines. Inflorescence to 10 ft/3 m high with ascending branches and yellow flowers. From near Parras, Coahuila, Mexico.

*Agave parviflora* Torr. Widely distributed in Sonora and Chihuahua, Mexico and in Arizona. A smallish attractive rosette with stiff narrow elongated dark green leaves having many white markings, margins with short white threads. Inflorescence to over 3¼ ft/1 m high with flowers two or four together. Tends to offset freely after flowering. Certain other species have similar characteristics. *A. toumeyana* Trel. from southern Arizona has leaves up to 10 in/25 cm long; and *A.t.* var. *bella* Breit. is more like *A. parviflora* but, if anything, even more compact and beautiful. *A. schidigera* Lem. from Michoacan, Mexico, has leaves up to 12in/30 cm long, uniformly spreading. A really beautiful hybrid between *A. filifera* and *A. schidigera* is a rarity of particular charm, known as *A.* × *'Leopoldii'* Hort.

*Agave pumila* de Smet. Possibly the smallest species of the genus being only about 2 in/5 cm in diameter and 1¼ in/3 cm high. Beautiful rosette, extremely compact, leaves about eight, fleshy, greyish-green, the underside being somewhat rounded, tapering abruptly to a short white spine. White margins with small teeth. Distribution uncertain but believed to originate from Mexico.

*Agave shawii*

*Agave shawii* Engelm. Has leaves 8–20 in/20–50cm long formed into a glossy-green compact rosette – the leaves with horny and spiny margins and a terminal spine to 1½ in/4cm in length. The inflorescence is borne on a stem about 10 ft/3 m long with greenish-yellowish flowers. From the Baja California.

*Agave stricta*

*Agave stricta* Salm-Dyck. One of the most attractive plants with long tapering narrow leaves, erect and slightly incurved forming a dense spreading rosette. Leaves about 14 in/35 cm long, thick at base and tapering to terminal spine, surface with parallel ribs or keels on both sides, greyish-green. Inflorescence to 6½ ft/ 2 m high with flowers in dense spike, white about ¾ in/20 mm long. Native of Mexico in the state of Puebla. There are other very similar species. *A. striata* Zucc., from Hidalgo, Mexico, has longer leaves and a less dense rosette. *A. echinoides* Jac. is a rare species of Mexican origin with a thick rosette of leaves about 6 in/15 cm long, narrowly ribbed with roughened margins and terminal spine about ⅛ in/3 mm long.

*Agave utahensis* Engelm. An erect compact grey-green rosette with stiff tapering leaves and pronounced terminal spine. Widely distributed throughout parts of Utah, California, Arizona, where it grows in desert and mountainous areas at 3,300–8,200 ft/1,000–2,500 m. Leaves to 6½ in/17 cm long and 1 in/2.5 cm wide, concave on upper side, convex below. Margins sinuate with teeth ⅜ in/10 mm apart, hooked, triangular ⅛ in/2 mm long. Inflorescence 8¼ ft/2.5 m high with yellow flowers 1 in/25 mm long. Several varieties of the species are recognized: *A. utahensis* var. *nevadensis* Engelm., an erect rosette with very long terminal spine to over 3 in/8 cm long, endemic to Clark Mountains, California, and Ivanpah Mountains, Nevada. *A. utahensis* var. *eborispina* (Hester) Breit. with light green leaves, ivory-white spine to 8 in/20 cm long, also from Nevada. *A. utahensis* var. *kaibabensis* (McKelvey) Breit., from Arizona, is a very large rosette to over 3¼ ft/1 m diameter, greyish-brown and long terminal spine with well-separated marginal teeth which curve backward or forward.

*Agave victoriae-reginae*

*Agave victoriae-reginae* T. Moore. One of the most outstanding plants in the succulent world! Found near Santa Catarina, Monterrey, Nuevo Leon and in certain other restricted areas of Coahuila and Durango. Rosette usually simple with leaves 6 in/15 cm long, long and narrow, with a blunted tip, thick, about 2 in/5 cm wide, slightly curved inward, concave on upper side and convex on lower surface with keel toward the tip; keel and margins with white bands and markings; terminal spine about ⅛ in/2 mm long, often with two minute spines. Inflorescence to 13 ft/ 4 m high, dense with creamy flowers usually three together. Several forms are recognized: *A. victoriae-reginae* forma *nickelsii* (Hort. ex Godd.). Trel. which used to be known as *A. fernandi-regis* Berg. has fewer leaves, more open rosette and leaves acute from base to apex; *A.victoriae-reginae* forma *ornata* Breit. is of smaller growth with brilliant white markings.

***Aichryson*** (Crassulaceae) are allied to *Aeonium* and endemic to the same areas. Annuals and biennials.
*Aichryson dichotomum* (DC.) Webb & Berth. Stems branching in pairs, hairy and succulent. Leaf spoon-shaped, bright green, sometimes purplish. Flower pale yellow.
*Aichryson villosum* (Ait.) Webb & Berth. Densely branched species, stems having white hairs, sticky. Leaves spatulate covered with long hairs. Flower golden-yellow.

***Alluaudia*** (Didiereaceae) originate from Madagascar. They have succulent trunks or stems, some with, but others without leaves. Rare and desirable!
*Alluaudia adscendens* Drake. A spectacular species, tree-like to 40 ft/12 m high. Thick, fleshy, becoming woody stem and few branches which are furnished with long conical thorns. Leaves rounded, somewhat heart-shaped. Long flower stalk with small insignificant flowers. Madagascar.
*Alluaudia dumosa* Drake. Large species with elongated stem, tree-like to 20 ft/6 m high. Branches freely. Usually without leaves, but with few solitary fleshy thorns. Flower insignificant, male flower globose, female oblong. Madagascar.
*Alluaudiopsis fiherenensis* H. Humb. & P. Choux. A tall graceful species rarely seen in cultivation. Elongated branches with solitary thorns. Leaves oblong-elliptical, sometimes more ovate, dark green. Inflorescence dichotomous with small flowers. Dioecious. Endemic to Madagascar.
*Alluaudia procera* Drake. The best known of this genus, tree-like species up to 40 ft/12 m or more high. Erect, few branches armed with longish thorns which widen toward the base. Leaves obovate, succulent. New leaves grow horizontally to start with and then vertically. Madagascar.

Other *Alluaudia* species include *A. comosa* and *A. humbertii* which have many characteristics similar to those mentioned, with individual peculiarities.

***Aloe*** (Asphodelaceae) is one of the most prominent genera of African succulents, represented by species of extreme dwarf habit to giant tree-like plants.
*Aloe albiflora* Guill. (syn. *Guillauminia albiflora*.) Small clumping species with compact rosettes. Long narrow leaves, tapering at apex, grey-green with many small white spots, margins with many closely set soft whitish teeth. Inflorescence simple with delicate white flowers, scented. An outstanding species which is native to Fort Dauphin Div., Madagascar.

*Aloe arborescens*

*Aloe arborescens* Mill. Grows to about 13 ft/4 m when in bloom. Leaves in a dense rosette – these to about 2 ft/60 cm long, dark greyish-green, concave toward the base and with sinuate-dentate margins. This spectacular species is one of the best known of the genus.

*Aloe aristata*

*Aloe aristata* Haw. Small grouping species with dense rosette of dark green leaves with scattered white spots. Inflorescence usually branched with lax reddish flowers. A well-known and attractive species from South Africa.
*Aloe cooperi* Bak. Plants usually solitary, but often clumping with grass-like leaves, long, slender, fresh-green with sometimes few spots near base. Leaves usually deciduous. Inflorescence simple, with conical raceme and pinkish and green flowers. Widely distributed in South Africa, Cape

Province to Natal.

*Aloe distans* Haw. A popular, well-known creeping species with many base offsets. Forms fleshy rosette, leaves bluish-green with whitish spots on both surfaces, and usually three teeth near apex on lower surface, margins with yellowish teeth. Inflorescence dichotomously branched, densely flowering with reddish blooms. West Cape Province, South Africa.

*Aloe doei* Lavr. Plants usually solitary. Rosette medium with dull green leaves with occasional white markings, margins with reddish-brown teeth. Inflorescence usually three-branched with conical raceme and flowers, yellow covered with white hairs – a feature of many of the south Arabian species. This is from arid foothills in the Subhaihi country.

*Aloe excelsa*

*Aloe excelsa* Bgr. A dense rosette of soft tapering leaves about 24 in/60 cm long with toothed margins. A tall inflorescence with bright reddish flowers. Zimbabwe.

*Aloe ferox*

*Aloe ferox* Mill. Tall-growing species with stem simple, often to 16½ ft/5 m high. Thick sword-shaped leaves with some-what spiny upper surface and more so on the back, margins with reddish or brown teeth. Single inflorescence with

branches, large reddish-orange flower, dense, cylindrical. Widely distributed throughout South Africa.

*Aloe haemanthifolia* Berg. So named on account of its resemblance to *Haemanthus*. A very rare species, stemless, with wide thick bluish-green leaves, rounded at apex. Grows at high altitudes on steep slopes. Inflorescence simple with red flowers. From high mountains near Franschoek, Cape Province, South Africa.

*Aloe haworthioides* Bak. Small stemless species to about 2 in/ 5 cm wide. Thin tapering leaves form dense rosette, leaves with prominent white markings on upper and lower surfaces and small white marginal spines. One of the most attractive of the genus but with somewhat insignificant orange-red flower from simple inflorescence. Central Madagascar.

*Aloe humilis* (L.) Mill. Small-growing species forming clusters. Rosettes about 2½ in/7 cm wide, leaves glaucous-green, tubercled with irregular white prickles, margins with soft white teeth. Inflorescence simple, scarlet flowers. East Cape Province, South Africa.

*Aloe longistyla* Bak. Stemless compact rosette about 9 in/ 23 cm wide. Leaves glaucous, lanceolate, both surfaces with whitish spines, margins with white teeth. Short inflorescence, simple, dense raceme with pinkish-red flowers. Central and southeastern regions of Cape Province, South Africa.

*Aloe niebuhriana*

*Aloe niebuhriana* Lavr. From the Arabian Peninsula, has a rosette of greyish-green leaves slightly flushed pale purple and a fascinating, unusual inflorescence of 2 ft/60 cm or more in length, bearing a head of pendulous greenish-yellow, sometimes reddish flowers and white-felted.

*Aloe parvula* Berg. Stemless rosette with blackish-green leaves with darkish spots, margins with softish white teeth. Inflorescence simple, lax raceme with reddish flowers. A beautiful species from central Madagascar.

*Aloe penduliflora* Bak. The leaves are pale-green, 12–16 in/ 30–40 cm long in the form of a rosette, pendulous flowers of yellowish-green on a slender inflorescence. Found on the island of Zanzibar.

*Aloe perryi* Bak. A low-growing species from Socotra. The rosette consists of up to 20 rather grooved, bluish-green leaves with horny, triangular teeth along the margins – forming a most attractive plant when in full flower. The inflorescence reaches about 24 in/60 cm high, carrying red flowers with greenish tips.

*Aloe polyphylla*

*Aloe polyphylla* Schoenl. ex Pill. A very rare and unusual species. Short stem forming spirally ascending rosette. Leaves grey-green, back surface with keel, margins with pale teeth. Inflorescence branched with greenish flowers having purplish tip. Lesotho.

*Aloe rauhii* Reyn. Another miniature species with grey-green leaves and numerous H-shaped spots. An open rosette with spreading leaves, margins with minute white teeth. Inflorescence simple with loose cylindrical raceme, flower rose-scarlet. On sandstone rock in southwest region of Madagascar.

*Aloe suzannae* R. Dec. Tall growing species of particular charm with leathery dark greyish-green leaves, slightly roughened, margins with brownish teeth. Inflorescence simple with cylindrical raceme, very elongated, with dense yellowish-rose flowers. As a young plant it is exceptionally attractive. Southwest Madagascar.

*Aloe tenuior* Haw. A 'climbing' species in bushes with branches to 10 ft/3 m long. Thin stems, losing its leaves near the base, and forming loose terminal rosette. Leaves glaucous-green with no markings, margins with white edge and teeth. Raceme cylindrical and tapering toward apex, flowers yellow. Eastern Cape Province, South Africa.

*Aloe variegata* L. Stemless species with many offsets and forming clumps. Leaves in 3 ranks, lanceolate, lower sur-face keeled, dark green with whitish spots and markings, usually in transverse bands. Margins with small white teeth. Inflorescence simple, sometimes branched, loose cylindrical raceme. The 'partridge breasted aloe'. Cape Province, South Africa.

**Aloinopsis** (Mesembryanthemaceae) is a dwarf species, with tuberous roots. Many leaf forms, but with few exceptions all are tuberculate. Includes about 17 species.

*Aloinopsis malherbei* (L. Bol.) L. Bol. Leaves erect, fan-shaped, truncate at tip, upper surface flat and back surface convex, margins and surfaces tuberculate. Flower brownish. Cape Province, South Africa.

*Aloinopsis peersii* (L. Bol.) L. Bol. Thick fleshy roots. Leaves two or four together, upper surface flat, back surface rounded, bluish-green. Flower yellow. Cape Province, South Africa.

*Aloinopsis schooneesii*

*Aloinopsis schooneesii* L.Bol. from the Willowmore Div. of Cape Province has bluish-green leaves, some of which remain subterranean – the tips are rounded triangular and very small. Flowers almost wax-like, yellowish-red.

**Amerosedum** (Crassulaceae) is one of the newly created genera concerned with a number of North American species.

*Amerosedum lanceolatum* (Torrey) Löve & Löve (syn. *Sedum lanceolatum* Torrey). It comes from the Rocky Mountains area and is more or less hardy in the northern hemisphere. Plants branch from the base with shoots about 2½ in/6 cm long bearing small densely set ⅜ in/1 cm long smooth leaves and golden-yellow flowers on 6 in/15 cm long stems.

**Ammocharis** (Amaryllidaceae) are large bulbous plants from tropical and South Africa – includes only five species.

*Ammocharis coranica* (Ker-Gawl.) Herb. Large bulbous species with strap-like leaves, green and spreading. Inflorescence on long flattish stem with umbels of rose-pink flowers. Leaves deciduous. In common with some other bulbous species, the flower precedes the leaves. From many areas of South Africa and Namibia.

*Anacampseros* (PORTULACACEAE) includes over 70 species, mainly from Africa, one Australian.

*Anacampseros alstonii* Schoenl. has a flattened caudex rootstock, leaves set in five straight rows and bearing pure white flowers about 1¼ in/3 cm across. Namibia.

*Anacampseros australiana* J. M. Black has thick tuberous roots, leaves in a rosette, bristly-hairy and bearing pink flowers. Australia.

*Anacampseros filamentosa* (Haw.) Sims has short leafy stems, the leaves covered with whitish threads. Flowers pink, about 1¼ in/3 cm across. Cape Province, South Africa.

*Anacampseros lubbersii* Bleck from Transvaal. A small rhizomatous plant with stems only ⅜ in/1 cm long bearing fleshy reddish leaves in a tight rosette. Flowers white.

*Argyroderma* (MESEMBRYANTHEMACEAE) are stemless plants, caespitose, and rarely have only one growth. Leaves ovate or semi cylindrical, smooth and glabrous. Well over 50 species are recorded, but many of these resemble each other very closely.

*Argyroderma framessi* L. Bol. Caespitose, growths with two leaves, upper surface oval, back surface roundish, smooth, blue-green. Flower pinkish-purple. Cape Province, South Africa.

*Argyroderma roseum* (Haw.) Schwant. Species with 1 or 2 growths. Leaves together at base and united halfway up, upper surface flat, lower surface convex, smooth, blue-green. Flower deep rose. Cape Province, South Africa.

*Beaucarnea* (AGAVACEAE) are caudex-forming, tree-like plants, closely related to *Nolina*. Flowers in a panicle, small, but several to a spike.

*Beaucarnea recurvata*

*Beaucarnea recurvata* (Lem.) Lem. (syn. *Nolina recurvata* Lem.). A tree-like plant from southeast Mexico about 20 ft/6 m high with pronounced globose base. Leaves elongated, thin and tapering and recurved about 3¼ ft/1 m long with smooth edges. Flowers inconspicuous, white.

Others of similar character, *B. bigelovii* Bak. from Sonora and *B. longifolia* Bak. from southern Mexico, are also tree-like species. *B. gracilis* Lem. is a somewhat smaller plant, but still tree-like, with straight leaves about 20 in/50 cm long and ¼ in/6 mm broad, grey with rough edges, endemic to south-central Mexico.

*Begonia* (BEGONIACEAE). Begonia species are to be found in many parts of the tropical and sub-tropical world. Only a few species are generally considered succulent, which again emphasizes the problem of deciding the *exact* definition of a 'succulent'. The species recognized have fleshy stems (others with similar stems or with fleshy [succulent] leaves have thus far been excluded). These include *Begonia caroliniaefolia* Regal (Mexico) with fleshy glossy-green leaflets, quilted with toothed margins; *Begonia conchaefolia* A. Dietr. (Costa Rica) having cupped, peltate and fleshy glossy-green leaves; *Begonia dayii* Ziesenn. (Mexico) succulent leaves with many chocolate-brown markings; *Begonia hidalgensis* L. B. Smith & Schubert (Mexico) with deep green fleshy leaves, somewhat kidney-shaped; *Begonia kenworthyi* Ziesenn. (Mexico) ivy-shaped bluish-grey fleshy leaves and stems.

*Begonia incana* Lindl. A Mexican plant from high altitudes, about 16,500 ft/5,000 m at Tierra Caliente, erect becoming shrubby, with succulent stems and large fleshy shield-shaped leaves covered with whitish scurf. Flowers pinkish-white.

*Begonia venosa* Skan. A large shrub-like plant from Brazil, often to 24 in/60 cm high or more. Stems and leaves covered with a white scurf. Leaves succulent, kidney-shaped. Flowers white.

Other South American species are recorded which merit acceptance as succulent plants. *B. epipsila* Brade, a Brazilian plant with succulent stems and roundish, fleshy bright green leaves, undersurface reddish and covered with whitish felt. Flowers white. *B. subvillosa* Klotsch., a beautiful species from Brazil having soft hairy succulent stems, velvety; ovate leaves, very pale green with toothed margins and large white flowers. *B. vellozoana* Walp. has very succulent leaves in varying colours from green to bronze and vivid whitish veins. Pinkish-white flowers.

*Bergeranthus* (MESEMBRYANTHEMACEAE) are stemless plants forming clusters, leaves semi-cylindrical with keel, smooth. Includes about 12 species.

*Bergeranthus scapiger* (Haw.) N. E. Br. Freely suckering, leaves forming loose rosette, 4½ in/12 cm long, pronounced edges, smooth, dark green. Flower golden-yellow. Cape Province, South Africa.

*Bergeranthus jamesii* L. Bol. More compact and low-growing with thick fleshy leaves, sword-like, upper surface flat, back surface has sharp keel, greenish-blue. Flower yellowish. Cape Province, South Africa.

*Beschorneria* (AGAVACEAE) are rosette plants from Mexico which in habitat quickly form large clumps. Inflorescence more or less paniculate.

*Beschorneria tubiflora* Kunth. Leaves up to 12 in/30 cm long and ¾ in/2 cm broad, roughened on both sides, rosulate, fleshy greenish-grey. Inflorescence 3¼ ft/1 m high with violet-red bracts and reddish-green tubular flowers. *B. bracteata* Jacobi has a very succulent rosette, thin fleshy leaves about 14 in/35 cm long, glaucous-green with rough margins. Inflorescence 6½ ft/2 m high with arching raceme, reddish bracts with yellowish-red flowers. Another species, *B. yuccoides* Hook. f. consists of rosette of about 20 leaves, 20 in/50 cm long and 2 in/5 cm wide, greyish-green, rough on margins and on underside. Inflorescence about 5 ft/1.5 m high, stem coral red and large reddish bracts and bright green flowers.

**Bombax** (BOMBACACEAE) includes only a few succulent species and these principally with thick fleshy stems.
*Bombax ellipticum* H. B. & K. A Mexican tree-succulent recorded from many parts of the north, central and more southerly areas, usually on limestone rocks. Has greenish caudex-like stem with greyish-brown bark and large green deciduous leaves. Flowers have purplish petals surrounding delicate soft pinkish stamens about 2½ in/6 cm long tipped with yellow anthers. Another species, *B. palmeri* Wats. is recorded as having a reddish caudex, but is in all other aspects very similar to *B. ellipticum* – they may be synonymous.
*Bombax malabaricum* DC. Has very spiny trunk of similar structure to *Adansonia*. Large palmate leaves with leaflets and pendulous red flowers in clusters. From many parts of Asia, India and the Far East. This should possibly be included under *Bombax ceiba* L.

**Bowiea** (LILIACEAE) is a bulbous group of succulents usually with very thin or thread-like stems, trailing or climbing. The onion-like bulb which remains exposed on the surface of the soil is a feature of the genus.

*Bowiea volubilis*

*Bowiea volubilis* Harv. ex Hook. Very large bulbs, dividing and developing groups, almost round and light green.

Long thin trailing stems with insignificant thin leaves and small greenish-white flowers. Rampant growing from early spring until late summer, then stems tend to wither and dry back. Endemic to South Africa.

**Brachystelma** (ASCLEPIADACEAE) includes many small growing species with very tuberous roots resembling a caudex. Stems and leaves are deciduous in resting season and plants should then be kept completely dry.
*Brachystelma grossarti* Dtr. Round tuber and branching to 8 in/20 cm long, erect. Leaves elliptical to 1¼ in/30 mm long. Flowers in umbels with longish stalks, and five recurved triangular lobes, yellow or greenish-yellow. Namibia.

*Brachystelma barberiae*

Several other species are now in cultivation and although of recent introduction have become much sought after. *B. foetidum* Schltr., *B. barberiae* Harv. ex Hook. and the even more miniature species, *B. pygmaea* N. E. Br., are of considerable interest.
*Brachystelma modestum* R. A. Dyer. Forming round tuber, generally subterranean and thin branches. Leaves small, oval-elliptical with minute hairs on upper surface. Flower simple or usually in pairs, spreading with five triangular recurved lobes, very dark red. Natal, South Africa.
*Brachystelma stellatum* Bruce & Dyer. Globular tuber, branching from the terminal, short and semi-erect. Leaves rounded about ⅜ in/1 cm long, minutely hairy, margins ciliate. Flowers from leaf axils, on short stalks, inside creamy-white and purple markings, five spreading lobes, yellowish with white hairs, oval triangular. Transvaal, South Africa.

**Brighamia** (LOBELIACEAE) is an Hawaiian genus of four species which have fleshy stems with terminal clusters of leaves and flowers.
*Brighamia insignis* A. Gray. A tall-growing plant to about 3¼ ft/1 m with a fleshy, unbranched stem. A terminal head of pale yellow flowers is surrounded by a rosette of bright green succulent leaves.
*Brighamia rockii* St. John. Attains 13 ft/4 m or more in

height. Flowers are whitish, symmetrical, with the scent of violets. Extremely rare in cultivation.

***Brownanthus*** (Mesembryanthemaceae) is an interesting and unusual genus, rather rare in cultivation. Much-branched, erect, often with nodes along the stems; only about six species are known.
*Brownanthus ciliatus* (Ait.) Schwant. Dwarf species, with many internodes giving the effect of being segmented. Leaves short and narrow. Flowers small, white. Cape Province, South Africa.
*Brownanthus pubescens* (N. E. Br.) Bull. Low-branching plant with spreading stems and internodes, leaves slender, erect, sub-cylindrical covered with small papillae. Flower white. Native to Namibia.

***Bulbine*** (Asphodelaceae) is an interesting genus of fleshy and very succulent plants generally with bright yellow flowers, rarely orange-red. In cultivation some are winter growing and flowering.

*Bulbine frutescens*

*Bulbine frutescens* L. Has thin, cylindrical, soft, grass-green leaves from elongated stems, forming lax clusters. Flower bright yellow, but there are other forms, one with white flowers and another with orange-red flowers described as *B. frutescens* 'Hallmark' Rowl., the origin of which is still undecided. Endemic to East London, Cape Province, South Africa.
*Bulbine lagopus* (Thunbg.) N. E. Br. From Cape Province, South Africa, has a 16 in/40 cm dark-green, almost rounded stem and carries several bright yellow flowers in a spike. The stamens are bearded toward the tip.

*Bulbine latifolia*

*Bulbine latifolia* (L.f) Haw. From southerly parts of Cape Province, has a rosette of soft fleshy leaves. Leaves to 12 in/30 cm long, the margins slightly curled inward. Flowers yellow.
*Bulbine mesembryanthoides* Haw. A real miniature with small caudex. Deciduous in winter. Leaves only ⅝ in/15 mm long, bright green and thickish, almost mimicking some of the stemless mesembryanthemums. Flower on slender stem, golden-yellow. Namaqualand and Cape Province, South Africa.

***Bulbinopsis*** (Asphodelaceae) is an Australian group very similar to the *Bulbine* species of Africa, originally included in *Bulbine*.
*Bulbinopsis bulbosa* (R. Br.) Borzi. Has fleshy basal leaves to about 12 in/30 cm long and a longer raceme of bright yellow flowers, each about ¾ in/2 cm wide with the six staminal filaments bearded yellow.

*Bulbinopsis semibarbata*

*Bulbinopsis semibarbata* Haw. A supposed annual species, but continuity can sometimes be obtained by rooting of cuttings. Loose inflorescence with yellow flowers. Easily grown from seeds. Endemic to Australia.

**Bursera** (Burseraceae) is a part of the 'incense-tree' family which includes a few succulent species, some tree-like, others of comparatively short growth, frequently with an obese stem.

*Bursera microphylla*

*Bursera microphylla* (Rose) A. Gray. Fairly widely distributed from the Colorado Desert to many parts of Sonora, Mexico. Commonly known as the 'elephant-trunk tree'. A tall tree-succulent to 33 ft/10 m high with thickish stem and branches consisting of soft wood with milky sap, thin yellow papery bark which is easily shed. Fernlike leaves which seem to be deciduous.

Other species include *B. fagarioides* with small insignificant heart-shaped leaves and small reddish flowers; *B. hindsiana* (Benth.) Engl., similar to the other species and having reddish papery bark.

**Calandrinia** (Portulacaceae) includes a few succulent species which boast quite attractive and colourful flowers.
*Calandrinia polyandra* (Hook.) Benth. From south and west Australia, has more or less ascending stems to 20 in/50 cm. Tall, fleshy, succulent, spatulate leaves about 1½ in/4 cm long and racemes of pink flowers each about ¾ in/2 cm across.
*Calandrinia spectabilis* Otto & Dietr. Native of Chile. A somewhat shrubby plant with elongated compressed leaves to 1½ in/4 cm long, pruinose. Flowers very beautiful, about 2 in/5 cm diameter, rich purple.

Several other South American species are recorded with similar habit and flower colour including *C. discolor* Schrad. (Chile); *C. ciliata* D.C. (Ecuador) and *C. umbellata* D.C. (Peru).

**Calibanus** (Agavaceae) has only one succulent species. It is an interesting rather than an attractive plant and something of an oddity.

*Calibanus hookeri*

*Calibanus hookeri* Trel. Native of Jaumava in Tamaulipas, Mexico, where it is found in hilly country hardly distinguishable from surrounding grasslands. Caudex generally underground, large globose about 12 in/30 cm diameter with thick corky bark. Branching from crown with many long grass-like leaves about 6 in/15 cm long. Branched inflorescence with numerous inconspicuous pinkish, somewhat purplish flowers.

**Calotropis** (Asclepiadaceae) appears to be monotypic and is found in desert areas of tropical Africa, India and Arabia.

*Calotropis procera*

*Calotropis procera* (Ait.) Ait. f. Desert shrub from the Arabian peninsula, 10 ft/3 m or more in height with large fleshy leaves to 8 in/20 cm long. Flowers of green and pink clustered in a terminal inflorescence. Fruits are large, inflated, obovate and spongy, about 6 in/15 cm diameter!

New species of the Asclepiadaceae are still being found. A choice dwarf plant recently discovered in the Saudi Arabian desert measures only about 3 in/8 cm high and 6 in/15 cm across. It has rounded fleshy leaves of deep-green, beautifully mottled, creamy-white flowers, followed by a typical follicle, and it is still nameless!

*Campanula* (CAMPANULACEAE) contains just one species which can be considered a borderline succulent.

*Campanula vidalii* H. C. Wats. A shrubby species to 10 in/25 cm high, much branched with succulent spatulate toothed leaves. Flowers in racemes, white with yellowish base, bell-shaped. Endemic to the Azores, Madeira.

*Caralluma* (ASCLEPIADACEAE) includes very many species, usually creeping plants, sometimes subterranean 'stolon'-like growths which spread and then appear above ground with erect stems. Very similar to *Stapelia*.

*Caralluma aperta* (Mass.) N. E. Br. Stems to 2½ in/7 cm high, often erect, sometimes prostrate, four-angled, bluntly dentate, greyish-green. Flowers on stalks at base of stems, oblong lobes, somewhat blunted, margins with fine papillae and darkish brown at bottom, yellowish and brownish furrows and many dots above. Namaqualand, and Cape Province, South Africa.

*Caralluma baldratii* White & Sloane. Stems simple or branching often from subterranean growths, four-angled, rather deeply furrowed, greenish-white and many reddish spots, margins toothed. Flowers pale maroon with pinkish-reddish spots and minute hairs, short pronounced lobes lanceolate. Ethiopia to Kenya.

*Caralluma burchardii* N. E. Br. Stems erect with many branches forming cushions, stems to 8 in/20 cm high, four-angled, edges, pronounced teeth, greyish to bluish-green. Flowers small in clusters, corolla glabrous, dark olive-green covered with whitish hairs, giving almost the effect of a greyish-blue flower. The Canary Islands.

*Caralluma dioscoridis*

*Caralluma dioscoridis* Lavr. Has creeping stems which root as they trail and so form clumps. Stems to 4 in/10 cm long, brownish-green, compressed-angular and sinuate-dentate. Flowers are borne on a stem about 1¼ in/3 cm long – generally solitary, occasionally 2 – the fleshy corolla about 2 in/ 5 cm across, creamy-white inside, pale-green outside, the whole covered with minute purplish hairs. Corona pale pink, about ⅓ in/8 mm across. A rare species from the island of Socotra.

*Caralluma dummeri* (N. E. Br.) White & Sloane. Stems somewhat four-angled but rounded with marginal teeth, pale greyish-green and red markings. Flowers several together on stalks about ⅝ in/15 mm long, cup-shaped, lobes spreading and tapering sharply, inside surface with hairs, outside rather smooth, darkish brownish-green. Tanzania and Kenya.

*Caralluma europaea*

*Caralluma europaea* (Guss.) N. E. Br. Erect stems and branches, four-angled with blunt edges slightly dentate, grey-green and many reddish spots. Flowers small in umbels, five ovate lobes, margins minutely ciliate, greenish-yellow, corona dark brown. Mediterranean countries and southern Spain. A well-known species with many varietal forms.

*Caralluma frerei*

*Caralluma frerei* (Dalz.) Rowl. Long known as *Frerea indica* until transferred to *Caralluma*. One of the few species with leaves. Stems somewhat rounded, spreading, rarely branched, olive-green, sometimes becoming pale green. Flowers at ends and along the branches, solitary with short stalk, petals broadly triangular with fine hairs, maroon to brownish. India.

*Caralluma mammillaris* (L.) N. E. Br. Branching from the base forming clusters. Stems stout to 5½ in/14 cm high, fresh green or brownish-green, five- or six-angled with spreading teeth. Flowers in clusters near apex of branches, corolla deeply five-clefted, lobes lanceolate and very narrow, margins recurved. Inside surface deep purple, outer surface whitish and many spots. Cape Province, South Africa.

*Caralluma retrospiciens* (Ehrenbg.) N. E. Br. One of the tallest species of the genus. Stems erect, smooth, four-angled almost horny edges, dentate, irregularly branched, pale greyish or olive-green. Flowers freely from tips of branches in umbels, lobes triangular-ovate, dark brown and very dark red cilia. Ethiopia, Somalia and certain Red Sea islands.

Many other species could be described; all have great visual appeal, and generally speaking are the most easily cultivated of the Stapeliaceae.

**Carpobrotus** (MESEMBRYANTHEMACEAE) is a well-known genus, many species of which are semi-hardy in northern Europe, and completely hardy in southern Europe. Much used for ground cover. Usually two-angled, branches prostrate and very stout leaves, three-angled. About 20 species.

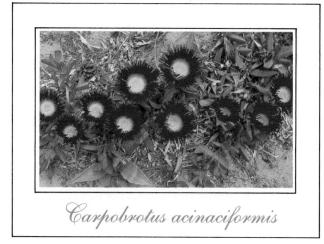

*Carpobrotus acinaciformis*

*Carpobrotus acinaciformis* (L.) L. Bol. 2-angled stems with short branches. Leaves fleshy, thick, sword-shaped, edges slightly rough, pale greyish-green. Flower large, carmine. Cape Province, South Africa.

*Carpobrotus edulis* (L.) N. E. Br. Leaves three-angled on elongated branches, spreading. This species is known as the 'Hottentot fig', the fruits of which are eaten in South Africa. Widely distributed throughout the world as a naturalized plant, flowers large in a number of colours, reddish, yellow, pinkish and purple. Cape Province, South Africa.

**Cavanillesia** (BOMBACACEAE) includes just one succulent species. Closely related to *Bombax*.

*Cavanillesia arborea* Sch. A large tree with very succulent barrel-shaped trunk, widening from the base, and then tapering toward the terminal end. Originates from dry forest areas of eastern Brazil, deciduous; its flowers are produced before the leaves. A rare and interesting plant.

**Cephalophyllum** (MESEMBRYANTHEMACEAE) are mostly prostrate plants, often caespitose, leaves in tufts, mostly elongated and angled and includes over 70 species.

*Cephalophyllum alstonii* Marl. Prostrate species, leaves in tufts, erect, generally sub-cylindrical with somewhat flattened upper surface to about 2½ in/7 cm long, grey-green. Flowers very beautiful, deep red. Cape Province, South Africa.

*Cephalophyllum cupreum* L. Bol. Prostrate creeping species, strong and fleshy. Leaves short, narrow and thick, tapering sharply with obscure keel, pale green. Very large flower, brownish-red and yellow. Cape Province, South Africa.

*Cephalophyllum serrulatum* L. Bol. Prostrate growing. Leaves 2½ in/7 cm long, flat on upper surface, keeled on back surface, becoming rounded, margins serrulate, bright green. Flower small, purplish-pink. Cape Province, South Africa.

**Ceropegia** (ASCLEPIADACEAE) species are extremely varied in flower character, resembling lanterns or parachutes. The majority are climbing or pendent plants, few are shrubby. Many have a very tuberous, caudex-like root system.

*Ceropegia ampliata* E. Mey. Thin-branched species, climbing. Leaves very small, soon falling. Flower very large to 2¼ in/ 6 cm long with a swollen, balloon-like base becoming tubular and purple petals united at the tips, inside of tube almost white with greenish nerves. Mozambique, Natal, South Africa and Namibia.

*Ceropegia devecchii* var. *adelaidae* Bally. A rare species from Kenya. The spreading broad triangular lobes of the corona are about ¼ in/5 mm long and wide, enclosed within the long intermediate lobes which are about 1 in/2.5 cm long.

*Ceropegia dichotoma* Haw. An erect cylindrical stemmed species to 3¼ ft/1 m high, greyish-green, divided into joint-like sections, and from the nodes developing greyish-green leaves during growing season. Flower toward terminal ends of branches, yellow with lobes remaining attached. The Canary Islands.

*Ceropegia elegans* Wall. A trailing species with elongate or oval leaves minutely ciliate, not fleshy. Flowers usually two together, cylindrical, expanding funnel-like, white and purple blotches, lobes remain united in the centre and are edged with dark hairs. India and Sri Lanka.

*Ceropegia fusca* C. Bolle. A very distinctive species somewhat resembling *C. dichotoma* in habit. Stems erect and then spreading to 16 in/40 cm high. Branches cylindrical constricting at joints, greyish or purplish. Leaves small, flowers brown and yellow. The Canary Islands.

*Ceropegia haygarthii* N. E. Br. A climbing, trailing species with strong stem, very succulent. Leaves on stalks, long-cordate. Flowers most attractive about 1½ in/4 cm long, tube curved at base and expanding funnel-like toward the tip, pale pink and purplish spots, the five lobes almost touch in the centre, then unite into a pistil-like stalk topped by red knob with whitish hairs. Endemic to Natal, South Africa.

*Ceropegia juncea*

*Ceropegia juncea* Roxb. A very succulent species from India and Indonesia. A twining, clambering plant with only small leaves, if any. The flower to about 1¼ in/3 cm long with a wide funnel-shaped tip, the lobes set on a somewhat triangular base.

*Ceropegia nilotica*

*Ceropegia nilotica* Kotschy. Species with tuberous roots, climbing and twining branches, four-angled. Leaves ovate, gradually tapering on short stalk, fleshy. Flowers with corolla to 1¼ in/3 cm long, clavate, dark brown – usually two-flowered. Lobes triangular, united at the tips, and brown hairs inside and yellow spots at the base. Ethiopia to Uganda.
*Ceropegia radicans* Schlecht. Succulent climbing species with long stems. Leaves about 1½ in/4 cm long, ovate, dark

green. Flowers solitary from leaf axils, in form tubular, widening toward the tip, where the erect lobes are united at the tips, purple, green and white. Cape Province, South Africa.
*Ceropegia robynsiana* Werderm. Climbing species, robust, fleshy with many nodes along the stems. Glabrous leaves, ovoid becoming pointed at tips. Flower, inflated balloon-like at base, above strongly constricted and expanding to whitish-green funnel with brownish spots and the long lobes, pointed, beak-like. West Africa.
*Ceropegia sandersonii* Decne. One of the most outstanding of the genus. Climbing succulent species having small ovate fresh green leaves. Flowers on short stalks like a parachute, green and mottled darker green corolla to 2½ in/7 cm long, expanding broadly funnel-like. Lobes at first narrow, then much widened and uniting at the sides, margins upturned with whitish hairs. Natal, South Africa.
*Ceropegia stapeliaeformis* Haw. Trailing species having thick stem, somewhat rounded and shortly jointed and many knots, greyish-green with purple mottlings and whitish spots. Flowers upturned and tube becoming funnel-like, widening broadly, lobes spreading, outer surface brownish with whitish spots, inner surface hairy, white. Cape Province, South Africa.
*Ceropegia woodii* Schlecht. Creeping with slender thread-like branches, forming tubers at nodes. Leaves heart-shaped, bluish-green, white marbled, two together. Flowers about 3¼ in/2 cm long, slightly curved, inflated at base, expanded above, lobes united at tip, purple. Natal, South Africa.

**Chamaealoe** (LILIACEAE) is a monotypic genus of consequence, closely related to *Aloe*.
*Chamaealoe africana* (Haw.) Bgr. Small rosette, grouping freely. Long slender pale green leaves with whitish spots on lower surface and margins with soft white teeth. Inflorescence simple, flowers greenish-white. Southern Cape Province, South Africa. This might be found to be inseparable from *Aloe* and consequently reclassified. It would then be transferred to Asphodelaceae.

**Cheiridopsis** (MESEMBRYANTHEMACEAE) species have many forms, from elongated leaf-pairs to small obovate pairs, which dry back during resting period and form a sleeve for the following leaf-pairs. Includes over 90 species.
*Cheiridopsis candidissima* (Haw.) N. E. Br. Much-spreading species forming cushions. Growths with one to two pairs of leaves, boat-shaped, flat upper surface, back surface rounded at lower end, then keeled, silver-grey. Flowers pale pink. Cape Province, South Africa.
*Cheiridopsis meyeri* N. E. Br. Short-stemmed, much-branched miniature species with small obovate leaves, light greyish-green, and numerous dark dots. Upper surface nearly flat, back surface semi-cylindrical, keel toward the apex. Flowers yellowish. Cape Province, South Africa.
*Cheiridopsis peculiaris* N. E. Br. A distinctive species usually with 1 growth and one to two leaf pairs. Lower pair usually prostrate, to 2 in/5 cm long and 1¼ in/3 cm wide, grey-

green. Succeeding growth at first erect with flat upper surface, rounded, keeled on back surface, thick, smooth. Flower yellow. Cape Province, South Africa.
*Cheiridopsis tuberculata* (Mill.) N. E. Br. Stemless with long narrow leaves, united at the base into a sheath or sleeve. Upper surface flat, back surface rounded and keeled toward the blunted tip, bluish-green. Flower yellow. Cape Province, South Africa.

**Chiastophyllum** (CRASSULACEAE) contains just one species of consequence; others within the genus must be omitted.
*Chiastophyllum oppositifolium* (Ledeb.) Bgr. A creeping succulent species very like *Umbilicus*, with roundish, oval leaves, somewhat dentate and narrowing at the base. Flower creamy-yellow. From high altitudes in the Caucasus. Completely hardy.

**Chorisia** (BOMBACACEAE) are spiny-stemmed, semi-forest tree-like plants which bear large attractive flowers. Native of South America and West Indies.

*Chorisia ventricosa*

*Chorisia speciosa* A. St. Hil. A tree-like species, its succulent trunk studded with stout sharp thorns. Leaves on long stalk, digitately compound toothed leaves. Flowers from the leaf axils, pink five-petalled flowers about 4 in/10 cm diameter with long hairs on the underside of the petals. Fruits are pear-shaped with silky floss around the seeds. Known as the 'floss-silk tree'. Native of Brazil. *C. ventricosa* N.M. is a very large tree with bottle-shaped trunk with top branches, all of which are spiny. Called the samuru tree in Argentina from where it originates, growing in dry forest areas. Flowers, pinkish or yellowish, the outside of the petals woolly.
   *Chorisia* species are reported from parts of the West Indies and they may be escapees from South America. In any event, although their existence can be substantiated, descriptive data are available.

**Cissus** (VITACEAE) is a large genus, but only few are truly succulent. In general climbing or clambering plants.

*Cissus cactiformis* Gilg. Climbing species with tendrils. Has large tuberous root, almost caudex and four-angled stems, sharply winged with pronounced constrictions and rough thorny edges, rather wavy. Leaves occasionally at internodes, deciduous. Fruits black. This is very similar to *C. quadrangularis*, and very likely a variety or perhaps synonymous. Savannah country, East Africa.
*Cissus quadrangularis* L. Climbing species with tendrils, stems fleshy, four-angled, constricted at the nodes, almost leafless, but sometimes few leaves at constrictions, three-lobed. Flowers green, followed by reddish-black berries. Tropical Africa, Arabia, South Africa, eastern India.
*Cissus rotundifolia* (Forsk.) Vahl. A climbing species with four-angled stems and somewhat rough, uneven corky edges. Leaves perennial, fleshy, rounded, greyish-green having serrate margins. Flowers very small, greenish, followed by red berries. Coastal regions of Tanzania.
*Cissus tuberosa* Moc. & Sesse ex DC. Native of Puebla, Mexico, where it is found at about 4,900 ft/1,500 m. A peculiar species with round, succulent caudex and vine-like growth of fleshy greyish-green joints producing aerial roots which seem to encourage swelling of stem joints. Leaves fern-like in shape, flowers insignificant.

**Commiphora** (BURSERACEAE) includes a few borderline species which may or may not be succulent; one only is considered a true succulent.
*Commiphora dulcis* Engl. A small tree with thick tuberous caudex, sparsely branched, spreading horizontally. Leaves very small, narrow with insignificant flowers. An interesting plant and a natural bonsai. Quartz rock face in Namib Desert, Namibia and South Africa.

**Conicosia** (MESEMBRYANTHEMACEAE) have many stems and branches, spreading or ascending, often with a caudex-like root. 10 species are recorded.
*Conicosia muirii* N. E. Br. Large fleshy caudex to 16 in/40 cm diameter. Stems prostrate, creeping, leaves long and narrow with a grooved surface, purplish-green. Flowers lemon-yellow. Cape Province, South Africa.
*Conicosia communis* (Edwards) N. E. Br. With fibrous roots developing woody stem with age. Leaves three-angled, long and narrow, and shorter on flowering branches. Flower very beautiful, pure yellow. Cape Province, South Africa.

**Conophyllum** (MESEMBRYANTHEMACEAE) is an interesting group allied to *Mitrophyllum*. Have only a short growing season. First pair of leaves forms the 'cone' and in dormant stage they very much resemble this. 'Cono' means cone-like. Includes about 25 species.
*Conophyllum grande* (N. E. Br.) L. Bol. With opposite two-angled keeled sterile leaves, about 3 in/8 cm long, upper surface flat, back surface rounded with blunted tip, light green. Flower pure shining white. Cape Province, South Africa.
*Conophyllum latibracteatum* L. Bol. Very tall species to nearly 28 in/70 cm high. Leaves about 4 in/10 cm long, narrow,

upper surface somewhat flattened, back surface rounded with blunt apex, deep green. Flower yellow. Cape Province, South Africa.

***Conophytum*** (MESEMBRYANTHEMACEAE) consists of dwarf plants, caespitose with shortened axis and branches. Body shape takes many forms – all consisting, however, of two united leaves. The new bodies are always formed within the old; they take sustenance from the older leaves until only the skin remains; this protects the new growth during resting period. In cultivation rest during spring. Flowers solitary on a short stalk, many colours. Nearly 300 species recorded. For classification purposes the genus has been divided into sub-genera, and again into series and sub-series, but these are not being included here.

*Conophytum bilobum* (Marl.) N. E. Br. Stemless, forming mats. Bodies somewhat heart-shaped, free only at the tips which are blunt and rounded, light green or whitish-green, edges red. Flower red. Cape Province, South Africa.

*Conophytum calculus* var. *calculus* (Bgr.) N. E. Br. An unusual caespitose species, bodies globose, fresh green to grey-green with no markings, often mostly enclosed in the brownish skins of older bodies. Flower yellow with brownish tips. Cape Province, South Africa.

*Conophytum concavum* L. Bol. Caespitose forming mats of several small bodies, rounded with flattish top, soft, minutely hairy, whitish with fissure compressed and hairy. Flower small, white. Cape Province, South Africa.

*Conophytum elishae* (N. E. Br.) N. E. Br. Caespitose forming cushions. Bodies thick, club-like, 2-lobed with many small dots, bluish-green. Flowers yellow. Cape Province, South Africa.

*Conophytum gratum* (N. E. Br.) N. E. Br. Caespitose forming cushions. Bodies somewhat pear-shaped with top slightly convex, fissure ¹⁄₂₅ in/1 mm deep, smooth, bluish-green with many minute greyish dots. Flower deep red. Cape Province, South Africa.

*Conophytum luisae*

*Conophytum luisae* Schwant. Forms loose cushions of more or less heart-shaped bodies consisting of two thick fleshy leaves

united for most of their length and lobed at the tips, and sparsely dotted. Flowers are bright yellow. Cape Province, South Africa.

*Conophytum luteum* N. E. Br. Clustering, forming cushions. Bodies small, somewhat pear-shaped, top flattish or convex with impressed fissure, greenish-grey and many dark green dots on upper surface with fewer on sides. Flower bright yellow. Cape Province, South Africa.

*Conophytum ovigerum* Schwant. Small species forming thick cushions. Bodies ovate and tapering toward the base, top rounded and indented toward the fissure, with dark dots, green. Flowers yellow. Cape Province, South Africa.

***Corallocarpus*** (CUCURBITACEAE) are considered caudiciform succulents, having thick, tuberous roots.

*Corallocarpus tenuissimus* Busc. & Musch. A much-branched, erect plant often with angled stems, very succulent. Leaves palmate into lobes. Slender peduncle having several whitish-yellow flowers. Fruit smooth, fleshy and rounded. From arid areas of South Africa and Zimbabwe.

*Corallocarpus glomeruliflorus* Schweinf. With thick club-shaped caudex branching from apex. Elongated branches, upper branches hairy. Leaves broad and rounded with toothed margins and somewhat undulate. Flowers dioecious – small, yellowish-green. Orange fruits, small, egg-shaped with longitudinal lines. Endemic to the Yemen.

***Coreopsis*** (COMPOSITAE) includes only one succulent plant.

*Coreopsis gigantea* (Kellog) Hall. A fleshy stemmed succulent plant from southern California, erect and stout, surmounted by a thick tuft of feathery leaves and corymbose inflorescence. This species is not difficult to grow and will retain its normal characteristics if rested completely in summer with very little water, and then encouraged to grow in cooler weather.

***Cotyledon*** (CRASSULACEAE) includes many species, shrubby or prostrate, usually compact with thick fleshy leaves and terminal inflorescence with pendent flowers.

*Cotyledon buchholziana* Steph. & Schuldt. Miniature branching species having cylindrical stems and branches, dark grey-green with brownish-red scale leaves; these soon disappear. Growing points spirally arranged, having small linear leaves. Inflorescence about ⅝ in/15 mm long with pinkish-purple flower. A rare species of considerable charm. Namaqualand and Cape Province, South Africa.

*Cotyledon cacalioides* L.f. A short, thick-stemmed, little branching plant. Stems tubercled, somewhat spiral. Leaves cylindrical-acute, greyish-green. Long inflorescence with many yellowish-red flowers. From the Karroo region of Cape Province, South Africa.

*Cotyledon jacobseniana* v. Poelln. A pretty semi-procumbent plant, much branched with brownish skin. Leaves small and thick, oblong, narrowing toward base and apex. Flower scape erect, thin with reddish-green blooms. Endemic to Namaqualand and Cape Province, South Africa.

*Cotyledon ladismithiensis* v. Poelln. Dwarf shrubby plant, freely branching. Leaves at terminal ends, very thick and fleshy, pale fresh green, obovate with dentate apex – the surface covered with minute white hairs. Inflorescence hairy with pendent apricot-yellow flowers. South Africa.

*Cotyledon orbiculata* L. Large thick-stemmed species, usually erect, sometimes procumbent. Leaves obovate covered with a waxy silver-whitish bloom, margins red. Long flower scape with yellowish-red blooms. There are several varieties of the species, with leaves and/or flowers differing. Endemic to Namibia.

*Cotyledon paniculata* L.f. Thick-stemmed tree-like species often to 5 ft/150 cm high. The swollen trunk is covered with thin papery brownish skin. Branches few, fleshy obovate leaves bluntly tapering, pale green with somewhat yellowish margins. Deciduous during resting season. Flowers red with greenish stripes. Karroo region of Cape Province, South Africa.

*Cotyledon papillaris* L.f. Low miniature species, much-branched. Leaves only few, somewhat wedge-shaped, or sub-obtuse, dark green. Margins rounded at base and sharp toward apex. Flowers on long scape, reddish-yellow.

Other varieties are recorded, *C. papillaris* var. *glutinosa* (Schoenl.) v. Poelln. where the flowers have sticky hairs, *C. papillaris* var. *robusta* Schoenl. & Bak. which resembles the species but more robust and *C. papillaris* var. *subundulata* v. Poelln. with leaves wavy toward the tip and reddish-brown. Karroo region of Cape Province, South Africa.

*Cotyledon schaeferana*

*Cotyledon schaeferana* Dtr. From Namibia and parts of Cape Province, South Africa. Stems are very short, rarely exceeding 1½ in/4 cm long, almost forming a small caudex – it branches freely and produces aerial roots. Leaves are glabrous, pale-greenish with distinct red lines. Flowers 1–3, a greenish corolla about ⅜ in/1 cm long with reddish lines and pinkish-lilac lobes.

*Cotyledon teretifolia*

*Cotyledon teretifolia* Thunbg. Grows to about 18 in/45 cm when in full bloom. It is from the Karroo area of Cape Province. Has slender greenish leaves, generally glabrous but sometimes densely white-hairy. The tall inflorescence carries bell-shaped pendent flowers.

*Cotyledon undulata*

*Cotyledon undulata* Haw. One of the most attractive of the genus, shrubby with opposite broad wedge-shaped leaves and distinctive crinkled apex, all stems and leaves covered with silvery-grey pruinose. Flower on long stalk, orange or golden-yellow becoming reddish near the apex. From Cape Province, South Africa.

**Crassula** (CRASSULACEAE) includes many species of considerable interest and variation, their attractiveness being centred more in their vastly differing foliage forms than in the flower, although when in full bloom they provide a most beautiful setting. Many *Crassula* species are non-succulent, others are aquatics, which are omitted here. The genus has been divided and sub-divided for classification purposes and particular references to this classification are not included. Several species of outstanding character are deserving of mention.

*Crassula barbata* Thunbg. Forming clusters of dense rosettes, usually curved inward, dark green, margins with many whitish hairs. Leaves almost rounded with fine point at apex. Flowers white, erect. A monocarpic species, old growth dies after flowering, but new growth develops from the base. From dry deserts of southern Africa.

*Crassula cephalophora* Thunbg. A short branching species forming flattish rosettes, leaves ovate and fleshy, flat upper surface and covered with whitish hairs, margins closely set with white cilia. Flowers yellowish. Well-distributed in Cape Province and Orange Free State, South Africa and Lesotho.

*Crassula cornuta* Schoenl. & Bak. Small species with densely leafed stems, fleshy, leaves keel-shaped, silver-grey. Short inflorescence with small white flowers. Namibia and Cape Province, South Africa.

*Crassula cotyledonis* Thunbg. Comes from Namibia, has oval basal leaves which are fleshy and white-felted. Stem is leafless, 4-angled, and bears white, yellowish or greenish-white flowers.

*Crassula falcata*

*Crassula falcata* Wendl. An attractive plant with thick, fleshy, somewhat flattened, oblong-falcate leaves, grey-green. Flower on fleshy stalk with many beautifully bright crimson or orange-red blooms. One of the best flowering species of the Crassulas. Cape Province to Natal, South Africa.

*Crassula hemisphaerica* Thunbg. Miniature species forming cushions, with round leaves, flat with raised tips, being closely set together and overlapping, giving rosette effect, dark grey-green, and with white ciliate margins. Flower white. Namibia.

*Crassula laticephala* Schoenl. A dwarf species from the Karroo Desert in South Africa. Leaves in 4-series, thick and slightly scurfy. Flowers in rounded heads, pure white.

*Crassula lycopodioides* Lam. A well-known species of many varietal forms, having thin brittle stems, leafed densely the whole length with pointed triangular scaly leaves, bright green. Flowers very minute, white. The species and varieties all originate from Namibia.

*Crassula pyramidalis* Thunbg. An attractive miniature, densely leafed in four rows, leaves being three-cornered, flat, of equal size, close together forming an attractive column. Flowers white, in clusters at apex of column. Namaqualand and Cape Province, South Africa.

*Crassula rupestris* Thunbg. A well-known species from the Karroo in South Africa. A small shrubby plant with woody stems and branches, thick fleshy leaves with reddish margins only about ¼ in/7 mm long. Flowers are small, pale pink or whitish. A plant of easy culture and suited for indoor decor.

*Crassula socialis*

*Crassula socialis* Schoenl. A somewhat tufted, bushy species from Cape Province, South Africa. Leaves are densely arranged in small rosettes about ¼ in/6 mm long and wide, thick, pale green and slightly narrow horny margins. Flowers white.

*Crassula tecta* Thunbg. A small-growing species, somewhat branched and closely set, fleshy semi-circular or boat-shaped leaves, dark green and covered with short but thick white hairs. Flowers white. Namibia and Cape Province, South Africa.

*Crassula tetragona* L. Resembling a miniature pine tree. An erect shrubby plant, few branches, slender and roundish. Leaves spindle-shaped, set closely together. Flower small, white. Eastern Cape Province, South Africa.

**Cucurbita** (CUCURBITACEAE) are mostly clambering plants with annual growth.

*Cucurbita foetidissima* H.B. & K. Has perennial caudex or tap-root with very elongated trailing stems bearing strong-smelling triangular leaves. Flowers are large, yellow like those of marrow. Yellowish fruits about 12 in/30 cm diameter. Known as wild pumpkin in southern states of the USA, where it is native.

*Cussonia* (ARALIACEAE) are evergreen, shrubby trees with caudex-like trunks which store moisture. Branches woody, flowers terminal.

*Cussonia spicata* Thunbg. Very swollen caudex, developing into a sizeable tree. Leaves soft green, digitately lobed, flowers in dense clusters and erect, elongated fruits. Distribution from South Africa to Tanzania.

Other species include *C. thyrsiflora* and *C. holstii*, both African species, and *C. myriacantha*, native of Madagascar.

*Cyanotis* (COMMELINACEAE) are fleshy-rooted plants, mostly of creeping prostrate habit. All native of tropical Africa and Asia.

*Cyanotis lanata*

*Cyanotis lanata* Benth. A densely leafy plant, very succulent and hairy to 2½ in/7 cm long from fleshy stems covered with wool. Flowers in clusters, generally purple or pink. Indigenous to many parts of tropical Africa.

*Cynanchum* (ASCLEPIADACEAE) is a more obscure member of this family, usually of climbing habit, having many thick branches and small flowers.

*Cynanchum marnierianum* Rauh. Low bushy species with many branches, dark green, covered by irregular tubercles and minute hairs. Leaves at internodes, deciduous. Flowers lantern-like, being five petals uniting at the tips, greenish-brown. Madagascar.

*Cynanchum messeri* (Buch.) Junelle & Perr. Climbing species, somewhat branched, woody, cylindrical, with roughened skin, reddish and waxy. Flowers small on short stalk, petals tapering, yellowish with short hairs on upper surface. Madagascar.

*Cynanchum perrieri* Choux. 4-angled branches, erect and leafless. Branches consist of swollen internodes, flowers small, pale greenish-white. Madagascar.

*Cynanchum rossii* Rauh. 4-angled or rounded stems, creeping growth forming dense clumps, dark green and a complete coating of curly hairs. Flowers solitary, having hairy peduncle, petals olive-green with white edges on the upper surface, yellowish-green on the lower, corona papillose, olive-green. Madagascar.

*Cyphostemma* (VITACEAE) are thick, fleshy-stemmed plants of the grape family, some forming almost a caudex-like trunk. All are of African origin.

*Cyphostemma bainesii* (Gilg & Brandt) Desc. With bottle-shaped trunk to 10 in/25 cm thick and 24 in/60 cm high or more, few stout branches, all very fleshy and covered with papery yellowish-green skin which peels readily on matured plants. Leaves green, coarsely serrate. Fruits red. Endemic to Namibia.

*Cyphostemma juttae* (Dtr. & Gilg) Desc. Long, thick and fleshy trunk up to 6½ ft/2 m high, smooth and yellowish-grey paper-like skin which peels with age. Divides into few branches at apex and has coarsely serrated irregular leaves, upper surface waxy green, underside with translucent hairs. Fruits yellow or red. Namibia.

*Cyphostemma seitziana* (Gilg & Brandt) Desc. Very swollen and often misshapen caudex-like stem up to nearly 6½ ft/2 m high. Few branches from near the apex. Trunk and branches with yellowish smooth skin. Leaves fleshy, long-ovate with pronounced serrate margins, grey-green, deciduous. Namibia.

Several other species of *Cyphostemma* are recorded, but in general most have characteristics similar to those mentioned. All are of easy culture but a minimum temperature of 50°F/10°C is advised for success.

*Dactylopsis* (MESEMBRYANTHEMACEAE) consists of only one known species, rare in cultivation.

*Dactylopsis digitata*

*Dactylopsis digitata* (Ait.) N. E. Br. Very succulent plant forming dense mats in habitat where it grows near salt pans. Leaves alternate to about 4½ in/12 cm long, thick, blunt, digitate, unevenly cylindrical, greyish-green. Flower small, white. Cape Province, South Africa. This species flowers during the winter.

**Dasylirion** (AGAVACEAE) consists of a few species from North and Central America which form a stem carrying a rosette of stiff, spiny and long leaves. All are of easy culture.
*Dasylirion longissimum* Lem. Large rosette on stem up to 6½ ft/2 m high with numerous elongated tapering leaves to over 5 ft/1.5 m long and only ¼ in/6 mm wide, upper surface somewhat convex and angled on lower surface. Inflorescence to 6½ ft/2 m high with whitish bell-shaped flowers. All species have much the same habit. *D. glaucophyllum* Hook. with bluish-grey leaves, slightly convex and prominent rib off-centre, margins with small hook-spines in both directions and whitish or greenish-white flowers. *D. acrotrichum* Zucc. with short thick stem topped by dense rosette of 3¼ ft/1 m long leaves and yellow spiny margins, flowers white. The 3 species mentioned are from eastern Mexico.

**Decaryia** (DIDIEREACEAE) are Madagascan plants – one of which is outstanding for its unusual characteristics.
*Decaryia madagascarensis* Choux. A tree with an erect trunk to 26 ft/8 m high. Branches spreading with many thorny twigs, zig-zag, succulent, and leaves rather small, sparse, fleshy, heart-shaped set under a pair of thorns, solitary. Flower small on short inflorescence.

**Delosperma** (MESEMBRYANTHEMACEAE) are generally shrubby plants, often thickly branched, spreading and prostrate forming mats. Of easy culture. Contains well over 100 species some of which are rare in cultivation.
*Delosperma aberdeenense* (L. Bol.) L. Bol. A compact-growing species forming dense clusters. Many branches with small acute leaves rounded on the back surface and flat on the upper surface. Flowers purplish. Cape Province, South Africa.
*Delosperma echinatum* (Ait.) Schwant. Dense bushy plants, with many branches. Leaves ovate-hemispherical covered with bristly papillae. Flowers solitary, yellow or creamy-white. Cape Province, South Africa.

**Dendrosicyos** (CUCURBITACEAE) is a monotypic genus containing a species sometimes referred to as the cucumber tree, on account of the shape of the fruits.
*Dendrosicyos socotrana* Balf. f. Large tree-like species with swollen trunk and white bark. Thin, somewhat pendent spiny branches and thistle-shaped leaves, rather rounded and palmate, dentate margins, papillose both sides. Flowers yellowish and glandular hairy fruits. Socotra. A very rare species.

**Diamorpha** (CRASSULACEAE) is one of several genera closely linked with *Sedum*. Leaves are set alternate along the many slender branches.
*Diamorpha cymosa* (Nutt.) Britt. A sedum-like plant generally accepted as an annual. Fleshy stems to about 4 in/10 cm high branching from the base with small oblong leaves and reddish flowers. North and South Carolina, USA.

**Didierea** (DIDIEREACEAE) are deciduous, thorny plants, often developing, tree-like proportions. Flowers are small, generally borne in cymes.
*Didierea madagascarensis* H. Baill. An erect species to 20–23 ft/6–7 m high. Branches only few with thorns which are sometimes solitary, often dense from leaf cushions and basal tufts of obovate leaves. Flower small, on short stalks from the thorny leaf cushions. A peculiar species of a distinctive genus. Endemic to Madagascar
*Didierea mirabilis* H. Baill. Tree-like to 13 ft/4 m high having very swollen trunk, resembling a caudex, often 24 in/60 cm wide. Erect and many branches spreading horizontally. Has dense leaf cushions, with long, sometimes curved, black thorns, linear leaves and male or female flowers. An extraordinary plant apparently closely related to *D. madagascarensis*. Madagascar.

**Didymaotus** (MESEMBRYANTHEMACEAE) recognizes only one species, rather rare in cultivation.
*Didymaotus lapidiformis* (Marl.) N. E. Br. Stemless and very succulent. Leaves 2 together, thick, about ¾ in/2 cm long 1¼ in/3 cm wide, triangular with rounded apex, upper surface flat, back surface with distinct keel, white-greyish-green. Flowers solitary from either side of the base of the growth, white with pinkish centre. The Karroo, Cape Province, South Africa.

**Dinteranthus** (MESEMBRYANTHEMACEAE) are stemless plants forming mats, stems with 1–3 pairs of leaves which are united at the base, whitish with large yellow flowers. Includes six species.
*Dinteranthus pole-evansii* (N. E. Br.) Schwant. Species with usually one growth. Leaf pairs united for half their length, upper surface flat, back surface rounded with keel, greyish-white, no dots. Flower deep yellow. Cape Province, South Africa.
*Dinteranthus wilmotianus* L. Bol. Usually with one growth and two leaves. Leaves small, upper surface somewhat flat and tapering, back surface rounded with one or two keels, smooth, greyish-pink. Flower golden-yellow. Cape Province, South Africa.

**Dioscorea** (DIOSCOREACEAE) includes a number of caudiciform species of interest to the more advanced collector.
*Dioscorea macrostachya* Benth. Member of the yam family from the forests of Fortin de las Flores, Vera Cruz, Mexico. A roundish, somewhat flattened caudex with long vine-like growth with panicles of yellowish-white flowers. *D. mexicana* Scheidw., reputed to be native of more northerly areas of Mexico, is very similar, but with much stouter stem growths, shining and only very few leaves.

**Diplosoma** (MESEMBRYANTHEMACEAE) consists of only 2 known species. Both are rare, interesting and uncommon in cultivation.
*Diplosoma leopoldtii* L. Bol. With unequal leaves, connate along part of one edge, semi-circular, upper surface somewhat flattened or convex with bluntly rounded angles and

tip, fleshy, smooth, darkish green marked, also transparent dots and lines. Flower purple. Endemic to Cape Province, South Africa.

**Dischidia** (ASCLEPIADACEAE) are closely related to *Hoya* and include some remarkable plants of unusual growth and habit. Most species are true epiphytes.
*Dischidia pectinoides* H. H. W. Pears. Thin trailing stems, rooting freely. Leaves opposite, oval-lanceolate and tapering to the tip, thick, urn-leaves like a mussel with many nerves and an opening at the base into which grows a root. The whole plant is grey-green. Small flowers at leaf axils, purplish-red. The Philippines.

*Dischidia rafflesiana*

*Dischidia platyphylla* H. H. W. Pears. A climbing vine with many thin branches. Leaves opposite, greyish-green, somewhat rounded or kidney-shaped. Flowers small, pitcher-shaped, ⅛ in/4 mm diameter, pale buff. The Philippines.
*Dischidia rafflesiana* Wall. With thin twining stems having opposite leaves starting small and rounded, later becoming large pitcher-like, hollow, fleshy-green outside, purplish inside, often frequented by ants in habitat. Flowers yellowish in umbels. Malaysia and Australia.

There are over 40 species recorded, all having very similar peculiarities; others of particular importance include *D. merillii* Becc. and *D. collyris* Wall.

**Dolichos** (LEGUMINOSAE) is one of the few genera of Leguminosae containing succulent species, usually in the form of a large caudex.
*Dolichos seineri* Harms. A plant almost unknown in cultivation. Has very large caudex, very fleshy. Stems form a bushy habit to about 3¼ ft/1 m high. Leaves in triplets, minutely hairy, soft. Flowers in racemes, very beautiful, bluish, like butterflies. Widely distributed in Namibia and south Angola.

**Dorotheanthus** (MESEMBRYANTHEMACEAE) are annuals, beautiful flowers of easy culture. Includes 11 species and a few varieties.

*Dorotheanthus bellidiformis*

*Dorotheanthus bellidiformis* (Burm.) N. E. Br. Small-growing species branching from the base with leaves usually basal, long, narrow, papillose, fleshy. Flowers on stalks, many colours – white, pink, red, orange, etc. Cape Province, South Africa.

**Dorstenia** (MORACEAE) is a genus that embraces a number of curious plants, not all of which are succulents. The true succulents are of great interest, and the flowers, although far from beautiful, are most fascinating.
*Dorstenia crispa* Engl. Cylindrical stem to over 12 in/30 cm high, swollen at base, dark green or blackish-green, glossy, with numerous papillose leaf bases. Branching from apex, leaves at terminal ends, oblong, with margins slightly dentate and curled. Inflorescence on longish stalk, 'heads' oval with 8 or 10 spreading bracts. Kenya.
*Dorstenia hildebrandtii* Engl. A species with compact fleshy caudex, sub-globose and succulent stem and few branches, olive-green. Leaves, elongated with undulate margins somewhat fleshy. Inflorescence solitary from leaf axils, 'heads' ovate ⅛ in/4 mm, set within eight bracts, ⅛ in/4 mm long and several smaller bracts. Endemic to Kenya.
*Dorstenia gigas* Schweinf. Thick fleshy stem, cylindrical, narrowing toward the apex to about 6½ ft/2 m high. Short smooth branches develop toward the top with leaves only at the ends. Leaves in whorls, oblanceolate, dark green on upper surface, lower surface slightly pubescent. Flower yellowish-green. Found on rock faces in Socotra. A rare and desirable species.
*Dorstenia gypsophila* Lavr. A recent discovery. about 4 ft/ 120 cm high. Stem somewhat thickened with greyish-white bark. Numerous branches, leaves in rosettes at terminal ends. Leaves ovate, cordate or cuneate, pubescent with margins undulate and dentate. Flower, heads small with seven to eight bracts to ½ in/8 mm long. Somalia.
Other species of *Dorstenia* are recorded, *D. foetida* (Forst.)

Lam. is closely related to *D. gypsophila* and originates from Kenya.

**Dracophilus** (MESEMBRYANTHEMACEAE) includes four species, all with fleshy leaves, forming cushions. Allied to the genus *Juttadinteria*.
*Dracophilus montis-draconis* (Dtr.) Dtr. Growths with two or three pairs of leaves, united at the base. Leaves three-angled with blunted edges and top about 1½ in/4 cm long. Surface slightly rough, bluish-green. Flowers solitary, white, sometimes pinkish. Namibia.

**Drimia** (HYACINTHACEAE) Jacq. have dense fleshy leaves from the base, forming a somewhat scaly bulb.
*Drimia haworthioides* Bak. Species with elongated succulent leaves from the base about ¾ in/2 cm long and ¹⁄₁₀ in/2 mm thick, dark green on upper surface, purplish grey on back surface. Leaves deciduous in resting period. Flowers from long stem, greenish-yellow or greenish-white. Endemic to South Africa.
*Drimia media* Jacq. ex Willd. From Cape Province, South Africa, a large bulbous species from which arise stiff semi-cylindrical leaves 4–10 in/10–25 cm long. Flowers borne on a long stem, several loosely arranged, brownish externally and silvery-white on the inner surface.

**Drosanthemum** (MESEMBRYANTHEMACEAE) includes over 100 species of shrubby plants, mostly prostrate, occasionally erect, leaves covered with small papillae resembling the genus *Drosera*, the sun-dew. Of easy culture and free-flowering.
*Drosanthemum dejagerae* L. Bol. An erect species to 6 in/15 cm high, many branches, younger ones with papillose hairs. Leaves small, thick, flat on the upper surface, somewhat keeled – wider at apex and papillose. Flowers purple. Cape Province, South Africa.
*Drosanthemum floribundum* (Haw.) Schwant. Cushion-forming species, creeping and branching. Leaves cylindrical and thicker toward the apex, light green. Flowers pale pink. Cape Province, South Africa.

**Dudleya** (CRASSULACEAE) is a genus consisting of about 40 species, divided into three sub-genera, *Stylophyllum, Dudleya, Hasseanthus*. All have rosette growth with persistent dried leaves at the base. Floral stems annual with sessile leaves.
*Dudleya attenuata* subsp. *orcuttii* (Rose) Moran. From Baja California with fleshy rounded green leaves covered with thick white pruinose. Flowers white, blushed pink.
*Dudleya densiflora* (Rose) Moran. A beautiful plant from San Gabriel Canyon, Los Angeles, California, with bright bluish-white farinose leaves forming rosettes of about 40 leaves on stems. Leaves almost round about 4 in/10 cm long. Flowers pinkish-white.
*Dudleya edulis* (Nutt.) Moran. The type species of the sub-genus *Stylophyllum*. Native of California and Baja California. Each rosette has 10–12 linear cylindric leaves, erect, bluish-green. Flowers white.

*Dudleya farinosa* (Lindl.) Br. & R. From coastal areas of California. Beautiful rosette about 4 in/10 cm diameter on stems often elongated, branching. Leaves green and farinose, sharp pointed and pale yellow flowers.

*Dudleya traskiae*

*Dudleya traskiae* (Rose) Moran. A Californian species, it has short, branching stems and a rosette comprising 25–30 oblong, pointed leaves – each leaf 1½–6 in/4–15 cm long and quite thick. Inflorescence up to 12 in/30 cm tall, branched, bearing yellow flowers.
*Dudleya variegata* (S. Wats.) Moran. From the area around San Diego, southern California, and Baja California. Type species of the sub-genus *Hasseanthus*. With a corm-like root-stock, typical of this sub-genus. Spatulate leaves about 2½ in/7 cm long and to nearly ⅛ in/4 mm thick forming loose rosette. Floral stem about 8 in/20 cm high with yellow flowers.
The genus comprises some of the most attractive succulents of North America. They are generally easy in cultivation, but great care is required when watering as a heavy drenching can remove much of the white farinose from the leaves.

**Duvalia** (ASCLEPIADACEAE) includes a number of species which are closely allied to *Stapelia*. Usually with prostrate stems, short and often thick or rounded, and frequently very pronounced corolla and annulus, with long flower stems.
*Duvalia caespitosa* (Mass.) Haw. Branching from the base. Stems to 1½ in/4 cm long somewhat rounded, four-angled. Flower from the middle or base of young growth, corolla greenish and brown, glossy, fleshy raised annulus, with minute hairs. Lobes spreading horizontally, edges folded back, ciliate toward the middle. Karroo, Cape Province, South Africa.

*Duvalia maculata.*

*Duvalia maculata* N. E. Br. Stems prostrate, forming clumps, angled with blunt edges and long teeth, darkish green. Flower from centre of new growth, corolla and lobes brownish-red, corolla ¾ in/20 mm, lobes ⅜ in/10 mm and folded right back, fleshy, and minute hairs. Annulus ⅜ in/ 10 mm, white with red spots. South Africa and Namibia.

*Duvalia polita* N. E. Br. An attractive plant with prostrate stems, darkish-green, six-angled, rather rounded, teeth having inclined tips and grooves over the teeth. Flowers from centre of growths, corolla with pale hairy ring in the middle, lobes broadly triangular, brownish-red, smooth. Namibia.

**Dyckia** (BROMELIACEAE) is a large genus of terrestrial bromeliads, many of which are considered borderline succulents.

*Dyckia sulphurea* C. Koch. A spreading rosette about 12 in/ 30 cm diameter, leaves about 8 in/20 cm long, dark green with silvery lines on the undersurface. Flower on long scape, sulphur-yellow, endemic to Brazil. *D. brevifolia* Bak. with rosette very similar to *D. sulphurea*, undersurface of leaves with whitish scales. Flowers yellow, somewhat tubular in shape and borne on long scape with recurved bracts. Also from Brazil. *D. altissima* Ldl. from northern Argentina and south Brazil has rosette of pale green leaves about 10 in/ 25 cm long with margins armed with prominent brown spines. Inflorescence rather horny, branched with bright yellow flowers.

Many other species have similar characteristics, some are especially outstanding such as *D. fosteriana* L. B. Smith, native of Brazil, an ornamental plant, small silvery-purple rosette with silvery marginal spines, bearing bright orange flowers. *D. chloristaminea* Mez. is unique inasmuch as it branches freely with very slender rosettes, almost grass-like leaves, rosettes stemless, offsetting from a common base. Endemic to Brazil. *D. remotiflora* Otto & Dietr. (syn. *D. rariflora* sensu Graham and sensu Lindl.) A well-distributed species in Uruguay, south Brazil and Argentina, rosette with leaves about 8 in/20 cm long, strongly recurved, margins with 1¼ in/3 cm long sharp spines. Inflorescence very

tall, mealy-white with deep orange-yellow flowers. *D. rariflora* Schult., a Brazilian plant not to be confused with *D. remotiflora*, is a rather small rosette with hard recurved leaves, green covered with greyish scales, margins with soft blackish spines. Tall inflorescence with only a few orange flowers. Many other plants are recognized including some newer discoveries, *D. hebdingii* L. B. Smith from Rio Grande do Sul, Brazil, with yellow flowers, and *D. marnierilapostollei* Mez., a Brazilian species of particular charm.

*Echeveria* (CRASSULACEAE) comprises one of the largest genera of North American succulent species, widely distributed throughout Mexico and Central America, with one species in Texas. Freely branched plants, rapidly forming clusters of varying shaped rosettes of fleshy leaves with smooth margins and generally with small pronounced tips. Inflorescence with several bracts and bell-shaped flowers on stalks.

*Echeveria agavoides* Lem. A fleshy rosette with rigid triangular-shaped pointed leaves, apple-green or greyish-green, margins sometimes reddish. Flower stalks 20 in/ 50 cm high with reddish flowers tipped yellow. Sometimes known as *Urbinia agavoides* Rose from San Luis Potosi, Mexico.

*Echeveria bracteolata* Lk., Klotzsch & Otto, from Venezuela. A plant very similar to *E. gibbiflora* DC. but having leaves alternate and horizontally spreading rather than rosulate. Very fleshy leaves, keeled on underside, pruinose. Flowers yellowish-red. Other South American species include *E. quitensis* (H. B. & K.) Lindl. from Ecuador, Colombia and Bolivia; *E. eurychlamys* (Diels.) Bgr., and *E. excelsa* (Diels.) Bgr., both native of Peru.

*Echeveria calycosa* Moran. From south of Uruapan, Michoacan, Mexico, with light green, spatulate, rounded leaves forming rather flat loose rosette of up to 25 leaves to about 4 in/10 cm diameter or slightly more. Tall floral stem about 8 in/20 cm long, flowers yellowish.

*Echeveria ciliata* Moran. A beautiful species from over 6,500 ft/2,000 m elevation at Canada Vetutla, Oaxaca, Mexico. Smooth glabrous leaves with very pronounced ciliate margins giving the effect of a continual feather-edge. A striking dense rosette having a silky appearance with floral stem to about 4½ in/12 cm long and reddish flowers.

*Echeveria columbiana* v. Poelln. From an altitude of over 9,900 ft/3,000 m near Vetas, Colombia. Branching with fleshy stems, rosettes at terminals, somewhat dense, wedge-shaped leaves with blunt tips, tapering, about 1¼ in/3 cm long. Long flower scape with yellow flowers. *E. ballsii* E. Walth. with short stems and thick, oblong-obovate leaves, bright green, tall inflorescence, often 2 to each rosette, yellow flowers, endemic to Colombia.

*Echeveria crenulata* Rose. Large rosette on short thickish stem, rosette of broad obovate leaves, grey pruinose, with reddish undulate margins to 12 in/30 cm long. Flower stem up to 40 in/100 cm long with yellowish-red flowers. Native of Mexico, near Cuernavaca, Morelos.

*Echeveria derenbergii* J. A. Purp. A popular and well-known species from southwest of Sierra de Mixteca, Oaxaca, Mexico. Small globular-shaped rosettes in clusters with many thick silvery bluey-grey-green leaves tipped red. Flowers on short stems, golden-yellow or reddish-yellow.

*Echeveria gibbiflora* De Cand. From south of Mexico City, a tall growing plant with long glabrous stem sometimes branched, topped with large rosettes of spoon-shaped greyish-blue leaves, tinted pink with reddish margins. Flower stem to 2 ft/60 cm long with reddish-yellow flowers. There are varieties of this well-known species: *E. gibbiflora* var. *metallica* (Lem.) Bak. with rounded leaves, bronze-coloured and intensely pruinose; *E. gibbiflora* var. *crispata* Bak. is similar to species but with wavy margins. One of the most outstanding forms is *E. gibbiflora* var. *carunculata* having blister-like warty protuberances on the upper surface.

*Echeveria globulosa* Moran. Probably from an altitude of 9,900 ft/3,000 m or more near Carrizal, Tlacolula, Oaxaca, Mexico. Compact rosette on short thick stem, clustering freely. Rosettes globose, somewhat depressed having up to 60 leaves bluish-green, spoon-shaped, ¾ in/2 cm or more long and ⅛ in/4 mm wide with reddish margins. Floral stems to 3 in/8 cm long, reddish, flowers yellow.

*Echeveria multicaulis*

*Echeveria multicaulis* Rose. Has a fairly dense rosette of dark green leaves with red margins – the leaves to 1¼ in/3 cm long. A tall inflorescence with many reddish flowers which are yellow on the inner surface. It is native of Guerrero, Mexico.

*Echeveria pilosa* J.A. Purp. Has a short stem which is reddish-felted, thick, pointed leaves in a loose rosette, densely and minutely white hairy. The flowers on a spike to 12 in/30 cm long – several to a stem – pale orange-red. From Mexico.

*Echeveria procera* Moran. A tall-growing species from La Muralla, Cerro Yucunino, Oaxaca, Mexico, at over 9,900 ft/3,000 m elevation. Stems to nearly 6½ ft/2 m tall, and to 1 in/3 cm thick! Rosettes at terminal ends about 10 in/25 cm diameter consisting of up to 30 leaves. Leaves oblong-obovate rounded at tips, to 4 in/10 cm long and ⅜ in/1 cm thick. Floral stem to over 3¼ ft/1 m tall, with up to 50 flowers to an inflorescence, flowers yellow.

*Echeveria pulidonis*

*Echeveria pulidonis* E. Walth. A yellow-flowering species from Hidalgo, Mexico. Leaves are in the form of rosettes which quickly offset. Leaves pale bluish-green with brownish edges.

*Echeveria rosea* (Bak.) Lindl. Apparently the only true *Echeveria* epiphyte. Frequents forest trees in eastern and central Mexico. Has very closely set spike of pinkish-red flowers borne from the centre of the rather loose rosette of slender lanceolate, greyish-green leaves.

This genus has been the subject of much research by prominent botanists and field collectors. The names of Reid Moran, Eric Walther and Tom McDougall number among those who originally contributed so much to the knowledge of these plants.

**Echidnopsis** (ASCLEPIADACEAE) is a group of rambling and misshapen plants, very irregular in their method of growth. Stems usually elongated with shorter branches, many angled and tubercled. Flowers very small.

*Echidnopsis cereiformis* Hook. f. Stem usually erect, rarely prostrate, spreading and forming large clusters. Branches and stems having many ribs with blunt, tubercled angles, darkish-green or brownish-green, tuberculate. Flowers very small, usually three or four, brown. Tropical Africa.

*Echidnopsis dammaniana* Spreng. Found in Ethiopia and Somalia. It has stems to about 8 in/29 cm long, very angular, bearing 2–5 flowers together on each stem. These are basically yellow with purplish-brown markings.

**Edithcolea** (ASCLEPIADACEAE) is closely allied to *Caralluma* but with particularly large flowers. A rare species in cultivation which seems to have difficulty surviving in most European climates.

*Edithcolea grandis*

*Edithcolea grandis* N. E. Br. Bushy plant up to 12 in/30 cm high. Stems somewhat erect, five-angled with many hard thorn-like teeth, greyish-green. Branches irregular, leafless. Flowers especially showy, solitary at branch tips on short stalk, circular in the centre with five triangular-ovate lobes 2 in/5 cm long joined together halfway to centre, yellow and numerous red or brown spots. Throat tuberculate round the deep tube with purple hairs. Kenya, Ethiopia and Somalia.

Another species is recorded from Socotra, *E. sordida* N. E. Br., which has similar characteristics except the flower colour, which is deep purple.

**Erepsia** (MESEMBRYANTHEMACEAE) are shrubby plants with fleshy, later woody two-angled stems. Leaves three-angled, with broad sides and prominent keel. Includes 36 species.
*Erepsia apera* L. Bol. Prostrate species forming compact shrub, elongated branches with internodes. Leaves falcate with sharp keel, sides flattened or convex and few dots. Flowers solitary, small, pink. Cape Province, South Africa.
*Erepsia gracilis* (Haw.) L. Bol. A tall erect plant to 2 ft/60 cm high, branches slender, reddish becoming grey. Leaves three-angled with short shoots at the axils, ¾ in/2 cm long, slightly incurved, narrowing toward the apex, recurving and producing a hook-like tip, fresh green with transparent dots. Flowers purple-rose. Cape Province, South Africa.

**Espeletia** (COMPOSITAE) are all native of South America. All are tall-growing, rare in cultivation.
*Espeletia grandiflora* Humb. & Bonpl. A short tree-like succulent to about 3¼ ft/1 m tall with short stem covered by old dried leaves and surmounted by a tuft of long leaves covered with numerous whitish hairs. An unusual plant rarely cultivated having insignificant flowers. Native of Colombia to Venezuela. Other species include *E. killipii* Cuatr. also from Venezuela, which is very similar but has a very erect rosette of leaves above the dried leaves.

**Euphorbia** (EUPHORBIACEAE) are very widely distributed – 'Spurges' are to be found the world over! Many diverse and unusual forms abound within the succulent species, all possessing the complicated flower structure typical of the *Euphorbia*, known as the cyanthium. While some species are bisexual, others are either male or female, and plants of both sexes are required to produce seeds. The fruit develops as a woody capsule containing three seeds, which when ripe are ejected with force. All species have milky sap; in some instances this can be exceedingly poisonous. Therefore great care must always be exercised in the handling of plants to ensure that the sap does not get into the eyes or open wounds. Other species are entirely harmless.

The genus has been divided into groups or sections for convenient classification, the main consideration being the peculiarities of the plant growth, not the flower. Extreme characteristics can be observed, from thorny bushes to giant columns resembling some cactus species, pencil-shaped stems to completely globular plants. Many species are armed with strong thorns, others are totally thornless.
*Euphorbia abdelkuri* Balf. f. A very rare species with dark grey-green stems and many branches. These are generally cylindrical with no thorns and possibly leafless. Young plants tend to develop with rather different growth, with wrinkled grey-green stems somewhat ribbed with pronounced angles and marginal protuberances. Abd al Kuri, Socotra.
*Euphorbia aeruginosa* Schweick. Branches bluish-grey or brownish-green with many brownish spines. Rounded stems, somewhat spirally twisted. A rare species from Transvaal, South Africa.
*Euphorbia bupleurifolia* Jacq. Usually with simple caudex, sometimes branching from the base with terminal leaves. Generally deciduous. Inflorescence on long stalk with greenish-yellow flowers. Cape Province and Natal, South Africa.
*Euphorbia cap-saintemariensis* Rauh. A dwarf species growing from a large tuberous root system. Branches freely from the crown of the tuber, nearly ⅜ in/1 cm thick, rounded or slightly angled and with scars from deciduous leaves, greyish-white. Leaves from the terminal forming a rosette – narrow, undulate and curved inward along the margins. Inflorescences bear two to four cyathia. From limestone rock at Cap Sainte Marie, Madagascar.
*Euphorbia cerifera* Alc. A tall cylindrical stemmed species from Sonora, Mexico, becoming shrubby with many erect waxy greyish branches and small reddish leaves soon deciduous. Flowers several together yellowish-white.
*Euphorbia cotinifolia* L. A West Indian tree-like species with long succulent stem to 20 ft/6 m high having soft flexible branches and broad ovate, coppery-brown thin fleshy leaves. Not often encountered in cultivation.
*Euphorbia crispa* (Haw.) Sweet. A rare perennial species with caudex root system, branching from the base. Leaves on long stalks, narrow, tapering, minutely haired. Margins undulate. A rare species from Van Rhynsdorp and Calvinia Div., Cape Province, South Africa.

*Euphorbia decidua*

*Euphorbia decidua* Bally & Leach. An unusual species with top-shaped caudex branching from the apex. Branches short, usually three-angled and very spiny. Deciduous. Little known in cultivation, but of easy culture and attractively miniature. Endemic to Zimbabwe and possibly Malawi.
*Euphorbia delphinensis* Ursch & Leandri. A thorny shrub, much-branched, ovate leaves with pronounced veins and undulated margins. An easily cultivated species with green flowers. Fort Dauphin, Madagascar.
*Euphorbia francoisi* J. Leandri. A low species with large tuberous root. Stems from the base, cylindrical with small spines. Leaves at terminal ends, undulate, tapering. Fort Dauphin, Madagascar.
*Euphorbia genoudiana* Ursch & Leandri. An interesting thorny bush with cylindrical stem and branching freely. Leaves pale green, small and elongated, usually in groups. Inflorescence with long peduncle with greenish-yellow cyathia. Mahafaly, Madagascar.

*Euphorbia grandicornis*

*Euphorbia grandicornis* Goebel. An outstanding species, large-growing with spiny three-angled stems, wing-like, with deep constrictions forming 'waists'. Angles curved and wavy with hard marginal edge. Stout spines, usually in

pairs. A spectacular plant. Natal, South Africa.
*Euphorbia lophogona* Lam. Shrubby species with many terminal leaves. Stem and branches tend to thicken toward the apex, very angled with attractive pink flowers. Fort Dauphin, Madagascar.

*Euphorbia milii*

*Euphorbia milii* de Moulin (syn. *Euphorbia splendens*). One of the best-known of the *Euphorbias*, sometimes called 'crown of thorns' and used as a houseplant. Shrubby plant, very spiny and leafy, with red flowers in profusion. Of easy culture. West and southwest Madagascar. There are other forms and varieties of this species with slightly varying growth and different coloured flowers.
*Euphorbia obesa* Hook. f. A popular and well-known species, spherical in shape with broad ribs creating shallow furrows. Beautifully marked with many reddish-brown and dark green lines running transverse and longitudinally – almost plaid-like. Plants dioecious. Graaff Reinet Div., Cape Province, South Africa.
*Euphorbia oncoclada* Drake. A totally spineless species, erect cylindrical stems, frequently divided into small joints or constrictions. Stems covered with leaf scars slightly indented. Small leaves, quickly deciduous. An uncommon species from Ejeda and Saint Augustin, Madagascar.
*Euphorbia opuntioides* N. E. Br. Resembling an *Opuntia*. Branches from the base with fleshy flattened and somewhat elongated joints with slightly crenate margins and a few insignificant slender spines. Pungo Andongo, near Candumba, Lower Guinea. Very rare in cultivation.
*Euphorbia pachypodioides* Boit. Resembling a *Pachypodium*, erect with fleshy club-shaped stems and terminal leaves and inflorescence with deep red flowers. Little known in cultivation, lime hills in Ankarana, West Madagascar.
*Euphorbia parvicyathophora* Rauh. A dwarf species from Madagascar only 4–6 in/10–15 cm tall. It has the smallest cyathia of all known species of this vast genus.
*Euphorbia phosphorea* Mart. One of the few South American species. An erect, somewhat stick-like plant with angled stems, jointed with very small terminal leaves. A species from Bahia, Brazil, which is said to shed phosphorescent

light due to a bacteria which is associated with this plant. Others include *E. caracasana sanguinea* Boiss., a bush-like plant native to Venezuela through to Peru having succulent stems with reddish branches and fleshy deep red oval leaves, becoming bluish-green in maturity with red veins and midrib. *E. sipolisii* N. E. Br., somewhat similar to the *E. phosphorea*. From the Minas Gerais, Brazil, an erect pencil-shaped stemmed plant, four-angled, jointed with small, soon deciduous leaves. Stems are dull green, the angles give the effect of blunted 'ribs'. Flowers red-maroon. *E. weber-bauri* Mansf., native of Cajamarca, Peru, is also of similar character to *E. sipolisii* and *E. phosphorea*. *E. neutra* Bgr. is a very large species endemic to Brazil. A succulent columnar plant, five- to six-angled, and constricted into longish joints set with pairs of short stout horny spines.

*Euphorbia poissoni* Pax. A branching species, very succulent with cylindrical stems and branches, 1¼–2 in/3–5 cm thick, somewhat tubercled, without thorns and greyish-green. Leaves at apex of branches, long and narrow. An unusual and rare species from the area of Jose, northern Nigeria and other West African countries.

*Euphorbia pteroneura* Bgr. A Mexican species with pencil-like stems, usually five- or six-angled, consisting of jointed sections between the leaf-bases. Leaves ovate-lanceolate, deciduous.

*Euphorbia fusca*

shrubby plant with thick stems and branches and very thorny and 5-angled. Native of Madagascar. *E. fusca* Marl. from Namibia and the Karroo Desert has a thick caudex and grows to about 12 in/30 cm tall. The branches are produced in a dense circle, spreading symmetrically to form a round compact plant. There is also a very pleasing cristate form sometimes seen. *E. multiceps* Bgr. from Cape Province, South Africa, has a large cone-like caudex from which arise numerous branches forming almost a dense 'mound' the branches covered with spirally-arranged tu-

*Euphorbia misera*

Other Mexican species include *E. misera* Benth., a miniature tree-like plant from Baja California with small heart-shaped leaves which are deciduous.

*Euphorbia rubella* Pax. One of the most dwarf plants of the genus, it comes from Somalia and Kenya and is only about 2 in/5 cm high with a subterranean caudex, only the tip of which protrudes above ground. Leaves appear as a small rosette at ground level. Cyathium rose-pink and white. *E. alcicornis* Svent., which is confused with *E. ramipressa* L. Croiz. and is possibly best referred to under that title, is a

*Euphorbia flanaganii*

bercles, each about ¼ in/4 mm long. *E. flanaganii* N.E.Br. is a well-known species from Cape Province – it has a caudex which protrudes above ground level and has many branches in rows symmetrically arranged to form a crown. It has small leaves about ¼ in/6 mm long which quickly fall.

*Euphorbia squarrosa* Haw. A low and very spiny succulent species with caudex. Has many spreading and procumbent stems, usually three-angled, dark green – frequently twisted, with greyish spines from the tubercles along margins. Kingwilliamstown Div., Cape Province, South Africa.

*Euphorbia trigona* Haw. An attractive tree-like erect plant, three- or four-angled, wing-like, dark green with white mottling. Margins with spines. Branches freely from the main stem. Namibia.

*Euphorbia turbiniformis* Chiov. One of the most unique species, a miniature with a top-shaped root and flat-rounded stem about 1½ in/4 cm diameter. Has central growing point with very small cyathium on short peduncles. Not easy in cultivation. Migiurtinia Province of Somalia.

*Euphorbia unispina* N. E. Br. Somewhat similar in many respects to *E. poissoni*, with cylindrical stems and branching freely, with a few thick leathery leaves crenate and notched at the apex, spreading at branch terminals. Stems with solitary spines. Generally distributed in West Africa, northern Nigeria and Zaire.

*Euphorbia xylophylloides* Ad. Brogn. ex Lem. An arborescent species with roundish stem, branching with compressed, almost flattened erect branches and joints, rounded at the apex. Small leaves develop but are quickly deciduous. Endemic to Madagascar.

**Faucaria** (MESEMBRYANTHEMACEAE) are mostly compact, fleshy plants and leaves furnished with marginal teeth. Flowers quite large, yellow, rarely white. Plants of good appearance and easy culture. Includes about 30 species.

*Faucaria candida* L. Bol. Leaves tapering, rounded in the upper part and more bluntly square in the lower. Back surface with keel, distinctly white and whitish lines on the lower surface, tip somewhat blunted. Margins with white teeth densely crowded. Flower white. Cape Province, South Africa.

*Faucaria felina* (Haw.) Schwant. Leaves rhomboidal, somewhat elongated, tapering gradually, keeled with whitish-grey dots and margins with curved pink teeth. Flowers yellow to orange. Cape Province, South Africa.

*Faucaria tigrina*

*Faucaria tigrina* (Haw.) Schwant. A very popular species

often called 'Tiger's Jaws'. Leaves about 2 in/5 cm long, rhomboidal-ovate, upper surface flat, undersurface rounded, tapering and keeled toward the apex, the tip forming a little 'chin', greyish-green with many white dots. Margins furnished with pronounced teeth, recurved and tapering to points. Flower golden-yellow. Cape Province, South Africa.

**Fenestraria** (MESEMBRYANTHEMACEAE) includes only two species with windows at the tips of the leaves. In habitat most of the leaves are buried.

*Fenestraria aurantiaca*

*Fenestraria aurantiaca* N. E. Br. Caespitose forming cushions. Leaves somewhat clavate, upper side slightly flat, back surface rounded and rounded tip, 1¼ in/3 cm long, smooth, fleshy, greyish-green. The leaf tip is almost transparent. Flower bright yellow. Cape Province, South Africa.

**Ficus** (MORACEAE) include a number of interesting species which commence as epiphytes and subsequently throw down roots to the soil and grow into shrubs or trees. Most of these are unknown in cultivation, but two are worthy of mention.

*Ficus decaisnei* Steud. (syn. *F. philippinensis*). A climbing epiphyte from the Philippines – with long elliptical fleshy leaves, becoming bushy with maturity.

Other species are recorded of this large genus which commence epiphytal, then throw down their roots and become sizeable trees or shrubs.

*Ficus palmeri* S. Wats. A species from Baja California, possibly synonymous with *F. brandegeei* Standl. With swollen whitish caudex-like base and multiple-stem growths having ovate leaves, somewhat pubescent. Flowers insignificant, but with interesting globose fruits.

*Ficus villosa* Blume. A creeping species with ovate dark green leaves and brown hairy margins. Yellow fruits are developed in clusters. From Malaysia.

*Fockea* (ASCLEPIADACEAE) includes a number of caudici-form species having large tuberous roots and many long thin clambering branches. Rare in cultivation.

*Fockea crispa* (Jacq.) K. Sch. Probably the best-known of the genus having round, turnip-shaped caudex, very warty and roughened up to 6½ ft/2 m diameter in habitat, much of which is buried underground. Leaves opposite, oval-acute, ¾ in/2 cm long, dark green, very wavy edges. Flowers 4 or 5 together, greenish with small brown spots. Karroo, Cape Province, South Africa. This species lives to a great age; several examples are to be found in botanic gardens throughout the world. Smaller plants are available for pot culture, and the great essential is a totally dry resting season.

*Fockea edulis* (Thunbg.) K. Sch. Large somewhat rounded caudex, covered with brownish skin. Branching freely from apex with glossy smooth leaves, dark green. Flowers yellowish-green. South Africa and Namibia. The tubers are said to be edible.

Other species are recorded, but have many similarities to those mentioned. *F. natalensis* is very similar to *F. edulis*. *F. multiflora* K. Sch. grows to great heights with thick succulent caudex, stems and branches. The sap is used for making rubber.

*Folotsia* (ASCLEPIADACEAE) are more or less clambering plants with smooth, segmented stems. They can be propagated easily from cuttings or seeds.

*Folotsia aculeatum* (B. Desc.) B. Desc. A slender trailing species, branching from the base, stems being segmented and covered with silvery-white powder. Inflorescence consists of several white terminal flowers. Native of Madagascar.

*Folotsia floribundum* B. Desc. A shrubby plant with numerous segmented branches, intertangling and forming masses. Inflorescence with terminal flowers, white and scented. Endemic to Madagascar.

*Frithia* (MESEMBRYANTHEMACEAE) is similar to *Fenestraria*, particularly in form of growth. Only one species.

*Frithia pulchra* N. E. Br. Small species, erect leaves, somewhat clavate, truncate at tip, translucent, window-like, greyish-green. Beautiful flowers, carmine-purple with white centre. Transvaal, South Africa.

*Fouquieria* (FOUQUIERACEAE) is an important group of shrubby and thorny succulents with deciduous leaves. This now includes the genus *Idria*.

*Fouquieria splendens* Engelm. Widely distributed throughout southern California and in many parts of northern Mexico. Spiny tree-like succulent with branches. Leaves small, oval and numerous bright red flowers at ends of stems. Known as the ocotillo shrub, it is popular in North America as a hedging plant. Other species include *F. diguetii* (var. Tieghem) J. M. Johnst. from Baja California; *F. fasciculata* H. B. & K., the type species of the genus, from north of San Cristobal, Hidalgo, Mexico, with almost bottle-shaped base, a rarity and ideal as a natural bonsai; *F. purpusii*, native of Oaxaca, resembles a small form of *Idria*.

*Fouquieria columnaris*

*Fouquieria columnaris* Kellog. The spectacular 'boogum tree' for long known as *Idria columnaris*, which is encountered in 'forests' near Bay of Sebastian Vizcaino in western–central part of Baja California. Huge tree succulent with heavy elongated caudex and numerous branches, greyish leaves and greenish-yellow flowers at apex of plant.

*Furcraea* (AGAVACEAE) are spectacular plants. The leaves are in the form of a huge rosette from the tip of the stem. Plantlets often form between the individual flowers.

*Furcraea bedinghausii* C. Koch. Very large succulent species forming large trunk topped by rosette of 30 or more elongated, leathery fleshy bluish-grey leaves about 3¼ ft/1 m long and 2¼ in/6 cm wide, with rough minutely dentate margins. Inflorescence to nearly 16½ ft/5 m high with drooping branches and flowers in loose panicles. Native of central Mexico. *F. cubensis* Vent., a Cuban species, has shorter stem with elongated sword-like leaves, rounded on lower surface and keeled, rough with marginal teeth almost straight about ⅛ in/3 mm long. Tall inflorescence to 16½ ft/5 m and pure white flowers.

*Gasteria* (ASPHODELACEAE) contains many and varied species, many of which are most difficult to determine, to a degree due to the remarkable differences which occur between young plants and mature ones. Gasterias very easily cross-pollinate, and in consequence many of the plants in cultivation are very likely hybrids and there is little

opportunity to know the parentage. All are very attractive and suitable as houseplants. Care must be taken not to presume correct naming. Only a few can be easily recognized.
*Gasteria armstrongii* Schoenl. A striking and sought-after species of character. Usually stemless, with thick glabrous leaves, sometimes almost as wide as it is long, mostly prostrate forming a rosette about 4 in/10 cm diameter. Leaves blackish-green or brownish, with whitish or green tubercles, margins with sharp keel toward the apex. Flower pinkish-red. Cape Province, South Africa.

*Gasteria batesiana*

*Gasteria batesiana* Rowl. One of the most outstanding and readily recognized species. Somewhat spiral rosette of triangulate-lanceolate leaves, very stiff and three-angled, with keel on back surface. Leaves darkish or olive-green with numerous greenish-white dots creating a roughened surface. Inflorescence reddish. From Natal.

*Gasteria liliputana*

*Gasteria liliputana* v. Poelln. A usually stemless species with rosette spirally arranged. A charming miniature plant, forming groups. Narrow oblong-lanceolate leaves of dark green, with a definite keel on the underside, greenish-white irregular spots on the upper surface, margins serrate, whit-

ish. Inflorescence red. From Peddie Road, near Grahamstown, Cape Province, South Africa.
*Gasteria neliana* v. Poelln. From Cape Province, has a distichous rosette of thick, bluntly triangular leaves of dark green with whitish-green blotches – to about 7 in/18 cm long.

*Gasteria poellnitziana*

*G. poellnitziana* Jacobs. Has a slightly spiralled rosette of narrow, elongated tapering leaves to about 8 in/20 cm long, the upper surface concave in the lower half – the whole covered with numerous whitish tubercles. Flowers on a long spike, reddish with green tips. From Cape Province, South Africa.

There are several others which merit reference and can be considered distinctive species – *G. maculata* (Thunbg.) Haw. and *G. verrucosa* (Mill.) Duv. can be recommended.

**Gerrardanthus** (CUCURBITACEAE) are mostly climbing plants arising from quite giant-sized caudices. All known species are from tropical Africa.
*Gerrardanthus macrorhizus* Harv. l.c. With urn-shaped almost round caudex to 12 in/30 cm diameter. Thin woody stems and branches, climbing. Leaves variable, triangular and lobed, sometimes rather rounded with pointed tip, thin but fleshy, darkish green. Flowers yellowish-brown. Fruit has obscure longitudinal angles, glabrous and smooth, becoming slender at the base. From arid regions of Kenya and Tanzania.

**Gibbaeum** (MESEMBRYANTHEMACEAE) consists of about 20 species of considerable interest as cultivated plants. Caespitose with shortened stems. Bodies have two fleshy leaves united together at the base, often very unequal lobes with cleft at the apex or lower down the side. Occasionally leaves are spreading.
*Gibbaeum album* N. E. Br. Forms clumps. Leaves variously long, fleshy, ovoid with fissure slightly open, leaves to nearly 1¼ in/3 cm long, keeled apex covered with minute hairs. Flowers white. Cape Province, South Africa.
*Gibbaeum dispar* N. E. Br. Cluster-forming. Bodies of 2

unequal-sized leaves, oval, somewhat keeled, grey-green with velvety hairs. Fissure very deep. Flower lilac-pink. Cape Province, South Africa.

*Gibbaeum heathii* (N. E. Br.) L. Bol. Forming clumps. Leaves whitish-green, obovoid to 1¼ in/3 cm high. Leaves compressed with fissure reaching centre of body. Flowers white, turning pink. Cape Province, South Africa.

***Glottiphyllum*** (MESEMBRYANTHEMACEAE) has over 60 species, and many have close resemblance to one another. Fleshy plants of easy culture. Too much watering tends to produce elongated unnatural growth. They should be grown fairly 'hard' when the most normal characteristics will be seen.

*Glottiphyllum album* L. Bol. ms. A branching species of unusual significance on account of the white flowers. Fleshy leaves, somewhat keeled, often of unequal length, tapering toward apex. Cape Province, South Africa.

*Glottiphyllum linguiforme* (L.) N. E. Br. Leaves distichous, lingulate, fleshy, glossy, green. Flower on short stalk, golden-yellow. This species particularly requires fairly dry conditions, otherwise it can become exceedingly flabby and uninteresting. South Africa.

***Graptopetalum*** (CRASSULACEAE) is closely related to *Echeveria*, forming rosettes either with or without stems. The main difference is centred in the flowers which are star-like, the petals being united up to the centre of the tube, then spreading almost horizontally and the petals having many dots or bands.

*Graptopetalum bellum*

*Graptopetalum bellum* (Moran & Meyran) D. Hunt. The erstwhile *Tacitus* which caused so much excitement when it was discovered in the mountains of Chihuahua, Mexico, a few years ago. A rosette plant of about 1 in/2.5 cm across, compact and almost flat to the ground. Flowers are in clusters of up to 15, each about 1 in/2.5 cm across, magenta-pink in colour.

*Graptopetalum filiferum* (S. Wats.) Whitehead. From Chihuahua, Mexico. A stemless miniature species forming clumps with numerous rosettes rarely more than 2 in/5 cm diameter

having up to 100 small spatulate leaves about 1¼ in/30 mm long and ½ in/12 mm wide, light green, rather greyish at times, margins minute, white papillose tapering and ending in a brown filiform bristle. Inflorescence about 3 in/8 cm long with flowers whitish with reddish spots.

*Graptopetalum paraguayense* (N. E. Br.) E. Walth. A Mexican plant regardless of its misleading specific name. A well-known species looking very much like an *Echeveria* with loose rosette of thick, fleshy, brittle leaves recurved on upper surface and keeled beneath, reddish-grey with silvery bloom. Rosette borne on long thick fleshy stem, firstly erect, becoming prostrate. Flowers white on long inflorescence.

***Greenovia*** (CRASSULACEAE) is closely related to *Aeonium* and endemic to the Canary Islands.

*Greenovia aurea* (C. Sm.) Webb & Berth. Forms close clusters with cup-shaped rosettes which tend to close tight during resting season. Leaves thin, spatulate and bluntly rounded at the tips, bluish-green, pruinose. Flower deep yellow.

*Greenovia dodrantalis* (Willd.) Webb & Berth. Dainty rosettes forming clusters with numerous spoon-shaped leaves, vivid bluish-green with waxy surface. Flower bright yellow.

***Haemanthus*** (AMARYLLIDACEAE) are exotic flowering bulbous plants with mostly thick fleshy leaves and are considered borderline succulents.

*Haemanthus albiflos* Jacq. A popular species with flowers like a shaving brush – white with golden anthers. Quickly grouping with evergreen leaves having ciliate margins. South Africa.

*Haemanthus coccineus* L. Species having a flattish bulb, producing deep red flowers with orange anthers before leafing. Usually has only two wide lingulate leaves annually which are deciduous. Fruit in the form of purple berries. South Africa.

***Haworthia*** (ASPHODELACEAE) consists of a great number of species and varieties with varying forms and peculiarities, usually of clustering habit, but a few remain solitary. The genus has been divided into many sections to enable better grouping of these complex species. All are of mainly miniature growth. Flower rather insignificant, usually whitish, rarely yellow.

*Haworthia blackburniae* Bark. Has loose rosette of narrow leaves, almost grass-like but firm, dark green and slightly grooved on the upper surface. Lower surface with blunt keel and margins with hard teeth. A desirable and sought-after species, but rarity makes it uncommon in cultivation. Oudtschoorn Div., Cape Province, South Africa.

*Haworthia bolusii* Bak. A very beautiful species with dense rosette of numerous incurved pale green leaves with terminal bristles. Upper surface with numerous lines, back surface keeled – margins and keel with long soft teeth and white bristles. Other species have similar characteristics, *H. setata* and its varieties in particular. Western parts of the Karoo, Cape Province, South Africa.

*Haworthia cooperi* Bak. A well-known and quickly grouping species. Pale green leaves, fleshy, oblong-lanceolate, with transparent green lines on both surfaces, margins very minutely toothed, keeled on back surface. From Somerset East, Cape Province, South Africa.

*Haworthia limifolia* Marl. Another very distinctive species together with the several varieties and forms which have their own peculiar characteristics. Firm rosette with shortish triangular leaves abruptly taper toward the apex. Leaves are greyish-green with many longitudinal lines and tubercles in transverse lines, keeled on the back surface. Still a rare species of great attraction. Cape Province and Transvaal, South Africa.

*Haworthia margaritifera*

*Haworthia margaritifera* (L.) Haw. An attractive, freely off-setting species from Cape Province, South Africa, with a rosette comprising thick, fleshy leaves of about 3 in/8 cm long. Both leaf surfaces are covered with small pearl-like tubercles. *H. ramosa* G. Smith. Short-stemmed plant which develops short rooting branches so as to quickly form large clumps of pale green rosettes. Cape Province, South Africa.

*Haworthia marumiana* Uitew. Leaves dark-green obovate to oblong lanceolate, tapering to terminal bristle. Upper surface with transparent lines and pellucid spots, usually oblong in shape, between the lines. Back surface with two keels. Leaf margins and keels have transparent teeth. From Ladysmith, Cape Province, South Africa.

*Haworthia maughanii* v. Poelln. A fitting partner to *H. truncata* – leaves form a rosette with the tips flattened, greyish-green, roughened by minute tubercles. Little Karroo, Cape Province, South Africa.

*Haworthia obtusa* var. *pipifera forma truncata* Jacobs. There are several forms and varieties of *H. obtusa*, and this is one of particular note equalled only by *H. obtusa* var. *dielsiana*. Leaves form tight rosette, are abruptly truncate, no keel, rounded with smooth margins or only minute teeth and no

bristle at apex. From Kingwilliamstown, Cape Province, South Africa.

*Haworthia reinwardtii* (SD) Haw. An outstanding species with several varietal forms. With spirally arranged leaves forming an elongated rosette, leaves darkish-green with many white or greenish tubercles. Well-known in cultivation – all varieties are of decided interest. Cape Province, South Africa.

*Haworthia truncata* Schoenl. Has a number of recognized forms, all with distichously arranged leaves, erect but sometimes curved inward, darkish or greyish-green, both surfaces tubercled. The tips of the leaves appear as if they have been cut off and are completely flat. A desirable and rare species from Oudtschoorn Div., Cape Province, South Africa.

*Haworthia uitewaaliana* v. Poelln. With dark green or greyish-green leaves, elongated and incurved towards the tip. Back surface with keel from near the base, keel and margins set with thick whitish tubercles. Namaqualand and Cape Province, South Africa.

**Hechtia** (BROMELIACEAE) are borderline succulents, and due to their xerophytic characteristics have been recorded as such, this genus being native of North America.

*Hechtia glomerata*

*Hechtia argentea* Bak. Stemless rosettes with dark glossy green leaves about 14 in/35 cm long covered with silvery whitish scurf on both surfaces and prominent sawtoothed margins. Long inflorescence with many greenish-white inconspicuous flowers. A number of other species, all Mexican, are of interest. *H. glomerata* Zucc., fleshy, dark green leaves with whitish scales on the lower surface and the upper surface often pale reddish-brown variegated, toothed margins and whitish flowers. *H. ghiesbreghtii* Lem., recurved leaves covered with silvery scales on both sides, the upper surface having brownish markings. *H. marnier-lapostellei* L. B. Smith is a dwarf species with short tapering silvery-grey leaves. *H. tillandsioides* L. B. Smith has elongated waxy green leaves, somewhat curling and very much resembling a *Tillandsia*.

*Hereroa* (MESEMBRYANTHEMACEAE) are easily grown species forming clusters or sometimes small shrubs. Includes 36 known species.

*Hereroa aspera* L. Bol. Shrubby plant to 3½ in/8 cm high, branches freely. Leaves semi-cylindrical, upper surface flat, underside rounded with blunted tip, with many pronounced dots, dark green. Flower yellow with reddish tips. Cape Province, South Africa.

*Hereroa nelii* Schwant. Growths with one to three pairs of leaves. Leaves falcate curved, 1¼ in/3 cm long. Upper surface flat, back surface keeled at tip, covered with tubercles. Flower yellow. Cape Province, South Africa.

*Hertia* (COMPOSITAE) is a small genus of fleshy-leaved plants with typical daisy-like flowers. Suitable for outdoor culture in Europe.

*Hertia cheirifolia* (L.) O. Ktze. A creeping glabrous grey-green shrub with fleshy purplish-green leaves having distinct veins. Flowers in panicles, yellow. Endemic to Algeria and Tunisia.

*Hesperaloe* (LILIACEAE) are tall plants with elongated flower stems, very similar to many of the *Yucca* species.

*Hesperaloe parviflora*

*Hesperaloe parviflora* Coult. A stemless plant with very long narrow pointed grooved leaves and whitish fibrous hairs along the margins. Flower scape to nearly 6½ ft/2 m long with bell-shaped pinkish-red flowers about 1¼ in/30 mm long. *H. funifera* Trel. is very similar but with longer scape and greenish-reddish flowers.

*Hoodia* (ASCLEPIADACEAE) are related to *Stapelias*. Not considered an easy plant in cultivation, requires good sunlight and airy conditions. Plants of distinction with most unusual flowers.

*Hoodia bainii*

*Hoodia bainii* Dyer. Stems erect with compressed tubercles, spirally arranged, rarely branching, greyish-green. Flowers at terminal ends, subcircular, the tips of lobes slightly raised, dull brownish-yellow. Cape Province, South Africa.

*Hoodia gordonii*

*Hoodia gordonii* (Mass.) Sweet. Species having many stems from central growing point, erect and firm, rarely branching. Has 12 to 14 ribs, irregularly longitudinal, furnished with tessellate tubercles and hard spines, greyish-green. Flowers usually at terminal end, subcircular with lobes hardly apparent, margins outcurved, brownish-pink with obscure furrows and rough. Cape Province, South Africa.

*Hoodia macrantha* Dtr. Stems erect forming clusters from central growing point to 32 in/80 cm high. Many ribs, sharply tuberculate. Flowers at terminal ends, subcircular, forming shallow bell-shape with tips of lobes somewhat recurved, purplish-yellow, the largest flowers of this genus being up to 8 in/20 cm across. From Namibia. Very rare in cultivation

*Hoodiopsis* (ASCLEPIADACEAE) are closely related to *Stapelia*, often forming large clumps. Uncommon in cultivation, but given good light and temperatures in excess of 55°F/12°C, they will thrive.

*Hoodiopsis triebneri* Luckh. An elegant species, erect stems branching from the base, eight- or nine-angled, very pronounced, with marginal teeth, light green and purplish lines. Flower solitary, bluntly star-shaped to about 4–4½ in/10–11 cm diameter, lobes flat spreading, margins recurved, outside surface greenish-pink, inside surface deep brownish-red, longitudinal grooves, all covered with papillae. Namibia.

**Hoya** (ASCLEPIADACEAE) are mainly climbing plants, only a few are shrubby while others are epiphytic. Most species are succulent; there are exceptions, but even some of these have a tendency to succulence, either in the stem or leaves. Known as the 'wax flower', some species have become popular as houseplants. This genus includes more species than is generally recognized; many are of easy culture. All species are fragrant.

*Hoya australis* R. Br. ex Trail. From Queensland, New South Wales, Australia, a trailing, robust climber with broad oval fleshy leaves 2–3 in/5–8 cm long and sparsely white-spotted. Flowers in umbels, whitish-pink with reddish centre with the scent of honeysuckle.

*Hoya bandaensis* Schltr. A rampant climber with very long stems and large oval pointed fleshy dark green leaves, glossy. Flowers in umbels on long stalks, white with reddish centre. Malaysia.

*Hoya bella* Hook. A well-known shrubby species, fairly straight stems and short branches, but sometimes drooping at the ends. Leaves small, thick, ovate-lanceolate, deep green. Flowers in umbels, white with purple centre. India and Malaysia.

*H. sikkimensis* Hook. and *H. parasitica* Wall. are also dwarf-growing species similar to *H. bella*, and might possibly be synonymous or a variety of this species.

*Hoya carnosa* (L.) R. Br. Trailing fleshy plant with elongated stems and branches. Leaves ovate-elongate and shortly tapering, dark green, fleshy and waxy. Flowers in pendent umbels, pink with reddish spots in centre. China and Australia. The species usually considered the 'wax flower'.

*H. carnosa* var. *marmorata* (syn. var. *exotica*) Hort. is in all parts the same as the species, but with yellow mottled or striped leaves. *H. carnosa* var. *variegata* de Vries. is also similar, but the leaves are white variegated. The flower in both instances is identical.

*Hoya carnosa* var. *compacta* Hort. An interesting, almost fasciated plant, generally of small growth and trailing. Leaves are somewhat twisted and curled, shorter than the species, the flower almost identical.

*Hoya coronaria* Blume. Oval, fleshy leaves with recurved edges. A robust climbing plant bearing large pale yellow flowers with bright red dots in the corona, several to an umbel. A native of Indonesia.

*Hoya engleriana* Hoss. A pendent species with thin stems, climbing or creeping. Leaves very small, elliptical, upper surface convex, dark green. Flowers in umbels usually four together, white with purplish centre. From Thailand.

*Hoya imperialis* Lindl. A trailing species with stems, leaf ribs and stalks covered with felt. Leaves very tough, elliptic, somewhat downy. Flowers very beautiful on pendent umbels, darkish purple with a greenish centre. Borneo.

*Hoya linearis* Wall. The most noteworthy epiphyte of this genus, has thin, almost thread-like leaves on pendent stems with scented whitish small flowers. Himalayas.

*Hoya longifolia* Wall. A smaller-growing species with slender stems and long linear leaves channelled above and roundish under. Flowers in umbels, delicate waxy-white and a rich carmine centre. A very distinctive species from the tropical Himalayas.

*Hoya macrophylla* Blume. Slow-growing species with twining habit. Leaves large, fleshy, ovate, light or coppery-green, tapering toward the tip, having prominent pale veins and a quilted surface. Flowers in umbels, white and papillate hairy. Java.

*Hoya moteskei*

*Hoya moteskei* Teijsm. Rampant climber with broad elliptic waxy leaves, somewhat leathery with irregular whitish spots and markings. Flowers in umbels, pinkish-white with maroon centre. Indonesia.

*Hoya multiflora* (Decaisne) Blume. A trailing plant, but more shrubby than some other species with large elliptic glossy leaves tapering sharply at both ends. Flower in umbels, straw-yellow with brownish centre. From Malaysia.

*Hoya obovata* Decaisne (syn. *H. kerrii*). A robust climber with stout stems. Leaves thick, fleshy and very succulent, heart-shaped to 3 in/8 cm long, dull green. Flowers in umbels creamy-white with rose-purple centre. Thailand, Java and possibly Fiji.

*Hoya pallida* Lindl. Long twining species having elliptic waxy leaves, pale green. Flowers in umbels, pale yellow with reddish centre. An unusual species and rare in cultivation. China.

*Hoya polyneura* Hook. For long known as *H. nepalense*. From

*Hoya polyneura*

*Huernia primulina* N. E. Br. An interesting species with short erect stems to 3 in/8 cm high, four- or five-angled, somewhat dentate and teeth which rapidly become blunted, pale greenish or greyish-green, with reddish spots. Flowers in clusters on short stalks, corolla has pale purplish tube and fleshy triangular lobes, broadly tapering, slightly recurved, inside yellow-white with a few blackish spots around throat. South Africa.

*Huernia schneideriana*

the Himalayan region of Nepal. The somewhat pointed leaves are a feature – these together with the rich reddish-brown of the corona and the yellowish-white of the corolla lobes create a species of particular interest. This comprises one of the most exotic climbing groups of succulents.

**Huernia** (ASCLEPIADACEAE) includes a great many species, having short stems and forming thickish clusters with many varied, colourful and unusual flowers.

*Huernia confusa* Phill. Erect five-angled stems, dull green, angles with short triangular teeth spreading acutely. Clusters freely. Flower on short stalk from near base of growths, corolla circular 1¼ in/3 cm, shallow tube, glabrous, pinkish with thick annulus, yellowish-green, spotted. Lobes triangular, short-tapering, pale green and reddish markings, slightly papillose. Transvaal, South Africa.

*Huernia schneideriana* Bgr. Stems to 7 in/18 cm long, five- to seven-angled, sparsely toothed, clustering, light green. Flower bell-shaped, outside surface brown, inside velvety-black with paler papillose margins and edges, lobes recurved. A popular species. Mozambique and Malawi.

*Huernia pillansii*

*Huernia zebrina*

*Huernia pillansii* N. E. Br. Stems forming clusters to 1½ in/ 4 cm high with spirally arranged ribs and soft maroon spines. Flowers from young stems on short stalk having five pronounced lobes, triangular and tapering, each to ¼ in/ 12 mm long. Outer surface yellow with reddish spots. Cape Province, South Africa.

*Huernia zebrina* N. E. Br. Thick clustering species, stems to 3 in/8 cm high, tapering toward the apex, green and flecked red, angled with reddish teeth. Flower on short stalks, broadly bell-shaped, narrowing around the mouth of the tube and a broad ring around the mouth. Lobes triangular, very acute. Rather small flowers, yellow with transverse purple bands. Natal and Transvaal, South Africa and Namibia.

*Huerniopsis* (ASCLEPIADACEAE) are low growing plants native to South Africa and Namibia, requiring the same attention as *Huernia*.

*Huerniopsis decipiens*

*Huerniopsis decipiens* N. E. Br. Stems semi-prostrate to 2½ in/7 cm long, four- or five-angled, rounded also sharp teeth, grey-green with purplish blotches. Flowers somewhat bell-shaped, triangular lobes and edges so recurved as to appear rounded, spreading. Inside surface purplish with yellowish spots, outside greenish and spotted.

*Hydnophytum* (RUBIACEAE) include some of the most remarkable of succulent plants with thick succulent bottle-like stems. Can only be grown epiphytically.
*Hydnophytum formicarium* Jacq. One of those peculiar epiphytic caudiciform succulents inhabited by ants. It has a smooth caudex up to 4½ in/12 cm diameter with many branches bearing fleshy, oval leaves, small white flowers and red berries. Native of Malaysia, where it grows in the branches of trees.

*Hypagophytum* (CRASSULACEAE) are cold-house plants with fleshy leaves set opposite. Related to *Sempervivum*.
*Hypagophytum abyssinicum* (Hochst.) Bgr. An unusual and attractive species with slender cylindrical stems arising from tuberous base, jointed, glabrous. Fleshy oval leaves, red-spotted margins. Flower whitish with reddish spots, in a somewhat flattened cyme. Ethiopia and Somalia.

*Ibervillea* (CUCURBITACEAE) are caudiciform plants of climbing habit, often by means of tendrils. Flowers rather insignificant and berry-like fruits.
*Ibervillea sonorae* (S. Wats.) Greene. A species with very swollen caudex, either globose or flattened producing a rampant vine-like growth. Fairly widely distributed in Mexico, particularly Sonora where it is found at the base of

thickets. Leaves small and insignificant, flowers small, yellowish.

*Impatiens* (BALSAMINACEAE) are usually considered herbaceous plants, but certain of the genus can be classified as succulents.
*Impatiens mirabilis* Hook. f. With fleshy pale green stems, later turning reddish-brown, very succulent – leaves grouping at the apex, somewhat ciliate and waxy. Flowers golden-yellow, large. Isle of Langkawi, Sumatra.
    A number of other species, obviously true succulents, are recorded – but these appear to be rare in cultivation, and very little is known about them. It is generally assumed they constitute 'stem' succulents. *I. balfouri* Hook. f. from west Himalayas has pink flowers and yellow spots. *I. holstii* Engl. & Warb., from Kenya and Tanzania with purple-scarlet flowers, is closely linked to the typical 'busy Lizzie', one of the most popular of this genus.

*Ipomoea* (CONVOLVULACEAE) have large rounded tuberous rootstock, short stems and typically convolvulus-like flowers.
*Ipomoea holubii* Bak. With large caudex (in habitat), usually buried. Grass-like leaves. Flower variable – from deep pink to dark purple. Widely distributed in north Transvaal, South Africa, on grasslands.
*Ipomoea inamoena* Pilg. Very large caudex with thick brownish skin. Leaves elongated, ciliate on the margins. Flowers from leaf-axils, lilac to white. Fairly widespread in parts of South Africa and Namibia.
*Ipomoea batatas* (L.) Lam. The well-known 'sweet potato' – having tuberous roots and succulent stems. Leaves variable, sometimes digitately lobed or ovate. Flowers pinkish-white. Originally from Asia.

*Ipomoea holubii*

Two other genera, *Merremia* and *Turbina*, are possibly identical to *Ipomoea* – and seemingly synonymous as far as the succulent species are concerned. *Turbina holubii* (Bak.) Meeuse is an example – although species so named have rather larger stem and leaf growths with larger, more purple flowers.

**Jatropha** (Euphorbiaceae) – not all species are succulent, but a few distinctive plants certainly come within that category, some in fact being extreme succulents.

*Jatropha macrantha* Müll. Arg. Endemic to central Peru at an altitude of over 6,500 ft/2,000 m. A beautiful flowering species to 3¼ ft/1 m high with glossy pinnate leaves usually from near-terminal ends of stems with pinkish-red flowers in clusters on short succulent stalk. *J. curcas* L. is a tall plant, indigenous to several parts of tropical America and the West Indies, tree-like to sometimes 20 ft/5 m high having a thick 'ivy-shaped' leaf, flowers yellowish-green. The seeds are used for their oil. *J. peltata* H. B. & K. from Amazonas, Brazil, through to Peru, a species to about 3¼ ft/1 m high with very succulent fleshy stem, leaves five-lobed. Flowers deep red.

*Jatropha multifida* L., a widely distributed species with narrowly segmented, pinnately lobed leaves and scarlet flowers, is but one of a number found native in the West Indies; others include *J. hastata* Jacq. and *J. pandurifolia* Andr. *J. berlandieri* Torrey is a native of Texas and has a round caudex-like base and annual growth from the apex with a charming red inflorescence.

*Jatropha podagrica*

*Jatropha podagrica* Hook. Native of Central America and the West Indies having short thickened trunk to about 2½ ft/ 75 cm high, greyish-green with shedding skin. Leaves from knobbly branches, peltate, three- to five-lobed, dark green and leathery about 7 in/18 cm long. Inflorescence much-branched with many scarlet flowers.

*Jatropha urens* L. Found in the West Indies. Fleshy, hairy stems and leaves which have the capacity to sting – locally called the 'horse nettle'. Flowers small, white.

**Kalanchoë** (Crassulaceae) is a genus of tremendous variety. Since *Bryophyllum* and *Kitchingia* have become merged with *Kalanchoë*, classification has divided the genus into three sections, *Kitchingia*, *Bryophyllum* and *Kalanchoë*. Species very widely distributed throughout many parts of the tropical and sub-tropical world.

*Kalanchoë beharensis*

*Kalanchoë beharensis* Drake del Cast. Tall slender stem, notched, becoming hard and woody, with brownish hairs. Leaves broadly arrow-shaped, lobed, fleshy, olive-green to dark green, brownish hairs on upper surface, whitish hairs on lower surface. Flowers yellowish-cream with purplish throat. Madagascar.

There are forms and varieties of this species – the forms involve the leaf colorations provided by the hairs. Some remain green or grey on the upper surface. Another varietal form, *K. beharensis* var. *glabra*, has wavy margins to the leaves, glaucous with no hairs, also from Madagascar. (Sect. Kalanchoë)

*Kalanchoë beauverdii* var. *beauverdii* Hamet. A climbing species with elongated leaves, blunt developing adventitious buds or 'plantlets' at the tip. Inflorescence has many flowers, deep violet or blackish-violet. South Madagascar.

Other varieties occur of this species, varying on account of flower and fruit. (Sect. Bryophyllum)

*Kalanchoë blossfeldiana* v. Poelln. Compact bushy plant, with erect stems and branches. Leaves glossy-green, small obovate, edged red, somewhat crenate toward apex. Flowers in clusters, bright red. Mont Tsaratanana, Madagascar. (Sect. Kalanchoë) This species has been used for hybridizing to produce some of the most popular houseplants in quite a range of colours.

*Kalanchoë brasiliensis* St. Hil. Of shrubby habit having stems covered with short hairs. Leaves ovate-lanceolate, tapering with serrated edges, upper leaves smaller with smooth edges. Terminal flowers in clusters, pink, the stalks being covered with dense hairs. Brazil. (Sect. Kalanchoë) *K. pinnata* (Lam.) Persoon is widely distributed in many parts of South America as well as the West Indies and most other tropical and sub-tropical parts of the world. An erect plant, very succulent to 3¼ ft/1 m high. Leaves at first simple, then pinnate with leaflets 3–5 together, oblong and rather bluntly tapering with crenate margins, flowers bell-shaped, hanging pendent on slender branching inflorescence, greenish on the outside becoming reddish toward the stalk and whitish tips to petals. (Sect. Bryophyllum)

*Kalanchoë farinacea* Balf. From Socotra, a compact plant with obovate leaves of pale green and pinkish margins. Flowers are bell-shaped, yellow and red. *K. jongsmansii* Hamet & Perr. from Madagascar is a spreading species with woody branches, fleshy leaves to 1½ in/4 cm long, and yellow flowers about 1¼ in/3 cm long – an ideal plant for hanging basket culture. *K. schumacheri* Koord. is thought to have come from Madagascar, but this is not certain. A semi-pendent species with bluish-green leaves and pale pinkish-purple flowers. There have been incorrect descriptions

*Kalanchoë synsepala*

given of this species over a period of many years. *K. synsepala* Bak. from central Madagascar has a few ovate-spatulate leaves 2½–5 in/6–13 cm long with undulating and dentate margins. There are several varieties recorded.

*Kalanchoë gastonis-bonnieri* Hamet & Perr. Large species, fleshy with large lanceolate leaves, margins coarsely crenate, surface whitish pruinose, especially on young growth. Flower pale pink. Endemic to Madagascar and also possibly Kenya. (Sect. Kalanchoë)

*Kalanchoë gracilipes* (Bak.) Baill. From Central Madagascar, with obovate elongated leaves with crenate edges. A true

epiphytic creeper – very rare in cultivation. (Sect. Kitchingia)

*Kalanchoë grandiflora* Wight & Arn. Erect species with obovate toothed leaves, covered with bluish waxy coating. Flowers yellow. One of the finest species, somewhat rare. East Africa and Eastern India. (Sect. Kalanchoë)

*Kalanchoë longiflora* Schltr. A robust erect species with 4-angled stems. Leaves oval to oblong and pronounced dentate in the upper part, very fleshy, pale grey-green or copper-coloured. Flowers pale orange with slight fragrance. Natal. (Sect. Kalanchoë)

*Kalanchoë mangani*

*Kalanchoë mangani* Hamet & Perr. Numerous woody stems and branches forming a thick somewhat prostrate or pendent shrub. Small leaves, fleshy, obovate, dark green, loosely arranged. Urn-shaped flowers brick red. Native of Andringitra, Madagascar. (Sect. Bryophyllum)

*Kalanchoë marmorata*

*Kalanchoë marmorata* Bak. Stout fleshy stem, erect, branching usually from the base. Leaves obovate with scalloped margins, pinkish or bluish-green, grey pruinose and many brownish mottlings. Flowers elongated, white. Somalia and Ethiopia. (Sect. Kalanchoë)

*Kalanchoë porphyrocalyx* (Bak.) Baill. From central Madagascar, with fleshy crenated but small leaves and developing aerial roots. Flowers usually pink but yellow-flowering species have been observed. (Sect. Bryophyllum)

*Kalanchoë pumila*

*Kalanchoë pumila* Bak. Bushy plant with erect becoming prostrate growth. Has closely set obovate leaves crenate in the upper part, purplish-grey with covering of white bloom. Flowers at terminal end, pitcher-shaped, reddish-violet or lilac. Popular species making excellent houseplant. From central Madagascar. (Sect. Kalanchoë)

*Kalanchoë rhombopilosa*

*Kalanchoë rhombopilosa* Mann. & Boit. A small distinctive species, mostly erect and little-branched. Small leaves somewhat triangular, rounded above, apex indented and sinuate, grey-green with silver and red markings. Flowers small, yellowish. There are other varieties of this species, *K. rhombopilosa* var. *alba* with wholly white leaves, and *K. rhombopilosa* var. *viridis* which has very thick, wider, deep or fresh green leaves. Madagascar. (Sect. Kalanchoë)

*Kalanchoë scapigera* Welw. An interesting and uncommon glabrous plant having thick stems and branches, with fleshy obovate leaves, margins entire, dark green or greyish-green. Leaves at apex of stems. Large red or orange-red flowers make this one of the most beautiful of the genus. Socotra and parts of East Africa. (Sect. Kalanchoë)

*Kalanchoë thyrsiflora*

*Kalanchoë thyrsiflora* Harv. Tall growing plant, up to 24 in/ 60 cm, with almost oval leaves densely arranged diagonally, light green, margins red. Stems and leaves are densely white pruinose. Flower urn-shaped, yellow. A very beautiful and desirable species from Transvaal, Cape Province, South Africa. (Sect. Kalanchoë)

*Kalanchoë tomentosa* Bak. Sometimes called the 'panda plant'. Has erect branching stems, densely leafy forming a compact shrub. Leaves spoon-shaped, entirely covered with white felt and the tips deep brown and dentate. There are a number of forms, some with small leaves, others having rather larger leaves than the species. Madagascar. (Sect. Kalanchoë)

*Kalanchoë tuberosa* Perr. A rare species with mealy-white stems and leaves. Leaves dentate, wavy margins about 1 in/ 25 mm long. Flower deep pink or rose. Madagascar. (Sect. Kalanchoë)

*Kalanchoë tubiflora* (Harv.) Hamet. Tall-growing species with slender erect stems, rarely branched. Stems greenish-brown, glabrous. Leaves narrow and almost cylindrical, grooved on upper surface and plantlets forming at the apex, greyish-green with pinkish and purplish blotches. Flowers reddish to purple. Madagascar. (Sect Bryophyllum)

*Kalanchoë uniflora* (Stapf.) Hamet. From forest areas of Ambre, Madagascar, with small fleshy leaves, crenate near the apex and having small reddish urn-shaped flowers. (Sect. Bryophyllum)

*Kalanchoë velutina* Welw. Fleshy-stemmed species, somewhat

creeping. Lower leaves ovate-lanceolate, upper leaves narrow and slightly rounded. All stems, branches, leaves and inflorescence short hairy, hence its name. Flower yellow to pink. From Tanzania, Angola and other parts of East Africa. (Sect. Kalanchoë)

*Kedrostis* (CUCURBITACEAE) are mostly creeping or clambering plants with fleshy rootstock. Flowers in panicles.
*Kedrostis africana* (L.) Cogn. Has become a well-known species. Large fleshy, whitish, tuberous root or caudex. Stems slender, climbing and branching. Leaves somewhat triangular in form, with lobes, fresh green, somewhat rough. Flower yellowish. Fruits deep orange, obscurely furrowed about ½ in/12 mm long, oval. South Africa and Namibia and parts of East Africa.
*Kedrostis nana* (Lam.) Cogn. Tuberous rooted with long slender stems and branches, climbing or prostrate. Leaves heart-shaped, rounded apex, margins slightly undulate. Flowers yellowish, small. Fruit red, oval with rounded base, smooth, about ⅝ in/16 mm long. South Africa.

*Kinepetalum* (ASCLEPIADACEAE) is a small genus of interesting plants with unusual flowers. Closely allied to *Ceropegia*.
*Kinepetalum schultzei* Schltr. Has very tuberous root, almost caudex-like. Many erect stems to 3¼ ft/1 m high, cylindrical, and minute hairs. Leaves long and narrow, somewhat grooved, tapering, green, covered with small hairs. Flowers have bell-shaped tube, with very thin, thread-like lobes about 1¼ in/3 cm long, white-spotted, green, with many purplish hairs. Namibia.

*Kingia* (XANTHORRHOEACEAE) is a monotypic genus with similarities to plants of *Xanthorrhoea*, the inflorescence presenting the contrasting difference.

*Kingia australis*

*Kingia australis* R. Br. Native of West Australia. Caudex to 6½ ft/2 m tall with long spreading toothed leaves. Inflorescence 12 in/30 cm long bearing rounded heads of white flowers 2–3 in/5–8 cm. Ovary and fruits densely white and hairy.

*Lampranthus* (MESEMBRYANTHEMACEAE) are shrubby plants, erect, prostrate or spreading. Of easy culture and very free-flowering. Embraces over 130 species.
*Lampranthus conspicuus* (Haw.) N. E. Br. Shrubby with thick creeping branches. Leaves incurved at branch terminals, about 2½ in/6 cm long, bright green often dotted, reddish tip. Flowers reddish-purple with cream centre. Cape Province, South Africa.

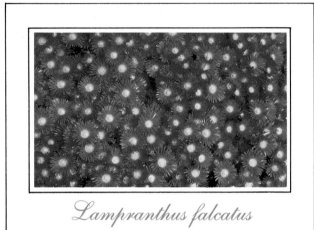

*Lampranthus falcatus*

*Lampranthus falcatus* N.E.Br. A species from Cape Province, South Africa which provides a mass of colour during the flowering season. The stems and branches are fairly low-growing, becoming very entangled as they develop. Flowers are pink, to almost ¾ in/2 cm across.
*Lampranthus roseus* (Willd.) Schwant. Erect spreading shrub to 2 ft/60 cm high. Linear leaves 1¼ in/3 cm long covered with translucent spots. Flowers in profusion, large, soft pink with yellow centre. Cape Province, South Africa.

*Lavrania* (ASCLEPIADACEAE) is a newly erected genus which is related to *Stapelia*.
*Lavrania haagnerae* Plowes. Comes from Namibia. It has a cylindrical stem to about 10 in/25 cm long with the flowers appearing near the base. The corolla lobes are yellowish-white with maroon spots and the corona bright red.

*Ledebouria* (HYACINTHACEAE) is a genus of some 30 species from South Africa, tropical Africa and India. Some are 'borderline' succulents, similar to some of the *Scilla* species mentioned here.
*Ledebouria ovalifolia* (Schrader) Jessop. A small bulbous plant with fleshy dark green leaves and stem. The leaves with maroon blotches on the underside. Stems to about 5 in/12 cm carrying small purple, pink or white flowers. From Cape Province, South Africa.
*Ledebouria floribunda* (Bak.) Jessop. Has a large bulb about

4 in/10 cm diameter, a soft fleshy stem about 20 in/50 cm long with broad purple-blotched leaves, 2–4 inflorescences bearing cream and green flowers.

**Lenophyllum** (CRASSULACEAE) is closely related to *Echeveria*, all rosette-forming with flowers single or few together at terminal ends of densely leafy stem.

*Lenophyllum acutifolium* Rose. Large rosette to 4 in/10 cm high with sword-like leaves tapering abruptly, upper surface furrowed. Flowers numerous, yellowish. A California species.

*Lenophyllum pusillum* Rose. Small rosette consisting of thick, fleshy, narrow leaves about ¾ in/2 cm long, keeled on back surface, reddish-green. Flowers solitary, yellow. Mexico.

**Lewisia** (PORTULACACEAE) includes many species which prove popular in cultivation. A number of these are indeed succulents with fleshy rootstock often caudex-like. Generally considered hardy.

*Lewisia brachycalyx* Engelm. Has a definite caudex, rather succulent leaves, lance-shaped, set in a loose rosette. Bears large pure white flowers. *L. rediviva* Pursh. is similar, varying mainly in leaf shape. North America.

*Lewisia cotyledon*

*Lewisia cotyledon* Robins. One of the better known species. This forms a dense rosette of several long leaves with red and white flowers borne in terminal panicles. It has been used extensively in hybridizing so that many shades of colour are now available. North America.

**Lithops** (MESEMBRYANTHEMACEAE) are pebble-like plants, often called 'living stones'. A very large genus of over 80 species and varieties from very dry desert regions where often they are almost buried or indiscernible in rock crevices. All species have a window-like top surface, so even when the plant is partially buried, the light can still penetrate into the plant for its survival. New growth develops at the axils of the old growth which withers and acts as a protective sheath for the new leaves, finally as only a skin. Not difficult to cultivate, but a very light position is essential for greatest success. Resting period is winter and early spring. For classification purposes the genus has been divided into two sub-genera: *Xantholithops* for those with principally yellow flowers and where the fissure does not extend over the whole body; *Leucolithops* to include white flowering species and with a fissure which divides the two leaves completely.

*Lithops bella* (Dtr.) N. E. Br. Forming clusters, bodies about 1¼ in/30 mm high with rather convex top surface. Has the colour of granite mimicking the environment from which it originates. Flower yellow. Namibia.

*Lithops comptonii* L. Bol. Clustering freely, bodies greyish-green up to 1½ in/4 cm with deep fissure making the leaves 'gape'. Top with window, amethyst with brownish and purplish markings and white spots in the 'islands'. Flower yellow. Cape Province, South Africa.

*Lithops dorotheae* Nel. Forming clusters, bodies obconical, dove-grey, with flat top, having translucent windows with many reddish and greyish markings. Flower yellow. Cape Province, South Africa.

*Lithops elisae*

*Lithops elisae* de Boer. Found in Cape Province, South Africa and areas bordering Namibia. The greyish-white bodies are about ¾ in/2 cm long with a definite fissure across the surface of each. Flowers white.

*Lithops julii* (Dtr. & Schwant.) N. E. Br. There are also two varietal forms of this species. Caespitose, somewhat conical with convex top surface, the fissure extending right across, pearl-grey. The margins of the fissure have dots on each side. Flower white. Namibia.

*Lithops opalina* Dtr. Somewhat constricted oval bodies with fissure extending right across, 1¼ in/3 cm high, bluish-white, top surface with purplish tint. Flower white. Namibia.

*Lithops optica* (Marl.) N. E. Br. Caespitose forming largish clump. Bodies greyish-white with pronounced fissure making cleft, leaf tips convex, spreading with whitish transparent windows. Flower white. There is a beautiful and rare form, *L. optica forma rubra* (Tisch.) Rowl., which is almost identical to the species, but the body is reddish-purple and the windows more apparent, flower white. Namibia.

*Lithops pseudotruncatella* N.E.Br. A popular and well-known species from Namibia. The bodies are either solitary or several together, compressed and truncate, varying in colour from greyish-brown to pale grey. Flowers are usually a bright yellow.

*Lithops salicola* L. Bol. Forming clusters, sometimes solitary. Bodies silvery-grey, oval with top surface convex and having large translucent greenish-grey or reddish windows, and numerous little greyish islands. Flowers white. Orange Free State, South Africa.

**Lobelia** (LOBELIACEAE) is a large genus of mostly non-succulents. The few exceptions are mainly from tropical Africa and constitute caudiciform plants.

*Lobelia rhynchopetala* (Hochst.) Hemsl. Caudiciform species having elongated fleshy trunk to about 13 ft/4 m high. Leaves long and wide developing palm-like fans at the terminal end. Endemic to Ethiopia and Tanzania.

**Lomatophyllum** (LILIACEAE) is closely related to the genus *Aloe* but seemingly was omitted when the new family title Asphodelaceae was erected. Usually forming branches with rosettes. All known species are from Madagascar and the island of Mauritius.

*Lomatophyllum citreum*

*Lomatophyllum citreum* Guill. Stemless plants with dark green leaves recurved and forming a loose rosette. Margins with triangular-shaped teeth. Has very attractive yellowish flowers.

*Lomatophyllum macrum* (Haw.) Salm ex Roem. & Schult. Large-growing species with sword-like leaves, tapering at the apex, bright green, margins with small red teeth. Flower reddish.

*Lomatophyllum orientale* Perr. Short-stemmed species with few leaves, elongated with marginal spines. Inflorescence simple with yellowish-red flowers.

*Lomatophyllum sociale* Perr. Species with many branches and loose rosette. Leaves elongated, narrowing at the base, dull green or reddish. Flowers carmine-red, fruits form berry-like in clusters.

**Luckhoffia** (ASCLEPIADACEAE) is a monotypic genus, the solitary species still considered a connoisseur's plant. Demands similar conditions as other South African species of this family.

*Luckhoffia beukmanii*

*Luckhoffia beukmanii* (Luckh.) White & Sloane. A rare member of the Stapeliaceae, erect stems branching from the base, tall, usually 8-angled with many blunted tubercles, greyish-green. Flowers at apex of branches, somewhat rounded and flat, greenish-pink on outside and inside papillate with black hairs, lobes brown and yellow spotted with longitudinal ribs, margins recurved, minutely ciliated. From Cape Province, South Africa.

**Melothria** (CUCURBITACEAE) are mostly climbing, creeping plants often with a very succulent rootstock. Flowers are small, followed by colourful berry-like fruits. Not all species are succulent.

*Melothria punctata* Cogn. (syn. *Zehneria scabra* [Lf.] Sond.). With greenish-grey caudex branching from apex, some-what woody, climbing with tendrils. Leaves ivy-shaped, rough and hairy. Flowers dioecious, yellowish. Small fruits, rounded and pointed at tip, crimson, ½ in/12 mm long. Widespread distribution in East and South Africa, parts of India, Malaysia and the Philippines.

**Mitrophyllum** (MESEMBRYANTHEMACEAE) is closely allied to *Conophyllum* but differing in the structure of the fruits. Most

species are rare in cultivation. Plant has similar leaf structure to the *Conophyllums*, one leaf pair rising from the lower pair, some which are united the whole length and others part way only, the former serving as a kind of 'sheath' for the latter. Includes only a few species, possibly no more than six and some are in doubt.
*Mitrophyllum mitratum* (Marl.) Schwant. Caespitose. Stems thick, fleshy, later becoming woody. Leaves very succulent, 3 in/8 cm long, rather triangular, and those spreading are slightly convex on the upper surface forming a deep furrow, back surface rounded and keeled. Flowers white with red tips to petals. Little Namaqualand and Cape Province, South Africa.

**Momordica** (Cucurbitaceae) are tropical climbing plants with fleshy rootstock and fruits far more attractive than the flowers! Only 3–4 species are recorded as true succulents.
*Momordica rostrata* A. Zinn. With fleshy succulent basal stem, irregularly ribbed. Branches thin, rambling, narrow palmate leaves. Flower deep yellow. Fruits somewhat spiny, pinkish-orange. Endemic to tropical East Africa.

**Monadenium** (Euphorbiaceae) have many similarities to *Euphorbia* and are well represented throughout East and South Africa, many central territories and coastal regions.
*Monadenium coccineum* Pax. An erect species, usually branching with five-angled stems, greenish-purple. Leaves glabrous and possibly deciduous. Flower bright red. From Tanzania north of Lake Eyassi on stony slopes.
*Monadenium lugardae* N. E. Br. Fleshy, cylindrical stems, glabrous and spineless, somewhat tessellated. Leaves form loose rosette at terminal ends, fleshy, obovate and serrated on marginal tips. Greenish flower.
*Monadenium stapelioides* Pax. Stems usually erect or semi-erect, cylindrical and generally unbranched. All stems have spirally arranged tubercles and leaf scar. Leaves near to apex, obovate and tapering towards the base. Flower greenish and pinkish-white. Tropical East Africa.
*Monadenium stellatum* Bally. A most unusual species, with single erect stems, cylindrical with many longitudinal grooves and pronounced tubercles, resembling stalks, horizontal from the stem. These are tipped with leaf scars and a few short spines. Leaves glabrous, deciduous, tapering toward the base, undulate toward the apex. Greenish-white flowers.

**Monanthes** (Crassulaceae) are small shrubby plants with leaves crowded at ends of branches. Flowers inconspicuous, but a delicately attractive genus. All from Madeira and the Canary Islands.
*Monanthes brachycaulon* (Webb & Berth) Lowe. Small, shrubby, with lax rosettes. Leaves fleshy, spatulate, somewhat flat. Inflorescence minutely hairy giving the effect of a cobweb. Flowers white.
*Monanthes polyphylla* Haw. Forms dense cushions of bluish-green rosettes, stems prostrate. Leaves small, club-shaped, and flower red.

**Monilaria** (Mesembryanthemaceae) are an interesting genus of semi-shrubby, low-growing plants, often jointed into small segments, leaves small, fleshy and generally sub-cylindrical. Closely related to *Mitrophyllum* and *Conophyllum*.
*Monilaria peersii* L. Bol. Shrubby to about 4½ in/12 cm high with several short branches and internodes. Leaves short, narrow with obscure keel near tip which is round at apex, covered with papillae, fresh green. Flowers white. Cape Province, South Africa.

**Monolena** (Melastomataceae) – just two species of these South American plants are recorded as succulents. These are rare in cultivation, but easily grown from seeds.
*Monolena primuliflora* Hook. f. An interesting caudiciform, leaf scars persisting giving a tubercled effect. Leaves large, smooth, dentate, red on underside and red veins. Pinkish flowers with white centre, usually three together. Colombia.

**Muiria** (Mesembryanthemaceae) includes just one rare species which is extremely succulent with short fibrous root system. Considered difficult in cultivation.

*Muiria hortenseae*

*Muiria hortenseae* N. E. Br. Growths consist of two completely united fresh green leaves forming what appears to be a globular body. Fissure hardly apparent until the flower is produced – this is solitary, pinkish-white. Karroo, Cape Province, South Africa.

**Myrmecodia** (Rubiaceae) are among the most fascinating of epiphytic succulents and require temperatures in excess of 60°F/15°C to grow satisfactorily.
*Myrmecodia echinata* Miq. is a smallish shrub-like plant with a large caudex which is rough and spiny. This is referred to as the 'ant plant'; the caudex has many hollows which serve as nests for stinging ants – and the caudex can be as much as 6½ in/16 cm in diameter. Fleshy stems arise from the caudex and have somewhat obovate fleshy leaves and small white tubular flowers. Followed later by red berries. Grows epiphytically on trees in Malaysia and Singapore. There are other species of this genus with the same habit, *Myrmecodia*

*platyrea* Becc. from New Guinea with a flatter caudex, and *Myrmecodia anatonii* Becc., an Australian species.

**Nananthus** (MESEMBRYANTHEMACEAE) consists of about 10 known species, all with very tuberous roots and tufted growth. Leaves distinctive with usually many white dots.
*Nananthus aloides* (Haw.) Schwant. Clumping from the base with many leaves which are lanceolate with a grooved upper surface, keeled toward apex, dark green with numerous white dots. Edges rather rough, also with dots. Flower on short stalk, yellow. Cape Province, South Africa.

*Nananthus transvaalensis*

*Nananthus transvaalensis* (Rolfe) L. Bol. Has leaves about 1¼ in/3 cm long and ⅜ in/1 cm wide covered with conspicuous tubercles along the margins. Flowers are borne solitary, yellow, about 1 in/2.5 cm across. From Transvaal, South Africa.

**Neoalsomitra** (CUCURBITACEAE) contains 2–3 species only which can be considered succulents. All plants of the genus are climbers.
*Neoalsomitra podagrica* Van Sten. Beautiful vine-like succulent with stems spindle-shaped, and at the base-swellings have blunt thorns homologous to leaf bases. Branches also develop this characteristic, until leaves appear. Leaves simple, then three- to five-foliate. Flowers yellowish green. The Philippines.

*Neoalsomitra sarcophylla* (Roem.) Hutch. A succulent vine with slender fleshy stems, much-branched, cylindric and pendent. Leaves elliptic-ovate, 3 to each petiole, channelled, succulent. Flower rather insignificant, greenish-yellow, but they are numerous and attractive as such. Fruits smooth, obtusely three-sided, sub-cylindric 2 in/5 cm long. A rare species of considerable merit from the Philippines, Thailand and Burma.

*Neohenricia sibbettii*

**Neohenricia** (MESEMBRYANTHEMACEAE) L.Bol. is a monotypic genus from the Orange Free State in South Africa. It is of easy culture and freely branches to produce large cushions.
*Neohenricia sibbettii* ǀL. Bol. Branches very freely – low growing, the leaves usually 4 together on each short stem, about ⅜ in/1 cm long and has many whitish tubercles. Flowers highly scented, night-flowering, pure white.

**Neorautenenia** (LEGUMINOSAE) are caudex-forming plants, mostly low-growing with soft, pubescent leaves and small flowers. Of easy culture.
*Neorautenenia ficifolia* (Benth.) C. A. Smith. Has large fleshy caudex, somewhat elongated with rough bark-like surface. Pale green leaves, tripartite, soft with prominent veins. Flowers small, pale yellow. Transvaal, South Africa. This is representative of just a few of the same genus which have been introduced into cultivation in recent years, and all have similar characteristics and are possibly synonymous.

**Notechidnopsis** (ASCLEPIADACEAE) is a new genus created to accept just a few species. Closely related to *Echidnopsis*, requiring similar cultural techniques.
*Notechidnopsis tesselata* (Pillans) Lavr. & Bleck. Previously known as *Echidnopsis framesii* White & Sloane. From Cape Province, South Africa. A prostrate plant, gradually becoming erect to about 4 in/10 cm tall, few branched which are rounded or six-angled with the angles divided into tubercles. Flowers purple. *N. columnaris* (Nel) Lavr. & Bleck (syn. *Echidnopsis columnaris* [Nel] Dyer & Hardy) has greenish-grey, eight-angled stems to 7 in/18 cm tall. The flowers are blotched-red externally, the inner surface white-hairy, yellowish-green with red spots. Cape Province, South Africa.

**Notoniopsis** (COMPOSITAE) is closely akin to *Senecio*. Few species are included. Of easy culture.
*Notoniopsis petraea* (R. E. Fries) B. Norden (syn. *Senecio*

*jacobsenii* Rowl.). This represents a genus erected in 1978. A fleshy creeping succulent from Kenya and Tanzania. The stems are about ⅜ in/1 cm thick and often branched, carrying thick oblanceolate leaves and heads of orange flowers. Other species of consequence include *N. implexa* (Bally) B. Norden, and the red-flowering *N. fulgens* (Hook. f.) B. Norden, still considered by many to be within *Senecio*.

**Ophthalmophyllum** (MESEMBRYANTHEMACEAE) is an interesting genus of about 18 species, stemless and very succulent with fibrous roots. Bodies fleshy with two leaves almost united, tips sometimes 'spreading' with windows.

*Ophthalmophyllum latum*

*Ophthalmophyllum latum* Tisch. Found in Cape Province, South Africa. The bodies consist of two very fleshy, swollen leaves united for most of their length, about 1 in/2.5 cm long and ¾ in/2 cm across, pale green in colour. Flowers are white, ¾ in/2 cm across.

*Ophthalmophyllum lydiae* Jacobs. Usually solitary with small obconical bodies about ¾ in/2 cm high with fissure forming a complete cleft at the top, olive-green and many transparent dots. Flower white, pink tips. Cape Province, South Africa.

*Ophthalmophyllum schlechteri* Schwant. Usually solitary, bodies cylindrical, flat top with pronounced fissure. Tops of lobes with transparent windows, green to reddish. Flower white. Cape Province, South Africa.

**Orbea** (ASCLEPIADACEAE) is a genus erected for certain species of the Stapeliaceae. All have angular stems and large flowers.

*Orbea ciliata* (Thunbg.) Leach. Previously known as *Diplocyatha ciliata*. Stems 2 in/5 cm long branching from the base forming clumps. Branches four-angled, with acute teeth, greyish-green and reddish markings. Flower about 3 in/8 cm from stalk, short campanulate funnelled tube with acute lobes, ovate, spreading, whitish, papillose edges and long white hairs, also in the centre of the tube, cup-shaped papillose annulus with thickish margins. From many areas of Cape Province, South Africa.

*Orbea cooperi* (N. E. Br.) Leach (syn. *Stultitia cooperi*). Stems erect to 1–1½ in/3–4 cm long, four-angled and pronounced teeth, greyish-green, mottled red and dark green. Flowers star-like, outside surface green and purplish stripes, smooth; inside surface wrinkled, yellow with purple lines, and small hairs on recurved margins. Cape Province, South Africa.

*Orbea semota*

*Orbea semota* (syn. *Stapelia semota*). Found in Tanzania, Kenya and Ruanda – a most variable species with 4-angled smooth, spotted stems to about 3 in/8 cm long. Flowers differ in colouring.

*Orbea variegata*

*Orbea variegata* (L.) Haw. (syn. *Stapelia variegata*). The well-known 'star flower'. Many branches in clusters and stems to 4 in/10 cm long, angled, spreading teeth, dark green. Flowers very showy, greenish-yellow with purplish-brown spots, lobes wrinkled having many transverse lines. Cape Province, South Africa.

*Orbeanthus* (ASCLEPIADACEAE) are creeping plants with attractive flowers with hairy corona. Closely allied to *Stultitia*. Cultural requirements similar.

*Orbeanthus conjunctus* (White & Sloane) Leach. Procumbent with many creeping branches to 6 in/15 cm long, four-angled, greyish-green, mottled deeper green and brown, angles with teeth. Flower bell-shaped, short lobes, smooth, pale purplish-brown and creamy-white. Transvaal, South Africa.

*Orbeanthus hardyi*

*Orbeanthus hardyi* (R. A. Dyer) Leach. Species with subterranean growths, somewhat prostrate stems, four-angled and pronounced teeth, pale green with brownish or darker green mottled. Flower campanulate having spreading recurved lobes, brownish-red, and yellowish-white spots; undersurface yellowish. Transvaal, South Africa.

*Orbeopsis* (ASCLEPIADACEAE) are closely allied to *Caralluma*. Distinguished by its umbel-like fascicles of flowers.

*Orbeopsis lutea* (N. E. Br.) Leach. Stems branching from the base forming clusters to 4 in/10 cm high. Stems four-angled, glabrous, sharply toothed, grey-mottled purple. Star-like yellow flowers with red cilia at edges. Transvaal, Cape Province and other parts of South Africa and possibly East Africa.

*Orostachys* (CRASSULACEAE) are fairly hardy plants, native of USSR and parts of east Asia. Closely related to *Sedum* and *Sempervivum*.

*Orostachys chanetti* (Lev.) Bgr. Small, light green fleshy rosette. Leaves of two different lengths, greyish-green to brown and brownish, apex tipped with fine bristle. Flower in dense pyramidal panicle, white with reddish markings on sepals. China.

*Orostachys spinosus* (L.) Bgr. A perennial species, grouping. Leaves form a strong rosette very similar to *Sempervivum*.

Leaves obovate wedge-shaped with spiny apex, greyish-green. Long inflorescence with yellow flowers. Endemic to East Asia.

*Othonna* (COMPOSITAE) contains a few succulent species, often with minutely hairy stems and leaves set opposite. Of easy culture.

*Othonna capensis* L. H. Bail. Creeping or procumbent species with many stems and branches. Leaves almost cylindrical, fleshy, slightly furrowed. Flower at terminal end, yellow. Eastern Cape Province, South Africa.

*Othonna euphorbioides* Hutchins. A dwarf succulent shrub with short stems, sparingly branched, covered with greyish powder. Leaves in tufts at end of branches, elongate-spatulate – like long spoons, light green, white pruinose and long white spines between the leaves. Deciduous. Flowers yellow on short stalk. From Namibia.

*Othonna herrei* Pill. Curious succulent with short thick stems notched by persistent leaf bases. Rarely branching. Leaves irregularly obovate, undulate, fleshy on short stalk, glaucous green, deciduous. Numerous small yellow flowers. Namaqualand, South Africa.

*Othonna lepidocaulis* Schltr. A very dwarf species, rarely branched, thick and roughened with persistent leaf bases. Leaves produced at the apex as small rosette, fleshy, linear about 2 in/5 cm long. Bright yellow flowers. A rare species from mountainous areas in Namaqualand and Cape Province, South Africa.

*Othonna pygmaea* Compt. Small, almost caudex base with short stem and branches. Fleshy succulent leaves, spatulate, somewhat obtuse, slightly crenate at the tips, deciduous. Inflorescence from apex of stem with short peduncle bearing yellow flowers. A very interesting miniature from rock faces, Clanwilliam Div., Cape Province, South Africa.

*Oxalis* (OXALIDACEAE) species are found in many parts of the world. The majority are somewhat succulent, others develop from a bulbous base. While species of the 'wood-sorrels' are to be found in Europe and Africa, the most interesting succulent plants are South American.

*Oxalis carnosa* Mol. Small shrubby plant with tuberous roots and thick fleshy stem with few branches. 'Clover-like' leaves from the terminal ends in clusters on longish stalks, bright green and fleshy. Flower stems from between the leaves, four or five in a cluster. Flower yellow. Native to coastal areas of Peru, Chile and Bolivia. *O. peduncularis* from Ecuador with fleshy petioles in rosettes at branch terminals and fleshy leaves. Flowers on long stem, deep yellowish-orange. *O. herrerae* Kunth. is a smaller edition of *O. peduncularis* H. B. & K., short stem with very thick fleshy leaf stalks and bright green leaves. Flowers rather smaller, yellow. *O. sepalosa* Diels. from Peru and Bolivia, stems to about 16 in/40 cm high and very much swollen at the base. Leaves densely arranged at the top with yellow flowers. *O. ortgiesii* Regel., from the Peruvian Andes, a succulent tree-like plant to about 20 in/50 cm tall with reddish-green leaves, maroon on the underside. Flowers yellow. *O. succulenta* Barn. An attractive small species with many branches and numerous small glaucous leaves having minute hairs on the under-surface. Native of Chile and Peru.

These plants are not difficult in cultivation – in fact if due attention is not given they can spread out of all proportions! They mainly require to be grown 'hard' – too much moisture encourages rampant growth and they quickly lose their attraction.

*Pachycormus* (ANACARDIACEAE) has soft woody stems which exude a white latex. Only one succulent species is recorded and this has a number of varieties.

*Pachycormus discolor*

*Pachycormus discolor* (Benth.) Coville. A native of Baja California and off-shore islands. Commonly known as the 'elephant tree' – an ideal plant for cultivation as a natural bonsai. A short, dwarfed swollen trunk with papery bark and branching quite freely with somewhat slender elongated branches and small leaves, deciduous. Flowers small, reddish or yellowish. During rest season the branches can be trimmed to encourage compact shape. An uncommon plant in cultivation. This is the only succulent within the plant family which includes several well-known non-succulents – *Mangifera indica*, the mango tree, *Harpephyllum caffrum*, the Kaffir plum, *Anacardium occidentale*, the cashew-nut tree, *Rhus vernix*, the poison ivy, and *Schinus molle*, the peppercorn tree, and it was into this latter genus that *Pachycormus* was originally placed.

*Pachycymbium* (ASCLEPIADACEAE) is a genus of few species, all with rhizomatous rootstock and unusual campanulate flowers. Allied to *Caralluma*.
*Pachcymbium lancasteri* Lavr. From the northeastern Transvaal, South Africa. A more or less erect plant with greenish-brown, four-angled stems 4 in/10 cm or more long with prominent teeth. Flowers bright golden-yellow.

Other species include *P. keithii* (syn. *Caralluma keithii*) and *P. carnosum* (syn. *Caralluma carnosa*), both of which are natives of Transvaal, South Africa.

*Pachyphytum* (CRASSULACEAE), which are related to *Echeveria*, generally have elongated rosettes, the flowers being the main characteristic. They are hanging, bell-shaped and enclosed in bracts on shortish stalks.
*Pachyphytum kimnachii* Moran. Native of the region around San Luis Potosi, Mexico, on mossy rocks at 5,900 ft/1,800 m altitude. Leaves glaucous, somewhat purplish, elliptic-oblong with rounded margins, to about 3 in/8 cm long forming elongated rosette on slender stem. Flower reddish and cream with greenish bracts.
*Pachyphytum oviferum* J. A. Purp. A beautiful and popular species called the 'sugar almond' plant, from Barranca Bagre, San Luis Potosi, Mexico. Fleshy, white pruinose, obovate, thick leaves to about 1¼ in/3 cm long and ¾ in/2cm wide, bluntly rounded at the tip, forming small rosettes at intervals along the usually prostrate fleshy branches. Flower reddish.
*Pachyphytum viride* E. Walth. A Mexican species with thick erect brownish stem to about 4 in/10 cm or more long. Leaves up to 20 at tip of stem, semi-cylindrical, blunt, pale green to about 4½ in/12 cm long. Flower reddish-green.
*Pachphytum werdermannii* v. Poelln. A distinctive species from near Jaumave, Tamaulipas, Mexico, having densely arranged leaves along stem up to 10 in/25 cm long. Leaves tongue-shaped, thick, somewhat recurved with bluntish tip, pruinose with pinkish shading, not forming a precise rosette. Flowers whitish-red with whitish bracts on long inflorescence.

*Pachypodium* (APOCYNACEAE) have created considerable interest since their introduction into cultivation. These succulent shrubby plants, all with fleshy trunks or caudices, are still considered rarities although two species are now being grown in Europe as useful houseplants.
*Pachypodium baronii* var. *windsori* (H. Poiss.) Pichon. An unusual species with almost globose caudex to about 3 in/8 cm diameter. Few branches, round with many spines and rough skin. Leaves at terminal ends, short stalk, thick, ovate and usually two together, opposite, margins crenate, about 2 in/5 cm long. Inflorescence between the leaves with red flowers. South Madagascar.
*Pachypodium bispinosum* (L.f.) DC. From Cape Province, South Africa – it has a large caudex with several stems and branches and can attain 18 in/45 cm in height. Stems bear thorns ⅜ in/1 cm long and narrow lanceolate leaves rough on upper surface, hairy below. Flowers pink or purplish.

*Pachypodium brevicaule* Bak. With stone-like fleshy swollen caudex often to 25 in/65 cm diameter. Leaves sessile, elliptical on short elevations 1¼ in/3 cm long, having few spines between leaves. Flower yellow. Madagascar.

*Pachypodium densiflorum* Bak. A multiheaded small caudiciform species, having many rounded branches covered closely with subulate spines. Leaves green with whitish felt on undersurface. Flowers very decorative, orange. Madagascar.

*Pachypodium geayi*

*Pachypodium geayi* Const. & Bois. Tree-like species, long slender stem to 33 ft/10 m high, fleshy with many spines, very dark or brownish-green. Leaves at apex, linear-lanceolate. Flowers white. From the dry western coastal areas of Madagascar at low altitudes.

*Pachypodium giganteum* Engl. Tall succulent tree-like plant to 20 ft/6 m high. Stem bottle-shaped, branching at apex, all furnished with many hard spines. Leaves sessile, ovate-elongate coming to a point, margins ciliate. Flower white, scented. Namibia.

*Pachypodium horomboense* H. Poiss. Low-growing species with caudex and many thick fleshy branches all with spines. Leaves oval to about 2½ in/6 cm long. Flower bright yellow, cup-shaped on long stem. Madagascar, where it grows on granite rocks.

*Pachypodium lamerei* Drake. An erect, sometimes much-branched species with conical fleshy trunk to 6½ ft/2 m high. Leaves 10 in/25 cm long and 1¼ in/3 cm wide. Flower white. From dry forest areas of Madagascar.

*Pachypodium lealii* Welw. Arborescent species, clavate, narrowing at the apex with numerous erect branches. Leaves small and narrow, set between stout spines, also

from shorter stems having somewhat larger leaf and less stout spines. Flower white at ends of branches. South Africa, Cape Province around Namaqualand.

*Pachypodium namaquanum* Welw. Tree-like succulent to nearly 6½ ft/2 m high. Stems fleshy and with many spines, only very rarely branched. Leaves develop in tufts at apex, smallish and undulated, deciduous in dry season. Flowers from leaf axils, numerous, velvety reddish-brown, striped yellow inside. Known as the 'ghost-men' by native population. Namaqualand and Cape Province, South Africa.

*Pachypodium rosulatum* Bak. Low and thick caudex, fleshy, branching with cylindrical and densely spined branches. Leaves at terminal ends, in form of rosette, narrow, oblanceolate. Flowers on long stalks, sulphur-yellow. Madagascar.

*Pachypodium saundersii*

*Pachypodium saundersii* N. E. Br. Caudex sometimes rounded, otherwise elongated to over 3¼ ft/1 m high. Leaves oblanceolate, dark green, undulate, from numerous twisted branches. Flower white with reddish stripes. Natal.

*Pachypodium succulentum* DC. Caudex short and thick with long tapering tuberous root, very succulent. Branches erect from the upper portion of the caudex. Leaves lanceolate, set at the base with two spines. Flower pale pink. Little Namaqualand and Cape Province, South Africa.

**Pectinaria** (ASCLEPIADACEAE) is related to *Piaranthus* and *Duvalia*. Low-growing species, with angled and tuberculate stems. Flowers with the corolla lobes connate at the apex having narrow openings between.

*Pectinaria asperifolia* N. E. Br. Freely clustering with many stems, often erect to 3 in/8 cm long, rounded with six to eight ribs consisting of sharp-tipped tubercles. Flower drooping, outside surface purplish-brown, inside white and purple dots. Cape Province, South Africa.

*Pectinaria saxatilis*

*Pectinaria saxatilis* N. E. Br. Forming clumps with somewhat procumbent stems, acutely four-angled to 2 in/5 cm long, angles compressed and furnished with acute teeth. Flowers in clusters from the younger shoots, ovate, lobes connate at the tips, blackish-purple and hairy. Cape Province, South Africa.

**Pedilanthus** (EUPHORBIACEAE) are very similar to *Euphorbia*, usually with deciduous leaves and bird-shaped red flowers. *Pedilanthus carinatus* Spr. Widespread in many of the West Indian islands, a shrubby plant often to 3¼ ft/1 m high, cylindrical stems, erect, green with obovate leaves, fleshy about 4¾ in/12 cm long and red bird-shaped cyathia. *Pedilanthus macrocarpus* Benth. From the Sonora Desert and Baja California, with erect thick succulent stems to about 3¼ ft/1 m high, tiny deciduous leaves. Bright red cyathia at terminal ends of stems.

**Pelargonium** (GERANIACEAE) is a genus including many true succulents, often with unusual stem growth.

*Pelargonium acetosum*

*Pelargonium acetosum* (L.) l'Her. A spreading shrubby species with slender branches, obovate leaves with slightly

*Pelargonium incrassatum*

crenate edges, but deciduous. Flowers borne on short stems, rose-pink. From near rivers in Cape Province, South Africa. *P.incrassatum* (Andr.) Sims. from southwest Cape Province has glabrous leaves, deeply pinnate and fleshy. The scape, bears clusters of large deep red flowers with deeper red stripes. The plant is about 6 in/15 cm tall when in bloom.

*Pelargonium echinatum* Curt. Small-growing species with erect fleshy branches, having many prominent stipules. Leaves three- to five-lobed somewhat rounded with crenate margins, greyish and rather hairy, on long stalk. Flowers on long peduncle, purple. Many parts of South Africa.

*Pelargonium juttae* Dtr. Small-growing species developing large caudex base. Branches freely on short stems with leaves on long stalks, dissected, semi-pinnate with hairy surface. A rare species from Namibia.

*Pelargonium paradoxum* Dtr. A very succulent species with thickened rounded fleshy stems with many leaf scars, light green or yellowish. Leaves develop near the tips of the branches, narrow and fleshy with curled and deeply crenate margins, grey-green and having short hairs. Flowers whitish in umbels. Namibia.

*Pelargonium sidifolium* (Thunbg.) Knuth. Similar to *P. echinatum*, but having no stipules. An easily grown species which branches freely with three- to five-lobed leaves, margins crenate. Flowers small, reddish-purple in clusters. Transvaal, South Africa.

*Pelargonium tetragonum* (L.f.) l'Her. A well-known succulent species, erect with thin angled stems, fleshy, pale green. Leaves 5-lobed, heart-shaped and crenate margins. Deciduous. Flowers pink and purple on long stalks. South Africa.

**Peperomia** (PIPERACEAE) is a large genus of over 500 species, many of which are truly succulent, in either root-stock, stems or foliage. Inconspicuous flowers borne in a terminal raceme. All of easy culture.

*Peperomia crassifolia* Bak. An erect species, fleshy, stiff with bright green stems. Leaves succulent, alternate, usually obovate to about 2½ in/6 cm long, fresh green, paler green on lower surface and pale midrib. Tropical Africa.

*Peperomia dolabriformis* Kunth. Species from Peru. Shrubby habit to about 4 in/10 cm tall, fleshy spatulate leaves folded together so that only the underside of the leaf is visible, the edges having a translucent appearance, creating a 'window' which allows light to penetrate. Flowers are inconspicuous, erect, catkin-like.

*Peperomia fosteri* Bak. From the Amazon Valley in Brazil, an attractive red-stemmed creeping species with thick leaves, short and elliptical.

*Peperomia prostrata* Hort. Williams, ex Gard. With small circular leaves, bluish-grey or brown in colour with distinct silvery markings – very attractive, but rare. Colombia.

*Peperomia rotundifolia* Dahlst. (syn. *P. nummularifolia*). From many of the West Indian islands where it totally inhabits trees. Very small, almost round leaves, fleshy and waxy on thread-like stems. *P. nivalis* Miq., a Peruvian species, with numerous leaves, keel-shaped, almost folded, forming rosettes. Leaves are scented like aniseed. *P. incana* A. Dietr., native of Restinga in Brazil, with fleshy stiff heart-shaped leaves, greyish and completely covered with whitish felt. A very succulent species. *P. ornata* Yuncker has short succulent stem with clusters of elliptical leaves on red stalks, and beautifully veined. Endemic to south Venezuela. *P. pereskiaefolia* H. B. & K. from northern Brazil and Venezuela with habit much resembling *Pereskia*. Succulent plant with obovate waxy leaves from reddish stems. *P. polybotrya* H. B. & K. originates from Colombia, erect succulent stem, vivid green leaves, purple-edged, thick, shield-shaped, inflorescence branched with multiple 'catkins'.

Many other species could also be included, *Peperomia pellucida* H. B. & K. and *Peperomia trinervula* DC. are but two.

Very widely distributed family of plants and the majority are succulents. Many are epiphytes.

**Philodendron** (ARACEAE) are mostly climbing plants with fleshy stems and leaves, often with very elongated, trailing roots. Ideal for home decor. About 300 species are recorded of this genus.

*Philodendron cannaefolium* Mart. Very succulent stems with deep green ovate leaves and red margins. A Brazilian species with creamy-white spathe and yellow spadix.

*Philodendron fragrantissimum* Kunth. Has large arrow-shaped leaves with many depressed veins. A beautiful and rare species with purplish-white spathe having an elusive fragrance. From eastern Venezuela and Guyana.

*Philodendron laciniosum* Schott (syn. *P. pedatum*). From northern Brazil and Guyana, epiphytic on trees or rocks. A climbing species, large leaves with three to five broad lobes and pronounced midrib. Spathe greenish-white and cream spadix.

*Philodendron rudgeanum* Schott. (syn. *P. cannifolium*). With beautiful lanceolate leaves, deeply channeled and having white spathe with yellow spadix. A showy species from Guyana.

*Philodendron saxicola* K. Krause. A beautiful species with leathery sword-shaped leaves. Usually saxicolous, but sometimes epiphytic on trees. A rare and unusual plant.

*Philodendron teretipes* Sprague. Has elongated sword-like leaves with many prominent veins, glossy-green with red margins. Colombia.

*Philodendron wittianum* Engl. From the Amazon rain forests above Manaus. Has oblong leaves similar to a *Musa* and about 20 in/50 cm in length. A creeping epiphyte with pale green spathe and cream spadix.

Due to the presence of aerial roots many might be considered epiphytic, but only those are noted which are totally epiphytal and succulent – and this only represents a small selection from a great number.

**Phytolacca** (PHYTOLACCACEAE) is a rather mixed group of plants, some tree-like or shrubby while others are just herbaceous plants; the roots of some of the latter are poisonous.

*Phytolacca dioica* L. Fairly well distributed throughout much of South America. A tall succulent tree with thick fleshy roots and equally fleshy trunk and branches. Leaves at terminals of branches somewhat spirally arranged, oval to elongated, tapering sharply at the tip about 10 in/25 cm long and about 6 in/15 cm wide, bright green with reddish veins. Flowers pendent on long stalks, whitish and inconspicuous.

**Piaranthus** (ASCLEPIADACEAE) are small-growing species usually with four-angled stems and blunt edges. Flowers erect on stalks, round corolla with bell-shaped tube, hairy triangular lobes.

*Piaranthus foetidus*

*Piaranthus foetidus* N. E. Br. Stems sub-globose to 1½ in/4 cm long with four and sometimes 5 angles, toothed edges, greyish-green, sometimes reddish. Flowers from near top of stems, outside greenish-red, fleshy and inside yellow with transverse lines and hairs. Cape Province, South Africa.

*Piaranthus globosus* White & Sloane. With procumbent stems, oval and obscurely four-angled with few small teeth along the edges, light green. Flowers have no tube, back surface glabrous, inside pale greenish-yellow with reddish spots, hairy. Cape Province, South Africa.

*Piaranthus pillansii* N. E. Br. Procumbent stems to 1½ in/ 4 cm long, club-shaped with four-angles rather obtuse. Light pinkish-green. Flowers in pairs, outside glabrous, inside yellowish-green, hairy. Cape Province, South Africa.

*Piaranthus ruschii*

*Piaranthus ruschii* Nel. Native of Namibia. A creeping or semi-erect plant with stems about ¾ in/1–2 cm long, greyish-green in colour and angled. The rounded corolla has slender lobes, greenish-yellow on the inner surface, with many small blackish blotches.

**Pilea** (URTICACEAE) includes many xerophytic plants, generally shade-loving, but not epiphytic. Several have succulent growth and are well-known as houseplants.

*Pilea globosa* Wedd. Peru and other Andean regions. Has small sub-globose leaves crowded toward tips of stems, only ⅛ in/3 mm long and broad. Upper surface hemispherical, somewhat flattened on lower surface. Flowers small, purple.

*Pilea peperomioides* Diels. An unusual species from Yunnan, China, growing at altitudes of 6,500–8,800 ft/2,000– 2,700 m. Stems densely set with stipules with spirally arranged fresh green, fleshy, almost orbicular leaves 1½– 2½ in/4–7 cm long and wide. Flowers are either male or female, greenish-cream suffused with pinkish-purple.

**Plectranthus** (LABIATAE) contains over 120 species, only a few of which are succulent in leaf or stem. Just one has a tuberous, fleshy rootstock.

*Plectranthus esculentus* N.E. Br. From many parts of tropical Africa, has tuberous roots (said to be edible), erect stems densely covered with minute white hairs and panicles of bright yellow flowers.

*Plectranthus prostratus* Gurke. Low-growing pubescent species with many soft branches. Leaves thick, soft and crenate about ½ in/12 mm long. Flowers in raceme, purple.

Tanzania. Many others of this genus are borderline succulents, perhaps *P. fischeri* Gurke the only species deserving mention as truly succulent.

**Pleiospilos** (MESEMBRYANTHEMACEAE) are popular plants with varying leaf shapes, clumping freely with large flowers, often scented. Includes over 30 species – all of easy culture.

*Pleiospilos bolusii* (Hook. f.) N. E. Br. Very succulent species, stemless with pairs of thick, stone-like keeled leaves 1½ in/ 4 cm long and nearly as broad. Leaves flattened on upper surface, light grey-green, with many darkish green dots. Flowers deep yellow. Cape Province, South Africa.

*Pleiospilos leipoldtii* L. Bol. Leaves of various shapes, generally obovate to about 2½ in/7 cm long, keeled at the bottom, pointed at apex, dullish green with numerous prominent dots. Flowers yellow, white centre. Cape Province, South Africa.

*Pleiospilos optatus* (N. E. Br.) Schwant. Much-branched from base, forming clumps. Leaves 2–4 in one growth to 1½ in/ 4 cm long, flattened on upper surface, rounded and keeled below tip, reddish-green with tinges of purple and numerous green dots. Flower yellow. Cape Province, South Africa.

*Pleiospilos willowmorensis* L. Bol. A popular and well-known species with 2–4 leaved growth, flattened upper surface somewhat sickle-like and keeled. Leaves of unequal lengths, purplish-green and covered with many dots. Flower yellow, white centre. Cape Province, South Africa.

**Plumiera** (APOCYNACEAE) are large shrub- or tree-like plants with fleshy thick stems and branches. A popular genus of South America and the West Indies which has been naturalized in many tropical regions of the world.

*Plumiera acuminata*

*Plumiera acuminata* Ait. A species distributed throughout much of Mexico, Central America and the West Indies. The typical 'Franzipani tree'. A succulent tree with fleshy stems and branches which exude a latex-like substance. Large green leaves which fall in rest season. Flowers very beautiful, dark cream with yellow centre.

*Plumiera acuminata* var. *purpurea* Ruiz. & Pav. Similar in most respects to the species, apparently native to several of the West Indian islands, having beautiful reddish-purple flowers. Another variety is *P. acuminata* var. *alba* L. from the Windward Islands and Leeward Islands having slender succulent stem and narrow leaves, long and tapering.

*Plumiera rubra* L. Similar in many respects to other species of *Plumiera*, native to the West Indies. A tree-like succulent with fleshy branches and large elongated leaves having panicles of deep red flowers with yellow throat from the terminal end of the branches. Native of Venezuela and possibly through to Peru.

**Poellnitzia** (ASPHODELACEAE) is separated from *Haworthia* and *Astroloba* because of the flower characteristics – only one species is included, but there are also a variety!.

*Poellnitzia rubiflora* (L. Bol.) Uitew. Dense-leafed rosette with elongated stems, offsetting from the base. Thick triangular leaves, blue-green or greyish, lower surface keeled, margins and keel with minute teeth. Long flower spike with orange-red flowers more similar to an *Aloe*. Southern Cape Province, South Africa.

**Portulaca** (PORTULACACEAE) is a well-known group of plants, some of which have been hybridized to good effect. There are a number which offer no attraction and have become pernicious weeds.

*Portulaca werdermannii* v. Poelln. A prostrate species from Bahia, Brazil, with oblong cylindrical leaves, set alternate, having many hairs in the leaf axils. Terminal flowers, purplish-red. *P. pilosa* L., distributed throughout much of tropical America, a beautiful prostrate plant with dense white hairs and small fleshy leaves. Flower reddish-yellow. *P. poellnitziana* Werd. from near Rio de Janeiro, Brazil, is very similar to *P. pilosa* but with more erect stems having whitish hairs, and bright yellow flowers. *P. grandiflora* Hook., a low, spreading plant with cylindrical leaves, fleshy and hairy. Flowers of various colours, yellow, red, purple, etc., often used as a decorative bedding plant for a sunny position and treated as an annual. Native of Brazil.

**Psammophora** (MESEMBRYANTHEMACEAE) includes only four species, low-growing, tufted with dense woody stems, branches often buried so only leaves are seen. Leaves sticky, bluish-green, and in habitat are covered with sand.

*Psammophora longifolia* L. Bol. Small species, tufted, growths with four to six leaves to over 1½ in/4 cm long and ½ in/12 mm wide, upper surface linear, flat and somewhat tapering, lower surface rounded with keel which is drawn forward over the upper surface, olive-green to brownish, surface rough, sticky and often sand-encrusted, a protection from undue transpiration. Flower white. From Namibia.

**Pseudolithos** (ASCLEPIADACEAE) is a small genus of greyish-green tuberculate, angled plants of particular interest to the advanced collector.

*Pseudolithos cubiforme* Bally. Has a stem with four blunt angles, angular tubercles and several greenish-brownish flowers in an umbel, pinkish hairy on the inner surface.

*Pseudolithos migiurtinorum*

*Pseudolithos migiurtinorum* (Chiov.) Bally (syn. *Lithocaulon sphaericum* Bally). With almost completely round or oblong stems, and totally covered with irregular tessellations, dull whitish-green when young, greyish-green on older plants. Flowers small in clusters, brownish-green. From Somalia.

**Pseudopectinaria** (ASCLEPIADACEAE) is a small genus closely related to *Stapelia*, requiring similar culture.

*Pseudopectinaria malum* Lavr. A relatively new discovery in Somalia. Very fleshy succulent stems, elongated and somewhat bluntly angled. Leaves insignificant and quickly fading. Flower borne on short pedicel, fleshy, circular, corolla purplish inside and papillose outside, incurved triangular lobes and yellow outer corona.

**Pterodiscus** (PEDALIACEAE) contains a number of species, mostly with thick fleshy stems and attractive flowers.

*Pterodiscus angustifolia* Engl. An interesting species having very fleshy base with many succulent branches, almost shrubby, purplish-green, to about 10 in/25 cm high. Leaves very succulent, narrow oblanceolate, deep green, margins usually undulate and dentate at apex. Flower deep yellow with purplish markings in the tube, scented. Tanzania.

*Pterodiscus aurantiacus* Welw. Irregularly shaped caudex to about 10 in/25 cm high and at the end short thickish branches, somewhat fleshy. Leaves elongate-lanceolate, wavy-edged with slight indentations, bluish-green. Flower yellow. Namibia and Angola.

*Pterodiscus procumbens* Burch. (syn. *Harpagophytum procumbens* [Burch.] DC). A trailing plant with fleshy tuberous roots and opposite leaves, pale greyish-green, lobed. Flowers from the leaf axils, red or purplish. Fruits brownish, barbed with recurved spines. South Africa.

*Pterodiscus luridus* Hook. Similar in many parts to *P. auran-tiacus*. Thickish-fleshy stem to about 16 in/40 cm high. Branches freely with oblong leaves, upper surface dark green, lower surface bluish. Flower yellowish with many red dots. Stem, branches, leaves, flowers somewhat pruinose. Cape Province, South Africa.

*Pterodiscus speciosus*

*Pterodiscus speciosus* Hook. A small fleshy-stemmed succulent with enlarged base, about 6 in/15 cm high. Leaves develop in the upper part, linear-oblong, dentate, dull green. Flowers purplish-pink. Cape Province, South Africa.

***Puya*** (BROMELIACEAE) are xerophytic plants closely allied to *Dyckia* and *Hechtia*. All are native of the Andes region, mostly at high altitudes. Of easy culture.

*Puya alpestris*

*Puya alpestris* Gay. Native of Chile. Large rosette over 3¼ ft/1 m diameter with long slender leaves about ¾ in/ 2 cm wide, having whitish scales on the lower surface and

very sharp, hard spiny margins. Long inflorescence with many upward-pointing branches, serrated bracts and large greyish-blue flowers. *P. chilensis* Mol. is also from Chile, develops a woody stem with age, often 3¼ ft/1 m or more tall from which the rosette growths develop. Leaves 3–4 in/80–100 mm long and 2 in/5 cm wide, margins with hard recurved spines. Tall inflorescence covered with brownish hairs and yellowish flowers. Other species include

*Puya raimondii*

*P. raimondii* Harms, one of the largest species of the genus from altitudes of about 13,000 ft/4,000 m in central and south Peru, almost hardy in some protected areas of Europe. *P. laxa* L. B. Smith, native of Argentina, has loose rosette of long narrow greyish velvety leaves developing on a much-branching plant. There are smaller growing species such as *P. nana* Wittm. from Bolivia and *P. medica* L. B. Smith which is endemic to Peru with bluish flowers. These are particularly useful for normal cultivation under glass.

***Pyrenacantha*** (ICACINACEAE) from East Africa includes a few root succulents, generally of climbing habit. Rare in cultivation.
*Pyrenacantha malvifolia* Engl. A species with very large caudex, often deformed, sometimes over 3¼ ft/1 m in diameter. Thickish stems develop from the apex of the caudex having only few leaves, flowers very small. Dioecious – fruits on female plants orange-red. Tanzania.
*Pyrenacantha vitifolia* Engl. A rare species having very large thickened, caudex-like rhizomes. Many branches, clamber-ing, with brownish-green skin. Leaves somewhat round, deeply lobed, dark green, deciduous. Flowers small from branch terminals. This plant is also dioecious – female plants have orange fruits. Kenya.

**Rabiea** (MESEMBRYANTHEMACEAE) is a species with fleshy roots and crowded branchlets. Leaves spreading, very dissimilar in appearance one leaf to another. Sharply tapering and keeled, usually with many wart-like white or brown dots. Flowers solitary. Includes only six species and a few varietal forms.
*Rabiea albinota* (Hae.) N. E. Br. Forming a dwarf succulent rosette consisting of six to eight triangled leaves, somewhat sabre-like, to about 4 in/10 cm long, flattened on upper surface and covered with many whitish warts. Flowers yellow. Cape Province, South Africa.

**Raphionacme** (ASCLEPIADACEAE) contains species which are either tuberous-rooted or with caudex. These are a recent introduction into cultivation and only a few of the nearly 30 species have yet been seen.
*Raphionacme galpinii* Schltr. Caudex to about 5½ in/14 cm diameter. Short annual stems to about 2½ in/7 cm long with elongated, pilose leaves about 1¼ in/3 cm long. Flower smallish, greenish-yellow. Transvaal, South Africa.
*Raphionacme hirsuta* (E. Mey.) Dyer. Large caudex to 8 in/20 cm diameter. Annual shoots appear from the apex producing small lanceolate leaves. Small flowers, purple. East Cape Province, Natal, Orange Free State and Transvaal, South Africa.

Other species are widely distributed throughout East, West, South Africa and Namibia – many are little known, but obviously are of considerable interest. *R. procumbens* Schltr. from Namibia has an exceptionally large tuber. *R. daronii* Berhaut from Ghana has almost a horizontally flattened caudex. *R. vignei* Bruce, also from Ghana with an almost vertical caudex, is very elongated and with greenish flowers.

**Rechsteineria** (GESNERIACEAE) includes a few root succulents of particular interest. Readily grown from seeds or division of rootstock.
*Rechsteineria leucotricha* Hoehne. With a thick rounded tuberous root often to 12 in/30 cm diameter which is mostly exposed. Stems densely covered with silvery hairs as are the broad obovate leaves set in the form of a whorl. The pinkish-orange flowers are terminal in centre of whorl. Native of Brazil.

**Rhombophyllum** (MESEMBRYANTHEMACEAE) recognizes only three species, shrubby or caespitose with tuberous roots, leaves somewhat rhomboidal, margins often with one or two teeth, otherwise entire.
*Rhombophyllum dolabriforme* (L.) Schwant. With leaves like stag's horns, wedge-shaped, spreading, upper surface flat and tapering, lower side semi-cylindrical with keel, green and translucent dots. Large flowers, golden-yellow. Cape Province, South Africa.

**Rhytidocaulon** (ASCLEPIADACEAE) is a small genus of fleshy-stemmed species, frequently tall-growing. Allied to *Echidnopsis*.
*Rhytidocaulon piliferum* Lavr. Erect stems and branches, four- to six-angled, bluntly tessellated, rough and covered with waxy papillae densely arranged, grey or brown. Leaves small, deciduous. Flowers fleshy, small, somewhat tubular with very narrow spreading lobes, whitish below, dark purple above. Somalia.

**Rochea** (CRASSULACEAE) includes only a few species similar to those of *Crassula* and possibly synonymous. Easily cultivated from seeds or stem cuttings.

*Rochea coccinea*

*Rochea coccinea* (L.) DC. A much-branched species with small pointed leaves on slender stems, closely set, green upper surface, red lower surface. Flowers numerous in cymes, scarlet. An attractive houseplant. South Africa.

**Rosularia** (CRASSULACEAE) are found in parts of Asia and USSR and are reasonably hardy. They are either root, stem or leaf succulents.
*Rosularia glabra* (Rgl. & Winkler) Bgr. With elliptical or spoon-shaped leaves with pointed apex forming bright green rosette. Flowers on short stalks, yellowish-red. Endemic to Turkestan.
*Rosularia modesta* (Bornm.) Parsa. From Iran, has a small, dense-leaved rosette arising from a caudex. A leafy stem produces an inflorescence of pink flowers.

There are several species of *Rosularia*; all are similar to *Sempervivums* and require similar culture but will not accept too much frost and snow.

**Ruschia** (MESEMBRYANTHEMACEAE) is one of the largest genera of Mesembryanthemums with about 350 species. Shrubby, somewhat erect but sometimes more prostrate and forming tufts. Branches often covered with dead leaf remains. Leaves of various shapes, elongated or rounded with pronounced keel, amplexicaul, very long sheath.
*Ruschia dualis* (N. E. Br.) L. Bol. Forming clusters up to

2 in/5 cm high with mature branchlets covered by dry leaves. Leaves two together, united near to base, upper surface flattened, back surface semi-circular and keeled with firm margins, greyish-green. Flowers small, deep pink. Cape Province, South Africa.

*Ruschia pygmaea* (Haw.) Schwant. A miniature species forming compact mats with short branchlets, one to two pairs of leaves, each pair different, the upper pair united at tip, the skin of which dries and covers the succeeding pair which have spreading leaves, rounded on upper surface and keeled below. Flowers small. Cape Province, South Africa.

**Sansevieria** (AGAVACEAE) are a widely distributed group embracing very many species, many of which are true succulents; indeed, some are epiphytic. We have authentic knowledge of only a few – new species are being discovered and remain, so far, undescribed. Some species have made ideal houseplants.

*Sansevieria canaliculata* Carr. A very slow-growing species, producing only two or three new leaves annually. These are medium-green, slightly curved and flexible with regular grooves longitudinally arranged. Flower whitish. Tropical Africa.

*Sansevieria cylindrica* Bojer. A most distinct species having sharp elongated cylindrical leaves, often with furrows, dull dark green. Flower stem short with very white flowers. Southern tropical Africa, Natal.

There are also varietal forms of this species, differing in the thickness of leaf, flower colour.

*Sansevieria grandis*

*Sansevieria grandis* Hook. f. From Somalia, with large broad obovate leaves, deep green with reddish margins and having numerous thick rhizomes. Flower in dense raceme, whitish, followed by greenish, turning black, berries. This and other species have been found in tropical East Africa in recent years – all epiphytic but still awaiting descriptions.

*Sansevieria hahnii* Hort. An interesting 'sport' of *S. trifasciata* var. *laurentii* found in New Orleans in 1939 with the habit of a low vase-like rosette, clustering freely from the base. Leaves dark green with pale green crossbands. Flower whitish.

*Sansevieria stuckyi* Godefr. Leb. With creeping rhizomes forming colonies. Leaves cylindrical to about 3¼ ft/1 m long with light green crossbands and mottling. Flower whitish. From the region of the Victoria Falls in Zimbabwe.

*Sansevieria thyrsiflora* Thunbg. Has thick, creeping rhizome sending up numerous rosettes of erect, flat, smooth leaves, tapering at the apex, upper surface slightly channelled, lower surface with slight keel. Flowers greenish-white, and sweetly scented. Southeast Africa.

*Sansevieria trifasciata* var. *laurentii* (Willd.) N. E. Br. A most attractive species, making an ideal houseplant – commonly known as 'mother-in-law's tongue'. Leaves sword-like, very erect with marginal yellow stripes and whitish crossbands. Flowers whitish. From Zaire, tropical Africa.

There are several other species worthy of note: *S. guineensis* Willd. from Nigeria, *S. pearsonii* N. E. Br. from Angola and the more miniature *S. parva* N. E. Br. from East Africa are of particular interest and merit, but there are many others also.

**Sarcocaulon** (GERANIACEAE) are small bushy plants closely allied to *Pelargonium*. Propagated by seeds or stem cuttings.

*Sarcocaulon burmannii* (DC.). Sweet emend. Rehm. Miniature bushy plant with many thick, somewhat spiny, greyish-green branches, small irregularly indented leaves and pinkish-white flowers. Bushmanland, South Africa.

*Sarcocaulon l'heritieri* (DC.) Sweet. Slender-stemmed dwarf shrub having many thin white spiny branches. Leaves are elongated heart-shaped, bright green. Small yellowish-white flowers. From the border of the Namib Desert in Namibia.

*Sarcocaulon multifidum*

*Sarcocaulon multifidum* R. Knuth. A beautiful miniature plant with thick branches growing horizontally. Stem without spines, leaves developing in small tufts, hairy, greyish-green. Flowers on long stalk, pink, much larger than the leaves. Namibia in mountainous country.

*Sarcocaulon rigidum* Schinz. Several varieties of this species, with differing characteristics dependent upon habitat conditions. The species is a spreading miniature shrub, very succulent stem and very spiny branches. Leaves all along the stems, two-lobed, deciduous. Flower scarlet with narrow petals. From the coastal region of Namibia.

**Sarcostemma** (ASCLEPIADACEAE) includes about 14 species, mainly with thin, somewhat elongated stems, often segmented, invariably leafless and with small flowers in umbels.

*Sarcostemma brunoniana* Wight & Arn. Having fairly strong twining stems, often prostrate, jointed with segments about 2 in/5 cm long, cylindrical, bright green. Flowers in umbels, white. India.

*Sarcostemma viminale* R. Br. Erect cylindrical branches, becoming rather pendent, jointed with triangular leaf scales, greyish-green. Flowers white in umbels. From tropical and sub-tropical Africa. The best known of the genus.

Descriptions of other species differ very little from those mentioned; the main distinction with some are the varying flower colours and size of flower. The distribution is most extensive – Asia, Africa and Australia, also in South America where perhaps the larger-flowering species are found.

**Sarcozona** (MESEMBRYANTHEMACEAE) is a small genus of low-growing plants, closely related to *Carpobrotus* and native of Australia. Leaves are flattened or angular, thick and fleshy. They require a position in full sun.

*Sarcozona praecox*

*S. praecox* (F. v. Muell.) S.T. Blake. Has purplish-grey leaves and particularly wrinkled surface. A compact plant, producing small pink flowers about ½ in/1.5 cm across. Occurs on flat sandy areas in South Australia.

**Sceletium** (MESEMBRYANTHEMACEAE) consists of 22 species and a few minor forms – somewhat unusual, often giving the effect of a papery skeleton-like structure caused by leaves persisting after withering. Spreading plants with prostrate stems and elongated rounded leaves, somewhat papillose when young. Species contain mesembrine, a poisonous drug.

*Sceletium archeri* L. Bol. Plant with short stems and elongated prostrate branches, slender with internodes. Leaves very succulent, erect, lanceolate, tapering toward apex, papillose, dull green, ½ in/12 mm long, sheath about ¹⁄₁₀ in/ 2 mm. Flower solitary, pale yellow. Cape Province, South Africa.

**Schwantesia** (MESEMBRYANTHEMACEAE) are compact plants, low-growing with leaves of various shapes and peculiarities. Plants have internodes encased in leaf-sheaths. Leaves of unequal pairs. Flower solitary. Includes 10 known species.

*Schwantesia acutipetala* L. Bol. Leaves short, narrow and fleshy, tapering sharply. Upper surface flat, lower surface rounded near base and sharply tapering toward apex, pronounced edges, smooth, bluish-green, sometimes reddish edges. Flowers yellow. Found in Namaqualand and Cape Province, South Africa.

*Schwantesia ruedebuschii* Dtr. A rare species forming clumps to 4 in/10 cm high. Leaves boat-shaped, upper surface almost flat or convex, back surface rounded near base with rounded margins, mottled-white with the tips expanding and furnished with thick blue teeth, brownish tip. A very attractive species, pale yellow flowers. Native of Namibia.

**Scilla** (HYACINTHACEAE) includes many bulbous species, some of which are very well-known in cultivation and are indeed considered hardy plants. Certain species have become recognized as succulents.

*Scilla pauciflora* Bak. Small bulbous plant, suckering freely. Leaves fleshy, pale green with deeper green markings. Flowers greenish. South Africa.

*Scilla socialis* Bak. Large bulb, very swollen base, suckering from the base with wide, short dark green fleshy leaves with many pale blotches and markings. Flower greenish-blue. South Africa.

*Scilla violacea* Hutchinson. Small bulbous species with swollen base, suckering freely. Slender fleshy leaves, upper surface olive-green with silver markings. Under-surface brownish-red. Flowers small, greenish-blue. South Africa.

**Sedum** (CRASSULACEAE) species seem numerous and are found in very many parts of the world including Europe and Africa, as well as the Americas, and these species are considered elsewhere. Many are relatively hardy, while others require certain protection from extreme cold and damp. For classification purposes the genus had been divided into sections and series, but these have to a great extent been superseded by a number of new generic titles, not all of which are fully acknowledged in this record.

*Sedum adolphii* Hamet. With curved ascending branches

with long fleshy thick yellowish-green leaves, tapering bluntly, margins often reddish in colour. Flowers white. Endemic to Mexico.

*Sedum allantoides* Rose. Shrub-like to 16 in/40 cm high with erect branches and horizontally spreading leaves, about ¾ in/2 cm long, almost cylindrical with blunt tip, greenish-white. Flowers whitish-green. Oaxaca, Mexico.

*Sedum backebergii* v. Poelln. An erect shrubby plant from central and south Peru about 2½ in/7 cm high with woody stems and many branches. Leaves bluish-green, alternate, oblong and rounded both sides with keel on lower surface, upper surface papillose. Flowers yellow.

*Sedum bellum*

*Sedum bellum* Rose. A caespitose plant with leaves formed into a rosette of pale green. Flowers are white, carried in a

*Sedum cupressoides*

lax cyme. From Mexico. *S. cupressoides* Hemsl. is also from Mexico – the little side-shoots forming an almost cypress-like growth. Flowers are borne singly or 2–3 together, pale

*Sedum multiceps*

yellow. *S. multiceps* Coss. & Dur. is native of Algeria – a small plant with very dense foliage, the leaves about ¼ in/6 mm long and papillose, the flowers yellow carried on very short branchlets.

*Sedum brevifolium* DC. Low perennial forming cushions of minute ovate leaves, white pruinose, flushed red. White flowers on short stalks. Europe and Morocco.

*Sedum craigii* R. T. Clausen. Small bushy plants, prostrate with fleshy stems and leaves. Leaves oblong, somewhat narrow with rounded tip, about 2 in/5 cm long, upper side almost flat, rounded on lower side, dark reddish-blue. Flowers white.

*Sedum dasyphyllum* L. Saxicolous. Low perennial, not rosulate, small opposite rounded leaves, fleshy, bluish-green, with short hairs. Flowers white. North Africa and southern and western Europe. A number of varieties of the species are recorded which have only slight differences from the species.

*Sedum frutescens* Rose. A miniature tree-like species with thick succulent stem and branching. Native of southern Mexico on lava flow between Mexico City and Cuernavaca. The stem is covered by thin papery bark which peels readily, with flat linear light green leaves and small white flowers. Two other species have similar habit, *S. tortuosum* Hemsl. and *S. oxypetalum* H. B. & K., but either stem colour is different or leaves slightly different shape – in the case of the latter, the flowers are red.

*Sedum hintonii* T. B. Clausen. One of the most beautiful of *Sedums* from Michoacan, Mexico. Leaves almost forming a rosette, ovate and rounded about ½ in/12 mm long, light green and densely covered with fine minute white hairs and white flowers. This plant is rare in cultivation.

*Sedum morganianum* E. Walth. A well-known species from Vera Cruz, Mexico, commonly termed the 'burro tail'. A pendent plant with long hanging stems covered with spindle-shaped silvery-blue leaves, thick and fleshy about

¾ in/20 mm long. Flowers at terminal ends in clusters, pinkish-purple.

*Sedum sieboldii* Sweet. A very graceful species with semi-pendent branches. Leaves sub-circular, set in whorls of three, glaucous blue, edged red. Flowers pink. Tends to lose all leaves and branches during resting season; these then grow again from the base. There is also a beautiful variegated form whose green leaves have yellow, cream and pink markings. Endemic to Japan.

*Sedum spectabile*

*Sedum spectabile* Boreau. A very popular species in cultivation, proving completely hardy in many European countries. It is native of China and parts of Korea and has fleshy roots, stems and leaves and bears a large somewhat flattened head of many pink flowers. This is currently recorded as *Hylotelephium spectabile* (Boreau) Ohba.

*Sedum spurium* Marsch. Bieb. A rambling species, mat-forming with thin reddish stems and many round green leaves, margins minutely hairy, rosulate. Flowers white, pink or red. Indigenous to the Caucasus.

**Sempervivum** (CRASSULACEAE) are rosette plants, forming cushions with colourful inflorescences of densely set flowers. Rosettes die after flowering. All are from mountainous regions of south and central Europe, Caucasus to Soviet Union, parts of Asia Minor and North Africa.

*Sempervivum arachnoideum* L. Leaves forming small rosettes, covered with hairs creating a cobweb effect. Flowers pinkish or reddish.

*Sempervivum ciliosum* Craib. Compact rosette, globose, with leaves ovate-lanceolate, greyish-green with margins and lower surface of the leaves ciliate. Flower yellowish.

*Sempervivum tectorum* L. Many sub-species and varieties according to geographical distribution. The 'house-leek'. Ovate cuspidate leaves, grey-green, tipped red. Flowers reddish or green.

**Senecio** (COMPOSITAE) is one of the larger genera of plants, a great number being succulents. Research is currently being carried out with a view to possible reclassification.

*Senecio chordifolius* Hook. f. A tall thrub with slender, elongated cylindrical leaves, slightly tapering at the apex, fresh green. Long flower scape of pale yellow flowers. Albert Div., Cape Province, South Africa.

*Senecio haworthii* (Haw.) Sch. Bip. Long known as *S. tomentosa*. Stems and branches either erect or semi-erect, covered with soft white wool. Leaves cylindrical and pointed and having white coating. Long flower scape with yellow flowers. Endemic to South Africa.

*Senecio macroglossus* DC. A variegated or green wax-vine, branching freely and climbing. Has small ivy-shaped leaves, succulent, variegations green and white or yellowish. Large yellow flowers. Green form endemic to Eastern Cape Province, South Africa, variegated form to Kenya.

*Senecio stapeliaeformis* Phill. An erect branching angular species, with purplish-brown and grey stems rising from the base, branches invariably underground at first. Angles five- to seven-toothed with minute leaves which quickly wither and leave cushions. Flower on long stalk, bright red. Eastern Cape Province, South Africa.

**Sesamothamnus** (PEDALIACEAE) are thorny succulents with swollen, fleshy stems and rootstock, mostly tall-growing. Propagation from seeds.

*Sesamothamnus guerichii* (Engl.) Bruce. Very succulent caudex, compact with papery skin, greyish-green. Many spiny branches, somewhat woody. Leaves small, spatulate, quickly deciduous. Flowers small, bright yellow. From Namibia.

*Sesamothamnus lugardii* N. E. Br. Low caudex with many semi-erect branches from base and sides forming a tree-like plant to about 6½ ft/2 m high. Branches succulent and tapering with few spines, leaves from the axils of the spines, small, somewhat oblong, greyish-green. Flowers whitish. Transvaal, Zimbabwe and other parts of tropical Africa.

**Seyrigia** (CUCURBITACEAE) are dioecious, clambering or climbing plants, generally with rather inconspicuous flowers.

*Seyrigia humbertii* Keraudr. Vine-like slender stems, somewhat four-angled, fleshy and covered with thick white wool arising from a rounded tuberous root. Has tendrils and very small pinkish-brown flowers. Fruits ovoid with pointed tips. Madagascar.

*Seyrigia gracilis* Keraudr. Tuberous root, rounded. Stems vine-like, slender and cylindrical, jointed branches with tendrils. Somewhat purplish-grey throughout. Flowers pale greenish-yellow. Fruits more or less conical. Madagascar.

**Sinocrassula** (CRASSULACEAE) are rosette-forming species, minutely haired. Mostly perennial, some biennials. Endemic to the Himalayas through to China.

*Sinocrassula yunnanensis* (Franch.) Bgr. Forming dense clusters of tight rosettes of many closely set fleshy pointed leaves, rounded on the back surface, dark green, finely papillose. Flowers whitish with red tips.

***Siphonostelma*** (ASCLEPIADACEAE) is a caudex-forming genus allied to *Ceropegia*. Rare in cultivation. Propagated by seeds, stem cuttings or division of rootstock.

*Siphonostelma stenophyllum* Schltr. Species with flattened caudex, few short stems from apex, somewhat jointed and minute hairs. Leaves narrow and elongated, dark green. Flowers small, bell-shaped with elongated lobes which unite above, brownish-green and yellow inside. Namibia.

***Stapelia*** (ASCLEPIADACEAE) is undoubtedly one of the best-known genera of succulent plants – all fleshy-stemmed with angular branches, usually four-angled, forming clumps and having remarkably attractive flowers.

*Stapelia asterias* Mass. With light green, soft downy, four-angled stems to 6 in/15 cm high, forming clusters. Flowers star-like, long dark brown lobes with transverse lines and reddish cilia. Karroo, Cape Province, South Africa.

*Stapelia clavicorona*

*Stapelia clavicorona* Verd. Stems to 12 in/30 cm long with compressed angles armed with teeth and sides deeply furrowed. Star-shaped flower, light yellow with purplish-brown transverse lines, margins partly ciliate. Transvaal, South Africa.

*Stapelia comparabilis* White & Sloane. Very succulent stems to 6 in/15 cm long, sometimes to nearly ¾ in/2 cm thick, four-angled, toothed. Flowers nearly 4 in/10 cm diameter, star-like hairy flowers, brownish-purple with yellowish transverse lines. Cape Province, South Africa.

*Stapelia erectiflora* N. E. Br. Slender four-angled stems, erect to about 5½ in/14 cm high, angles with small distant teeth, pale green. Flower on long stalk, small about ½ in/12 mm purplish, and densely covered with white hairs. Cape Province, South Africa.

*Stapelia gigantea* N. E. Br. Stems angled, ascending, thick and fleshy to 8 in/20 cm high, small teeth on angles, dull green, velvety. Flower very large to 14 in/35 cm diameter, pale yellow with many undulate, crimson transverse lines.

Natal, Transvaal and Zululand, South Africa.

*Stapelia grandiflora* Mass. Has clavate stems, angled with teeth, very erect to 12 in/30 cm high, dark green and densely soft-hairy. Flowers large to 6½ in/16 cm across, flat, deeply lobed, purple-brown and purplish and whitish hairs on margins of lobes. Cape Province, South Africa.

*Stapelia hirsuta* L. With erect stems, clustering to 8 in/20 cm long, four-angled and minute teeth, dark greyish-green, soft-hairy. Flowers rather large to 5 in/12 cm, star-like, yellowish-red with many purplish hairs on margins and lobes having transverse lines of purplish-red. Cape Province, South Africa. This species has many varietal forms.

*Stapelia kwebensis* N. E. Br. Fleshy erect stems, branching freely from the base to 5½ in/14 cm high, four-angled, pronounced dentate with small 'leaves', fresh green. Flowers from near the base, smallish, star-like, on stalks, chocolate-reddish, fleshy with many wrinkles and transverse lines. Transvaal, South Africa.

*Stapelia kwebensis* var. *longipedicellata* Bgr. Similar to the species, but flowers are longer-stalked – lobes dark brownish-black on inner surface and very wrinkled. Botswana.

*Stapelia leendertziae* N. E. Br. Slender and erect stems, loosely clustering, slightly angled with small fleshy teeth and minutely papillose. Flowers have bell-shaped tube about 2½ in/6 cm long and pointed recurved lobes, dark purple, covered with dark purple hairs. Transvaal, South Africa.

*Stapelia mutabilis* Jacq. Stems to 5½ in/14 cm high, clustering, thick with pronounced teeth, greyish-green. Flowers roundish with recurved lobes, yellowish and purplish transverse lines and margins ciliate. South Africa.

*Stapelia nobilis* N. E. Br. A much-branched species with stems to 5½ in/14 cm long, pale green, angles have minute teeth and slightly hairy. Flowers star-shaped with bell-shaped tube, yellow, reddish transverse lines, back surface purple. From Transvaal, South Africa.

*Stapelia pillansii* N. E. Br. Branching freely into clusters, stems 4½ in/12 cm long, bluntly angled with few teeth. Flowers star-shaped and having slender lobes, purplish-brown, fleshy, smooth. Back surface covered with soft hair and purplish hairs or margins. Cape Province, South Africa.

*Stapelia virescens* N. E. Br. With erect, greenish-grey stems, brownish mottled, bluntly angled and small teeth. Flowers like starfish, flat, lobes spreading and margins recurved, yellowish-green with covering of small pointed papillae, outside whitish-tinged purple. Cape Province, South Africa.

This comprises one of the most colourful groups of succulents and those recorded are typical of the exotic nature of the flowers – others of the genus are no less fascinating. The great disadvantage associated with these plants is the evil smell of the flowers, resulting in their being referred to as 'carrion plants'.

***Stapelianthus*** (ASCLEPIADACEAE) includes only a few species with distinctive stem shapes, many angled and smallish flowers. Closely related to the genus *Huernia*. All known species are endemic to Madagascar.

*Stapelianthus insignis* B. Desc. From southwest Madagascar, has 4-angled prostrate stems to about 8 in/20 cm long, reddish-grey with darker blotches. Flowers solitary on short stems with multicoloured flowers of white, red, green, yellow and purple – in either shades or blotches.

*Stapelianthus madagascarensis*

*Stapelianthus madagascarensis* (Choux) Choux. Stems greyish-green, somewhat erect to 4 in/10 cm long, six- to eight-angled, dentate with pronounced teeth and spiny tip. Small flower, bell-shaped, reddish, spotted purplish, with papillae, tube narrow, lobes tapering.

*Stapelianthus pilosus* (Choux) Lavr. & Hardy (syn. *Trichocaulon decaryi* Choux). An attractive and unusual species covered with numerous hair-like conical tubercles, stems erect or prostrate to 7 in/18 cm long. Flower from base of stems on stalk, broadly bell-shaped, reddish, with minute hairs, lobes tapering, triangular.

**Stomatium** (MESEMBRYANTHEMACEAE) comprises about 40 species of easily grown, attractive leafed plants, fragrant, nocturnal flowers. Forming clusters, short-stemmed with two pairs of leaves often of unequal length, keeled towards the apex, somewhat tuberculate.

*Stomatium agninum* (Haw.) Schwant. Branching species with soft, boat-shaped, grey-green leaves, upper surface flat, lower surface convex and keeled, three-angled, margins, few teeth. Flowers yellow. Cape Province, South Africa.

*Stomatium fulleri* L. Bol. Stemless, clustering to about 20 in/ 50 cm high. Leaves somewhat three-angled, flat on upper surface, the tip recurved, back surface convex and keeled at apex, edges with few teeth, both surfaces rough, the lower has many whitish warts. Flowers yellow. Cape Province, South Africa.

**Streptocarpus** (GESNERIACEAE) are beautiful flowering plants, but the majority of the many species are not succulents and excluded here.

*Streptocarpus saxorum* Engl. Stems very succulent with dark rich green fleshy leaves and large purplish flowers, Tanzania. Less succulent species include *S. kirkii* Hook. f. and *S. hirsutissimus* E. A. Bruce, both endemic to tropical Africa.

**Stultitia** (ASCLEPIADACEAE) are related to *Stapelia* – separated on account of the flower characteristic. *Stultitia* have flowers which show a distinct ring around the mouth of the tube. Includes only a few species.

*Stultitia araysiana* Lavr. & A. S. Bilaidi. Stems to 3 in/8 cm long, spreading and forming clusters, four-angled with conical teeth, greyish-green also brown spots. Flowers star-like, with slender lobes, deeply set, margins rounded, inside surface bright red-brown, shiny, tubercles densely arranged with short white bristle, outside surface greyish-green, tuberculed. South Yemen.

**Synadenium** (EUPHORBIACEAE) is a small group of tree-like succulents, very much branched with many large leaves, evergreen in habitat, sometimes deciduous in cultivation.

*Synadenium capulare* (Boiss.) L. C. Wheeler. A large shrub up to 6½ ft/2 m high with many succulent branches having numerous leaf scars. Wide wedge-shaped leaves, somewhat ovate, bright green. Inflorescence branched with yellowish-green flowers. A very poisonous plant from the Transvaal and Natal, South Africa, and also Swaziland.

*Synadenium grantii* Hook. f. The best-known of this genus, tall and erect with many branches. Large bright green leaves, ovate-spatulate, margins finely dentate. Flower brownish-red. Uganda, Tanzania and Zimbabwe.

There is a most beautiful variety, *S. grantii* var. *rubra*, with all the characteristics of the species, but with maroon-red leaves.

**Talinum** (PORTULACACEAE) is an interesting group of mainly tuberous rooted plants. Flowers are borne terminally, but short-lived. Propagation from seeds or stem cuttings.

*Talinum guadalupense* Dudley. One of the rarest of· succulents from Guadalupe Island off Baja California. A compact very fleshy plant having thick globose misshapen caudex with greyish skin, which readily peels. Branches irregular bearing ovate-spatulate leaves about 2 in/5 cm long, fleshy, bluish-green, edged red. Inflorescence with oval bracts and pinkish flowers.

Talinum includes many other species of extreme succulence, many of which are North American. *Talinum parvulum* Rose & Standl. and *T. paniculatum* (Jacq.) Gaertn. are perhaps among the better-known and of easy culture.

**Tavaresia** (ASCLEPIADACEAE) was for many years known as *Decabelone* and includes a few species of distinctive characteristics making them easily distinguishable from others of the Stapeliaceae.

*Tavaresia angolensis* Welw. (syn. *Decabelone elegans* Decne.). Stems six- or eight-angled, spreading teeth each with three whitish spines. Flowers several together from the base of the dark greenish stems, corolla tube curved 3 in/8 cm long, lobes triangular, recurved and tapering to short point. Outside yellowish and many brownish spots, inner with numerous papillae within the tube and minute hairs. Angola.

*Tavaresia grandiflora* (K. Sch.) Berg. (syn. *Decabelone grandiflora* K. Schum.). Stems 10- to 14-angled, tubercled with white bristle-like spines at tips of tubercles. Flowers from base of the greyish stems, corolla curved to 5½ in/12 cm long, lobes spreading, broadly triangular and tapering to point. Outside surface has minute papillae, somewhat rough, yellowish and brownish spots and furrows, inner surface with many papillae. Namibia.

**Telfairia** (Cucurbitaceae) are caudiciform plants of climbing habit. Very much desert natives requiring long periods of dormancy in winter.

*Telfairia occidentalis* Hook. f. Stout caudex and fleshy roots. Climbing vine with rounded branches. Leaves five-foliate, elliptic-ovate, many veins, margins dentate, bright green. Flowers small, whitish flushed purplish-red at throat. Fruits large and ovoid-oblong to about 23½ in/60 cm long, deeply channelled or furrowed, greenish-yellow. A distinctive species from deserts of West Africa.

*Telfairia pedata* (Smith) Hook. A thick tuberous, fleshy root. Stems woody, perennial, branching freely. Leaves three- to seven-foliate, ovate-oblong tapering at tips, margins usually very dentate – upper surface smooth, lower surface rough. Flowers purplish. Fruit green, very large, furrowed. From the deserts of South and East Africa, Madagascar.

**Testudinaria** (Dioscoreaceae) have one outstanding feature – the large caudex covered with corky bark, irregularly distributed or in large raised wart-like protuberances. The caudex is fleshy and with age can grow to well over 3½ ft/1 m thick.

*Testudinaria elephantipes* (l'Her.) Lindl. A popular and important species with large caudex and angled protuberances. Long vine-like growth, very branched with small green leaves, somewhat triangular or often three-lobed. Flowers insignificant. A South African plant from near Little Kommaggas. Commonly known as 'the elephant's foot'.

*Testudinaria sylvatica* (Eckl.) Kunth. Caudex much flatter than *T. elephantipes*, often completely flat and having the appearance of being just dead wood. Stems tend to be deciduous, these are thin and elongated, branching freely with pronounced triangular leaves, and insignificant flowers. Endemic to many parts of South Africa.

**Thompsonella** (Crassulaceae) are peculiar plants closely akin to *Echeveria*; the flower scape is lateral from the axils of older leaves, has many minute bracts, and flowers are in a loose single spike.

*Thompsonella platyphylla* Br. & R. From Guerrero, Mexico. A stemless rosette about 4½ in/12 cm long, flattish and about 1½ in/4 cm broad, leaves greyish with red margins. Flowers pinkish-red on panicle. *T. minutiflora* Br. & R. from Oaxaca and Puebla, Mexico, is smaller in every respect with rather lax spike and reddish flowers.

**Titanopsis** (Mesembryanthemaceae) includes about six extremely attractive species with unusual leaf markings. All are dwarf-growing, clumping freely with terminal flowers on long stalk and bracted.

*Titanopsis calcarea* (Marl.) Schwant. Forming clustering rosettes of spreading leaves with fleshy roots. Leaves greyish, spatulate, resembling pieces of limestone, to 1 in/2.5 cm long, covered with greyish-white tubercles. Flowers yellow. Cape Province, South Africa.

*Titanopsis schwantesii* (Dtr.) Schwant. Dwarf clustering species forming mats. Leaves light bluish-grey, somewhat inclined to 1¼ in/3 cm long. Wide at base, tri-cornered near apex, most of the upper part and sides covered with roundish yellow-brown warts. Flowers yellow. From Namibia.

**Tradescantia** (Commelinaceae) is a well-known genus containing 30–40 species, a few of which are succulents. Of easy culture. Propagation by cuttings.

*Tradescantia navicularis* Ortg. Half-creeping succulent species with short segmented stems. Leaves boat-shaped, grey-green set in two ranks, often purplish on the underside. Flowers purplish-pink. From Peru.

*Tradescantia sillamontana*

*Tradescantia sillamontana* Matuda. From northeast Mexico, forms small cushions of white-hairy velvety leaved stems about 2½ in/6 cm long – the leves about ¾ in/2 cm long and slightly plicate. Flowers are pinkish-mauve.

**Trematosperma** (Icacinaceae) contains only a very few species with a caudex base. Very rare in cultivation but can be propagated from seeds sown in a high temperature of over 70°F/22°C.

*Trematosperma cordatum* Urb. A succulent caudiciform,

caudex up to 10 in/25 cm diameter, greyish. Few cylindrical fleshy branches, many small hairs. Leaves heart-shaped, elongated, prominent veins. Flowers insignificant. Somalia.

**Trichocaulon** (ASCLEPIADACEAE) have thick fleshy often globose or cylindrical stems with densely arranged tubercles. Flowers rather small, from between the tubercles. Most species are still rare in cultivation.

*Trichocaulon cactiforme*

*Trichocaulon cactiforme* N. E. Br. Stems cylindrical or oval-cylindrical, densely tuberculate, greyish-green. Flower at apex, pale yellow, spotted red, short lobes spreading.

*Trichocaulon keetmanschoopense*

*Trichocaulon keetmanshoopense* Dint. Stems globose about 6 in/15 cm long, greyish- or purplish-brown, covered with rounded tubercles. Flowers small, yellowish with brownish spots, lobes broadly ovate, tapering abruptly. Namibia.
*Trichocaulon meloforme* Marl. Stem almost round or oval, greyish-green with blunt obtuse tubercles. Flower near

apex, somewhat campanulate, inner surface yellow spotted purplish, lobes broad, oval and tapering abruptly, under-surface dark reddish. Namibia.
*Trichocaulon pedicillatum* Schinz. Thick cylindrical stems completely tubercled with minute bristle. Greyish-green. Flowers from near apex, small, dark brown and reddish, spreading lobes and inner surface with minute papillae. Namib Desert, Namibia.
*Trichocaulon pillansii* N. E. Br. Stems branch freely, many angled but generally cylindrical, grey-green, covered with tubercles and bristle at tip. Flowers several together, yellowish, campanulate with lobes spreading. Cape Province, South Africa.

**Trichodiadema** (MESEMBRYANTHEMACEAE) has 31 species of shrubby plants having peculiar leaves covered with papillae on the surface and with spreading glistening bristles at the tip, forming a 'diadem'. Of easy culture with many small flowers of different colours.
*Trichodiadema barbatum* (L.) Schwant. Turnip-shaped roots with many prostrate branches. Leaves small, slightly re-curved, grey-green and wart-like papillae. Leaf tip with black bristles. Flowers about 1¼ in/3 cm, vivid red. Cape Province, South Africa.
*Trichodiadema densum* (Haw.) Schwant. A popular, well-known species with very fleshy rootstock, almost a caudex. Short stems forming tufts with leaves crowded together ¾ in/20 mm long and ⅛ in/4 mm thick, dark green with numerous papillae, the tip with long radiating white bristles. Flowers about 1¼ in/3 cm, violet-red. Cape Province, South Africa.

**Tripogandra** (COMMELINACEAE) contains but few species, closely allied to *Tradescantia*. Only one species seems to be cultivated, and is of easy culture.

*Tripogandra warscewicziana*

*Tripogandra warscewicziana* (Kumph & Boucke) Woodson. An attractive rosette plant with dark green fleshy leaves developing from thick succulent stems. Leaves are some-what recurved, elongated with the base clasping the stem.

The long-lasting flowers of rich purple are carried on a branched inflorescence in clusters. Endemic of Guatemala.

**Tumamoca** (CUCURBITACEAE) are climbing, twining plants arising from a tuberous caudex base. Not often seen in collections, but readily propagated from seeds.
*Tumamoca macdougallii* Rose. A scrambling plant from Arizona with thick, partly subterranean caudex very similar to Ibervillea. Annual branches with thin leaves. Has male and female flowers, male three to six together, female solitary, pale yellow. Yellowish-red berry-like fruits about ¼ in/10 mm diameter.

**Turbina** (CONVOLVULACEAE) is a small genus of plants very closely related to the tuberous rooted *Ipomoea*. Some are decidedly climbing plants, others have an underground tuberous rootstock which produces semi-prostrate foliage and quite large colourful flowers.

*Turbina holubii*

*Turbina holubii* Raf. Has a subterranean, rounded tuber – and it is the rootstock which gives this an association with succulent plants. Leaves are very slender, grass-like, and deciduous. Flowers are large, 2–3 in/5–8 cm long, funnel-shaped, purplish-red in colour, borne on very short stalks. Native of South Africa. This appears to differ very little from certain tuberous rooted species of *Ipomoea*.

**Ullucas** (BASELLACEAE) is a genus of few species – mostly with tuberous rootstock and of climbing, trailing habit. Propagation from seeds or division of tubers.
*Ullucas tuberosus* Caldas. An interesting species having large tuberous root and succulent vine-like stems. Leaves generally heart-shaped, sometimes roundish, thick and fleshy. Small whitish flowers in loose racemes. The red tubers are said to be edible. Chile and Peru.

**Vanheerdea** (MESEMBRYANTHEMACEAE) are clump-forming with extremely succulent leaves similar to those of many of the genus *Gibbaeum*, always symmetrical, keel and margins finely dentate, bodies sub-globose. Includes four species.
*Vanheerdea roodiae* N. E. Br. L. Bol. Bodies to about 1 in/2.5 cm high, semi-globose, fleshy leaves partially united. Inner surface flat, outer surface rounded and distinctly keeled at tip, pale green with minute whitish hairs. Flowers orange-yellow. Bushmanland and Cape Province, South Africa.

**Villadia** (CRASSULACEAE) contains many succulent species of trailing, creeping habit. The rootstock is tuberous, flowers small but not unattractive.
*Villadia andina* (Ball.) Baehni & MacBr. A low, small-clustering species native of Peru. Leaves semi-globose and very small. Flowers with short stalks, blackish-red. *V. berillonana* (Hamet) Baehni & MacBr. from an altitude of 9,900 ft/3,000 m at Ayacucho, Peru, has short stems with greyish-green fleshy leaves, almost round. Flowering stems longer, very succulent with yellow flowers. *V. grandyi* (Hamet) Baehni & MacBr. from Chachapoyas, Peru, an erect plant with stems to 1¼–1½ in/3–4 cm long with roundish leaves, more long than wide with blunt tip. A rather long flowering stem with leaf-like bracts, few yellowish flowers.

**Welwitschia** (GNETACEAE) contains just the one solitary species, a plant considered totally unique. Can be grown successfully from seeds, but very slow-growing.
*Welwitschia bainesii* (Hook. f.) Carr. This legendary plant is from the desert areas of Namibia and Angola. Endemic to coastal regions where its main sustenance is derived from the surface dew which settles daily, the result of hot days and cold nights. Has huge thick woody caudex and long tap-root with two thick and fleshy succulent leaves, strap-like to 20 ft/6 m long, glaucous, and waxy-green, with parallel veins growing from the base, not the apex. Inflorescence cone-like on stalk, female green, male reddish-brown.

**Xanthorrhoea** (XANTHORRHOEACEAE) are extraordinary plants known in Australia as 'blackboys'. Tall, elegant plants with spreading foliage and elongated inflorescences. Propagation from seeds.
*Xanthorrhoea australis* R. Br. A tree-like species to 6½ ft/2 m

tall – the leaves over 3¼ ft/1 m long and widely spreading and drooping. Flowers in the form of a long spike which often attains 10–13 ft/3–4 m in length, bearing numerous densely set creamy-white flowers.

*Xanthorrhoea preissii*

*Xanthorrhoea preissii* Endl. Has a basal trunk or caudex to 16½ ft/5 m long, sometimes branched and wide-spreading grass-like leaves to over 3¼ ft/1 m long. The long stem bears a spike of white flowers. All species of the genus are native of Australia.

**Xerosicyos** (CUCURBITACEAE) contains only a few species with succulent leaves and stems. Flowers insignificant followed by small somewhat rounded fruits.
*Xerosicyos danguyi* Humb. A climbing succulent with tendrils branching from the base, cylindrical stems. Leaves almost round, fleshy, margins entire. Flower small, whitish. Madagascar. Called the 'penny plant'.
*Xerosicyos perrieri* Humb. A climbing species, smaller than *X. danguyi*, having cylindrical stems with alternate rounded, somewhat pointed greyish-green flat leaves, margins entire. Tendrils opposite leaves. flowers small, white. Madagascar.

**Yucca** (AGAVACEAE) are very much the giant 'lilies' of North America. There are many species, mostly tree-like, having thickened stems and rosettes of stiff leaves and generally huge inflorescences. They make spectacular specimens. Some are semi-hardy.
*Yucca faxoniana* Sarg. (syn. *Samuela faxoniana* Trel.). Tree-like species with long stems up to 13 ft/4 m high, thick and only rarely branching. Leaves at apex, about 3¼ ft/1 m long, strap-like, with white threads on margins, somewhat grooved with short tapering end. Inflorescence forming pyramid shape with both large bracts and white flowers. Found in northern Mexico and Texas.
*Yucca rigida* (Engelm.) Trel. from Mapimi, Mexico, bluish

leaves, up to 10 ft/3 m high. *Y. baileyi* Wooton & Standley is a smaller species from Arizona and New Mexico; *Y. neomexicana* Wooton & Standley another smaller growing species from mountains of New Mexico, USA and *Y. schottii*

*Yucca brevifolia*

Engelm. one of the most showy plants with spectacular fruits from Animas Mountains, Mexico. *Y. whipplei* Torrey a native of southern California, flowers only once and dies. *Y. gilbertiana* (Trel.) Rybd. comes from central Nevada. *Y. filamentosa* L. is one of the most distinctive, having sword-shaped leaves edged with curly white hairs and creamy-white flowers on a 10 ft/3 m high stem. *Y. aloifolia* L. – its varieties 'Marginata' and 'Tricolor' are also among the most attractive of this extraordinary family. One species above all others, *Y. brevifolia* Engelm., the 'Joshua tree', is widely distributed in southern USA and many parts of northern Mexico.

**Zygophyllum** (ZYGOPHYLLACEAE) are a comparatively small genus, but widespread from Namibia northward to areas of North Africa and the Canary Islands.
*Zygophyllum aurantiacum* Lindl. From southern Australia, grows to about 12 in/30 cm or more tall and forms small bushes. The leaves are green, very succulent, borne in opposite pairs. The flowers are yellow, with 4 pronounced petals.
*Zygophyllum clavatum* Schltr. & Diels. Low-growing, much-branched and fairly densely covered with very small leaves. Flowers are minute, yellowish. Namibia.
*Zygophyllum fontanesii* Webb. & Berth. An unusual succulent shrub with fleshy leaves, bearing many pinkish flowers and four-angled whitish fruits. Canary Islands.

# Cacti and Succulents as Houseplants

*I*N AN AGE when plants have become an integral part of interior decoration – in fact, accepted as a most essential factor in home ornamentation – succulent plants in general have an important function, with so many pertinent qualities to recommend them.

For years succulents have been used as houseplants – sometimes, perhaps, without the owner really being aware of this. *Sansevieria trifasciata* var. *laurentii* (mother-in-law's tongue), *Aloe variegata* (the partridge-breasted aloe), *Hoya carnosa* (the wax plant), Christmas cactus – *Schlumbergera truncatus*, species and cultivars, remembering also the Easter cactus; these are just a few selected at random which can be found in many homes, and very worthy attractions they prove to be.

There is also the fact that in more recent times, when a high percentage of the population are compelled to become city or town dwellers – often living in flats or in limited accommodation where there is no garden – the need for houseplants becomes even greater.

No real problems are likely to be encountered in caring for succulent plants in the home. The modern house is generally well equipped with ample lighting and also has the advantage of a warm, dry atmosphere – and these factors play a great part in ensuring successful culture. It is true that frequently succulents grown indoors can achieve equally successful results as with any other houseplant – in fact better than many – both as regards growth and flowering. Yes, it is well to remember that all succulents flower, and, what is even more important, many of the finest flowering succulents are readily adaptable as houseplants.

For over 100 years, cottage windows have been brightened by the lovely blooms of *Epiphyllum ackermannii*. To be precise, this is a cultivar produced in the early 1800s and without question one of the finest outcomes of man's endeavour in the realm of cross-pollination. This same remarkable houseplant is still seen adorning countless window-sills, continuing to be most floriferous, producing, year after year, on a matured plant, up to 100 large scarlet flowers during the spring and early summer. During the last two decades the sphere of *Epiphyllum* cultivars – erstwhile *Phyllocactus*, sometimes referred to as 'orchid cactus', this being due to their truly exotic flowers – has developed and expanded. Where for years there seemingly were only the beautiful *Epiphyllum ackermannii* and perhaps the small flowering *Epiphyllum* 'Deutsche Kaiserin', with its masses of delicate shell-pink flowers, today these exotics are obtainable in almost every colour – except green and blue – highly scented, white or cream, sweetly perfumed yellows (still considered something of a rarity), pink varieties from pastel shades to deepish rose, peach and pale orange ranging to even deeper reddish-orange, crimson, scarlet, cultivars with purple, mauve or lilac blooms and many choice multicoloured varieties. With only trifling exceptions they are proving to be ideal houseplants.

Perhaps it is appropriate to discuss these a little further. Many people have made a practice of putting these *Epiphyllums* outside in a shady position from soon after flowering is finished until early autumn. This is a very commendable arrangement – but it must be remembered they will require regular watering and attention, as well as protection from garden pests such as slugs, snails, woodlice,

*Epiphyllum Hybrid*

*Epiphyllum: 'Carnation'*

etc. Before any seriously cold weather commences, place the plant in a light position indoors and buds should begin to form from early winter. Subsequently from early spring onward – possibly until well into summer – they should provide a succession of beautiful flowers.

Some cultivars can be particularly recommended:

### Epiphyllum
'Ackermannii hybridus' – the old-fashioned cultivar, scarlet.

'Alba superbus' – large white and scented.

'Bliss' – large flower, pastel orange.

'Carnation' – a choice variety, carnation pink with rose centre.

'Cooperii' – large perfumed white.

'Dante' – multicoloured, orange, red and magenta.

'Deutsche Kaiserin' – shades of pink, smallish flower.

'Fiesta' – rich flame orange.

'Glamour girl' – buttercup-yellow, exceptionally fine.

'Guatemala' – deepest red and purple, large flower.

'Impello' – open flower, lilac and mauve.

'King Midas' – one of the finest. Golden-yellow with deep orange stripe.

'Maharajah' – deep purple.

'Princess Grace' – even deep pink, symmetrical cup-shaped flower.

'Queen Anne' – yellow and cream, scented.

'Regency' – very large, scented, cream.

'Sun goddess' – beautiful dust-orange.

'Thalia' – multicoloured, red, purple and magenta.

'Zoe' – begonia-pink, very choice.

There are nurseries which specialize in *Epiphyllums* and which offer those mentioned above, together with a great many more beautiful varieties, all as easy as one another in cultivation, and each having equally lovely flowers.

Mention has already been made of Christmas cactus. Here again considerable developments have been made to perfect new coloured varieties. The original is the outstanding 'rich magenta', and it would prove extremely difficult to procure a more rewarding houseplant than this well-loved plant. We live in days when the demand is for 'something different' – and so with the Christmas cacti a good colour range of these late autumn- and winter-flowering plants can now be obtained. Some are not so readily available, but a thorough search of a specialist nurseryman's catalogue will probably be an aid to locating some of them. Confusion still exists as to the correct nomenclature of these cacti. For years they have been known as *Zygocactus* (this is not incorporated within *Schlumbergera*). *Zygocactus truncatus* was wrongfully considered to be the magenta flowering plant so popularly grown. It was then found to be a hybrid of *Zygocactus truncatus* and *Schlumbergera russelianum*, and the name of *Schlumbergera* × *'Bridgesii'* became associated with the plant. Since then further complications have stalked it; insofar as suggestions being put forward purporting different origins – true to say, 'it's had a rough ride'. However, whatever the name or parentage, it still holds right of place as the accepted and popular Christmas cactus. These require much the same treatment as *Epiphyllums*. A period out-of-doors can be advantageous and an encouragement to flower production, but in early autumn they should be set in a position indoors in readiness for flowering. A word of warning, and this is very important. Buds will begin to appear in late autumn – from that time it is unwise to reposition the plants as far as light is concerned. Great disappointment has been expressed when the buds have fallen off – and turning the pot around can possibly be one of the main causes. The best plan is to place a marker – a label is suitable – in a given position in the pot and thus you have the means of determining that the plant always faces

*Epiphyllum: 'Queen Anne'*

*Epiphyllum: 'Thalia'*

*Schlumbergera: 'Lilac Beauty'*

the same direction in relation to the light, wherever it is placed. The situation as regards natural light should remain the same throughout the flowering period. This may not be the only cause of bud-drop – under-watering or over-watering can also cause problems; likewise a draughty position can create havoc. Watch for these dangers and remember it is possible for a whole season's flowering to be lost on any of these accounts.

The following selection of Christmas cacti can be recommended:

*Schlumbergera truncatus* – a parent of the original Christmas cactus – magenta.

× 'Lilac beauty' – lilac petals with white throat.

× 'Frankenstoltz' – deep rose-pink with whitish throat.

× 'Weihnachtsreude' – pastel orange with tinges of magenta.

× 'Noris' – a robust variety with magenta and red-orange flowers.

× 'Wintermärchen' – almost white, slightly shaded pink.

*delicatus* (a species), small flower on small plant, white.

× 'Bridgesii' – the typical Christmas cactus, magenta.

× 'Gold charm' – the first good yellow variety produced.


*Rhipsalidopsis gaertneri*, better-known as the 'Easter cactus', is, of course, a spring-flowering species and was at one time considered a *Schlumbergera*. Another spring flower is *Rhipsalidopsis rosea*; this and hybrids between the two species require much the same treatment as *Epiphyllum* and *Schlumbergera*. The ancestors of all those mentioned were rain-forest plants, enjoying conditions which left no room for long periods of drought. Equally so in the home: never let the roots become completely dry – it is dangerous and can cause withering. The best way to retain moisture is to stand the pot in a saucer containing peat or vermiculite, and take care to keep this constantly moist. During the growing and flowering seasons plants should be watered moderately, and in very warm weather an overhead spray can be a great asset, but be careful of incessant wetness which can be disastrous. Fertilizing is very helpful,

especially when the flower buds form. Many proprietary brands can be used for this purpose, but it would appear that any fertilizer prepared for tomato crops is beneficial to these cacti and encourages both growth and blooms.

It must not be presumed that any cactus or succulent is automatically a suitable subject for house culture. This is far from true. There are numerous exceptions, and guidance from an expert should be sought. Some plants are temperamental and require a great deal of understanding, coupled at times with very peculiar and rigid cultural demands such as could not be provided in ordinary house conditions – in other words, they are not readily adaptable. Nevertheless, the urge can sometimes be too strong, and the challenge too great! In which case, be sure to select the brightest position possible, coupled with facilities to give higher temperatures, and success may be achieved – but be prepared for disappointments. One word of encouragement, however: many excellent collections of succulents have been maintained in bay windows, where maximum light is guaranteed.

*Schlumbergera bridgesii*

A built-in window box might well be contemplated for succulents – but here we are veering toward greenhouse culture, and much that applies to greenhouses would equally refer to a glazed window-box – and this is dealt with elsewhere.

Certain rules should be constantly observed if successful culture of cacti and succulents as houseplants is to be achieved.

(i) All plants prefer a reasonably light position; remember light is a major essential; without it plants can become etiolated and 'soft'. It is an even greater necessity than warmth.

(ii) Correct watering is all-important. If a minimum room temperature of 61°F/16°C is maintained, then water freely throughout the growing season, and, out-of-season, just keep the root system moist, not wet. It is not necessary to dry succulents out completely. *Never* apply water when the compost is already moist. Give the plants the opportunity of using up the moisture you've given already – after all, they are succulents able to store water against possible drought – that is their nature and this must always be accepted and encouraged.

If a much lower temperature applies, say, down to 45°F/70°C, then a complete rest is necessary; only *Epiphyllum*, *Schlumbergera* and similar species should remain just moist.

It has become almost a creed to presume that water must be given from below; in other words, the pots stood in water and allowed to absorb their fill. This is all right, but not essential. There is no reason why watering should not be effected by overhead spraying, and this method helps to keep the plants clean and free from dust.

*Rhipsalidopsis rosea*

*Rhipsalidopsis gaertneri*

When watering, water well – not a teaspoonful every day or so; this only tends to give the plant 'indigestion', and is really one of the speediest ways of encouraging root rot and plant destruction. Learn the difference between so-called *regular* watering and *necessary* watering. There can be no stipulated time lag in this respect – more plants have been lost through wrong watering and over-watering than were ever lost by under-watering. If in doubt – *don't*. As an aid to correct watering, the use of a hydrometer can be recommended – purchasable from many garden shops and centres – and a convenient 'do or don't' implement. Rain water? Read what has been said about this elsewhere.

(iii) Fertilizing is important for all houseplants; succulents are no exception. Applications every three or four weeks during the growing season are advisable and only apply when the soil is already moist. This enables the fertilizer to percolate freely throughout the container and be readily assimilated.

(iv) When repotting is necessary – and this can be a frequent occurrence – it is best attended to in spring. If it is advisable to transfer into a larger container, then carefully up-turn the pot, tap gently so that the whole ball of soil is loosened and can be easily removed, inspect for root decay and cut away any damaged roots. Check also for pests, which can be equally dangerous. Then place into new container, filling in around with fresh compost. It is sometimes wiser to remove much of the old surface soil and replace

with new. If the same-sized pot is to be used, then it is imperative to remove some of the old soil from sides and surface; inspect thoroughly, and treat as above.

Another popular method for growing plants indoors is the use of a trough or bowl – where several plants are grown together. Miniature gardens have become exceedingly popular in recent years, and so often succulents are the acceptable choice of plants for this purpose. One important thing must be borne in mind – the plants selected must be capable of growing happily together, or have a kinship. A specialist nurseryman could advise on this. For example, it would be most unwise to include a Christmas cactus with *Aloe variegata* – they have distinctly different requirements. Species of *Hatiora*, *Epiphyllum*, *Rhipsalis* and *Peperomia* would make good companions. Likewise *Aloe variegata* would live ideally with species of *Notocactus*, *Echinocereus*, *Parodia* and *Crassula*. If in doubt, seek the help of an expert.

Preparation of the bowl or trough must have careful thought and planning. Firstly, choose the right container. Anything less than 4 in/10 cm deep is not really serviceable.

Most containers of this sort have no drainage holes as this might make them impracticable in other respects. Therefore the base should be freely spread with crocking, e.g., broken pieces of clay pots or very small washed gravel – all to a depth of not less than 1½ in/4 cm. This crocking, together with charcoal chippings to keep the soil sweet, can act as a reservoir and very often the roots will go down into the crocking for surplus moisture which may have accumulated. This also calls for extremely careful watering – it's so easy to give too much – and the crocked area must not become a constant 'pool'. When the plants are resting, the container will require very little water at all. This is another instance when a hydrometer would be very useful.

No succulent plant should ever be used in bottle gardens. This literally means the automatic extermination of the plant – it is certainly one of the quickest ways to kill – be it a cactus, epiphytic or otherwise, or any other variety of succulent, from jungle or from desert. Bottles weren't meant for cactus – or cactus for bottles!

# Greenhouse Culture

HERE IS MUCH to say in favour of the greenhouse. In many parts of the world a favourable climate exists for the year-round cultivation of succulents out of doors, but this is not always the case! If our natural surroundings do not provide the required climatic conditions for the successful growing of succulents, then the only alternative is to create them – and what better than a greenhouse?

It is true to say that it was never intended by nature that we should grow plants under glass – or, for that matter, in pots. However, these two go hand-in-hand to give to the plant enthusiast the scope to grow and enjoy such exotics as may capture his imagination. By this means success can be achieved if due attention is given to detail – an understanding of the plants and what they require, the use of personal initiative and enterprise.

## GREENHOUSE DESIGN

First, the greenhouse. Make sure it is sound and strong, a well-built construction, leak-proof, with proper provision for ventilation, the roof not too low – or, for that matter, not too high; a slightly raised floor is useful, enabling surplus moisture to seep away at, or below, floor level, and has a reliable heating system.

The question is asked, 'Which is best, wood or metal?' This is really a matter of choice. It is considered that wood might be warmer, but, of course, wood can rot, so take every care in treating all timbers. Likewise, metal tends to be cold – but perhaps more durable, and again, metal can rust, so be sure a rust-proof alloy is supplied; alternatively, satisfactory preservatives should be applied. Whichever is selected, it is wise to have the greenhouse erected on a concrete base so that neither wood nor metal bars have direct contact with the soil.

The glazing is very important – the use of wide panes of glass and narrow glazing bars ensures maximum light, and if the glass is taken to almost ground level, it serves to make 'under the bench' a very useful area.

Substitutes for glass are now finding a ready market. Light polythene to provide double glazing has much to commend it, but to use the heavy plastic sheeting, which tends to become almost opaque in only a short time, is not advised as, above all, it can restrict the benefits derived from sunlight. The greenhouse is mainly an 'enclosure' to protect plants from excessive rain and extreme cold – that, and little else – and nothing should allow the advantages of good sunshine to be lost.

## VENTILATION

Ventilation is a most important factor to consider. If correct attention is not given to this aspect, all manner of problems can arise. Condensation is one of the biggest difficulties to combat – and it is most frequent that drips, be it from condensation or from faulty construction, find their way onto the plant or plants which matter most. Drips are a menace and must be avoided at all costs. Correct ventilation serves to make such problems almost non-existent. Very few greenhouses are supplied with sufficient vents. It might be argued that vents offer a welcome to leakages from outside elements – but good vents can be fitted and weatherproofed – and frankly you cannot have too many vents. Fresh air never killed plants.

We live in fortunate days of automation. Automatic temperature-controlled 'openers' can be fitted to any vent, which will then open and close according to the thermostatic setting. This is truly a labour-saver and worthy of every consideration, especially when a greenhouse may have to be left all day; it might be chilly in the morning, and not advisable for vents to be opened, or very little. Then, as the day warms up, and ventilation is really necessary, vents open accordingly – then start closing when the thermostat instructs. Whether or not automatic methods are adopted, it cannot be stressed too greatly that any process which allows for an oppressive or stagnant air condition proves injurious to the plants. Remember we are considering the requirements for succulent plants – and it is well to recall that such plants or their forebears originated from wide open spaces. We cannot reproduce such vast expanses, but we should strive to get as near the bright, breezy conditions as possible. Brief mention has been made of leaky vents – and this equally applies to any fault in the structure which allows for rain seeping in. If you have such a greenhouse, there are suitable sealers produced commercially which will help to solve these difficulties – any good garden store would gladly advise and recommend suitable products for the purpose.

I have known of some constructions with doors at both ends. This is a good thing, and opens up another method of ventilation. What better could be expected on a sultry day than to have doors open at either end to allow for a through current of air? However, a danger does lurk here – in fact more than one danger. This can also be the cause of draughts under certain circumstances, so must not be considered a 100% alternative to window vents. Another danger is from animals or birds which might have easier access through a door than through a window – and they can cause a great deal of damage. Netting can be fixed to the window vent quite easily to keep out birds or insects, but this is not always so easily done with doorways; but it is not, of course, impossible. It is a thought to consider.

## HEATING

Heating is also a matter of paramount importance – a factor to consider seriously when trying to grow succulents successfully. There are so many methods available: some old-fashioned which have stood the test of time and experience; others which sound remarkably good, and perhaps are, but they still have no background of practical experience, and using new methods must throw the onus very much onto the shoulders of the greenhouse owner. Well, what is best to use? It is a matter of taking your choice.

Pipe heating has been tested for generations and, undoubtedly, if carefully installed and maintained (that goes for the boiler and the pipes) it would take a great deal of effort to find better – and this form of heating can be fuelled by coal, coke, gas or oil, coupled with thermostatic control. Air heating has become increasingly popular both with commercial growers and amateurs; it is clean, efficient and, if everything has been done correctly – the right capacity air heater, ducting and any other detail carefully checked – possibly one of the finest foolproof methods of heating yet invented. Hot air reaches to every corner of the house in a matter of seconds from the moment the heater comes on. Convector heaters, portable ones, are ideal for the small greenhouse – oil or electric, it does not matter, but do be certain the capacity of the heater is sufficient to do the job required. The heater cannot be blamed if it was not guaranteed for the area of greenhouse.

Beware of stoves which were not intended for greenhouse heating! There is no true economy in using an old electric fire or oil stove which is no longer wanted for any other purpose. Dangers lurk in such equipment. I have seen beautiful collections of well-kept succulents become completely blackened overnight due to a faulty oil stove, not intended for the purpose, which has blown out black smoke for hours until soot has covered everything. If you want to get the full benefit from heating, then use the right equipment and have it installed correctly.

It is easy to talk about heating and almost at once the impression is given that succulents must have constant heat. This is not so. There are exceptions, of course, but such exceptions are nearly always in the minority and can be catered for separately without undue expense caused by keeping all-round high temperatures. During the rest periods which invariably coincide with the colder months of winter, the majority of plants will be quite content with 45°F/7°C or a lift to say 50°F/10°C would assuredly be welcome. Such is the necessary maximum. More tender plants, requiring higher temperatures, can have a small section separated from the rest of the greenhouse, using polythene or glass, and can have supplementary heating easily installed. A small electric bulb, in a waterproofed holder, with a clay flowerpot set over it as a cover, will radiate sufficient additional heating for a small area at little expense.

To summarize as regards heating – it cannot be stressed too often that any equipment used must be without fault, kept clean and checked regularly. Oil, gas, electric, coke – all are excellent forms to use – but without due care of the apparatus they can prove dangerous to the users and disastrous to the plants.

## CHOICE OF PLANTS

If you are going to grow cacti and succulents in your greenhouse do not mix them up with tomatoes, ferns or grape-vines. Useful and decorative as these might be, they are not the most suitable companions for cacti and succulents, even though it has been known for certain succulent plants apparently to flourish mixed in with cucumbers and chrysanthemums, plus the tomatoes. This is really 'one up' for the poor succulents which try to tolerate any conditions and suffer many discomforts to survive. Keep a succulent house for succulents. These warnings are possibly unnecessary, as most collectors find their greenhouses so often over-full with succulents that other things would not have a chance.

Cultivation of succulents under glass is reasonably simple if common sense and very obvious guide-lines are followed. If the purpose is to grow a mixed collection of cacti and other succulent plants, then this should not present undue problems, but one great factor must be recommended, that the selection of plants is such that all the species will grow well together, requiring or accepting the same conditions – temperature, watering, resting and environment. This means: (a) What surroundings would the plants have enjoyed in nature? (b) Are they 'desert' plants, used to full light for most of the year? (c) Would they accept the same resting period? Alternatively, there are plants which would flourish better in shade or partial shade, and this particularly applies to rain forest and jungle plants, and then a different approach to 'resting' must be adopted. It is not wise to mix the two groups in one greenhouse unless suitable preparations have been made to accommodate them in varying conditions. Partitioning is easy to erect and this can be in any durable material; possibly plastic sheeting is to be preferred above all else. It is simply a matter of trying to understand what you are growing. Lack of attention in these respects can cause many disappointments and frustrations.

## SHADING

A passing mention has been made earlier regarding shading. This is an important matter when it comes to successful growing. The conditions developed in the greenhouse, well-ventilated as it may be, can sometimes, in very hot oppressive weather, be totally foreign to what would occur in habitat even in the hottest and driest season. Scorch cannot be overlooked, and while ventilation goes two-thirds of the way to offsetting this, good shading provides the other third safeguard. To set minds at rest, shading will not be detrimental to flower producing!

It is customary for greenhouses to be erected facing east and west. This is considered the best situation to gain the benefit of full light and, of course, maximum light is an essential requirement. However, sunshine, as opposed to light, will have every opportunity of pervading the greenhouse, and, as it has to travel through glass, this can, at times, be much magnified, hence scorching, and nothing disfigures a plant more quickly and more permanently.

Therefore, shading is a *must* and can be done easily and effectively. It is possible to make or purchase blinds which are undoubtedly the best of all methods – hessian is a very suitable material and fairly cheap. Slatted blinds offer another splendid system. The process usually resorted to is painting the glass with a special compound which can be purchased from garden stores. If this is used, then follow the directions for mixing and applying – but wait until the necessity arises before doing the job – it becomes a rather semi-permanent method and so often the need for removing it, when duller and colder weather descends, is overlooked. Don't leave it to wash off on its own accord – it might not happen. It is easier to give shade than to give sunshine; too much shade can damage plants, or make them grow 'soft', and surplus moisture tends to hang around just a little too long if shading remains unnecessarily.

When the collection is a mixed one, it is advisable to apply some method of shading throughout the brighter months to protect the area set aside for 'shade-lovers'. Such plants can accept a measure of surplus moisture, but not too much – they are used to a high humidity and moist conditions, and if these are not made available it will mean the plants can wither, or, to say the least, look very unhappy. On the other hand, if the whole collection is for these varieties, then the question of shading is simplified and the only time it will not be needed are the months when sunshine and light are least available – late autumn, winter and just the very beginning of spring.

## WATERING

Successful growing does demand certain chores. Automation has not supplied a totally foolproof method of dealing with these. It is a manual effort, one which must be systematically undertaken. Watering is of great consequence. Haphazard watering is dangerous; you must know what you are doing. The question arises, 'When and how often do plants need watering?' It is totally impossible to determine this by any system of prior planning. We are not able to foresee weather conditions and changes – a period of heatwave can dry out pots in a few hours, while even in so-called summer, a pot may remain moist for many days. So water when the soil is dry, then water well. A little, whether it wants it or not, is a dangerous practice and ultimately spells disaster.

During winter and early spring, it is advisable to restrict watering almost entirely, and if a very low temperature of under 45°F/7°C is maintained, total dryness must be effected. By the end of the rest period the soil may have become hard, as well as dry, and if soil-less composts have been used, a problem may be presented in getting the soil moist again, more so when dealing with a peat-based compost. However, wetting agents can be obtained. These are mixed with the water for the first application, so the soil will more readily absorb moisture. It is known that certain washing-up liquids make excellent wetting agents and do no harm to the plants. It is not essential to use rain water; in fact, if it is impossible to guarantee the cleanliness of rain water, then it is much better to use tap water at all times. While there may be a certain amount of lime in it, this can be easily offset, and it is certain that no direct infection by undesirable bacteria, algae and the like is encouraged. The idea that tepid water must be used in colder weather is yet another fallacy. Water direct from the tap can be used without fear. One final word on this subject. Light overhead spraying is very beneficial in hot weather; this should be given in the evenings, after the sun has gone down, and will have the effect of creating humidity similar to dew, which is an encouragement to growth and flowering.

A very different method of watering is required in the case of shade-loving plants, including epiphytes and *Epiphyllum* hybrids. The resting period does not occur as with desert plants. Lack of water spells impending danger. If the root system dries out, then the tendency is for it to dehydrate and rot. This rotting can even be encouraged by the renewal of watering. Therefore, such plants must be kept moist – *not* wet – at the roots throughout the year. Root rot is one of the most prevalent difficulties encountered, and while this might be due to other conditions, it is undoubtedly true that the main cause is allowing the plant to dry out. The roots seem to shrivel almost immediately, so that when watering is renewed they have lost the capacity of taking up moisture – and so rot sets in.

One aspect has not yet been mentioned. There are certain South African and sub-tropical plants which are winter growers; they stay dormant all the summer months, then come into leaf from early autumn onward and subsequently into bloom. Here is an instance where an understanding of the plant is tremendously important. If it is growing, then it must be watered. Unfortunately it has not been possible to change the habits of these plants in cultivation so that they forget their seasons. This factor will call for higher temperatures and winter watering – in other words, what is done for succulents in the summer must be provided for these winter growers during the colder weather. If such provision cannot be made, it is better not to indulge in such luxury plants.

## POTTING & SOILS

The subject of potting and soils can be made a very complex matter, and this is certainly not the intention here. However, a very practical and sensible approach is essential. No subject has encouraged more arguments among gardening addicts than the question of compost. What satisfies one is totally unacceptable to another. When it comes to succulents, some gardeners endeavour to relate their growing media to that which applies in nature, and, really, this just cannot make sense. To emulate nature precisely would require the use of many varying soil formulas. In addition there would be a demand for extremely varying growing conditions – varying from one species to another. No plants grow in sheer sandy deserts where rainfall is non-existent, but they often survive in impoverished soil, on stony wastes, on cliff faces and mountain ridges – frequently where water is at a premium and where they are often kept waiting months or even years for rain.

On the other hand, some succulents enjoy a comparatively comfortable existence, where conditions are conducive to the production of handsome plants with magnificent growth. So back to the compost formula. How can you produce a compost which on the one hand is a 'survival' mixture, and on the other hand is one which is to encourage fantastic growth and development? Frankly, a survival growing mix is not sufficient; here it is possible to improve on nature, and the plants will readily respond. It should be the pride and ambition of any grower to do something better than would occur in habitat. So use a compost which grows plants and grows them well. In these days it is possible to purchase many branded composts ideally suited to the majority of cacti and succulents.

The age of soil-less composts is very much with us. With very few exceptions, succulents relish these. Nevertheless, certain factors must be borne in mind. A porous mixture is a 'must'. Therefore, any soil-less compost must have a good proportion of very sharp-washed sand, preferably small washed coarse gravel, as much as 30% or more of the bulk. If the compost is commercially prepared without this ingredient it need be no problem to add, but the mixing must be done thoroughly. Soil-less composts are prepared with nutrients which last only for a matter of weeks, but excellent results can be achieved in that short period. Therefore, additional fertilizing must be undertaken at regular intervals, otherwise the plant will eventually succumb. It is usually considered wise and necessary to fertilize every three or four weeks throughout the growing season – a thriving plant needs plenty of food.

One aspect of major importance must be remembered before leaving the subject of soil-less composts, and that is watering. Great care must be given to this, especially if plastic pots are in use. These require less water than clay pots, and it is so easy to over-water. Soil-less composts demand excellent drainage and more will be said about that later; otherwise, excessive dampness can encourage sciara fly, one of the most dangerous pests to be avoided, as succulents have no natural immunity against this sort of problem.

Many other popular soil mixtures are commercially available, some of long-standing repute with much to recommend them. These are usually prepared according to prescribed formulas supplied by eminent research establishments, and if the ingredients are correctly proportioned and no carelessness has been allowed in the preparation, they have the quality of growing excellent plants. An increasing difficulty today is that of getting good-quality loam, an ingredient in all such composts. The fields of many countries are still suffering the after-effects of herbicides, fungicides, pesticides and so many other 'cides' which have built up in the soil and to a degree contaminated it – a fact which causes concern. Be certain the supplier of your compost is himself satisfied with the product he is selling and will stand by it. A good compost is excellent – a not-so-good compost is invariably bad and will not contribute to good growing.

Here are just a few comments to summarize what has already been referred to, together with a few rules which, if observed, can save many a heartache.

If you use plastic pots – they are cheap to buy, easily cleaned, and equal to any clay pots in successful growing – be sure to crock the pot well. It is not a matter of covering the hole to stop the soil falling out – the hole wasn't put there for that purpose. Crocking should be of sufficient depth to allow surplus moisture to percolate freely and escape through the drainage hole. Too shallow crocking means the compost is liable to press too heavily and harden, which will tend to create a complete 'seal' at the bottom of the container. Stagnation can then set in, and succulents cannot tolerate 'wet feet'.

## FERTILIZERS

Be sure you use the right fertilizers, prepared correctly for the greatest benefit to the plants. Too much nitrogen certainly promotes growth but does not influence flowering. Don't feed a scraggy plant or a dehydrated one – it will probably want a lot of 'hospital' treatment before it can receive nutrients again. Ascertain why it is in this condition. Examine the roots; they may be rotten and therefore incapable of taking up moisture at all. Only a plant growing well will take nutrients – the response will be rapid.

Cacti and succulents are sometimes said to flourish on neglect. This is not so. They may survive, but not flourish. One only has to leave a plant unattended or uncared for over a period of a few months, or even weeks, and the result will be only too apparent. Furthermore, it is unlikely ever to be the same again, however much kindness may be showered upon it afterwards. On the other hand, when due attention is given to its needs, the reward justifies the effort. Remember, once a plant is placed in a container its success or failure is in the hands of the grower; it cannot water, feed or do much to help its own survival; the thinking and effort must be ours.

## PROPAGATION

There is an increasing interest in the propagation of succulents. This is by no means a difficult task, and there are various methods whereby plants can be increased at relatively little cost.

Very few plants can compete with succulents for easy, almost 'do-it-yourself' propagation. So often it is heard 'You just break a piece off and it will grow'. That is almost correct if not taken too literally. Several cacti species – *Opuntias* probably offer the finest example – provide endless scope for increase by removing the pads which root so easily. This equally applies to *Epiphyllums* or *Euphorbias* – and hosts of other species – when, for the purpose of propagating, a small section can be removed, allowed to callus, then set in a light and very porous compost and stood in a semi-shady position until a root system has developed. If such cuttings are taken in warm weather they will require no other form of heating, but if the operation takes place during periods of inclement conditions then the use of a propagating frame, with some sort of under heat, is recommended. Watering must not be overlooked during the rooting period, but extreme care must always be exercised. Too much water will rot the cutting, while too little will encourage dehydration. Many species of globular cacti will develop offsets naturally. While it is not a wise thing to take them off indiscriminately for the purpose of propagation, it is nevertheless a fact that such offsets from *Echinopsis, Lobivia, Mammillaria, Rebutia* and others with similar habits will quickly root if treated as suggested for *Opuntias*, etc. With *Echinopsis* and some other genera, the 'pups' come away from the parent very easily and mostly have their roots already. If, however, the need arises literally to sever the offset, then treat this operation with due care. Using a very sharp knife, let the wound be as small as possible. Dusting the cut surfaces with sulphur powder is one way to safeguard against infection. Remember, the need to allow the wound to callus is very important. Incidentally, most succulents have a watery sap which very soon heals. There are some *Euphorbia, Ceropegia* and *Hoya* species which have milky sap – latex – and this can ooze for some time after the cut has been made, often to the detriment of both plant and cutting. It is best to dip the cutting in cold water immediately. This will have the rapid effect of stopping the flow of sap. It is not always so easy to deal with the parent plant, but a can of water can be used to spray over the cut section which will quickly staunch the 'bleeding'.

Another method of propagation is grafting. This should not be done for the sake of grafting. If a plant grows well on its own roots why bother to graft? Grafting is mainly used for propagating plants which are themselves inclined to be temperamental or very slow growing on their own roots, or are most effective-looking when grafted; in the latter category is the Christmas cactus, when a stately 'standard' has much to commend it! Recent years have seen the introduction and development of seedlings minus chlorophyll. Chlorophyll is what produces the green colouring – or perhaps it should be said the *correct* colouring – in plants, mainly as it applies to the plant body. When a few thousand seeds are sown, some species have a tendency to develop a few 'freaks' – little red, yellow or white plant bodies which feed on the cotyledon; then normally, when the cotyledon dies, the little seedling dies too; it hasn't the means of looking after itself. The idea of trying to save these little seedlings originated in Japan, so that now we have 'red-knobs' (they are even termed 'strawberry knobs'), yellow, orange or white knobs. There is an elusive attraction about them. When they were first introduced there was rare excitement. A new sort of plant had been developed by man's skill, but it was also rumoured that it was a result of radiation, one of the after-effects of the atom bombs dropped on Japan. Whether we like them or not is immaterial – the fact is simply that such subjects

can *only* survive by grafting. Another new venture into the realm of grafting has been undertaken by a leading German university where annual and biennial species of succulents have been grafted on perennial stock, the result being a perennial 'annual'. Let grafting be undertaken only when there is a worthwhile end product.

Care must be taken in the selection of suitable stock. Most globular cacti, species of *Trichocereus* or *Harrisia* are very satisfactory. In such grafts the union is effected by a horizontal cut, with provision made for the scion to be held in position securely until the union is complete – usually a matter of only a few days. The use of an elastic band is ideal. When dealing with Christmas cacti and similarly epiphytic plants, the best stock is *Hylocereus, Selenicereus, Peireskiopsis* or *Pereskia* – or even *Opuntia*. A young but strong and erect stock should be selected about 10 in/25 cm or more in length depending upon the height required for the 'standard'. Here the method of grafting is by a slit or 'V' shaped cut; the scion should have the skin of the section to be inserted carefully removed and then be immediately set in the cleft and held in position by a cactus spine. The sap of the scion and that of the stock will encourage a quicker and more satisfactory union.

The correct time for grafting is late spring and early summer months. Stand the grafts in a warm, shady and airy place, keep moist, and the results should be satisfactory.

The other method of propagation is, of course, by seed. This, after all, is the most natural and most satisfying. It can prove an exciting experience and nothing is more stimulating than to look at fully matured flowering plants and have the great satisfaction of realizing they were grown by you from seed.

Packets of mixed seed are frequently offered commercially. Seeds can vary tremendously in size: from dust to seeds as large as peas. They may have different periods of germination and these factors can produce difficulties. Most specialist nurseries now offer named varieties of cacti and succulent seed; this is the better way, and in any case you will know what you are growing. As long as moisture and warmth are provided, together with a somewhat close atmospheric environment, seeds will germinate quite quickly. A shady position is recommended at first, and once the seedlings are through they should be given more light, but not too much at one time – carrying through the process gradually. Prepared seed composts are obtainable and can be thoroughly recommended; this is easier and safer than trying to prepare your own. Very small seeds should be lightly scattered and left uncovered, but with larger seeds the usual policy is to cover to the approximate size of the seed – the larger the seed the deeper the covering. After sowing, soak the container thoroughly, preferably by immersion in water, but not too much or the top layer of soil, with the seeds, may float away. Then cover with a sheet of glass and paper, place either in a propagator or in a place away from direct sunlight where a temperature of 70°F/22°C can be maintained throughout the period of germination. Never let the soil dry out, but discriminate between the soil being moist and being wet.

Following germination, the main concern is to see that the seedlings do not rot. Once they are given further light there is the great fear of damping off – and as with most things, prevention is better than cure. It is no problem to purchase, either from a garden store or pharmacist, such items as Chinosol (Potassium oxyquinoline sulphate) or Cheshunt Compound, both of which are well-established and well-recommended preventatives. They should be mixed with water and lightly sprayed over the tray of seedlings at the first watering after germination. It is then a matter of getting the seedlings accustomed to more light, but again a gradual process is best. Together with light, give more ventilation and reduce the temperature little by little so they learn to accept the normal conditions which would apply to mature plants.

Seedlings should be encouraged to grow all the time – that is, for at least nine months continuously so as to enable them to be of sufficient size to accept the resting period requirements associated with the particular species. If adequately high temperatures can be maintained throughout the succeeding winter, there is no reason why the seedlings should not be allowed to continue growing right through to the following winter. Don't be too anxious to prick out the seedlings; wait until they can be handled easily and have taken on the appearance of the parent plant. While it is best to sow seeds thinly, the fact remains that even if the small plants appear to be overcrowded they will come to no harm if left untouched for quite a long while – at least to the stage when they can be readily pricked out into trays or individual pots.

After all this, when is the best time to sow? If you have the means to maintain sufficient warmth, then mid-winter is a good time. By the time the seeds have germinated and are able to accept full light and ventilation, the spring months will have come and from then on, with correct attention, they should not look back. If, on the other hand, it is not possible to make this provision for heat, then it is certainly wiser to wait until early spring before sowing.

We hear about growing from seed in an airing cupboard. This is all very well if you remember they are there; they can easily be forgotten – 'out of sight, out of mind'. However, if you do use this method, place the whole tray, after it has been thoroughly moistened, into a plastic bag and seal it. This will at least conserve the moisture, but be sure to watch carefully, and when the seeds have germinated, place the tray in a lighter position and so continue as with seeds grown in a propagator.

Yes, the greenhouse can prove a wonderful asset. Look after it and use it to its fullest capacity, but remember the snags which may develop if due care is not given to detail, and have the necessary remedies on hand for emergencies.

## PROPAGATION

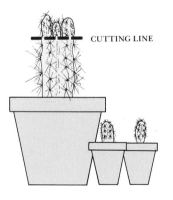

MANY SUCCULENTS can be propagated from cuttings, which may also improve plants' shape and encourage basal growth. The red lines on the opuntia (below left) and echeveria (below right) show where the cuts can be made. Let the cuts heal before rooting offsets in a mixture of equal parts peat and sharp sand.

BECAUSE THEY HAVE their own internal water supply, succulents are not so disturbed by a temporary stoppage in water flow and lend themselves readily to vegetative propagation by division, offsets, suckers, cuttings or grafting.

This globular cactus can be increased two ways. The top section may be cut off (above left) and the cutting left in an airy, light shelf until a protective callus has been formed over the wound.

(Some growers recommend dipping the cut in a rooting powder.) After callusing has taken place, insert the top section in a new pot. To prevent rot, do not bury the base too deeply.

The plant that has been divided will grow new offshoots (above right) from the top of the stump. These may also be cut off and rooted in smaller pots. Use a rooting compost of equal parts sifted sharp sand and peat.

# Pests and Diseases

*I*T IS UNFORTUNATE that no form of plant life is totally immune from pest and disease problems, and while succulents are relatively secure from many aspects of infestation, there are difficulties which may be encountered and must be resolved.

Diseases as such are few, and these are likely to affect only certain families or species. Frequently these disorders can be avoided altogether if due consideration is given to cultural requirements. So often the conditions which encourage disease are due to carelessness on the part of the grower.

The wisest policy is prevention. With the introduction of modern techniques it is reasonably simple to reduce pest penetration to a minimum and to a great degree provide the plant with efficient resistance against the more common diseases. Systemic insecticides and fungicides are assets to the grower, and if used wisely and in strict accordance with the producer's instructions, excellent results can be achieved. Systemics become operative soon after they are applied, and remain potent for a considerable period afterward. If the plants are clean and healthy to start with, the use of systemics is undoubtedly the easiest and most effective method to keep them that way.

With only few exceptions, succulents are not marked or damaged by the application of insecticides or fungicides, systemic or otherwise, so long as the manufacturer's recommendations are observed. The more sensitive plants are invariably mentioned by the manufacturer, who advises against the use of the pesticide in such cases. Species of *Crassula, Kalanchoë, Echeveria* and certain other leaf-succulents can be blemished if due care is not maintained. This must be kept uppermost in the mind when considering the use of malathion or any proprietary brand of insecticide containing this chemical.

It is not proposed to mention any particular brand by name, only the chemical involved. In certain instances, non-chemical remedies are preferable and due regard is given to this.

SCALE INSECT. Resembles a minute 'limpet' – this is the female form which sucks the sap and lays her eggs. In due course the grubs move around until the females take the form of 'limpets' – and so the process continues. This pest can cause tremendous disfigurement to the plant. Systemics provide long-term protection. Oil-emulsion based spray will give rapid clearance of the pest – but this can remove the 'bloom' from leaf and stem surfaces in certain species.

SCIARA FLY. Most frequently associated with peat-based preparations – one of the few drawbacks to soil-less composts. Minute black flies – sometimes called 'mushroom flies' – which lay their eggs and when hatched the little white grubs eat the roots of seedlings and fleshy plants and into the base of the plant. Commercial treatments are available.

SLUGS AND SNAILS. Night prowlers causing great damage and disfigurement. Many killing compounds on the market either in liquid form or pellets – all equally efficient.

WOODLICE are more of a nuisance than a pest – although the young are known to eat seedlings and young growth. There are many commercial preparations to deal with them.

APHIDS. Green-fly and black-fly can do immeasurable harm to young growth and flower buds. Systemic insecticides are effective and can afford long-lasting protection.

WHITE FLY. A dangerous and persistent pest which attacks leaf succulents in particular, usually on the back of leaves. When the plant is 'brushed' they fly off in clouds, only to return again. Difficult to eradicate. Smokes are most effective, but should be used **STRICTLY** in accordance with the manufacturer's instructions. Dangerous if misused.

ANTS. While they do no real harm in and of themselves, they are a nuisance and considered to encourage aphids, mealy-bugs, etc. There are many products available to deal with ants.

Other pests are met with occasionally: caterpillars, earthworms, mice, etc. These are best dealt with by more manual means.

## PESTS

MEALY-BUG. Has the appearance of a very small woodlouse about 1/16 in/2 mm long, covered with a white mealy substance. The eggs are contained within the white tufts which are usually in close proximity. When only a small infestation is apparent apply methylated spirit (or better still, 1 part nicotine to 30 parts methylated spirit) to the affected area by means of a small camel-hair brush. This will immediately remove the white coating and kill the pest. Alternatively, (a) *Nicotine* as a spray using 1 fl oz/0.025 l to 10 galls/4.5 l of water; (b) *Malathion* diluted as prescribed on container, or Malathion as an aerosol; (c) *Systemic* preparations whereby the plant absorbs the poison and the pest dies in consequence.

RED SPIDER. This is not a spider at all, and not really red. More appropriately called 'spider mite'. Orange in colour, minute, almost too small for the naked eye to see, colonizing and becoming surrounded with very fine webs. The pest sucks the sap, resulting in disfigurement of the plant body or reddening of the leaves.

The problem is usually caused by too-dry conditions and bad ventilation; spider mites can only thrive in a hot and close environment. *Prevention* can be achieved by a more humid atmosphere and good ventilation, or at least these will act as deterrents. Systemics are effective and can provide a means of prevention.

ROOT MEALY BUG. A white dusty-looking substance around the root system and frequently noticeable on the inside of the container. A dangerous pest requiring urgent attention – will eat the roots and work its way into the base of the plant, particularly young fleshy plants. Can be washed off completely by fierce jets of water. It is wise to wash the roots totally clear of soil, then dip into a malathion solution before repotting. Systemic pesticides can immunize the plant if applied before infestation, and dosed periodically thereafter. Repeated dosages can also effect a cure.

EEL WORM, or nematodes. Do not often affect small collections. The roots are contaminated and become swollen, developing small nodules. Drastic action is necessary. Cut away all infected roots, or take cuttings from the plant and re-root, destroying the original plant entirely. Chemical treatment is dangerous, protective clothing necessary.

## DISEASES

Very few diseases and disorders affect healthy plants; the use of fungicides usually offers protection or cure, but good cultivation is the best remedy.

BLACK ROT. Appears to be most prevalent with stapelias and epiphytic cacti. The blackening of the stem generally occurs at or just below soil level. The cause is not too certain but is considered to have an association with a high nitrogen content in the soil. The remedy also is not definite but a copper-based fungicide will possibly help. The best solution is to take clean cuttings, allow to callus and re-root, experimenting with a somewhat different soil medium.

BASAL-STEM ROT. Closely akin to black rot. The rot seems to arise from foot damage or disorders – sometimes due to being too cold or excessive watering, and no fungicide can offset this condition. Take clean cuttings, dust with sulphur powder, and allow to callus before setting for re-rooting.

ROOT DISORDERS. These problems can be quickly appreciated when the plant fails to grow and shows signs of shrivelling. This can be due to wrong watering, too much or too little; under-potting, or a general souring of the soil. The use of charcoal chippings with the crocking will help to avert the last difficulty. Re-potting is necessary, examining the roots, trimming where required, and re-potting into good compost, and remember to crock and crock well.

Other aspects of damage to succulents have been considered in previous chapters – bud-drop with Christmas cacti, scorching because of bad ventilation, damping off of seedlings, – these and other headaches can be avoided if due regard is given to cultural requirements for greenhouse subjects.

## WARNING

In conclusion it is well to remember that the chemicals used are toxic – be careful how they are handled – that the dosage is correct – and generally it is wise to wear some form of protective clothing. Care should be exercised as to where chemicals are stored – well away from children and pets. The dosage should comply with the instructions – also the time and the method. In this way damage to plants and humans will be avoided – there is no wisdom in trying to solve one problem and creating another!

# Directory of Families and Genera

This directory lists genera and sub-genera which are currently accepted in botanical nomenclature and have been validly published, or are generally recognized in horticulture. Where names which are now considered obsolete are listed, indication is given of current generic title in brackets.

This record is reasonably complete, and an endeavour has been made to provide a comprehensive guide to those plant families whose genera include succulent plants.

Plants are listed alphabetically by family, generic title, authorship, distribution.

The naming of plants may need some explanation to those unfamiliar with international conventions for nomenclature. A plant name consists of three parts: 1) the name of the genus, e.g., *Acanthocereus*, 2) the specific name, e.g., *pentagonus*, and 3) the name of the person who gave the plant that name; this normally appears in an abbreviated form, and a list of authors will be found at the end of the book. In the case of *Acanthocereus pentagonus*, this name was given to the plant by Br. and R. The currently correct name for this plant is therefore *Acanthocereus pentagonus* Br. & R. This plant, however, was originally known under another name

and this gives rise to confusion. The plant was originally named by Linnaeus and his initial therefore precedes the initial of the current author. The full name therefore becomes *Acanthocereus pentagonus* (L.) Br. & R. The name which Linnaeus gave the plant appears as a synonym – in this case, *Cactus pentagonus* (L.). The entry therefore appears as: *Acanthocereus pentagonus* (L.) Br. & R. (syn. *Cactus pentagonus* L.)

In general, the book is so organized that the genera are arranged within their sub-tribes and tribes. Occasionally it has been necessary to depart from this arrangement and in these cases the sub-tribe is given in brackets, following the generic, specific and author's name, e.g., *Opuntia quimilo* Sch. (Platyopuntia).

NOTE: *Ficoidaceae–Aizoaceae*
*Ficoidaceae* has been superseded by *Mesembryanthemum*. *Aizoaceae* is partially retained and currently only the genera *Aizoanthemum* and *Sesuvium* are included.

For the purposes of this directory all are listed under *Mesembryanthemum*.

## Agavaceae
*Agave* L. USA, MEXICO, C. AND S. AMERICA, WEST INDIES.
*Beaucarnea* Lam. MEXICO.
*Beschorneria* Knuth MEXICO.
*Calibanus* Rose C. AND E. MEXICO.
*Dasylirion* Zucc. USA (SOUTHERN STATES), MEXICO.
*Furcraea* Vent. MEXICO, WEST INDIES.
*Hesperaloe* (see Liliaceae)
*Littaea* (Tagl.) Bak. MEXICO, C. AMERICA (sub-genus)
*Manfreda* (Salisb.) Bak. USA, MEXICO (sub-genus)
*Nolina* Machx. (see *Beaucarnea*)
*Samuela* Trel. MEXICO, USA (SOUTHERN STATES).
*Sansevieria* Thunbg. TROP. AFRICA, INDIA, WEST INDIES, MADAGASCAR, ETC.
*Yucca* L. MEXICO, USA.

## Aizoaceae – see *Mesembryanthemum*

## Amaryllidaceae
*Ammocharis* Herb. S. AFRICA, ANGOLA, NAMIBIA.
*Haemanthus* L. TROP. AND S. AFRICA.

## Anacardiaceae
*Pachycormus* Cov. BAJA CALIFORNIA, MEXICO.

## Apocynaceae
*Adenium* Roem. & Schult ARABIA, TANZANIA, KENYA, SOCOTRA.
*Pachypodium* Lindl. NAMIBIA, ANGOLA, MADAGASCAR.
*Plumiera* L. TROP. AMERICA, MEXICO, WEST INDIES.

## Araceae
*Philodendron* Schott S. AMERICA, WEST INDIES.

## Araliaceae
*Cussonia* Thunbg. MADAGASCAR, TROP. AFRICA.

## Asclepiadaceae
*Asclepias* L. S. AND C. AFRICA.
*Brachystelma* R. Br. S. AFRICA.
*Calotropis* R. Br. E. AFRICA, ARABIA.
*Caralluma* R. Br. S.W. MEDITERRANEAN REGION, ARABIA, ETHIOPIA, SOCOTRA, INDIA AND PARTS OF N.E. AND E. AFRICA.
*Ceropegia* L. C. AND S. AFRICA, INDIA, MADEIRA, CANARY ISLANDS.
*Cynanchum* L. C. AND S. AFRICA, MADAGASCAR.
*Decabelone* Decne. NAMIBIA.
*Decanema* Decne. MADAGASCAR.
*Desmidorchis* M. Gilbert MIDDLE EAST.
*Dipolcyatha* N. E. Br. (see *Orbea*)
*Dischidia* R. Br. INDIA, AUSTRALIA, PHILIPPINES.
*Drakebrockmania* White & Sloane SOMALIA.
*Duvalia* Haw. S. AFRICA, NAMIBIA.
*Echidnopsis* Hook. C. AND S. AFRICA, ARABIA, SOCOTRA.
*Edithcolea* N. E. Br. KENYA, SOCOTRA, SOMALIA, TANZANIA.
*Fockea* Endl. KAROO DESERT TO ANGOLA.
*Folotsia* Cost. & Bois. MADAGASCAR.
*Frerea* Dalz. E. INDIA (see *Caralluma*)
*Hoodia* Sweet S. AFRICA, NAMIBIA, ANGOLA.

*Hoodiopsis* Luckh. NAMIBIA.
*Hoya* R. Br. MALAYSIA, CHINA, INDIA, AUSTRALIA.
*Huernia* R. Br. S. AND E. AFRICA, ETHIOPIA, ARABIA.
*Huerniopsis* N. E. Br. S. AFRICA, NAMIBIA.
*Karimbolea* B. Desc. S. AFRICA.
*Kinepetalum* Schltr. S. AFRICA.
*Lavrania* Plowes NAMIBIA.
*Lithocaulon* Bally E. AFRICA (see *Pseudolithos*)
*Luckhoffia* White & Sloane S. AFRICA.
*Notechidnopsis* Lavr. & Bleck S. AFRICA.
*Ophionella* Bruyns S. AFRICA.
*Orbea* (Haw.) Leach S. AFRICA.
*Orbeanthus* Leach S. AFRICA.
*Orbeopsis* Leach NAMIBIA, E. AND S. AFRICA.
*Pachycymbium* Leach S. AFRICA.
*Pectinaria* Haw. S. AFRICA.
*Piaranthus* R. Br. S. AND S.W. AFRICA.
*Pseudolithos* (Bally) Bally SOMALIA.
*Pseudopectinaria* Laur. SOMALIA.
*Quaqua* (N. E. Br.) Bruyns S. AFRICA.
*Raphionacme* Harv. E. AFRICA.
*Rhodiola* C. AND S. EUROPE.
*Rhytidocaulon* Bally E. AFRICA.
*Sarcostemma* R. Br. TROP. ASIA AND AFRICA, AUSTRALIA, NAMIBIA.
*Siphonostelma* Schltr. S. AFRICA.
*Stapelia* L. TROP. AND S. AFRICA, NAMIBIA, KENYA, TANZANIA, INDIA.
*Stapelianthus* Choux MADAGASCAR.
*Stapeliopsis* Pillans S. AFRICA.
*Stultitia* Phillips S. AFRICA.
*Tavaresia* Welw. C. AND S. AFRICA, NAMIBIA.
*Trichocaulon* N. E. Br. S. AFRICA, NAMIBIA, MADAGASCAR, SOMALIA.
*Tridentea* Leach S. AFRICA.
*Tromotriche* Leach S. AFRICA.
*Whitesloanea* Chiov. SOMALIA.

### Asphodelaceae
*Aloe* L. N. TO S. AFRICA, MADAGASCAR.
*Aprica* Wills (see *Haworthia*)
*Astroloba* Uitew. S. AFRICA.
*Bulbine* L. S. AFRICA, E. AUSTRALIA.
*Bulbinopsis* Borzi. E. AUSTRALIA.
*Gasteria* Duval. S. AFRICA, NAMIBIA.
*Guillauminia* A. Bertrand MADAGASCAR.
*Haworthia* Duval. S. AFRICA, NAMIBIA.
*Poellnitzia* Uitew. S. AFRICA.

### Balsaminaceae
*Impatiens* L. MALAYSIA.

### Basellaceae
*Ullucus* Calas PERU, CHILE.

### Batidaceae
*Batis* L. USA.

### Begoniaceae
*Begonia* L. BRAZIL, MEXICO.

### Bombacaceae
*Adansonia* L. MADAGASCAR, NAMIBIA, AUSTRALIA.
*Bombax* L. MEXICO.
*Cavanillesia* Ruiz. & Pav. E. BRAZIL.
*Chorisia* H. B. & K. S. AMERICA, WEST INDIES.

### Bromeliaceae
*Abromeitiella* Mez. ARGENTINA, BOLIVIA.
*Bromelia* L. WEST INDIES, MEXICO, S. AMERICA.
*Dyckia* Schult. S. AMERICA.
*Hechtia* Klotzsch. MEXICO, USA.
*Puya* Mol. CHILE, ARGENTINA, COLOMBIA.

### Burseraceae
*Bursera* Jacq. MEXICO, USA.
*Commiphora* Jacq. NAMIBIA.

### Cactaceae
*Acanthocalycium* Backeb. ARGENTINA.
*Acanthocereus* (Bgr.) Br. & R. MEXICO, COLOMBIA, GUATE-MALA, BRAZIL.
*Acantholobivia* Backeb. (see *Lobivia*)
*Acanthorhipsalis* (K. Schum.) Br. & R. ARGENTINA, BOLIVIA, PERU.
*Akersia* Buin. (see *Borzicactus*)
*Ancistrocactus* (K. Schum.) Br. & R. (see *Ferocactus*)
*Andenea* Kreuz. (see *Lobivia*)
*Anhalonium* Lem. (see *Ariocarpus*)
*Anisocereus* Backeb. (see *Pterocereus* and *Escontria*)
*Aporocactus* Lem. MEXICO.
*Aporocereus* Fric & Kreuz. (see *Aporocactus*)
*Archiebnerella* Buxb. (see *Mammilliaria*)
*Arequipa* Br. & R. (see *Borzicactus*)
*Arequipiopsis* Kreuz. & Buin. (see *Arequipa*)
*Ariocarpus* Scheidw. MEXICO.
*Armatocereus* Backeb. PERU, ECUADOR, COLOMBIA.
*Arrojadoa* Br. & R. BRAZIL.
*Arthrocereus* Bgr. BRAZIL.
*Astrophytum* Lem. MEXICO, USA.
*Austrocactus* Br. & R. ARGENTINA, CHILE.
*Austrocephalocereus* (Backeb.) BRAZIL.
*Austrocylindropuntia* Backeb. (see *Opuntia*)
*Aylostera* Speg. (see *Rebutia*)
*Aztekium* Böd. MEXICO.
*Azureocereus* Akers & Johns (see *Browningia*)
*Backebergia* Bravo MEXICO.
*Bartschella* Br. & R.(see *Mammillaria*)
*Bergerocactus* Br. & R. MEXICO, USA.
*Binghamia* Br. & R.(see *Haageocereus*)
*Blossfeldia* Werderm. BOLIVIA, ARGENTINA.
*Bolivicereus* Card. (see *Borzicactus*)
*Bonifazia* Standl. & Steyern (see *Disocactus*)
*Borzicactella* Ritter (see *Borzicactus*)
*Borzicactus* Riccob. ECUADOR, PERU.

*Brachycalycium* Backeb. (see *Gymnocalycium*)
*Brachycereus* Br. & R. GALAPAGOS ISLANDS.
*Brasilicactus* Backeb. (see *Notocactus*)
*Brasilicereus* Backeb. BRAZIL.
*Brasiliopuntia* (K. Schum.) Bgr. (see *Opuntia*)
*Brasiliparodia* Ritter (see *Notocactus*)
*Bridgesia* Backeb. (see *Weingartia*)
*Brittonia* Houghton ex. C. A. Armstr. (see *Hamatocactus*)
*Browningia* Br. & R. PERU.
*Buiningia* Buxb. BRAZIL.
*Cactus* L. (see *Melocactus*)
*Calamorhipsalis* K. Schum. (sub-genus)
*Calymmanthium* Ritter PERU.
*Carnegia* Br. & R. non Perkins USA, MEXICO.
*Castellanosia* Card. BOLIVIA, PERU.
*Cephalocereus* Pfeiff. MEXICO.
*Cephalocleistocactus* Ritter (see *Cleistocactus*)
*Cephalophorus* Lem. (see *Pilosocereus*)
*Cereus* Mill. S. AMERICA.
*Chamaecereus* Br. & R. (see *Lobivia*)
*Chiapasia* Br. & R. (see *Disocactus*)
*Chilenia* Backeb. (see *Neoporteria*)
*Chileorebutia* Fric (see *Neoporteria*)
*Chilita* Orcutt (see *Mammillaria*)
*Cinnabarinea* Fric ex Ritter (see *Lobivia*)
*Cipocereus* Ritter (see *Pilosocereus*)
*Cleistocactus* Lem. BOLIVIA, ARGENTINA, PARAGUAY, URUGUAY.
*Clistanthocereus* Backeb. (see *Borzicactus*)
*Cochemiea* (K. Brandeg.) Walton (see *Mammillaria*)
*Coleocephalocereus* Backeb. BRAZIL.
*Coloradoa* Boiss. & Davids. (see *Pediocactus*)
*Consolea* Lem. (see *Opuntia*)
*Copiapoa* Br. & R. CHILE.
*Corryocactus* Br. & R. PERU, BOLIVIA.
*Corynopuntia* F. Knuth (see *Opuntia*)
*Coryphantha* (Engelm.) Lem. MEXICO, USA.
*Cryptocereus* Alex. MEXICO, COSTA RICA.
*Cullmannia* C. Distefano (see *Wilcoxia*)
*Cumarinia* (F. Knuth) Backeb. (see *Neolloydia*)
*Cumulopuntia* Ritter (see *Opuntia*)
*Cutakia* Backeb. (see *Arthrocereus*)
*Cylindropuntia* (Engelm.) F. Knuth in Backeb. (see *Opuntia*)
*Cylindrorebutia* Fric & Kreuz. (see *Rebutia*)
*Deamia* Br. & R. (see *Selenicereus*)
*Delaetia* Backeb. (see *Neoporteria*)
*Dendrocereus* Br. & R. CUBA.
*Denmoza* Br. & R. ARGENTINA.
*Digitorebutia* Fric & Kreuz. ex. Buin. (see *Rebutia*)
*Discocactus* Pfeiff. BRAZIL, BOLIVIA, PARAGUAY.
*Disocactus* Lindl. GUATEMALA, HONDURAS.
*Dolichothele* (K. Schum.) Br. & R. (see *Mammillaria*)
*Ebnerella* Buxb. (see *Mammillaria*)
*Ebneria* Backeb. (see *Monvillea*)
*Eccremocactus* Br. & R. COSTA RICA.
*Echinocactus* (Link & Otto) Br. & Rose MEXICO, USA.
*Echinocereus* Engelm. MEXICO, USA.

*Echinofossulocactus* Lawr. MEXICO.
*Echinomastus* Br. & R. (see *Neolloydia*)
*Echinopsis* Zucc. BOLIVIA, BRAZIL, PARAGUAY, ARGENTINA.
*Encephalocarpus* Bgr. MEXICO.
*Eomatucana* Ritter (see *Matucana*)
*Epiphyllanthus* Bgr. (see *Schlumbergera*)
*Epiphyllopsis* Bgr. (see *Schlumbergera*)
*Epiphyllum* Haw. C. AND S. AMERICA, WEST INDIES, MEXICO.
*Epithelantha* (Web.) Br. & R. MEXICO.
*Erdisia* Br. & R. (see *Corryocactus*)
*Eriocactus* Backeb. (see *Notocactus*)
*Eriocereus* (Bgr.) Ricco. ARGENTINA, BRAZIL.
*Eriosyce* Phil. CHILE.
*Erythrorhipsalis* Bgr. BRAZIL.
*Escobaria* Br. & R. USA, MEXICO.
*Escontria* Rose MEXICO.
*Espostoa* Br. & R. PERU.
*Espostopis* Buxb. (see *Austrocephalocereus*)
*Euescobaria* Buxb. (see *Escobaria*)
*Eulychnia* Phil. CHILE.
*Eurhipsalis* K. Schum. (sub-genus)
*Facheiroa* Br. & R. BRAZIL.
*Ferocactus* Br. & R. MEXICO, USA.
*Floresia* Krainz & Ritter (see *Weberbauerocereus*)
*Floribunda* Ritter (see *Pilosocereus*)
*Frailea* Br. & R. BRAZIL.
*Glandulicactus* Backeb. (see *Ancistrocactus*)
*Goniorhipsalis* K. Schum. (sub-genus)
*Grusonia* F. Reichenb. (see *Opuntia*)
*Gymnanthocereus* Backeb. (see *Browningia*)
*Gymnocactus* Backeb. (see *Neolloydia* and *Thelocactus*)
*Gymnocalycium* Pfeiff. ARGENTINA, PARAGUAY, BOLIVIA, URUGUAY.
*Gymnocereus* Backeb. (see *Browningia*)
*Haageocereus* Backeb. PERU.
*Hamatocactus* Br. & R. (see *Ancistrocactus* and *Ferocactus*)
*Harrisia* Britt. USA, JAMAICA, CUBA, HAITI.
*Haseltonia* Backeb. MEXICO.
*Hatiora* Br. & R. BRAZIL.
*Heliabravoa* Backeb. MEXICO.
*Helianthocereus* Backeb. (see *Trichocereus*)
*Heliocereus* (Bgr.) Br. & R. MEXICO, GUATEMALA.
*Hertrichocereus* Backeb. (see *Stenocereus*)
*Heteropodium* Backeb. (see *Lepismium*)
*Hickenia* Ritter (see *Parodia*)
*Hildewintera* Ritter (see *Borzicactus*)
*Homalocephala* Br. & R. (see *Echinocactus*)
*Horridocactus* Backeb. (see *Neoporteria*)
*Hummelia* Backeb. (see *Monvillea*)
*Hylocereus* (Bgr.) Br. & R. WEST INDIES, VENEZUELA, MEXICO, PERU.
*Hymenorebutia* Fric ex Buin. (see *Lobivia*)
*Islaya* Backeb. (see *Neoporteria*)
*Isolatocereus* (Backeb.) Backeb. (see *Stenocereus*)
*Jasminocereus* Br. & R. GALAPAGOS ISLANDS.
*Krainzia* Backeb. (see *Mammillaria*)
*Lasiocereus* Ritter PERU.

*Lemaireocereus* Br. & R. (see *Pachycereus* and *Stenocereus*)
*Leocereus* Br. & R. BRAZIL.
*Lepidocoryphantha* Backeb. (see *Coryphantha*)
*Lepismium* Pfeiff. BRAZIL, PARAGUAY, ARGENTINA.
*Leptocereus* (Bgr.) Br. & R. CUBA.
*Leptocladodia* Buxb. (see *Mammillaria*)
*Leuchtenbergia* Hook. MEXICO.
*Leucostele* Backeb. BOLIVIA.
*Lobeira* Alex. (see *Nopalxochia*)
*Lobivia* Br. & R. BOLIVIA, ARGENTINA, PERU.
*Lophocereus* (Bgr.) Br. & R. MEXICO.
*Lophophora* Coult. MEXICO.
*Loxanthocereus* Backeb. (see *Borzicactus*)
*Lymanbensonia* Kimn. PERU.
*Machaereocerus* Br. & R. (see *Stenocereus*)
*Maihuenia* Phil. ARGENTINA, CHILE.
*Maihueniopsis* Speg. (see *Opuntia*)
*Malacocarpus* Salm-Dyck non Fisch. & May (see *Notocactus*)
*Mamillopsis (Morr.)* Br. & R. (see *Mammillaria*)
*Mammillaria* Haw. MEXICO, USA.
*Mammilloydia* Buxb. (see *Mammillaria*)
*Marenopuntia* Backeb. (see *Opuntia*)
*Marginatocereus* (Backeb.) (see *Stenocereus*)
*Maritimocereus* Akers & Buin. (see *Loxanthocereus*)
*Marniera* Backeb. (see *Epiphyllum*)
*Marshallocereus* Backeb. (see *Stenocereus*)
*Matucana* Br. & R. PERU.
*Mediocactus* Br. & R. BOLIVIA, PARAGUAY, MARTINIQUE, PERU.
*Mediolobivia* Backeb. (see *Lobivia*)
*Melocactus* (Tourn.) Link & Otto MEXICO, WEST INDIES, BRAZIL, PERU, VENEZUELA.
*Micranthocereus* Backeb. BRAZIL.
*Micropuntia* Daston (see *Opuntia*)
*Mila* Br. & R. PERU.
*Mirabella* Ritter (see *Acanthocereus* and *Monvillea*)
*Mitrocereus* (Backeb.) Backeb. MEXICO.
*Monvillea* Br. & R. BRAZIL, PERU, BOLIVIA, PARAGUAY.
*Morangaya* Rowl. MEXICO.
*Morawetzia* Backeb. (see *Oreocereus*)
*Myrtillocactus* Cons. MEXICO, GUATEMALA.
*Navajoa* Croiz. (see *Pediocactus*)
*Neoabbottia* Br. & R. HAITI, DOMINICAN REP.
*Neobesseya* Br. & R. MEXICO, USA.
*Neobinghamia* Backeb. PERU.
*Neobuxbaumia* Backeb. MEXICO.
*Neocardenasia* Backeb. (see *Neoraimondia*)
*Neochilenia* Backeb. (see *Neoporteria*)
*Neodawsonia* Backeb. MEXICO.
*Neoevansia* W. T. Marsh (see *Peniocereus*)
*Neogomesia* Cast. (see *Ariocarpus*)
*Neolloydia* Br. & R. USA, MEXICO, CUBA.
*Neolobivia* Ritter (see *Lobivia*)
*Neomammillaria* Br. & R. (see *Mammillaria*)
*Neoporteria* (Br. & R.) Don & Rowl. CHILE, PERU.
*Neoraimondia* Br. & R. PERU.
*Neowerdermannia* Fric CHILE.

*Nichelia* Bullock (see *Neochilenia*)
*Nopalea* Salm-Dyck. (see *Opuntia*)
*Nopalxochia* Br. & R. MEXICO.
*Normanbokea* Klad. & Buxb. (see *Turbinocarpus*)
*Notocactus* (K. Schum.) Bgr. BRAZIL, URUGUAY, ARGENTINA.
*Nyctocereus* (Bgr.) Br. & R. MEXICO, NICARAGUA, GUATEMALA.
*Obregonia* Fric & Bgr. MEXICO
*Oehmea* Buxb. (see *Mammillaria*)
*Ophiorhipsalis* K. Schum. (sub-genus)
*Opuntia* Mill. N., C. AND S. AMERICA, WEST INDIES.
*Oreocereus* (Bgr.) Ricco. ARGENTINA, BOLIVIA, PERU.
*Oroya* Br. & R. PERU.
*Ortegocactus* Alex. (see *Neobessaya*)
*Pachycereus* (Bgr.) Br. & R. MEXICO.
*Parodia* Speg. BRAZIL, ARGENTINA, BOLIVIA, PARAGUAY.
*Pediocactus* Br. & R. USA.
*Pelecyphora* Ehrenb. MEXICO.
*Peniocereus* (Bgr.) Br. & R. USA, MEXICO.
*Peireskia* Steud. (see *Pereskia*)
*Peireskiopsis* Br. & R. MEXICO.
*Pereskia* (Plum.) Mill. BOLIVIA, PERU, MEXICO.
*Peruvocereus* Akers (see *Haageocereus*)
*Pfeiffera* Salm-Dyck. BOLIVIA, ARGENTINA.
*Phellosperma* Br. & R. (see *Mammillaria*)
*Philippicereus* Backeb. (see *Eulychnia*)
*Phyllocactus* Link (see *Epiphyllum*)
*Phyllorhipsalis* K. Schum. (sub-genus)
*Pilocanthus* B. W. Benson & Backeb. (see *Pediocactus*)
*Pilocereus* Lem. non K. Schum. (see *Pilosocereus*)
*Pilocopiapoa* Ritter (see *Copiapoa*)
*Pilosocereus* Byl. & Rowl. BRAZIL, WEST INDIES, PERU, MEXICO, VENEZUELA.
*Piptanthocereus* (Bgr.) Riccob. (see *Cereus*)
*Platyopuntia* Web. (sub-genus)
*Polaskia* Backeb. MEXICO.
*Porfiria* Boed. (see *Mammillaria*)
*Praecereus* Buxb. (see *Monvillea*)
*Pseudoacanthocereus* Ritter (see *Acanthocereus*)
*Pseudocoryphantha* Buxb. (see *Coryphantha*)
*Pseudoespostoa* Backeb. (see *Espostoa*)
*Pseudolobivia* (Backeb.) Backeb. (see *Lobivia*)
*Pseudomammillaria* Buxb. (see *Mammillaria*)
*Pseudomitrocereus* Bravo & Buxb. (see *Mitrocereus*)
*Pseudopilosocereus* Diers & Esteves S. AMERICA.
*Pseudonopalxochia* Backeb. (see *Nopalxochia*)
*Pseudorhipsalis* Br. & R. COSTA RICA, MEXICO.
*Pseudozygocactus* Backeb. (see *Hatiora*)
*Pterocactus* K. Schum. ARGENTINA.
*Pterocereus* MacDoug. & Mir. MEXICO.
*Puna* Kiesling ARGENTINA.
*Pygmaeocereus* Johns. & Backeb. PERU.
*Pygmaeolobivia* Backeb. (see *Lobivia*)
*Pyrrhocactus* (Bgr.) Backeb. (see *Neoporteria*)
*Quiabentia* Br. & R. ARGENTINA, BRAZIL, BOLIVIA.
*Rapicactus* Buxb. & H. Oehme (see *Neolloydia*)
*Rathbunia* Br. & R. MEXICO.

*Rauhocereus* Backeb. PERU.
*Rebutia* K. Schum. BOLIVIA, ARGENTINA.
*Reicheocactus* Backeb. (see *Neoporteria*)
*Rhipsalidopsis* Br. & R. BRAZIL.
*Rhipsaphyllopsis* Werderm. (see *Rhipsalidopsis*)
*Rhipsalis* Gaertn. S. AMERICA, WEST INDIES, MADAGASCAR, ETC.
*Rhodocactus* (Bgr.) F. Knuth BRAZIL, GUATEMALA, COSTA RICA, WEST INDIES, ETC.
*Ritterocereus* Backeb. (see *Stenocereus*)
*Rodentiophyla* Ritter (see *Eriosyce*)
*Rooksbya* Backeb. (see *Neobuxbaumia*)
*Roseocactus* Bgr. (see *Ariocarpus*)
*Roseocereus* Backeb. (see *Eriocereus*)
*Samaipaticereus* Card. BOLIVIA.
*Schlumbergera* Lem. BRAZIL.
*Sclerocactus* (Br. & R.) Benson (see *Pediocactus*)
*Selenicereus* (Bgr.) Br. & R. MEXICO, ARGENTINA, CUBA, HAITI, COSTA RICA, ETC.
*Seticereus* Backeb. (see *Borzicactus*)
*Seticleistocactus* Backeb. (see *Cleistocactus*)
*Setiechinopsis* (Backeb.) de Haas ARGENTINA.
*Soehrensia* Backeb. (see *Trichocereus*)
*Solisia* Br. & R. (see *Mammillaria*)
*Stenocactus* (K. Schum.) A. Bgr. (see *Echinofossulocactus*)
*Stenocereus* (Bgr.) Ricco. MEXICO.
*Stephanocereus* Bgr. BRAZIL.
*Stetsonia* Br. & R. ARGENTINA.
*Strombocactus* Br. & R. MEXICO.
*Strophocactus* Br. & R. BRAZIL.
*Submatucana* Backeb. (see *Matucana*)
*Subpilocereus* Backeb. COLOMBIA, VENEZUELA, GRENADA, CURAÇAO.
*Sulcorebutia* Backeb. BOLIVIA.
*Tacinga* Br. & R. BRAZIL.
*Tephrocactus* Lem. (see *Opuntia*)
*Thelocactus* (K. Schum.) Br. & R. USA, MEXICO.
*Thelocephala* Y. Ito (see *Neoporteria*)
*Thrixanthocereus* Backeb. PERU.
*Toumeya* Br. & R. (see *Pediocactus* and *Turbinocarpus*)
*Trichocereus* (Bgr.) Ricco. BOLIVIA, ARGENTINA, PERU, ECUADOR.
*Trigonorhipsalis* Bgr. (sub-genus)
*Turbinocarpus* (Backeb.) Buxb. & Backeb. MEXICO.
*Uebelmannia* Buin. BRAZIL.
*Utahia* Br. & R. (see *Pediocactus*)
*Vatricania* Backeb. BOLIVIA.
*Weberbauerocereus* Backeb. PERU.
*Weberocereus* Br. & R. COSTA RICA, PANAMA.
*Weingartia* Werderm. ARGENTINA, BOLIVIA.
*Werckleocereus* Br. & R. (see *Weberocereus*)
*Wigginsia* D. M. Porter (see *Notocactus*)
*Wilcoxia* Br. & R. (see *Echinocereus*)
*Wilmattea* Br. & R. GUATEMALA, HONDURAS.
*Winteria* Ritter (see *Borzicactus*)
*Winterocereus* Backeb. (see *Borzicactus*)
*Wittia* K. Schum. (see *Disocactus*)

*Wittiocactus* Rauschert (see *Disocactus*)
*Yungasocereus* Ritter (see *Sampipaticereus*)
*Zehntnerella* Br. & R. BRAZIL.
*Zygocactus* K. Schum. (see *Schlumbergera*)

*Campanulaceae*
*Campanula* L. MADEIRA, CANARY ISLANDS.

*Chenopodiaceae*
*Allenrolfia* Kuntze USA, ARGENTINA.
*Arthrocnemum* Moq. INDIA, TROP. AFRICA.
*Microcnemum* Ung.-Sternb. SPAIN.
*Pachycornia* Hook. f. AUSTRALIA.
*Salicornia* L. S. EUROPE, N. AFRICA, NAMIBIA.
*Salsola* L. S. EUROPE, AUSTRALIA, C. ASIA, ETC.
*Suaeda* Dumort COASTAL REGIONS, EUROPE, AMERICA, S. AFRICA, CANARY ISLANDS, MADEIRA.

*Commelinaceae*
*Cyanotis* D. Don. ASIA, TROP. AFRICA.
*Tradescantia* L. N. PERU.
*Tripogandra* Raff. GUATEMALA.

*Compositae*
*Baeriopsis* J. T. Howell GUADALUPE.
*Cacalia* Cass. (see *Senecio, Othonna*)
*Coreopsis* L. USA (CALIFORNIA).
*Coulterella* Vasey & Rose BAJA CALIFORNIA, MEXICO.
*Espeletia* Mutis ex Humb. & Bonpl. PLATEAUX OF ANDES, VENEZUELA TO COLOMBIA.
*Gynura* Cass. KENYA AND TANZANIA.
*Hertia* Less. TUNISIA.
*Kleinia* L. (see *Senecio*)
*Notonia* DC. (see *Senecio*)
*Notoniopsis* Nordenstam E. AFRICA.
*Othonna* L. S. AFRICA, NAMIBIA.
*Pteronia* L. S. AFRICA, NAMIBIA.
*Senecio* (Tourn.) L. N. AND S. AFRICA, MALAYSIA, MEXICO, MADAGASCAR, CANARY ISLANDS, ETC.

*Convolvulaceae*
*Ipomoea* L. S. AFRICA, NAMIBIA.
*Merremia* Dennst. S. AND E. AFRICA, NAMIBIA.
*Turbina* Raff. E. AND S. AFRICA.

*Crassulaceae*
*Adromischus* Lem. S. AFRICA, NAMIBIA.
*Aeonium* Webb. & Berth. CANARY ISLANDS, MADEIRA, N. AFRICA.
*Afrovivella* Bgr. ETHIOPIA.
*Aichryson* Webb. & Berth. CANARY ISLANDS, MADEIRA, AZORES.
*Aizopsis* Grulich N. ASIA.
*Amerosedum* Löve & Löve N. AMERICA.
*Asterosedum* Grulich S. EUROPE.
*Breitungia* Löve & Löve N. AMERICA.
*Bryophyllum* Salisb. (see *Kalanchoë*)

*Chiastophyllum* (Ledeb.) Stapf. CAUCASUS.
*Chetyson* Löve & Löve E. USA.
*Clausenellia* Löve & Löve E. USA.
*Cockerellia* Löve & Löve E. USA.
*Cotyledon* L. ARABIA, ETHIOPIA, S. AFRICA, NAMIBIA.
*Crassula* L. S. AND TROPICAL AFRICA, MEDITERRANEAN COASTS, ETC.
*Dasystemon* DC. (see *Crassula*)
*Diamorpha* Nutt. USA.
*Diopogon* (see *Jovibarba*)
*Dinacria* Harv. S. AFRICA.
*Dudleya* Br. & R. S.W. STATES OF USA, BAJA CALIFORNIA AND SONORA, MEXICO.
*Echeveria* DC. MEXICO, TEXAS, USA, C. AMERICA, ETC.
*Etiosedum* Löve & Löve EUROPE.
*Gormania* (Britt.) Löve & Löve W. AND N. AMERICA.
*Graptopetalum* R. MEXICO, USA (ARIZONA).
*Greenovia* Webb. & Berth. CANARY ISLANDS.
*Hjaltalinia* Löve & Löve EUROPE, N. AFRICA.
*Hylotelephium* Grulich N. ASIA.
*Hypagophytum* Bgr. ETHIOPIA.
*Jovibarba* Opiz. EASTERN ALPS, BALKANS, ETC.
*Kalanchoë* Adans, S. AFRICA, TROP. W. AFRICA, NAMIBIA, INDIA, MADAGASCAR, MALAYSIA, TROP. AMERICA, WEST INDIES.
*Kitchingia* Bak. (see *Kalanchoë*)
*Lenophyllum* R. MEXICO, USA (SOUTH).
*Macrobia* (Webb & Berth) Kunkel CANARY ISLANDS.
*Megalonium* (Bgr.) G. Kunkel CANARY ISLANDS.
*Meterostachys* Nakai JAPAN, KOREA.
*Monanthes* Haw. CANARY ISLANDS, MADEIRA.
*Mucizonia* (DC.) Bgr. C. AND S. SPAIN, CANARY ISLANDS, MOROCCO.
*Oliveranthus* Rose (see *Echeveria*)
*Oriosedum* Grulich N. EUROPE, N. ASIA, MEDITERRANEAN.
*Orostachys* Fisher N. ASIA, JAPAN, KOREA.
*Pachyphytum* Link, Klotzsch & Otto MEXICO.
*Pagella* Schoenl. S. AFRICA.
*Perrierosedum* (Bgr.) Ohba MADAGASCAR.
*Petrosedum* Grulich N. EUROPE.
*Pistorinia* DC. IBERIAN PENINSULA, N. AFRICA.
*Poenosedum* Holub. N. AFRICA, MEDITERRANEAN.
*Prometheum* (Bgr.) Ohba USSR, ASIA MINOR.
*Pseudorosularia* Gurgen. USSR.
*Pseudosedum* (Bois.) Bgr. C. ASIA.
*Rhodiola* L. NORTH EUROPE TO ARCTIC.
*Rochea* DC. S. AFRICA.
*Rosularia* (DC.) Stapf. ASIA MINOR, CAUCASUS, HIMALAYAS.
*Sedella* Löve & Löve EUROPE.
*Sedum* L. N. EUROPE, GT. BRITAIN, C. AFRICA, MADAGASCAR, PERU, BOLIVIA, MEXICO, N. AMERICA, E. ASIA, MEDITERRANEAN-AREA.
*Sempervivella* Stapf. HIMALAYAS.
*Sempervivum* L. C. AND S. EUROPE, CAUCASUS TO USSR., ASIA MINOR, N. AFRICA.
*Sinocrassula* Bgr. HIMALAYAS, CHINA.
*Spathulata* (Boris.) Löve & Löve USSR, CAUCASUS.

*Thompsonella* Br. & R. MEXICO.
*Tillaea* Calderon MEXICO.
*Tillaeastrum* R. (see *Tillaea*)
*Tolmachevia* Löve & Löve C. AMERICA.
*Tylecodon* Jaarsveld S. AFRICA.
*Umbilicus* DC. S. EUROPE, W. ASIA, CANARY ISLANDS, W. AND E. AFRICA, EGYPT.
*Urbinia* Br. & R. (see *Echeveria*)
*Vauanthes* Haw. S. AFRICA.
*Villadia* Haw. MEXICO, PERU, GUATEMALA.

## Cruciferae
*Caulanthes* S. Watts. N. AMERICA.

## Cucurbitaceae
*Acanthosicyos* Welw. NAMIBIA.
*Alsomitra* Roem. TROP. AFRICA.
*Anisosperma* Manso. BRAZIL.
*Apodanthera* Arn. USA, MEXICO.
*Cephalopentandra* Chiov. ETHIOPIA.
*Ceratosanthes* Burm. S. AMERICA, W. INDIES.
*Corallocarpus* Hook. ARABIA, S. AND E. AFRICA, MADAGASCAR.
*Cucurbita* L. USA, MEXICO.
*Dendrosicyos* Balf. f. SOCOTRA.
*Echinocystis* Torr. & Gray USA, MEXICO.
*Gerrardanthus* Harv. KENYA AND TANZANIA.
*Ibervillea* Greene MEXICO.
*Kedostris* Medic. E. AND S. AFRICA.
*Melothria* L. S. AND E. AFRICA, MADAGASCAR.
*Momordica* L. KENYA AND TANZANIA.
*Neoalsomitra* Hutchins. PHILIPPINES, BURMA, THAILAND.
*Pisosperma* Sond. E. AND S. AFRICA.
*Seyrigia* Kerauda. MADAGASCAR.
*Telfairia* Hook. W., S. AND E. AFRICA, MADAGASCAR.
*Trochomeria* Hook. TROP. AND S. AFRICA.
*Trochomeriopsis* Cogn. TROP. AFRICA.
*Tumamoca* R. USA (ARIZONA).
*Xerosicyos* H. Humb. MADAGASCAR.
*Zehneria* Endl. S. AFRICA.

## Didiereaceae
*Alluaudia* Drake S.W. MADAGASCAR.
*Alluaudianopsis* H. Humb. & Choux MADAGASCAR.
*Decaryia* Choux MADAGASCAR.
*Didierea* H. Baill. MADAGASCAR.

## Dioscoreaceae
*Dioscorea* L. S. AFRICA, MEXICO.
*Testudinaria* Salisb. S. AFRICA.

## Euphorbiaceae
*Dactylanthes* Haw. (see *Euphorbia*)
*Elaeophorbia* Stapf. W. TROP. AFRICA, ANGOLA, SIERRA LEONE.
*Euphorbia* L. AFRICA, CANARY ISLANDS, SRI LANKA, MEXICO, BRAZIL, ETC.
*Jatropha* L. TROP. AFRICA, MADAGASCAR, TROP. C. AND S. AMERICA, WEST INDIES, ETC.

*Monadenium* Pax. E. AND S. TROP. AFRICA, ETHIOPIA, KENYA, ZIMBABWE.
*Pedilanthus* Neck. WEST INDIES, BAJA CALIFORNIA, MEXICO.
*Stenadenium* Pax. TANZANIA. (see *Monadenium*)
*Synadenium* Boiss. E. AFRICA.

**Ficoidacae** – see **Mesembryanthemum**

**Fouquieraceae**
*Fouquiera* H.B. & K. MEXICO, S. CALIFORNIA, USA.
*Idria* Kellog (see *Fouquiera*)

**Geraniaceae**
*Pelargonium* L'Her. S. AFRICA, MADAGASCAR, NAMIBIA.
*Sarcocaulon* (DC.) Sweet S. AFRICA, NAMIBIA.

**Gesneriaceae**
*Rechsteineria* Hoehne BRAZIL.
*Streptocarpus* Lindl. TROP. AFRICA.

**Gnetaceae**
*Welwitschia* Hook. NAMIBIA.

**Hyacinthaceae**
*Drimia* Jacq. S. AFRICA.
*Ledebouria* Roth. S. AFRICA, INDIA.
*Litanthus* Harvey S. AFRICA.
*Scilla* L. S. AFRICA, MEDITERRANEAN REGION.

**Icacinaceae**
*Pyrenacantha* Wright. E. AFRICA.
*Trematosperma* Urb. SOMALIA.

**Labiatae**
*Aeolanthus* Mart. TROP. AFRICA.
*Coleus* Lour. ARABIA, TROP. AFRICA, E. MALAYSIA, MADAGASCAR.
*Plectranthus* L'Her. E. AFRICA.

**Leguminosae**
*Dolichos* L. NAMIBIA.
*Neorautenenia* Schinz S. AFRICA.

**Liliaceae** – see also *Asphodelaceae* and *Hyacinthaceae*
*Bowiea* Harv. ex. Hook. E. AND S. AFRICA.
*Chamaealoe* Bgr. S. AFRICA.
*Chortolirion* Bgr. S. AFRICA, NAMIBIA.
*Hesperaloe* Engelm. MEXICO, USA (TEXAS).
*Lomatophyllum* Willd. MADAGASCAR, MAURITIUS.

**Lobeliaceae**
*Brighamia* A. Gray HAWAII, USA.
*Lobelia* L. Ethiopia, WEST INDIES.

**Melastomataceae**
*Monolena* Triana. COLOMBIA.

**Menispermaceae**
*Stephania* Lour. TROP. W. AFRICA, ANGOLA, CONGO, ETC.

**Mesembryanthemum** L. All genera are indigenous to Africa – from Egypt, Algeria, Arabia – Ethiopia and N.E. Africa generally – Zimbabwe and tropical West Africa, to Namibia, throughout South Africa, including mainly Cape Province, Orange Free State and Transvaal. Only three genera are recorded elsewhere – in Australia (Tasmania), New Zealand (St Helena), and Chile. Some species are to be found in other areas, but these have been transported and become naturalized.
Abbreviations: CP (Cape Province). TR. (Transvaal). OFS (Orange Free State). SA (South Africa). NAM. (Namibia). MEDIT. (Mediterranean region).

*Abryanthemum* Necker (see *Carpobrotus*)
*Acaulon* N.E. Br. (see *Aloinopsis*)
*Acrodon* N.E. Br. CP.
*Aethephyllum* N.E. Br. CP.
*Agnirictus* Schwant. (see *Stomatium*)
*Aistocaulon* var. Poelln. (see *Aloinopsis*)
*Aizoanthemum* Dietr. ex Friedr. ANGOLA, NAM.
*Aloinopsis* Schwant. CP.
*Amoebophyllum* N.E. Br. CP., NAM.
*Amphibolia* L. Bol. CP.
*Anisocalyx* L. Bol. CP.
*Antegibbaeum* Schwant. CP.
*Antimima* N.E. Br. (see *Ruschia*)
*Apatesia* N.E. Br. CP.
*Aptenia* N.E. Br. SA. (arid coastal areas)
*Arenifera* Herre CP., NAM.
*Argeta* N.E. Br. (see *Gibbaeum*)
*Argyroderma* N.E. Br. CP.
*Aridaria* N.E. Br. (see *Nycteranthus*)
*Aspazoma* N.E. Br. CP.
*Astridia* Dietr. & Schwant. CP., NAM.
*Bergeranthus* Schwant. CP
*Berrisfordia* L. Bol. CP.
*Bijlia* N.E. Br. CP.
*Bolusanthemum* Schwant. (see *Hereroa*)
*Braunsia* Schwant. (see *Ruschia* and *Echinus*)
*Brownanthus* Schwant. CP., NAM.
*Calamophyllum* Schwant. SA.
*Callistigma* Dietr. & Schwant. NAM.
*Carpanthea* N.E. Br. CP.

*Carpobrotus* N.E. Br. CP. (also AUSTRALIA, TASMANIA AND CHILE)
*Carruanthus* Schwant. CP.
*Caryotophora* Leistn. SA.
*Cephalophyllum* (Haw.) N.E. Br. CP., NAM.
*Cerochlamys* N.E. Br. CP.
*Chasmatophyllum* Dietr. & Schwant. CP., OFS., NAM.
*Cheiridopsis* N.E. Br. CP., NAM.
*Circandra* N.E. Br. (see *Erepsia*)
*Cleretum* (N.E. Br.) Rowl. SA.

*Conicosia* N.E. Br. CP.

*Conophyllum* Schwant. CP.

*Conophytum* N.E. Br. CP., NAM.

*Corpuscularia* Schwant. (see *Ruschia* and *Delosperma*)

*Crocanthus* L. Bol. (see *Malephora*)

*Cryophytum* N.E. Br. (see *Mesembryanthemum, Micropterum* and *Eurystigma*)

*Cylindrophyllum* Schwant. CP.

*Dactylopsis* N.E. Br. CP.

*Deilanthe* N.E. Br (see *Aloinopsis*)

*Delosperma* N.E. Br. ETHIOPIA, CP., TR., OFS., ZIMBABWE, N.E. AFRICA.

*Depacarpus* N.E. Br. (see *Meyerophytum*)

*Derenbergia* Schwant. (see *Conophytum, Gibbaeum* and *Ophthalmophyllum*)

*Derenbergiella* Schwant. (see *Mesembryanthemum*)

*Dicrocaulon* N.E. Br. CP.

*Didymaotus* N.E. Br. CP.

*Dinteranthus* Schwant. CP., NAM.

*Diplosoma* Schwant. CP.

*Disphyma* N.E. Br. CP. (also AUSTRALIA, NEW ZEALAND, TASMANIA)

*Dorotheanthus* Schwant. CP.

*Dracophilus* Dietr. & Schwant. CP., NAM.

*Drosanthemopsis* Rauschert CP.

*Drosanthemum* Schwant. CP., NAM.

*Eberlanzia* Schwant. CP., NAM.

*Ebracteola* Dietr. & Schwant. NAM.

*Echinus* L. Bol. CP.

*Ectotropis* N.E. Br. CP.

*Enarganthe* N.E. Br. CP.

*Erepsia* N.E. Br. CP.

*Esterhuysenia* L. Bol. CP.

*Eurystigma* L. Bol. CP.

*Faucaria* Schwant. CP.

*Fenestraria* N.E. Br. CP., NAM.

*Frithia* N.E. Br. TR.

*Gibbaeum* Haw. CP.

*Glottiphyllum* Haw. CP.

*Gymnopoma* N.E. Br. (see *Skiatophytum*)

*Halenbergia* Dietr. NAM.

*Hallianthus* H. Hartmann SA.

*Henricia* L. Bol. (see *Neohenricia*)

*Hereroa* Dietr. & Schwant. CP., NAM.

*Herrea* Schwant. CP.

*Herreanthus* Schwant. CP.

*Hydrodea* N.E. Br. NEW ZEALAND, NAM.

*Hymenocyclus* Dietr. & Schwant. (see *Malephora*)

*Hymenogyne* (Haw.) N.E. Br. CP.

*Imitaria* N.E. Br. CP.

*Jacobsenia* L. Bol. & Schwant. CP.

*Jensenobotrya* Herre NAM.

*Jordaaniella* H. Hartmann CP.

*Juttadinteria* Schwant. CP., NAM.

*Kensitia* Fedde CP.

*Khadia* N.E. Br. TR.

*Lampranthus* N.E. Br. CP.

*Lapidaria* Schwant. NAM.

*Leipoldtia* L. Bol. CP., NAM.

*Lithops* N.E. Br. CP., NAM.

*Litocarpus* L. Bol. (see *Aptenia*)

*Machairophyllum* L. Bol. CP.

*Macrocaulon* N.E. Br. (see *Carpanthea*)

*Malephora* N.E. Br. CP., OFS., NAM.

*Marlothistell* Schwant. (see *Ruschia*)

*Maughania* N.E. Br. CP.

*Maughaniella* L. Bol. CP.

*Mentocalyx* N.E. Br. (see *Gibbaeum*)

*Mesembryanthemum* L. emend L. Bol. CP., NAM.

*Mestoklema* N.E. Br. CP.

*Meyerophytum* Schwant. CP.

*Micropterum* Schwant. CP.

*Mimetophytum* L. Bol. CP.

*Mitrophyllum* Schwant. CP.

*Moniliaria* Schwant. CP.

*Mossia* N.E. Br. TR.

*Muiria* N.E. Br. CP.

*Muirio-Gibbaeum* Jacobs. CP.

*Namaquanthus* L. Bol. CP.

*Namibia* Dietr. & Schwant. NAM.

*Nananthus* N.E. Br. CP., TR., OFS.

*Nelia* Schwant. CP.

*Neoaridaria* Schwant. (sub-genus, see *Nycteranthus*)

*Neohenricia* L. Bol. OFS.

*Neorhine* Schwant. CP.

*Nycteranthus* Necker CP., NAM.

*Octopoma* N.E. Br. CP.

*Odontophorus* N.E. Br. CP.

*Oophytum* N.E. Br. CP.

*Ophthalmophyllum* Dietr. & Schwant. CP., NAM.

*Opophytum* N.E. Br. ALGERIA, EGYPT, ARABIA, TROP. W. AFRICA, CP.

*Orthopterum* L. Bol. CP.

*Oscularia* Schwant. CP.

*Ottosonderia* L. Bol. CP.

*Peersia* L. Bol. (see *Rhinephyllum*)

*Pentacoilanthus* Rappa & Camarrone (see *Mesembryanthemum, Psilocaulon* and *Nycteranthus*)

*Perissolobus* N.E. Br. (see *Machairophyllum*)

*Pherolobus* N.E. Br. CP.

*Phyllobolus* N.E. Br. CP.

*Piquetia* N.E. Br. (see *Kensitia*)

*Platythyra* N.E. Br. CP.

*Pleiospilos* N.E. Br. CP.

*Polymita* L. Bol. CP.

*Prenia* N.E. Br. CP.

*Prepodesma* N.E. Br. (see *Aloinopsis* and *Hereroa*)

*Psammophora* Dietr. & Schwant. CP., NAM.

*Pseudobrownanthus* Ihlen & Bittrich NAM., SA.

*Psilocaulon* N.E. Br. CP., NAM.

*Punctillaria* N.E. Br. (see *Pleiospilos*)

*Rabiea* N.E. Br. CP., OFS.

*Rhinephyllum* N.E. Br. CP.

*Rhombophyllum* Schwant. CP.

*Rhopalocyclus* Schwant. (see *Leipoldtia*)
*Rimaria* N.E. Br. (see *Vanheerdea*)
*Roodia* N.E. Br. (see *Argyroderma*)
*Ruschia* Schwant. CP., NAM.
*Ruschianthemum* Friedr. CP.
*Ruschianthus* L. Bol. NAM.
*Saphesia* N.E. Br. CP.
*Sceletium* N.E. Br. CP.
*Schlechteranthus* Schwant. CP.
*Schoenlandia* L. Bol. (see *Delosperma*)
*Schwantesia* Dietr. CP., NAM.
*Scopelogena* L. Bol. CP.
*Semnanthe* N.E. Br. CP.
*Sesuvium* L. E. AFRICA.
*Skiatophytum* L. Bol. CP.
*Smicrostigma* N.E. Br. CP.
*Sphalmanthus* N.E. Br. (see *Nycteranthus*)
*Stayneria* L. Bol. CP.
*Sterropetalum* N.E. Br. (see *Nelia*)
*Stigmatocarpum* L. Bol. (see *Dorotheanthus*)
*Stoeberia* Dietr. & Schwant. CP., NAM.
*Stomatium* Schwant. CP., OFS.
*Synaptophyllum* N.E. Br. NAM.
*Tetracoilanthus* Rappa & Camarrone (see *Aptenia*)
*Thyrasperma* N.E. Br. (see *Apatesia*)
*Tischleria* Schwant. CP.
*Titanopsis* Schwant. CP., NAM.
*Trichocyclus* N.E. Br. (see *Brownanthus*)
*Trichodiadema* Schwant. CP., BFS., ETHIOPIA.
*Vanheerdea* L. Bol. CP.
*Vanzijlia* L. Bol. CP.
*Verrucifera* N.E. Br. (see *Titanopsis*)
*Wooleya* L. Bol. CP.
*Zeuktophyllum* N.E. Br. CP.

**Molluginaceae**
*Hypertelis* E. Mey. ex Fenzl. S. AFRICA, NAMIBIA.

**Moraceae**
*Dorstenia* Plum. KENYA, SOCOTRA.
*Ficus* L. BAJA CALIFORNIA AND SONORA, MEXICO.

**Moringaceae**
*Moringa* Burm. NAMIBIA.

**Oxalidaceae**
*Oxalis* L. S. AMERICA.

**Passifloraceae**
*Adenia* Forsk. E. AFRICA, SOMALIA, NAMIBIA, MADAGASCAR.
*Modecca* Lam. (see *Adenia*)

**Pedaliaceae**
*Harpagophytum* CD. ex Meissn. S. AFRICA.
*Holubia* Oliv. S. AFRICA.
*Pedaliodiscus* Ihlenf. E. AFRICA.
*Pedalium* Royen KENYA, TANZANIA, ETHIOPIA, SOCOTRA, MADAGASCAR, ETC.
*Pterodiscus* Hook. SOMALIA, KENYA, SUDAN, S. AFRICA, NAMIBIA.
*Sesamothamnus* Welw. KENYA, NAMIBIA, C. AND TROP. AFRICA.
*Rogeria* J. Gay ex Delice TROP. AFRICA, NAMIBIA.
*Uncarina* Stapf. MADAGASCAR.

**Phytolaccaceae**
*Phytolacca* L. S. AMERICA.

**Piperaceae**
*Peperomia* Ruiz. & Pav. WEST INDIES, S. AMERICA, MADAGASCAR, ETC.

**Portulacaceae**
*Anacampseros* L. C. AFRICA, NAMIBIA, KENYA, TANZANIA, S. AUSTRALIA.
*Calandrinia* H. B. & K. AUSTRALIA, USA TO CHILE.
*Ceraria* Pears. & E.L. Stephens S. AFRICA, NAMIBIA.
*Lewisia* Pursh. WESTERN USA., C. AMERICA, BOLIVIA.
*Portulaca* L. S. AFRICA, S. AMERICA, AUSTRALIA, WEST INDIES.
*Portulacaria* Jacq. S. AFRICA.
*Sedopsis* J.W. Willis E. AFRICA.
*Talinopsis* A. Gray MEXICO, SOUTHERN USA.
*Talinum* Adans. NAMIBIA, MEXICO, WEST INDIES.

**Rubiaceae**
*Hydnophytum* Jacq. NEW GUINEA.
*Myrmecodia* Jack. MALAYSIA, AUSTRALIA.

**Scrophulariaceae**
*Castilleva* Mutis ex L.f. MEXICO, GUADELUPE IS.
*Chamaegigas* Dietr. NAMIBIA.
*Dermatobotrys* H. Bol. S. AFRICA.

**Umbelliferae**
*Crithmum* L. MADEIRA, CANARY ISLANDS, MEDITERRANEAN COASTS OF SPAIN AND PORTUGAL.

**Urticaceae**
*Pilea* Lindl. PERU.

**Violaceae**
*Hymenanthera* R. Br. NEW ZEALAND, AUSTRALIA.

**Vitaceae**
*Cissus* DC. S. AFRICA, NAMIBIA, TROP. AFRICA, MEXICO.
*Cyphostemma* B. Desc. MADAGASCAR.

**Xanthorrhoeaceae**
*Kingia* R. Br. AUSTRALIA.
*Xanthorrhoea* Sm. AUSTRALIA.

**Zygophyllaceae**
*Augea* Thunbg. S. AFRICA, NAMIBIA.
*Zygophyllum* L. CANARY ISLANDS.

# Appendix of Authors' Names

*Principal authors of Succulent Plant Descriptions.*

AKERS, JOHN  *Akers*
ALEXANDER, E. J.  *Alex.*

BACKEBERG, Curt  *Backeb.*
BAEHNI, C.  *Baehni*
BAILEY, L. H.  *L. H. Bailey*
BAKER, J. G.  *Bak.*
BALFOUR, Prof. Isaac Bayley  *Balf. f.*
BALLY, Peter R. O.  *Bally*
BEAUVERD, Gustave  *Beauv.*
BECCARI, O.  *Becc.*
BENSON, B. W.  *B. W. Benson*
BENSON, Lyman  *L. Bens.*
BERGER, Alwin  *Bgr.*
BIGELOW, J.  *Bigel.*
BOEDEKER, F.  *Boed.*
BOISSEVAIN, C. H.  *Boissev.*
BOISSIER, P. E.  *Boiss.*
BOLUS, Dr. Louisa  *L. Bol.*
BORG, John  *Borg*
BRANDEGEE, K.  *K. Brandeg.*
BRANDEGEE, T. S.  *Brandegee*
BRAVO, Dr. Lelia  *Bravo*
BREDEROO, J. A.  *Bred.*
BRITTON, Dr. N. L.  *Britt.*
BRITTON & ROSE  *Br. & R.*
BROWN, Dr. N. E.  *N. E. Br.*
BROWN, R.  *R. Br.*
BRUCE, E. A.  *Bruce*
BUINING, Albert F. H.  *Buin.*
BUXBAUM, F.  *Buxb.*
BYLES, R. S.  *Byl.*

CANDOLLE, Aug. de  *DC.*
CARDENAS, Dr. Martin H.  *Card.*
CASTAÑEDA  *Cast.*
CASTELLANOS, A.  *Castell.*
CAVANILLES, A. J.  *Cav.*
CELS, J. P. M.  *Cels*
CHOUX, P.  *Choux*
COGNIAUX, C. A.  *Cogn.*
COMPTON, R. H.  *Compt.*
COULTER, Th.  *Coult.*
COVILLE, F. V.  *Cov.*
COWPER, Denis  *Cowper*
CRAIB, W. G.  *Craib*
CROIZAT, Leon  *Croiz.*
CULLMAN, Dr. W.  *Cullm.*

DALZELL, N. A.  *Dalz.*
DAMS, E.  *Dams*

DANGUY, P.  *Dan.*
DECAISNE  *Decne.*
DECARY, R.  *R. Dec.*
DECKEN, C. C. von der  *Decken*
DESCOINGS, B.  *B. Desc.*
DIELS, F. L. E.  *Diels*
DIETRICH, A. G.  *Dietr.*
DON, G.  *G. Don*
DONALD, John D.  *Donald*
DRAKE, S. A.  *Drake*
DYER, R. A.  *R. A. Dyer*

EHRENBERG, C. G.  *Ehrenb.*
EICHLAM, F.  *Eichl.*
ENGELMANN, George  *Engelm.*
ENGLER, Dr. A.  *Engl.*

FORBES, J.  *Forb.*
FÖRSTER, C. F.  *Först.*
FOSTER, Robert C.  *Foster*
FRIC, A. V.  *Fric*
FRIEDRICH, H.–C.  *Friedr.*
FRIES, R. E.  *R. E. Fries*

GALEOTTI, H. G.  *Gal.*
GARDNER, C. A.  *Gard.*
GILG, Ernest F.  *Gilg*
GILLIES, J.  *Gill.*
GOEBEL, Prof. K. von  *Goebel*
GOSSELIN, R. Roland  *Goss.*
GRAY, Asa  *A. Gray*
GRIFFITHS, Dr. D.  *Griff.*
GRISEBACH, A.  *Griseb.*
GUILLAUMIN, A.  *Guill.*
GURKE, Dr. A. R. L. M.  *Gurke*
GUSSONE, G.  *Guss.*

HAAGE, F. Jr.  *Haage Jr.*
HAMET, Prof. Dr. R.  *Hamet*
HARMS, H.  *Harms*
HAWORTH, Adrian H.  *Haw.*
HILDMANN, H.  *Hildm.*
HOCHSTETTER, C. F.  *Hochst.*
HOOKER, Sir Wm.  *Hook.*
HOPFFER, C.  *Hopff.*
HORTICULTURAL ITEM  *Hort.*
HOSSEUS, C. C.  *Hoss.*
HUMBERT, H.  *H. Humb.*
HUMBOLDT, BONPLAND & KNUTH  *H. B. & K.*
HUTCHISON, P. C.  *Hutchison*

JACOBSEN, H.  *Jacobs.*
JOHNSON, H. & KIMNACH, M.  *Johns & Kimn.*

JOHNSTON, J. R. *J. Johnston*

KARWINSKY, Baron Wilhelm von *Karw.*
KER-GAWLER, J. Bellenden *Ker.-Gawl.*
KESSELRING, W. *Kesselr.*
KIMNACH, Myron *Kimn.*
KLOTZSCH & OTTO *Klotzsch & Otto*
KNUTH, F. M. *F. Knuth*
KOCH, C. *C. Koch*
KOTSCHY, Theo. *Kotschy*
KRAINZ, H. *Krainz*
KRAUSE, K. *K. Krause*
KREUZINGER, K. G. *Kreuz.*
KUNTZE, O. *Kuntze*

LABOURET, J. *Lab.*
LAGERHEIM, N. G. von *Lagerh.*
LAMARCK, J. *Lam.*
LAUTERBACK, L. *Lauterb.*
LAVRANOS, J. *Lavr.*
LAWRENCE, G. *Lawr.*
LEACH, L. *Leach*
LEANDRI, Prof. Dr. J. *Leandri*
LEHMANN, Charles A. *Lehm.*
LEMAIRE, C. *Lem.*
LINDBERG, S. O. *Lindb.*
LINDLEY, Dr. J. *Lindl.*
LINK, H. F. & OTTO, C. F. *Link & Otto*
LINNE, Carl (LINNEAUS) *L.*
LODDIGES, C. *Lodd.*
LÖFGREN, Dr. A. *Löfgr.*
LUCKHOFF, Dr. J. *Luckh.*

MARLOTH, Dr. R. *Marl.*
MARTIUS, C. F. von *Mart.*
MEYER, E. H. F., *E. Mey.*
MILLER, Philip *Mill.*
MIQUEL, F. *Miqu.*
MONVILLE, M. de. *Monv.*
MOORE, T. *T. Moore*
MORAN, Dr. Reid V. *Moran*
MUEHLENBERG, G. H. E. *Muehlenb.*

ORCUTT, C. R. *Orcutt*
OTTO, C. F. *Otto*

PFEIFFER, Dr. L. *Pfeiff.*
PHILIPPI, R. A. *Phil.*
PICHON, M. *Pichon*
POELLNITZ, Dr. Karl von *Poelln.*
POISSON, H. *H. Poiss.*
POSELGER, H. *Poselg.*
PURPUS, Dr. J. A. *J. A. Purp.*

QUEHL, L. *Quehl*

RAUH, Prof. Dr. W. *Rauh*

RAUSCH, W. *Rausch*
REYNOLDS, George *Reyn.*
RICCOBONO, V. *Riccob.*
RITTER, F. *Ritter*
ROSE, Dr. J. N. *Rose*
ROWLEY, Gordon D. *Rowl.*

SALM-REIFFERSCHEID-DYCK, J. *Salm-Dyck*
SCHINZ, H. *Schinz*
SCHLECHTER, F. R. *Schlecht.*
SCHOENLAND, S. *Schoenl.*
SCHOTT, H. W. *Schott*
SCHULDT, H. *Schuldt*
SCHUMANN, Prof. Karl *K. Schum.*
SCHWANTES, Dr. G. *Schwant.*
SHURLEY, E. W. *Shurley*
SLOANE, Boyd L. *Sloane*
SMITH, C. A. *C. A. Smith*
SMITH, Lyman B. *L. B. Smith*
SPEGAZZINI, Dr. Carlo *Speg.*
ST. HILAIRE, A. F. de *St. Hil.*
STANDLEY, P. C. *Standl.*
STAPF, F. M. or O. *Stapf*
STEARN, Wm. T. *Stearn*
STEIN, B. *Stein*
SWARTZ, P. *Swartz*
SWEET, R. *Sweet*

THUNBERG, Carl Peter *Thunbg.*
TORREY, J. *Torr.*
TOUMEY, Prof. J. W. *Toumey*
TRELEASE, W. *Trel.*
TURPIN, Dr. François J. P. *Turp.*

UITEWAAL, A. J. A. *Uitew.*
URBAN, Dr. I. *Urb.*
URSCH & LEANDRI *Ursch & Leandri*

VAUPEL, D. *Vaup.*
VELLOSO, J. M. de C. *Vell.*
VERDOORN, I. C. *Verdoorn.*
VOLL, Otto *Voll*

WALTHER, E. *E. Walth.*
WALTON, F. A. *Walton*
WATSON, S. *S. Wats.*
WEBER, A. *Web.*
WEINGART, W. *Weing.*
WELWITSCH, F. *Welw.*
WENDLAND, J. C. *Wendl.*
WENIGER, H. L. *Weniger*
WERDERMANN, E. *Werderm.*
WHITE & SLOANE *White & Sloane*
WIGHT and ARN *Wight & Arn*
WILLDENOW, C. L. von *Willd.*

ZUCCARINI, J. G. *Zucc.*

# Glossary of Terms

| | |
|---|---|
| *acantha-* | spine, thorn or prickle |
| *acaul-* | without a stem |
| actinomorphic | symmetrical in form |
| acuminate | becoming pointed |
| acute | pointed |
| *albus* | white |
| anther | the pollen-bearing part of the stamen |
| *areole* | a 'cushion-like' growing point of a cactus |
| *austro-* | southern |
| axil | the angle between stem and branch |
| *azureus* | blue |
| *bellus* | beautiful, lovely |
| *brachy-* | short |
| bract | a modified or reduced leaf |
| bristle | a stiffened hair |
| *caespitose* | forming clumps |
| calcareous | referring to chalk or lime |
| *callus* | the tissue which forms over a cut |
| calyx | outer portion of a flower which surrounds the base, formed of sepals |
| capitate | possessing a 'head' |
| capsule | the dried fruit |
| caudex | the fleshy or woody section which develops at or below ground level, possessing terminal growing points |
| caudiciform | possessing a caudex |
| cephalium | a densely spined 'head' to certain mature cacti |
| cordate | heart-shaped |
| corolla | the petals of a flower |
| corona | the centre of the flower which surrounds the stamens and style – the crown |
| cotyledon | seed-leaf or leaf in embryo |
| crispate | having undulating edges to leaf or flower petals |
| cristate | referring to 'monstrosus' growth development in plant or flower |
| cultivar | a cultivated form, variety – a hybrid |
| cuspidate | cusp-shaped or pointed |
| cyanthium | refers to the peculiar construction of a flower (generally *Euphorbia*) – formed of flowers surrounded by bracts |
| dentate | toothed |
| digitate | spreading from a single point |
| dioecious | unisexual |
| distichous | arranged in two vertical rows |
| diurnal | day-flowering |
| *echino-* | spiny – like a hedgehog |
| endemic | regularly or only found in (a certain place) |
| ensiform | sword-shaped |
| entire | (with leaves) margins smooth |
| epiphyte | growing on other plants but not parasitic |
| etiolate | growing incorrectly through lack of light |
| exotic | refers generally to tropical or sub-tropical plants |
| exserted | protruding from |
| falcate | sickle-shaped |
| family | a taxonomic grouping of similar genera |
| farinose | having a mealy appearance |
| *flavi-* | yellow |
| floccose | having woolly hairs |
| fugacious | short-lived, temporary |
| *fulgens* | shiny |
| genus | taxonomic grouping of similar species |
| glabrous | without hair or wool covering, smooth |
| glaucous | covered with a wax-like bloom |
| globose | globular, spherical |
| glochid | hairs or bristles (as with *Opuntia*) |
| hastate | shaped as an arrow-head |
| head | a close-set group of flowers |
| *helio-* | refers to the sun |
| *hexa-* | six |
| hirsute | rough, fairly bristly, hairy |
| humus | decomposed organic matter |
| hybrid | the resultant 'cross' between two different species |
| imbricate | overlapping |
| inflorescence | a flowering stem bearing multiple flowers |
| internode | section of stem between two nodes |
| involucre | a series of bracts surrounding the inflorescence, forming an envelope |
| joint | a section of stem from which a leaf or branch grows |
| keel | a ridge on leaf or petal |
| labiate | having a 'lip' |
| lacerate | deeply divided or torn |
| laciniate | divided into slender sections or lobes |
| lateral | refers to the sides |
| latex | a milky sap which exudes from stems or leaves |
| leaflet | a small leaf or section of a pinnate leaf |
| linear | with parallel edges |
| lobe | a more or less rounded section of leaf or flower petal |
| lustrous | glossy |
| marbled | marked with unequal blotches |
| margin | the edge of a leaf or petal |
| membranous | papery, thin |

| | | | |
|---|---|---|---|
| midrib | the central vein (of a leaf) | serrate | a small-toothed or saw-like edge |
| monotypic | the solitary type (only one species within the genus) | sessile | having no stalk, attached directly by the base |
| naturalized | refers to plants which flourish freely away from their natural habitat | simple | solitary – one part only |
| | | sinuate | wavy-edged |
| nerve | a vein | spathe | a large bract often subtending a bud |
| obtuse | rather blunt or partially rounded | species | an individual item within the grouping of a genus |
| offset | a section of plant capable of rooting | | |
| orbicular | more or less circular or spherical | spicate | like a spike |
| ovate | broad elliptic, wider toward the base, egg-shaped | spine | a stiff or hard outgrowth of a stem |
| | | stalk | the more or less erect growth which supports leaves or flowers |
| palmate | shaped like a palm-leaf | | |
| panicle | a several-flowered inflorescence | stellate | star-like |
| pectinate | arranged comb-like | stigma | the tip of the style |
| peduncle | the (flower) stalk | stolon | a horizontal stem above or below ground which roots and produces new plants |
| pendent | inclined downward | | |
| perennial | plants living beyond two years | | |
| perianth | the complete flower | striate | grooved or lined longitudinally |
| petiole | leaf stalk | sub-genus | a sub-division of a genus |
| pinnate | compound leaves divided into opposite leaflets | sub-species | plants with similarities but differing in certain characteristics |
| plicate | pleated – folded fan-like | subtend | immediately below |
| plumose | feathery, a covering of very fine hairs | subulate | awl-shaped, slender and tapering |
| procumbent | trailing or resting upon the ground | succulent | able to store nourishment in the tissues |
| prostrate | trailing the ground | synonym | titles which are already known under differing names |
| pruinose | covered with a wax-like bloom | | |
| pseudocephalium | a single-sided cephalium | terete | cylindrical |
| pubescent | densely covered with minute hairs | tuber | swollen section of the root or underground stem |
| raceme | a number of individual flowers forming an inflorescence | | |
| | | tubercle | a small tuber-like swelling or growth |
| recurved | curved backward | tunicate | having concentric layers |
| reflexed | curved downward | turbinate | shaped like an inverted cone or top |
| regular | uniform (as with symmetrical flowers) | type | a species which constitutes the taxon of a genus |
| resting period | the period of dormancy | | |
| reticulate | a network formation | umbel | an inflorescence where the peduncles emerge from a single point |
| rhizome | a stem formation at or below ground level | | |
| | | undulate | with wavy margins |
| rib | longitudinal ridge on stems – often applied to veins of leaves | *vagans* | wandering |
| | | variety | a plant which has slightly distinguishing features from the species |
| rosulate | rosette-like | | |
| *sanguini-* | the colour of blood | *versi-* | variously |
| *sarco-* | fleshy | viable | able to survive and develop |
| saxicolous | refers to plants growing on rocks (saxatile) | vilous | with a covering of soft but long hairs |
| | | *virens* | green |
| scale | a thin leaf-like structure | vittate | striped longitudinally |
| scandent | climbing | *volubilis* | twisting, twining |
| scape | a leafless stalk | *vulgaris* | ordinary, common |
| *schizo-* | divided | wart | an irregular growth |
| scion | the section used to insert into the stock when grafting | whorl | a group of leaves surrounding a stem at one level |
| *sclero-* | inclined to be hard | wool | dense covering of soft hairs |
| *scopa* | broom-like tuft of hairs | *xantho-* | yellow |
| *seleni-* | refers to the moon | *xero-* | very dry |
| self-fertile | fertilization within the same flower to produce viable seeds | *zebrinus* | striped, zebra-like |
| | | *zygo-* | joined |
| sepal | the leaves which encompass the flower bud – a part of the calyx | zygomorphic | having a single plane of symmetry |

# Societies & Bibliography

## SOCIETIES

Throughout the world there are societies and establishments that function for the precise purpose of furthering the interest in cacti and other succulent plants. In most instances periodicals are offered which contain information for the particular benefit of the collector. The English-speaking world is extremely fortunate in this respect. Those listed below accept international membership. Each organization issues its own regular publication and distributes to its respective membership, or by subscription.

*British Cactus & Succulent Society*
19 Crabtree Road, Botley, Oxford OX2 9DU, England

*Mammillaria Society*
26 Glenfield Road, Banstead, Surrey SM7 2DG, England

*Epiphytes*
1 Belvedere Park, Gt. Crosby, Merseyside L23 0SP, England

1508 San Remo Drive, Pacific Palisades, CA 90272, USA

*Cactus & Succulent Society of America*
1675 Las Canoas Road, Santa Barbara, CA 93105, USA

*South African Aloe & Succulent Society*
P.O. Box 1193, Pretoria 0001, South Africa

*Aloe, Cactus & Succulent Society of Zimbabwe*
P.O. Box 8514, Causeway, Salisbury, Zimbabwe

*Australian National Cactus & Succulent Journal*
P.O. Box 572, Gawler, S. Australia 5118, Australia

*New Zealand Cactus Society*
Kumeu, Auckland, New Zealand

## BIBLIOGRAPHY

'Ashingtonia' (Holly Gate Reference Collection).

Backeberg, Curt, *Die Cactaceae* (6 vols.), Gustav Fischer, Jena (1958–62).

Benson, Lyman, *Native Cacti of California*, Stanford Press, California (1969).

Breitung, A. J., *The Agaves*, Cactus & Succulent Society of America Handbook (1968).

Britton, N. L. & Rose, J. N., *The Cactaceae* (4 vols.), Carnegie Institute, Washington (1923).

Barbhuizen, B. P., *Succulents of South Africa*, Purnell, Cape Town (1978).

Barthlott, W., *Cacti*, Stanley Thornes Ltd., Cheltenham (1977).

Haage, Walther, *Cacti & Succulents*, Vista Books (1963).

Jacobsen, Herman, *Handbook of Succulent Plants*, Blandford Press, London (1960).

*Journal of the National Cactus & Succulent Society* (vols. 1–28), Quarterly.

*Journal of the Cactus & Succulent Society of America* (vols. XXXV–LVIII), Abbey Garden, California. Bi-monthly.

*Journal of the African Succulent Plant Society* (vols. 1–7). Publication now ceased.

Rauh, Prof. Dr. W., *Bromelien 2*, Ulmer (1973).

Reynolds, G. W., *Aloes of Tropical Africa & Madagascar*, South Africa Book Fund (1950).

Reynolds, G. W., *Aloes of South Africa*, South Africa Book Fund (1950).

Schwantes, Dr. G., *Flowering Stones & Midday Flowers*, Benn, London (1957).

Werdemann, E., *Brazil & its Columnar Cacti*, Abbey Garden Press (1942).

White, A. C., Dyer, R. A., Sloane, B. L., *Succulent Euphorbiaceae*, Abbey Garden Press (1941).

# General Index

# Plant Index